———— City Folk ————

NYU SERIES IN SOCIAL AND CULTURAL ANALYSIS
General Editor: Andrew Ross

Nice Work If You Can Get It: Life and Labor in Precarious Times
Andrew Ross

City Folk:
English Country Dance and the Politics of the Folk in Modern America
Daniel J. Walkowitz

City Folk

*English Country Dance and
the Politics of the Folk in
Modern America*

Daniel J. Walkowitz

NEW YORK UNIVERSITY PRESS
New York and London

NEW YORK UNIVERSITY PRESS
New York and London
www.nyupress.org

© 2010 by New York University
All rights reserved

Library of Congress Cataloging-in-Publication Data

Walkowitz, Daniel J.
City folk : English country dance and the politics of
the folk in modern America / Daniel J. Walkowitz.
p. cm. — (NYU series in social and cultural analysis)
Includes bibliographical references and index.
ISBN-13: 978-0-8147-9469-2 (cl : alk. paper)
ISBN-10: 0-8147-9469-6 (cl : alk. paper)
1. Country dance—United States—History. 2. Folk dancing—United States—History.
3. Dance—Social aspects—United States—History. 4. Folk dancing, English. I. Title.
GV1623.W4   2010
793.3'1973—dc22   2009044351

New York University Press books are printed on acid-free paper,
and their binding materials are chosen for strength and durability.
We strive to use environmentally responsible suppliers and materials
to the greatest extent possible in publishing our books.

Manufactured in the United States of America

10 9 8 7 6 5 4 3 2 1

To
Lucy Miriam Turner-Walkowitz
And the next generation of country dancers

Contents

Abbreviations   ix
Preface   xi
Acknowledgments   xv

Introduction   1

I   ANGLO-AMERICAN URBAN FOLK REVIVALS

1. Revival Stories   15
2. Orderly Bodies: Dancing New York, 1900–1914   42
3. Orderly Bodies: Dancing London, 1900–1914   68
4. Planting a Colony in America   90
5. The American Branch   117

II   LIBERALISM AND FOLK REIMAGININGS

6. The Second Folk Revival   161
7. Re-Generation   206
8. Modern English Country Dance and the Culture of Liberalism   238

Conclusion   261

Notes   275
Bibliography   309
Index   323
About the Author   335

Abbreviations

BACDS	Bay Area Country Dance Society
CD*NY	Country Dance * New York
CDM	Community Dance Manual
CDS	Country Dance Society of America
CDSS	Country Dance and Song Society of America
ECD	English Country Dance
ECDDP	English Country Dance Documentation Project
EFDS	English Folk Dance Society
EFDSS	English Folk Dance and Song Society
HTC	Harvard Theatre Collection, Houghton Library, Harvard College Library
MECD	Modern English Country Dance
PCD	Princeton Country Dancers
SCFCH	Smithsonian Center for Folklife and Cultural Heritage
SFPALM	San Francisco Performing Arts Library and Museum
UNH-MC	University of New Hampshire, Milne Collection
VWML	Vaughan Williams Memorial Library, Cecil Sharp House, London, England

Preface

Folk dance groups seemingly are in an ever-constant search for new bodies, especially to augment the persistent short supply of male dancers. In that spirit, in March 1993, some friends with whom I was doing Scandinavian dancing every Wednesday evening at a synagogue on East 14th Street in New York City urged me to join them at a Tuesday-evening session of English Country Dancing at the Metropolitan-Duane Methodist Episcopal Church on 13th Street and Seventh Avenue. I had a full day of teaching on Tuesdays, so I thought I would be ready for some relaxation. And the church was very convenient; I lived only a few blocks away.

Other than one or two dances, which had entered the International Folk Dance repertoire, I had never done any English dancing. Still, I suspected that I would enjoy the form. The previous year, while spending a year teaching in Baltimore, I had come to enjoy a kindred dance form: contra dance.

Dancing in numerous folk dance venues was not unusual. As was my custom, wherever I happened to be I joined the local International dance group. In Baltimore, it met weekly at Johns Hopkins University. That spring I also danced with the local Balkan dance performance troupe, Narod. Balkan dance is performed with lines of men and women; sometimes they dance together, sometimes separately. Groups of each are needed, but not necessarily in even numbers. Country dancing, however, is couple dancing (as is Scandinavian), and near the end of my year in Baltimore the women of Narod convinced me to join them at Lovely Lane Church for an evening of contra dancing.

I remember that first venture as exhilarating and intimidating. The musicians—typically a fiddler, a banjo picker, a guitarist, and a piano player—rocked. The music seemed like familiar country square dance music, and the caller zipped through instructions that bore some resemblance to grade-school "do-si-dos" and "left and rights," but the women spun and "twizzled," ad-libbing extra turns and lunges that dazzled me. I dare say I did not leave anyone dazzled the few weeks I danced there, but I did find I loved the music and the dancing.

Back in New York the next year, in the wake of the putative end of the Cold War, the tumultuous breakup of the Soviet Union after 1989, and the consequent resurgence of nationalism, I found the International dance community had become a small uptown dance group focusing on Balkan dance, a relatively difficult, vigorous dance tradition of line dances in often complicated, quick patterns.[1] The location was inconvenient, but I think in retrospect I also did not appreciate that the group seemed to have become more antiquarian and nationalist than internationalist.

My turn away from Balkan dance reflects my interest in the politics of the folk, an interest deeply rooted in my personal history. I have folk danced since I was a young boy. I was introduced to folk dance through my parents and at "red diaper" summer camps in the early 1950s. These were "International" folk dances, dances from many lands that we danced as an expression of international solidarity with "common folk." As such, I grew up feeling the dances were integral to Left political culture and important on a personal and familial level to what I experienced, in the age of Reagan, as an increasingly beleaguered Left political community. The decline and narrowing of the International dance community in New York in the early 1990s, then, coincided with my decision to try English Country Dance (ECD).

Changes in folk dance practice and the dance community have variously bemused and agitated me as a participant-observer. Growing up in a left-wing family and in the folk culture of the 1950s and 1960s—a period that I analyze in the second half of this book—I experienced folk song and dance as part of a vital political culture. I enjoyed folk dancing as part of a Left community that walked picket lines together in the afternoon and sang folk songs "of protest" while doing so. Moreover, when I danced the "Danish Masquerade," I for the moment left the world of affluence and political instability and became the peasant, gentry, or aristocracy that the three parts of the dance aped. Similarly, when I joined a circle that was dancing a Croatian "Kolo Dance" to celebrate a wedding, I joined the men in teasing the women, once again imagining myself in another culture, in another time and place. The dance, then, was a carnivalesque experience in which, as in acting (which was my other passion), dancers became at one with "another" community of the "common people."

In the late 1960s, I believed that the political meaning of this culture was being lost, a notion that was, in retrospect, quite imperfect. Nonetheless, when I turned to English Country Dance in the early 1990s, I looked again for the political and emotional possibilities of folk imaginings in the dance. Interestingly, English Country Dance immediately struck me as embodying different imaginings in quite complex ways. I was hard-pressed to find many historical English dances that celebrated a ceremonial occasion for the community or its members (deaths, war, courting) or seasonal change (harvests, plantings). Rather, dances were named for places or groups ("Drapers' Gardens," "Well Hall") or famous personages such as dancing masters at the time ("Jacob Hall's Jig" or "Mister Isaac's Maggot"), and the choreography and bodily expression rarely had any relationship to the title. To be sure, I did find that some modern choreographers writing new dances in the traditional style were naming dances after current events or special occasions, but for the most part, the cultural expression of ECD came from the carriage, styling, and tempo or the dance—it was in the bodily expression of the genre, not for a "story" it told about an event.

There were, however, two sets of class origins that offered me confusing but fertile ground for taking myself out of the present when dancing. One, advanced by revivalists in the early nineteenth century, represented the dance as "peasant"; the other, which depicted dancers as gentry, shaped the way many people at the end of the century imagined the dance and was seen in the widely viewed mid-1990s television and film dramatizations of Jane Austen novels. Both, however, had very different political valences from the proletarian imaginings I remembered animating International Folk Dance in the 1960s. And it is the difference between International Folk Dance and English Country Dance imaginings that directs my fascination with charting in this book the evocative, multivalent, and changing politics of the folk and left-liberal political culture in the United States.

My role as oral historian and participant-observer, of course, complicates my voice in this story. Since 1999, I have been engaged with colleagues at the Smithsonian Center for Folklife and Cultural Heritage (SCFCH) in an ECD documentation project. Stephanie Smith, a folklorist and archivist at the SCFCH, Charles Weber, the SCFCH's ethnographic videographer, and I, under the auspices of the Country Dance and Song Society of America (CDSS), have completed video oral histories with approximately seventy dancers, musicians, choreographers, and callers. I have conducted further, and often quite lengthy, telephone interviews with another dozen people. Moreover, we have dozens of additional hours of footage of these people "speaking" with their bodies, that is to say, dancing. English Country Dance is more restrained than some popular social dances in which people get down and dirty. ECD is usually done at arms' length, and the footage shows participants speaking with their bodies about pleasure, respectability, sexuality, discipline, and the boundaries of sociability. The challenge is to hear what they say.

But folk dancers and, more specifically, those in the English dance community on both sides of the Atlantic, are more than subjects and partners; they are friends for whom I hold the highest regard. I have danced, dined, and shared weekend and week-long dance events with many of these people for the past fifteen years, and Stephanie Smith has done so for many years more. Smith also teaches English Country Dance for the Washington, DC, dance community, and I occasionally call dances in New York City. That is, we interview people with our own informed sense of the dance and often of an interviewee's personal history. Our joint presence in most interviews meant we tried to check our insiders' knowledge and allow interviewees to tell their own story, although as my research evolved, I pressed many of them to think about the questions of race, class, and political engagement that concerned me but that may not have been on their agenda.

Many interviewees have candidly entrusted their views and stories with me, and I believe I honor their perspective in the honest telling of the history's challenges, ironies, and contradictions alongside its delights. I participate quite fully in the cultural forms described and analyzed. (In the late 1990s, I had custom made for myself an elegant circa-1735 gentry costume of chocolate silks to wear to festive dance balls.) I share the dance community's concern for its future. And neither they nor I nor the future of the country dance movement are well served by pieties. The ECD community's joys and pleasure are mine, but so are their contradictions my contradictions, their foibles my foibles.

Finally, I listen to my storytellers but must acknowledge that in editing the text I am the grand narrator with my own experiences: indeed, as a folk dance teacher, performer, and recreational dancer, I could as easily be the subject of the interview as the interviewer. Of course, on a fundamental level, the historian always tells his or her own story in constructing an apparently seamless narrative from diverse data. But the questions I asked, however open ended, reflect questions that have long interested me as a member of the dance community, so my own voice and perspective—indeed, our voices are never silent—implicitly if not explicitly shaped the interviews, much as it shapes the story that follows.

Acknowledgments

Over the course of the decade in which I began to collect material for this book and to interview dancers, choreographers, musicians, and leaders, I also danced regularly. As a participant-observer, in truth I am indebted to all in this national and international dance community. Most of the people with whom I spoke knew of my project and spoke freely with me, sharing insights and stories with candor and a sense of joy for the project. Their generosity of spirit allowed me the too-rare opportunity to unite my worlds of play and work, and I thank them for it. Some in particular extended themselves in offering materials from their personal archives, reading sections relevant to their own experience, or with lengthy email recollection. I undoubtedly will have forgotten some, but I thank them all, including David Chandler, Paul Friedman, Yonina Gordon, Sharon Green, Robin Hayden, Judy Klotz, Gene Murrow, Liz Snowden, Allan Troxler, Ed Wilfert, and all those who have enriched the discussion on the ECD listserv hosted by Alan Winston.

The historical research at the core of this book was made possible through the gracious and accommodating research staffs at libraries on both sides of the Atlantic. I wrote drafts of most chapters while happily ensconced in the British Library each June and in the Wertheim Room of the New York Public Library at other times. Both libraries are amazing places with extraordinary collections that merit more public support. Librarians at Harvard's Houghton Library and Boston University responded to my queries and forwarded research material in a timely way, and Michael Nash, the director of the Tamiment Library at New York University, as always, was a good friend to the project (and to me). I also wish to thank the research staffs at the New York Public Library's dance collection at Lincoln Center and at the San Francisco Performing Arts Library and Museum. But two librarians, in particular, extended themselves to me and deserve special mention: Roland Goodbody, manuscript curator for special collections at the University of New Hampshire, and Malcolm Taylor, the librarian at the Vaughan Williams Memorial Library at Cecil Sharp House in London. Malcolm and his assistants, especially Elaine Bradtke, accommodated my repeated requests for help deciphering Cecil Sharp's handwriting and offered endless hints at relevant nuggets in their collection that would enrich this study.

I was also the beneficiary of financial and intellectual support from several institutions. New York University research grants allowed regular travel to London and provided administrative support to transcribe many of the video oral histories used in the project. The T. Baker Foundation provided a series of grants to the ECD documentation project that made possible on-location interviewing and videotaping in Massachusetts, New Hampshire, New York, Washington, DC, and in England. And, most memorably, the Humanities Center at Stanford University hosted me for a year in which a core group of ethnomusicologists were present. It was an extraordinarily helpful year in which the project gestated, for which I thank the director, John Bender, the staff, and the community of fellows, including Paul Berliner, Laura Chrisman, Louise Meintjes, Marc Perlman, Kevin Platt, Rob Reich, Sandra Richards, Janice Ross, and Debra Satz.

The ECD community includes many academics and independent scholars, and they played a prominent role in reading drafts of the manuscript for me: Jennifer Beer, David Millstone, Stephanie Smith, and Allison Thompson. Each refined and elaborated the argument in countless ways, for which I am deeply indebted. Stephanie Smith and Charlie Weber, the librarian and videographer, respectively, at the Smithsonian Center for Folklife and Cultural Heritage, have partnered with me since 1999 in the video documentation project and oral histories on which I draw extensively in the latter chapters, and they are coproducing the program for public television that draws on this book and that footage. Their collaboration has of necessity bled into this book, and they deserve credit accordingly.

Of course, other historians also graciously gave of their time to offer careful readings of part or all of the manuscript. Victoria Phillips Geduld and Ronald D. Cohen offered helpful correctives to a draft on the second folk revival and the Cold War. The historian Linda Tomko's gendered account of the early years of the first revival was a constant source of inspiration, as was her careful reading of various chapters. My colleagues at NYU Andrew Ross and Thomas Bender helpfully read a penultimate draft. One colleague in particular, however, merits special thanks: Michael Frisch. He gave the entire manuscript a close reading twice, each time providing a virtual chapter-length set of the sharply analytic comments that are his hallmark. Sparing no criticism, he was also consistently supportive and directive with suggestions, and I hope the book lives up to his high standards.

Eric Zinner at NYU Press remains one of the few editors today who reads manuscripts and works with his authors. I knew this by reputation before I gave him this book, and his interventions confirmed the fact. He and his staff have been consistently supportive and helpful.

Finally, I have the good fortune to have benefited from the support of the unusually capable academic family business. My daughter and son-in-law, Rebecca Walkowitz and Henry Turner, each a distinguished literary scholar, provided wisdom, close readings, and a loving embrace through even my surliest moments. Judith Walkowitz, of course, has been my rock. She read too many drafts to count, each with the great intelligence she brings to her own work. Most important, she is my partner in the larger struggles in life that we share and love, including our new granddaughter, Lucy Miriam, to whom this book is dedicated.

Introduction

Virtually every schoolgirl educated in the United States in the twentieth century grew up doing folk dancing, though few probably thought of it as a substantive part of their educational experience. My wife, Judith, for instance, who grew up in suburban Long Island in the 1950s, remembers folk dance as one of the preferred gym options for girls; you did not have to change or take a shower in the middle of the day. In the class, she learned a variety of dances from many lands. Children's favorites such as the "Mexican Hat Dance" and, probably because of the Jewish background of the community, familiar Israeli folk dances such as "Mayim, Mayim" or "Do Di Li" alternated with some "American" folk dance favorites such as "Pop Goes the Weasel."

Judith was the subject of a practice of teaching folk dance to girls that had roots early in the century. As early as 1897, Mary W. Hinman taught a combination of ballroom and folk dance to both sexes at Chicago's Hull House, and ten years later, the principal at PS 15 in Manhattan crowed that some sixty "healthy, happy" fifth-grade girls in the Burchenal Athletic Club regularly performed fifteen northern European dances, from the Irish jig to the Hungarian csardas, Swedish frykdalspolska, Russian comarinskaia, and a minuet. By 1909, Elizabeth Burchenal, who directed the teachers who ran the club and was just becoming chair of the Folk-Dance Committee of the Playground Association of America, claimed to have trained over 250 (female) public-school folk dance teachers. These teachers, in turn, taught the dances to more than twenty-four thousand public-school girls.[1]

Schoolboys sometimes participated in the dancing, but educators thought it to be an especially appropriate regime for girls, and it often became a regular part of their physical-education program. So, although I recall folk dancing as a schoolboy in the 1950s in northern New Jersey public schools, my memories are of being taught dances such as "The Virginia Reel" to accompany specific holiday programs. "The Virginia Reel" was taught as part of Thanksgiving festivities as an American traditional dance inherited from our colonial ancestors. Our teachers did not know that the dance was actually a modified version of the classic English country dance "Sir Roger de Cloverly." To our teachers—and to us—it was an authentic "American" product.[2]

As these personal anecdotes suggest, both the roots of English Country Dance and its development into a foundational folk dance movement in the United States have been obscured. Organized in March 1915 under the guidance of the English folklorist Cecil Sharp, the American Branch of the English Folk Dance Society is the oldest folk dance organization in the United States. Nearly a century later, it continues to thrive. At the outset of the twenty-first century, its descendant, the Country Dance and Song Society of America (CDSS), boasts over 250 affiliate groups and several thousand members. In addition, there are hundreds of other unaffiliated groups. Significantly, though, CDSS as an umbrella organization reflects the twinned notion of dances such as "The Virginia Reel"/"Sir Roger de Cloverly" as American and English; the organization includes ECD and kindred folk dance forms, square and contra (or American Country Dance), as part of an Anglo-American folk dance tradition and national cultural identity.

On any night of the week, one can country dance in virtually any metropolitan area of the country. The majority of the CDSS clubs are dedicated to contra dance, but several thousand English Country dancers gather weekly in locations as disparate as Fairbanks and Atlanta. In each genre, dancers take a partner and typically line up across from one another in longways sets that can be as long as the room permits, although English is more likely also to use shorter sets of two, three, or four couples. The usual pattern is for two couples to dance with each other in the line for thirty-two bars of music, and then each couple progress up or down the set, repeating the pattern with another couple. English and American music is quite different, however, and each evokes different body movements. Both genres use traditional tunes, but much English music is drawn from classical and baroque composers such as Henry Purcell and George Frederick Handel and from modern composers such as Baltimore's Jonathan Jensen, who works in that vein. The English classical music tends to be more lyrical and the dancers "stately," evoking what the folk revivalist Cecil Sharp called "gay simplicity." In contrast, contra music is more energetic, mostly relying on Irish and Scottish jigs and reels and, more recently, old-time southern mountain music, and the dancers move more with gay abandon.

For most of the twentieth century, then, American children grew up learning to folk dance, and English Country Dance as a dance tradition advanced an Anglo-American national identity as white, Anglo-Saxon, and Protestant.

City Folk traces the history of the changing racial, ethnic, and class profile of the people who joined in that project and examines the cultural politics that attracted them to it.

Folk Modernism

The title *City Folk* points to two conjunctions of the urban and popular: the folk as an imagined subject from the rural past that contemporary and largely urban-suburban dancers revive; and the folk as the urban culture of the revival dancers themselves. This double reference intends to trouble longstanding anxieties among dancers and folklorists about both authenticity and the identity of the folk, because although the origins of folklore and anthropology informed the politics of the folk for early revivalists, the disciplines have not agreed on who constitutes the folk. For instance, folklorist Theresa Buckland has pointed out that Sharp, who dominated the early history of English Country Dance on both sides of the Atlantic and cast a long shadow over how the tradition was understood, simply adopted the "survival theory" of the folk developed in James Frazer's influential *The Golden Bough* (1890) that was to shape folklore studies well into the twentieth century.[3] Frazer's views, like many of Sharp's, have since been discredited by a new generation of folklorists, and today folklore remains divided: traditionalists privilege an "essential" rural folk presumed to express in their essence the native spirit of a pristine society, while modern folklorists assert a more plastic, evolving notion rooted in constantly changing or "invented" traditions that are not class or region specific.[4] The traditional view remained prevalent through much of the twentieth century, however, and by celebrating the folk as the bedrock of pure, natural, "primitive" roots unsullied by the "modern," urban, industrial world, made it easy to see the folk dance movement and its proponents as quintessentially antimodern.

The characterization of the folk as antimodern, however, though not wrong, misses the mark. Not only does it ignore these people's cosmopolitan outlook and commitment to "progress," but it replicates the historical tendency to see modernism and antimodernism as binaries, rather than as intermeshing tendencies. In English Country Dance, the antimodern "primitive" folk were an instrument to create a modern Anglo-American citizen. The premodern would be the tool of the modernizers.[5] Thus, writing about Progressive reformers, the historian Andrew Camberlin Reiser notes that the term *antimodern* is used by dominant groups who benefit (sometimes indirectly) from the power of corporate capital. These reformers, like those who led the folk dance revival and whose wives, daughters, and sons flocked to the new American dance venues, were generally part of the rise of the new business and managerial elite located in C. Wright Mills's new white-collar middle class. These were people, as the historian Marina Moskowitz has perceptively observed, invested in growth—and in stability. That is, they were structural reformers, not social levelers; they encouraged upward mobility but retained an abiding faith in the status quo. Thus, with vast numbers of dissenting immigrants pouring into urban "rookeries" at the turn of the century, early-twentieth-century elites searching for "natural" or premodern sources of "authentic" experience turned to folk dance to win the allegiance of subordinate groups to a common set of "American" values and attitudes in the culture. Some of them, such as, most notably, Henry Ford, turned to square dance, as an Americanizing project. Others "recovered" English Country Dance as the fount of Anglo-American culture.[6]

The historian Allan Howkins argues that those who revived the dance in England were not folklorists but new suburbanites who were moved "to live, or rather, invent English country life."[7] Howkins is of course correct about the revivalists' "invention." But as the historians Eric Hobsbawm and Terence Ranger have observed in their important 1983 book, *The Invention of Tradition*, all traditions are invented, and "authenticity" is amorphous at best. In presuming traditions have a stable, essential meaning in some golden past, Howkins merely invokes an element of the older essentialist paradigm of the folk.

Challenging the hegemony of the dominant paradigm, *City Folk* takes the alternative modern view, seeing the folk as rooted in a local culture with its own political resonance. The folk need not be ancient or only of a peasantry, and the cultural life of an urban bourgeoisie is no less "genuine." A folk tradition is no less "real" for being constantly revised or "invented" in ways that are fundamental to its essence. So although even Sharp came to view country dance as having lost its peasant origins by the late seventeenth century as it moved "upstairs" to parlors and drawing rooms for balls and performance by the gentry and nobility, one could argue instead that the dance represented then the culture of the gentry "folk."[8] Thus, the "folk process" is one in which local community cultures give each tradition its own inflection, and its history (changing over time) and individuals give it further individualized, historical expression.[9]

So all cultural forms in this study are expressions of a folk, and as a folk dance genre, English Country Dance expresses what its devotees and collectors imagined to be "Englishness" abroad and what they imagined as the

Anglo-American roots of "American" culture in the United States. But the debate over English Country Dance as a folk dance is less interesting to me as a test of authenticity than for how it illuminates who patrols the boundaries of "authenticity" and how they do it.[10]

English Country Dance, as the title *City Folk* means to suggest, is folk dance of the urban bourgeoisie but, more so, of a liberal class fraction that has carved out a place for itself in the helter-skelter, heterogeneous modern city. Liberalism, what the historian Daniel Rodgers has described as the transnational Anglo-American reform project to make the "reality" of the city rational and thinkable, was arguably the dominant ideology of the twentieth century. Settlements, folk culture, arts and crafts, and, in turn, English Country Dance embodied—figuratively and literally—solutions to the liberal problematic of the twentieth century. And although historians have charted liberalism's rise and fall as a political and economic system and more recently have noted how it was implicated in the culture wars of the 1980s and 1990, they have less appreciated how liberalism has been invested in cultural institutions. *City Folk* uses the folk dance movement as a prism through which to examine what I call the culture of liberalism.

The Politics of the Folk and Modern Liberalism

People in the modern era who chose to do English Country Dance—in contrast, for example, to those schoolchildren who were assigned it—have been a social and political breed apart. Folk dancers located themselves outside the mainstream of popular culture, but they did so in explicit relationship to aspects of that culture they found problematic. At the same time as some sought what several contemporaries called a "safe haven" or "refuge" from mainstream culture, they and others engaged in missionary activity to change it or offer what they believed to be a salutary alternative. The English Country Dance movement in both England and the United States fits that paradigm: the founding generation worried about the injurious moral and physical dangers that the "tango craze" and unchaperoned dance halls would have on everything from women's reproductive organs to working-class immigrants' respectability.

The distinctive class position and politics of these country dance communities also marked them as a world apart from the new immigrant denizens of the urban metropolises. In class terms, these communities constituted a particular fraction of affluent professional-technical workers, and their politics reflected the changing tides of liberalism in the twentieth-century United

States and England. Fabian socialists and progressive social reformers played major roles in the development of the English folk dance movement on both sides of the Atlantic early in the century, and interviews and surveys document the central place of left-liberals reared in the midcentury second folk revival in the more recent history.

Liberalism advanced in English Country Dance alongside a tide of nationalism, and both were expressed in the folk revival that swept across western Europe and the United States at the end of the nineteenth and the early twentieth centuries. Native-born elites in urban industrial centers feared immigrant "others" they saw "flooding" into cities. "Superior," "civilized" societies, they believed, had a mission to "uplift" the poor or, failing that, to remake them, and the folk revival became an instrument of a project that was nationalist, imperialist, and, at home, a form of domestic colonialism.[11] In England, for instance, the folk revival in dance centered on the English folk tradition as a native source of Englishness, in which dancers would embody the "peasant" folk as the bedrock of pure, natural, "primitive" roots unsullied by the "modern," urban, and industrial. As I suggested earlier, Cecil Sharp believed the dances he recovered harked back to the farmhouses, village greens, and dancing booths of the annual fairs of medieval times and even to the "primitive" maypole dances. The "gay simplicity" of country dances and ballads, Sharp believed, contrasted with what the immigrant poor experienced in the bawdy, boisterous music halls. So, not surprisingly, it was Sharp who led the fight to have the folk repertoire made a permanent part of the school curriculum as an expression of the redemptive power of essential Englishness. This redemptive project was the work of liberalism: in doing and teaching English Country Dance, participants perform liberalism with the governance of space as a moral project, by creating, moving, and administering space to make it knowable, stable, and dependable. Folk dance associations were a cultural crucible in which liberals elaborated disciplinary regimes.[12]

The story of English Country Dance in the United States replicates these cultural politics. Sharp, who founded the American Branch of the English Folk Dance Society, advanced the dances as nominally about Englishness; but he and his Anglo-American followers appreciated that the dance tradition was equally about Americanism. As arbiters of American culture, East Coast WASP Brahmins, whose ancestors came from the British Isles, celebrated English Country Dance as part of an Anglo-American dance tradition and as the root of "American" contra and square dance. Progressive Era social reformers committed to Americanization saw these English dances as "respectable" and healthy alternatives to the sultry tango and wild, vertiginous spinning of the waltz and polka popular among immigrants. These reformers were equally anxious to make the structured environment of settlements, schools, and playgrounds an alternative to the dance halls, regarded by them as unchaperoned dens of inequity. Revivalists, then, on both sides of the Atlantic, paternalistically patrolled popular culture as part of political project to assimilate the immigrant working class. And though the elite English Country Dance community was itself a small community, the group had considerable social and political capital. In their articulation of English folk dance as an alternative to the rhythms, sounds, and expressions of sociability in the popular culture, dancers expressed "respectable" cultural signifiers, a socially resonant style of being American, of what we might call cultural citizenship.

Almost a century later, English Country Dance continued to define itself in no small part in relation to urban popular culture. The racial composition in particular of American and to a lesser extent English cities, had changed in the interim, of course, gaining new Black and Hispanic majorities. But the composition of the dance community changed as well, as "white ethnics" assimilated. As liberal elites, English Country dancers tried to live in and make sense of increasingly multiracial urban twentieth-century America. Some dancers expressed the desire to seek an alternative to the "speed-and-greed" culture or to the intense pulsating rhythms of "aerobic" music, each suggesting how fast-paced, hip-hop urban culture might have become modern metonyms for anxieties that devotees a century earlier had attributed to the music hall or the tango craze. A "modern" English Country Dance movement that emerged at the end of the twentieth century and in the new millennium reflected on the politics of liberalism and its relation to the problem of racism as it marked country dancing in the postwar city. In oral histories, many dancers spoke of finding a "refuge" in the enduring ties of an ideal (and idealized) dance community. But the history of English Country Dance in the United States highlights the contradictions within liberalism that made "community" as much about exclusion as inclusion. The English Country Dance community, in creating and celebrating itself and its dance floor as "safe spaces," had to come up against the countervailing impulses of modern liberal culture that welcomed some people and kept others at a distance.

City Folk focuses on the revival history of English Country Dance in the United States. The American story, however, is a transnational one. Major figures and ideas move back and forth across the Atlantic, and most especially in this account, between England and the United States. More particularly, as the urban imaginary informed the dance movements, leaders and ideas flowed between London and New York. The book follows that movement and ultimately tries to explain the irony that in the early twenty-first century, according to accounts by dancers from both sides of the Atlantic, English Country Dance flourishes more in the United States than it does in England.

This history begins in seventeenth- and eighteenth-century England and its American colony. The conventional origin story of the revival celebrates Cecil Sharp's encounter with Headington Morrismen in Oxfordshire on Boxing Day 1899. Sharp subsequently arrived in 1914 to "revive" America, but of course, as a British colony, colonial Americans knew that English Country Dance and the tradition persisted continuously in kindred forms in the southern mountains and New England countryside into the revival era. Chapter 1 of this book recounts these origin stories.

Part I then continues with paired chapters that trace Americans in England during the revival and then the English who, in turn, went to the United States to spread the English Country gospel. Class concerns animated these affluent dance reformers who worried about what they imagined as the dissolute culture of the poor. But there was a gendered hue to these worries as well, which equally marked the history of the dance community in the opening decades of the twentieth century. Thus, as the male "expert," Cecil Sharp came to dominate how the dances were taught and embodied. His lessons were advanced both by wealthy American women reformers who traveled to England to be certified by him and by women devoted to him who followed him to the United States to run the American movement. During an era of suffrage militancy for which Sharp had no tolerance, English Country Dance offered women leadership positions and public roles, but from a particular class position and in deference to a male idol. At the same time, Sharp vanquished other leaders with alternative embodiments of the dance, especially if they were strong women. Thus, Sharp and his followers advanced a white, Anglo-Saxon cultural hegemony, but it was also a deeply gendered and class story with which future generations of dancers would have to engage. Women trained and certified by Sharp directed and shaped the American Branch and its successor, the Country Dance (and after 1964, Song) Society of America, until the late 1960s in his image: it remained a small and largely Anglophile community of well-heeled, white Anglo-Americans.

Part II picks up the story in midcentury with the emergence of the second folk revival. It continues the transnational center of this history but reverses the flow. As the first revival moved from England to the United States, square dancing and new internationalist folk songs of the second revival transformed the English community, and they did so almost two decades before they revived the American movement. The key to the difference lay in both the internationalist political message central to the second folk revival and the particular virulence of the Cold War in the United States.

Part II begins with a counternarrative of a path *not* chosen by English Country dancers: International Folk Dance. This discussion builds on the idea that people are drawn to different folk dance traditions for different reasons and that they also invest the dances with their own meanings. The Nazis, for instance, invoked the *volk* as the spirit of Aryan superiority during the same decades that the communists celebrated the folk as carriers of an international proletarianism that could inform a radical political culture. Indeed, invocations of the folk could serve both nationalist and internationalist visions. Thus, in the 1950s, International Folk Dancers and ethnics at Polish American clubs could both dance the mazurka, but for each group the dance had vastly different meaning. For the former, it may have been the only Polish dance of some thirty dances done that evening and was an expression of the solidarity of people of many lands; for the latter, it was part of an evening of Polish dances dedicated to preserving "Polishness" until the homeland would be "liberated" from the communists.[13]

English Country Dance was in this context a national dance. An International Dance might teach the English dance "Hole-in-the-Wall," but it would be followed by dances from other countries, such as a Russian two-step, a Hungarian czardas, an Irish set dance, or perhaps, the Scottish dance "Road to the Isles." In Britain, English Country Dance expressed "Englishness," not a broader Britishness, a reality that Celts such as British-Irish, Welsh, or Scottish nationals would not miss. In the United States, English Country Dance's privileging of the English origins of the nation as a foundational Anglo American national tradition similarly minimized participation by Irish Americans, who constituted large communities in eastern cities such as Boston and New York, where English dance groups flourished. Thus, English Country Dance in the United States existed in changing relationship to the International Dance alternative, at times hostile and at times sympathetic, and the politics of "internationalism" provided a challenging counterpoint to the more nationalist and avowedly apolitical politics of the English Country Dance community.

With the waning of the more virulent domestic constraints of the Cold War and the rise of the back-to-land counterculture in the early 1970s, a contra boom brought a new generation of young people into the Country Dance and Song Society. It did not hurt that the infusion of these people coincided with new leadership of the American organization. The shift, however, followed changes that had transformed the dance scene in England. The English dance community lost many male dancers in the war, and the leader of the English Folk Dance and Song Society instituted a couples-only policy and began to emphasize square dance and less fussy "community" (or "traditional" or "barn") dances that did not require much teaching or styling. American soldiers stationed in Britain popularized square dancing, but it was a photo of Princess Elizabeth and Prince Philip square dancing at a reception at Canada House that transformed the English dance scene. Thousands lined up to square dance at Cecil Sharp House in London, dramatically broadening the size and social profile of the community there. The new policies had implications for the future of the dance community, a theme explored in the last chapters of the book.

The story concludes, however, with the history of the new generation of people who transformed the American ECD community from the 1970s forward. Many dance newcomers had little or no family roots in England. Joining the dance from an international dance and song tradition, they had to remake the national tradition to serve them. One way they did so was by elaborating a new "modern" variant on the English dance tradition with new tempos, style, and embodiments for both older and newly written dances. In other ways, however, these newcomers resembled their predecessors in the English Country Dance movement. They, too, were a relative elite, but one drawn from a slightly different class of professional and technical workers. As significant was their political profile: they overwhelmingly self-identified as left-wing or liberal. In a neocon political world dominated by Thatcherism and Reaganism, where "liberal" had become a dirty "L Word," the ECD community constituted a safe haven for these folks, a place apart. They took this place on the road, however. Reflecting the new consumerism of the era, the leisure time of the many older dancers, and the bourgeois preferences of this urbane class fraction, dancers participated in a national and even global dance community, traveling to weekly balls and to week-long dance camps across the country and on dance holidays abroad. And if they could not travel, they transported themselves by plugging into MP3 players and listening to CDs made by renowned English Country Dance bands.

The new, commodified English Country Dance experience may, however, have come at a steep price. The urban and suburban folk in the contemporary English Country Dance community worry about their ability to reproduce themselves, yet the consumer dance culture sends messages to outsiders of the community's distinctiveness. For left-liberal and urbane English Country dancers remain enmeshed in the contradictions of the modern liberal imaginary: they identify with the city even as they exist in an uneasy place apart. The classical tunes that accompanied the dances and the leisure-world activities of the dance community remain affluent markers of the class fraction who promote the dance and do it as a recreational adjunct of their life, much as are the stately posture, gestures, attire, and conventions of the dance. These signifiers convey "white" and relatively elite messages about the English Country Dance community's class and culture. To be sure, the community broadened over the twentieth century, but its cultural markers sustain much of the penumbra of its Anglo-Saxon national origins. So although the fare for a contemporary local dance event is typically not extravagant, greater participation in dance community events raises both the cultural and financial ante. It remains to be seen, as the dance community seeks to expand its base, if and how it will engage the inclusive-exclusive contradictions of modern liberalism and, in doing so, determine its future.

Part I

Anglo-American Urban Folk Revivals

1

Revival Stories

> These old forms of dancing, which have been worked out in many lands and through long experiences, safeguard unwary and dangerous expression and yet afford a vehicle through which the gaiety of youth may flow. Their forms are indeed those which lie at the basis of all good breeding, forms which at once express and restrain, urge forward and set limits.
> —Jane Addams, 1910[1]

Boxing Day 1899. Cecil Sharp, the music master at Ludgrove, a boys' preparatory school mainly for Eton, was spending the Christmas holiday with his wife's family at Sandfield Cottage, Headington, just east of Oxford. Sharp's career up to then had been one of modest achievement; the son of a London slate merchant, he could, in fact, have been described as downwardly mobile. Ill health and a nervous disposition, from which he seemed to suffer throughout his life, forced him to drop out of public school in 1874. He subsequently completed a degree in mathematics at Clare College, Cambridge, but with little enthusiasm or any particular distinction. Seeing him at sixes and sevens, his father sent him to Australia to sort out his career. There, apparently having inherited his mother's love for music, he found his métier as a music teacher, at one point briefly teaching the royal princesses. Now, as Sharp looked out the window at the snowy Christmas scene before him, an extraordinary musical sight came into view that would forever transform him and the history of English Country Dance. His biographers describe what Sharp would always refer to as "the turning point of his life": "eight men dressed in white, decorated with ribbons, with pads of small latten-bells strapped to their shins, carrying coloured sticks and white handkerchiefs; accompanying them was a concertina-player and a man dressed as a 'Fool.'" The concertina player "struck up an invigorating tune, the like of which Sharp had never heard before," and as the men jumped and cavorted, waving their handkerchiefs, "the bells marked the rhythm of the dance."[2]

Sharp was witnessing the morris dance "Laudnum Bunches." When the quarrymen finished, they picked up their sticks and danced "Bean Setting," followed by three other dances. Their performance having concluded, the men apologized for being out that day; they knew the proper time was Whitsun, but they were out of work and danced in the hope of gaining a few pennies. There is no record of how Sharp responded to their need, though one imagines he understood the rules of deference, class, and charity, especially at Christmas. It was the dancing, however, and not the men's need that captivated Sharp: according to his collaborator and secretary, Maud Karpeles, "He felt that a new work of beauty had been revealed to him." The concertina player, a young man of twenty-seven named William Kimber Jr., agreed to help Sharp transcribe these five dances and more the next day, and the rest is, as they say, history. Sharp, usually credited as one of the leaders, if not the leader, of the folk revival in England and the United States, spent the rest of his life collecting folk song and dance; William Kimber was his first and foremost informant.[3]

Like all good foundational stories, the Boxing Day revelation has taken on a life of its own in the history of the folk revival. The site even has a historical plaque commemorating the event. In the following decade, Sharp emerged as the head of the English folk dance movement, and in the subsequent struggle over leadership and authority over the movement, the story stands as a tale told by the winner, as history usually is. To be sure, Cecil Sharp was an extraordinary man who embarked on extraordinary adventures in England and the United States. He was also a man who did remarkable and pioneering work in documenting, transmitting, and building English Country Dance on both sides of the Atlantic. Although he was never particularly rich, he had all the advantages of an elite Cambridge education and combined the traits of a thoroughgoing bourgeois with those of the intellectual mandarin class: that is, his materialism was tempered by a patrician disdain to be too public about the need for money. Lingering effects of his provisional association with Fabian socialism meant he brought a fundamental sympathy with the working class and rural folk to his work, but he did so with more than a patina of paternalism. This tension was also at the core of the liberal problematic in the United States in the Progressive Era, and it makes Sharp's career a metonym for the culture of liberalism.

Sharp's achievements in collecting song and dance should not be minimized, although historians have disagreed on the nature and impact of his political attitudes toward his respondents. At one end are the critics who see Sharp as a misogynist, elitist, and Puritan. These views range from criticism

William Kimber, Jr. (Reproduced courtesy of EFDSS)

by the historian David Harker that Sharp's project was less about folk revival and recovery than about social control and fabrication—the invention of the folk as a reductio ad absurdum. Critical but more appreciative is Henry D. Shapiro's patronizing portrayal of Sharp's collaboration in the United States with the folklorist Olive Dame Campbell and his proselytizing for the "inherent value of the naïf culture of Appalachia."[4] Against these views, folklorist-historians Archie Green and David Whisnant have put forth compelling evidence of Sharp's progressive views. They paint a picture of Sharp the collaborator as consistently evenhanded and responsible, and noting his Fabian socialism, both reference his 1920 letter to the Russell Sage Foundation's John Glenn in support of the Welsh miners' strike. The miners had struck, Sharp wrote, because of their "determination not to work for anybody's profit. . . . Capital they say should be well rewarded but no more, and should not make surplus profits." Continuing on a personal level, Sharp wrote, "I feel that the

Revival Stories | 17

organization of industry has somewhere or other to be radically changed. Men won't work like slaves with the fear of unemployment constantly before their eyes." With the memory of events in eastern Europe fresh in mind, he concluded that there was "enough discontent to lead a dozen revolutions."[5]

However, Sharp's biographers (hagiographers is probably more accurate), Maud Karpeles and Fox Strangways, were the first to acknowledge the limits of Sharp's Fabian socialism. Sharp supported the Liberals and, later, Labour. But Karpeles remembers that he liked to "air his Radical views and 'pull the legs of the Tories,'" and his characterization of himself as a "conservative Socialist" seems spot on. He joined the Fabian Society in December 1900, but he also enrolled in the Navy League. His intellectual tastes further reflected the lengths and limits of his progressive cosmopolitanism: he loved Schöpenhauer and Ibsen and admired the modern dancer Ruth St. Denis and the Diaghilev Ballet. At the same time, he opposed capital punishment and female suffrage, though Karpeles, his devoted assistant and ever his defender, insisted he mostly opposed the suffragettes' militancy.[6] The record is less equivocal: he gave token support to his sister, the bohemian and militant suffragist Evelyn Sharp. They infrequently corresponded, but she wrote him upon her release from Holloway prison, where she had been force fed: "I quite agree to the absurdity of quarrelling because we differ on Woman Suffrage; but then, I never thought of such a thing. For one thing, I have yet to be convinced that you are a confirmed 'Anti.'"[7] In fact, though Sharp may have supported suffragists in theory (and if they assumed passive, deliberative roles), he opposed their assertive practice. His one letter on the subject reveals his wariness. His hostility and anxiety about the subject was sufficiently pressed on Helen Storrow, a benefactor to Sharp and the American Country Dance movement and grande dame of the Boston English Country Dance community, that she felt compelled to warn him in 1915 about the women he would meet when he was to teach country dance at Wellesley College. Writing Karpeles about the forthcoming encounter, Sharp mused nervously, "The W. [Wellesley] people are all suffragists Mrs. Storrow says and have behaved like the maniacs of that persuasion!"[8]

Indeed, the historian Georgina Boyes's view of Sharp as one who "politically, philosophically and in personal terms . . . disliked change" seems on the mark. Boyes, though focused on the folk revival in England and not in the United States, provides a careful feminist and radical analysis of Sharp and the contested political world of prewar London. She reminds us that the traditions he transmitted, as in all such conversions, were inventions shaped by his frustrated social aspirations and class and gender prejudices. Still, though he never appeared out of character as the English gentleman, this often quite sickly man nonetheless completed a series of remarkably rigorous travels through Appalachia to gather folk songs. Sharp's social distance from his respondents never seemed to stymie his collecting: walking the mountain valleys, the collector continually established rapport—and even won affection—with rural poor people who shared their tunes with him. But, then, having learned their songs and dances, Sharp would replicate the strategies he had followed in England, a hint of which is evident in the paternal deference that characterized his Boxing Day meeting with the Headington quarrymen: he might give them a few "honest pennies" they sought, but he would return to the metropolis, put on his waistcoat, and present the folk songs and dances in respectable dress both actual and metaphorical; in a remarkable class transmogrification, he took "tradition" from the "peasantry," dressed it up, and trained "respectable" elite women to teach immigrants from "peasant" backgrounds in settlement houses the "proper" form that supposedly conveyed the innate spirit of the country folk.[9]

This was Sharp the missionary to others; what is striking about his travels in the United States between 1914 and 1917 is the equal passion he generated among recreational dancers committed to English Country Dance for their own pleasure. To be sure, the bourgeois elite whom Sharp attracted to his emergent dance community shared the sociopolitical mission that had driven Sharp. They, too, were impelled to preserve the "authentic," "natural" spirit of the "peasantry" and reinvigorate the English "race." Yet at the same time, many of these same devotees worked in the playgrounds and settlements to help immigrant children preserve and respect their own cultures, in good part as a way of teaching them respect for their parents and tradition. Against these cultures, the folk dance teachers trained by Sharp and his acolytes asserted the majesty and vitality of Anglo-English culture in English Country Dance—and by extension, the vigor of English political and social institutions.

Cecil Sharp is a central player in this story, but he properly belongs aside the story of many others. Although the Boxing Day foundational story places Sharp at the center of the folk revival, where he surely belongs, it obscures the way he got there and the significant role of some important other figures he sought to diminish in order to establish his own authority, women such as New York's Elizabeth Burchenal and London's Mary Neal. Such women went on to have distinguished careers, but often despite rather than because of Sharp. Still, these conflicts dramatize the significance of gender to this story—both in the traditionally coupled structure of the dance and in the significantly new public roles taken on by women in the dance revival that is highlighted by Burchenal, Neal, and many other women, most notably Boston's Helen Storrow and Louise Chapin, Sharp's collaborator and assistant Maud Karpeles, Chicago's Mary Wood Hinman, and two Sharp student-teachers who settled in the United States after his death to direct his efforts there, Lily Conant (née Roberts) and May Gadd.

But first, I turn to the transformations of the city that excited Progressive reformers such as these women to seek the renovation of the urban spirit and the "race" in the revival of English Country Dance. Because the culture of liberalism is both personal and political, this chapter focuses on the social and economic conditions at the end of the nineteenth century and early twentieth century that drew the liberal professional class in the United States and England to this project. It also illustrates the larger transnational context for the revivals that Cecil Sharp helped organize in both England and the United States around English Country Dance.

This chapter does not proceed with a strictly historical account. It introduces some of the major threads that weave together to provide the complex fabric that is the history of English Country Dance in the twentieth century. After a review of the material conditions in the industrial city at the end of the nineteenth century, in which calls for revival echoed, the chapter moves between themes that interweave at different stages in the history, and often to different effect. The discussion moves from discourses on the body to histories of reform to the folk revival, but one theme is never far from another. Concerns voiced by Progressive reformers over dangers from and to gendered bodies cross with interests in social control and cultural amelioration. And the romantic views of peasants and the folk mix with Anglo-Saxon and white imperial ambitions to revitalize the "race."

City Trouble

The transformation of England and the United States into urbanized centers of industrial and finance capital by the beginning of the twentieth century disrupted familiar patterns of daily life, social relations, and public culture and generated new social and cultural anxieties. In the first half of the nineteenth century, the rise of industrial capitalism and the market economy transformed independent artisanal work relations into dependent wage labor in routinized workplaces. Historians' images of "Satan's Strongholds" in industrial villages and of the grinding poverty that accompanied metropolitan industrialization in New York and London have captured the disruptive character of this transformation.[10]

After 1880, as industry became increasingly characterized by oligarchy and monopoly, industrialists and manufacturers continually fought to lower costs to survive in the increasingly competitive marketplace. They had a range of strategies, but most came down to either increasing production quotas or employing cheaper labor. Taylorism, the breaking down of tasks into "efficient" small pieces that could be easily learned and repeated at faster and faster speeds, was one answer; deskilling work, displacing work with machines or employing low-paid women, African Americans, children, or immigrants desperate to earn some money, was another. Migrants from the South, often African Americans, provided one source of cheap labor, but the massive influx of immigrants from eastern and southern Europe to cities such as Chicago and New York provided the largest source of such labor. Many of them were "swarthy" Mediterraneans or Semites; moreover, often they were Catholic or Jewish and spoke foreign tongues. Some were people who had been pushed off failing farms in Ireland or New England; others arrived to avoid repressive political regimes, whether it was conscription into the Czar's army, pogroms, antiradicalism (e.g., accompanying the Revolutions of 1848), or southern lynch mobs. Often desperate, they were simultaneously attracted by the promise of a new life and decent job. Of course, as often as not, the job was not so decent, because under the ruthless pressures of competition, manufacturers continually cut wages, increased production quotas, and displaced anyone who objected with someone who would be more compliant (and, not uncommonly, who was willing to work for less).[11]

As significant as the transformations in economic life were the class tensions they unleashed. The working class had been "made" in the 1830s in both countries, but as manufacture expanded, class differences became the grammar of the everyday struggle for daily survival for majorities of the population at the end of the century. The economic crisis of the 1870s in both countries—the first industrial depression—hastened the decline felt by workers and emphasized awareness of the differences between dependent labor and the elites and middling sorts above them. For example, following on the fears excited by news of the Paris Commune in 1871, business-oriented city fathers enacted vagrancy laws, transforming the respectable tradition of the tramping artisan into the new figure of the disreputable tramp.[12] Workers, not surprisingly, resisted what they understood as encroachments on their jobs and their ability to feed their families with militant trade unions and bitter strikes. Indeed, as the century drew to a close, populists and socialists (and anarcho-syndicalist movements on the horizon) raised concerns of class warfare—the "classes versus the masses"—in both England and the United States.

Equally important to the class antagonism were heightened gender anxieties that accompanied the changing social relations wrought by industrialization. Financial need both attracted and pushed working women into factories during early industrialization; by midcentury, those who had no such need created an ideology that condemned such work outside the home as immoral, what historians have called the Cult of True Womanhood. True Womanhood ideology of the privileged class complained about the suspect morality of "factory girls," while it took the luxury of celebrating woman in the hearth as mother and wife. Of course, working-class parents, dependent on their own and their children's labor to survive, also worried that their young daughters working in factories, no longer under their daily supervision, were at risk from dangerous machines and lecherous male overseers.

By early in the twentieth century, and regularly thereafter, the shift from production to service work, distribution, and consumption unleashed new anxieties about the role of women at work and at home. The rise of white-collar clerical and service, such as the burgeoning of the garment industry to meet the rising consumer ethos, gave women new visible roles both in the sweated labor and in the social-service industries that arose to redress it. There were class inflections to gendered policy, to be sure, as affluent wives and daughters joined with trade-union women to advance maternalist protective legislation for factory girls and children (but not for working-class men, whose leaders were themselves often only too happy to remove the threat of cheap female labor).

The class and gendered anxieties set in motion by the turn-of-the-century industrial transformations had one more characteristic critical to this story: ethnic identity. Industrial capitalism's intensifying drive for more and cheaper labor also transformed the urban character of England and the United States, and the role of foreigners in the city only increased old-timers' anxieties about the changes. In the United States, new immigrants from eastern, central, and southern Europe took the place of the Irish, Scots, English, Germans, Nordics, and French Canadians who had dominated earlier immigration. The Irish as foreigner continued to occupy a large place in the English imaginary, but he was joined by the Jew and the Italian by the end of the century. These newcomers, one seen as "swarthy," the other as "olive-skinned" Mediterranean, were thus racial "others" with accents, languages, and customs that those who were already present found strange.

The influx of migrants and immigrants also intensified the pace of urbanization and renewed the traditional romance with rural values on both sides of the Atlantic. In England, the 1851 census reported that as many people lived in cities as in the country, with 8.95 million in each sphere; in 1881, it reported that two-thirds of the population was urban.[13] In the United States, the federal census announced the split seventy years later in 1920, but the census pronouncement that the frontier had disappeared in 1890 was equally momentous. As Frederick Jackson Turner warned historians in his presidential address to the American Historical Association in 1893, the end of the frontier sounded the death knell to the foundational American democratic experience as it closed the "safety valve" that had provided release from the pressure of overheated urban life.[14]

The putative end of the frontier and coincident growth of cities quickened the interest in the recuperative power of rural idylls, represented in images of the Village Green and the Yeoman Farmer that had long been seen as the repositories of national virtue. The early asylums of the 1830s, for example, were described as "retreats" located on the city outskirts in rural settings where they were thought to provide a relief from urban anomie, neurasthenia (which was more often diagnosed for upper-class women), and crime induced by the pressures of city life. And most famously, of course, Foucault has highlighted the supervisory character of the inmate body in these institutions in his analysis of the architecture of the Panopticon.[15] The development of the immigrant city (whether it be Chicago and New York or Manchester and London) over the course of the rest of the century further threatened the historical importance Englishmen and Americans credited to rural life and, if anything, intensified these rural idylls. Thus, revivalists across northern Europe and the United States embraced folk traditions, in all their art forms, to capture a vital "pure" essence from the countryside that could rejuvenate the dissipated modern urban industrial body.

Bodies at Risk

By the turn of the century, many urban reformers had come to understand urban industrialization as a crisis of the body. Cramped factory conditions characterized the new mass-production industries in which workers remained tethered to machines for upward of twelve hours a day, six days a week, in debilitating conditions. Seen as "teeming hoards," the urban bourgeoisie worried about immigrants who crowded the streets of London and New York and filled cramped tenements, strained the educational system, and taxed sanitation and public services. To be sure, reformers moved to implement new tenement laws and city planning, but changes did little to alleviate the cramped conditions of those who continued to crowd into them. Teenagers and young adults continued to work ten or more hour days in confining factories. Labor legislation increasingly freed many children from factories, but the new kindergartens and public schools now confined them in regimented days at cramped desks. Thus, reformers saw working-class bodies massed in dank rooms, confined into factories, and crowded into schools for long hours in small cramped desk spaces. And leisure-time activities were no less worrisome. Unchaperoned girls and boys gadding about in the streets were one problem; of greater concern was the temptation of the dance halls, where liquor and the vertigo of the "spieling" (fast-turning pivot) dances threatened loss of control.[16]

These worries, which were compounded by fears about the fragility of the female body, radical politics, the suspect moral values of a militant working class, and the imperial needs of the nation, gave increased urgency to the new Progressive reform movement. A complex movement, Progressives sought to ameliorate the ways in which urban industrial life confined bodies and jeopardized democracy. Progressives' answers employed "efficient" plans implemented by "experts," at the same time as they sought to bring their own sense of order to control over it. Their concerns, often focusing on play in all its physical and moral varieties, took them from considerations of Physical Culture to Modern Dance and then to Folkdance and English Country Dance in particular. Worried about the debilitating effects of city life, factories, and immigrant "peasant" cultures for urban success, they focused on those for whom they thought they could have the greatest impact: children, who were thought to be more easily organized and malleable than adults.[17]

Working men had fought for shorter hours and public schools since the 1830s and '40s, but many families depended on labor from their children. Starting in Massachusetts in the early 1880s, professional educators and industrial reformers, with scarce attention to family economy, led the fight to get children out of factories and into schools. Appropriately, that same decade witnessed the development of the kindergarten movement to give working-class children an early introduction to American urban socialization. Subsequent protective labor legislation during the Progressive Era completed the process of requiring public education for children.

Getting children out of factories merely raised other questions: What was to be done at school to counter the debilitating conditions of constricting desks and day-long confining routines? What was to be constituted as a "meaningful," that is, "constructive," form of play? and Who was to teach it? The questions, like the answers to them, were transatlantic. One set of answers combined beliefs in the rehabilitative power of nature ("fresh air") and survival skills rooted in handcraft and ingenuity with imperial ambitions of the American and British empires. Thus, reformers such as Sir Robert Stephenson Smyth Baden-Powell (1857–1941) initiated the Boy Scouts in England in 1908; Girl Guides were established there two years later. Meanwhile, in the United States, Daniel Carter Beard (1850–1941), in order to keep the spirit of the pioneers alive, in 1905 created Boy Pioneers (it had evolved from his Society of the Sons of Daniel Boone), the largest boys club in the country. And in 1911, Beard organized the American Boy Scouts.

Organizations for girls soon followed. Juliette Gordon Low met Baden-Powell in 1911, the same year the Girl Guides were established. A year later, Low established the Girl Scouts of America, and that same year Luther Halsey Gulick Jr. (1865–1918) and his wife, Charlotte, held the founding meeting of the Camp Fire Girls of America in Vermont.[18] These groups were part and parcel of movements to create "productive" play based on notions of craft tradition drawn from the virtues of "pioneer" life. The groups were also integral to the imperial moment as they created reward systems (badges) for completing skills seen as essential to muscular Christianity for men and domestic Christianity for women. So, not surprisingly, these groups and the people such as Gulick and others who joined him, played important roles in various efforts to develop folk dance as a feature of healthy play for young boys and girls in the city during these same years.[19]

Two other major Progressive Era sites were the center of reformers' focus on children's bodies: the settlement and the playground or schoolyard. The Settlement House movement began with the establishment of Toynbee Hall in 1884 by Samuel Augustus Bennett, the canon of St. Jude's Church in the Whitechapel district of London's East End. Named for the social reformer Arnold Toynbee, its origins reflected the combination of Christian and socialist missions to the poor that characterized much transatlantic Progressive Era reform. The social reformer and Ethical Culture leader Stanton Coit (1857–1944) visited Toynbee Hall in 1886 and the next year opened the first settlement house in the United States, Neighborhood Guild, on the Lower East Side in New York. In 1888, Jane Addams and Ellen Gates Starr visited Toynbee Hall, and by the next year they had opened Hull-House in Chicago to provide education and social services to the immigrant communities there. Within a decade, the settlement movement had spread widely in both countries; the United States counted over a hundred settlements by 1900 and more than four times that number a decade later. Many of the most famous were led by socialist-inspired women such as Lillian Wald and Mary Simkovitch, who pioneered public-health efforts and public-housing reform; the majority operated in the shadow of the Charity Organization Society and focused more on self-help. All sought to be "helpful" in teaching immigrants how to adjust or survive better, combining skills in language and budgets with lessons on interclass dialogue and cooperation as the basis of democracy.[20]

The second reform space created at this time—the schoolyard or playground—was equally significant as a site for play. Boston opened the first playground—three piles of yellow sand in a yard of the Children's Mission—in 1885. By 1899, thirteen cities had opened them. New York City opened thirty-one supervised playgrounds between 1899 and 1906, when Gulick and Henry S. Curtis organized the Playground Association of America (PAA).

Curtis has been credited with originating the idea of a Playground Association. A student of the renowned Clark University child psychologist G. Stanley Hall, Curtis traveled to England in 1902 to study the recreational system there. He found its reliance on gymnastics too militaristic and determined to create an American system more oriented toward team play that would be more democratic. Appointed director of the New York City playground system, he found himself working closely with the director of the city's public-school physical-education program, Luther Gulick.[21]

Gulick, the New York medical doctor who, as I have already noted, with his wife established the Camp Fire Girls in 1911, had taught at Springfield International YMCA Training School when James A. Naismith, at Gulick's request to create an indoor game that was not too rough, invented basketball there in 1891.[22] A decade later, Gulick found himself in the modern city, "where there is as much need for fighters as there ever was" but where boys have "been made lax." The "modern city," he complained, produces "ease, mushiness, softness" in the world. Adults have baseball, yachting, and hunting (though presumably not in the city!); hence, he continued, boys need boxing and football: "If there ever was the need for a stiff-backed boy, it is in the modern city."[23] Gulick's initial response was to found the New York Public Schools Athletic League (PSAL), for which in 1903 he became the first director of physical training. But Gulick also realized that his major problem was not the boys: most schools already had the physical education programs in place for boys. Rather, the pressing need was a program for girls. As Curtis stated, "From every point of view the girls are our great national problem." Man's work has become more subject to mechanization, but not women's. Girls tend to "sit about and gossip or play jackstraws" if no provision is made for them; "vigorous health and a good physique are always among the chief charms of women, . . . [and] childbirth has become more and more difficult with succeeding generations." The result for women, he warned, is greater sterility, dread of childbirth, and less ability to nurse babies. And the answer is play: "the school and community need to put very much greater emphasis on play and physical activity for girls, especially during the period before puberty."[24]

Gulick's answer was the Girls' Branch of the PSAL. Founded by Jessie Bancroft in 1905, with the support of two prominent wealthy reformers, Grace Dodge and Ellen Speyer, much of the leadership fell to Elizabeth Burchenal, a woman who as a pioneer of the American folk dance movement is a major part of this story.[25] But Gulick had a second institutional response as well: in Washington, DC, on April 12, 1906, Gulick and Curtis founded the Playground Association. The president of the United States, Teddy Roosevelt, was made honorary president of the association, and the muckraking reformer Jacob Riis was made honorary vice president. Gulick served as president and Curtis as secretary and acting treasurer. The group quickly moved to enact legislation in New York State mandating minimums for school recesses and physical education. And within two years, they had national results: by 1907, fifty-seven cities reported that they had 836 playgrounds for which maintenance costs were $904,102.[26] The New York Branch, headed by Gulick, was an eclectic group that counted among its leaders Curtis and Progressive settlement leaders such as Lillian Wald and Mary Simkovitch, as well as the conservative Boston philanthropist James Lee, who supported the Immigration Restriction League.[27]

What, however, was to be done in the playgrounds? For possible answers, reformers looked to various programs for enriching the culture of the body through movement that had emerged in the nineteenth century, both in Europe and North America: exercise and dance.

Physical Culture

Most working people could not escape to the countryside, so reformers sought alternatives to fresh air and rural space in exercises that could be practiced in relatively small internal facilities. The answer, drawn from strong, "manly" conceptions of the northern European (and white) body, came from physical culture and what in the schools came to be known as physical education.

Luther Gulick emphasized how muscular exercise could address the twin problems of urbanization and industrialization on worker bodies. Urbanization had transformed daily life: less than 4 percent of Americans had lived in cities and villages in 1790; 40.2 percent in 1900 no longer lived in "country districts." Certain eastern states had become virtual urban enclaves with no green space: in Massachusetts in 1900 only 8.5 percent lived in rural areas, and in New York, Connecticut, and New Jersey, the figure was only about 25 percent. At the same time as Gulick bemoaned the lack of rural space for exercise, he observed that the growth of machine production resulted in fewer muscular movements by workers, and those they did make were often repetitive. Trade unionists might complain about routinized work in confined spaces, but Gulick's concern was that modern industrial life had replaced more arduous farm labor with work that involved little more in his mind (as he did none of it) than "tending machines."[28]

Gulick rehearsed the gendered systems of gymnastic practices that had grown up in the United States during the nineteenth century, on which one could draw for training the male and female body.[29] The earliest forms, attributed by Gulick to the Germans and Swedish, emphasized gymnastic exercises that could produce the healthy male body in particular. The first of these, pioneered by the Prussian "father of gymnastics," Friedrich Ludwig Jahn (1778–1852), early in the nineteenth century, was introduced to the United States (and presumably to England) by German refugees from the failed revolution of 1848.[30] A second system, named after the founder of Swedish Gymnastic Movements, Peter Henry Ling (1776–1837), gained favor in the 1870s. In contrast to the German emphasis on muscular development for men, the Ling system focused on suppleness.[31] By the turn of the century, a third form of exercise emerged, an "American system" pioneered by Harvard medical doctor Dudley A. Sargent. Celebrating the "well-rounded body," Sargent worked with his male students at the college and developed a system of weight machines to tailor physical training to an individual's body shape and needs.[32]

Finally, a fourth exercise system that followed the work of the Frenchman François Delsarte (1811–1871) gained currency at the turn of the century as a system of "harmonious gymnastics" for the female body. Less a form of physical exercise than a set of gentle movements and breathing techniques, the Delsarte method reflected how gendered and class-specific routines came to characterize turn-of-the-century concerns with the healthy body: it was thought most appropriate for elite female bodies, for which hard physical work was considered neither appropriate nor usual.

The Americanized form of the Delsarte system produced gendered "relaxed harmonious bodies" in keeping with concerns that had emerged over the course of the nineteenth century about what the physician Edward H. Clarke in 1873 had warned of as emotional and physical dangers to women's reproductive organs. In his 1873 book, *Sex in Education: A Fair Chance for Girls,* Clarke warned that exercise routines and coeducation more generally stressed women's unique fragile physiognomy. Women, he explained, are distinguished from men in reproductive organs, and these organs are at their most formative stage in the early teens. Citing seven cases of young women who exerted themselves in study and work (trying to succeed "like a man"), in which he found reproductive systems suffered, Clarke concluded that girls between fourteen and eighteen years old should not study as much as boys. Young women, he continued, jeopardize their "special apparatus" when they use as much "brain work as boys." Woman is "dowered with a set of organs specific to herself," and therefore, in the "interest of the race," coeducation should proceed with different regimes for boys and girls.[33]

Turn-of-the-century reformers embraced the gentle movements of the Delsarte exercise regime as an alternative bodily regime. After studying with Delsarte in Paris, theater innovator Steele MacKaye (1842–1894) developed a program for training actors in his New York acting company that replaced gymnastics equipment with deep-breathing exercises and training in graceful methods of reclining and fainting. Genevieve Stebbins (1857–1914?), a onetime actress and collaborator with Steele, popularized this system of techniques in her book, *Delsarte System of Expression*, and institutionalized it in the New York School of Expression, which she founded at Carnegie Music Hall in 1893. Her book, reprinted six times by 1902, reflected the substantial popularity of the system among the educated reading public. As important, as the focus on fainting suggests, the Delsarte method mirrored the gendered and class nature of emerging physical education. Even as reformers mobilized to teach immigrant girls to combat the enervating effects of industrial urban living, the Delsarte system addressed the neurasthenia-prone elite female body.[34]

Educators worked to institutionalize these developments in physical culture in the last quarter of the nineteenth century as physical education tailored for men and women. In the United States, Sargent's programs become cornerstones of new Normal Schools that began as single-sex schools for girls or for boys in the 1860s. By the 1880s, these new schools were training teachers for public-school physical-education programs. Such training became an integral element of teacher education generally and explains how it is that college-level dance programs became institutionalized in schools of education.

Reformers emphasized that bodily education was important for those who were beyond school years as well, and exercise became a cornerstone of the YMCA movement that emerged on both sides of the Atlantic during this era. Writing in 1920, Gulick approvingly noted that five hundred YMCA gyms with one hundred thousand members had been established in the United States since 1870. The underlying goal of moral virility may have meant little more than cold showers and clean living, but these gyms provided planned regimes of exercises that varied by the person's age, individual needs, and targeted muscles.[35]

Gymnastics, military training, and manly sport produced the healthy, more elite male body, whether that of the Harvard boys or the upper ranks of the growing white-collar managerial and professional labor force. And the Delsarte system taught graceful contained body movement to the comparable class of women in women's colleges and female academies and to the burgeoning numbers of "middling" white-collar would-be professionals—the growing corps of teachers, social workers, and nurses in the new service economy. The Delsarte techniques, however, also informed an emerging movement in modern dance that heralded a new respectable public role for women's bodily display at the turn of the century. As a socially acceptable form of activity, modern dance was also the one dance form that many young affluent women of the new middle classes brought with them when they first encountered English Country Dance.

The origins of modern dance also lay in this period and constituted a variation on physical exercise, albeit for elite women in particular. Modern dance provided an alternative model to the manly physicality associated with gymnastics on the one hand and the questionable (at best) morality of risqué music hall burlesque on the other. Women who pioneered this dance, such as Loie Fuller (1862–1928), Ruth St. Denis (1879–1968), and Isadora Duncan (1877–1927), in order to claim respect for their performance as an aesthetic art form rather than as a debased erotic, had to negotiate the male gaze and the often thin line between traditions of burlesque and music hall "hootchie-kootchie" dance and their "art." "Aesthetic" dance, they averred, emphasized grace, often combining Delsarte fluidity with the allures of the scantily clad burlesque queen, representing classical figures such as Salome. But as important as their bodily movement, these artistes, as historian Linda Tomko points out, established a new sanctioned public role for women. These modern dance pioneers, speaking with their bodies in a respectable manner and capitalizing on the traditional role of woman teacher in primary schools, won the authority to teach the modern dance as well.[36]

Gymnastics, sports, and the military for men and Delsarte exercises and modern dance for women gave elites a range of bodily exercises, but they did not address the social question of the age: how were working-class immigrant bodies to be disciplined? These exercise regimes could counter the stultifying monotony of office life and the country club or the impersonal and imposing brick-and-concrete urban metropolis that Fritz Lang so graphically represented in his 1927 film of that title. What bodily regimes, though, could meet the needs of the working class cooped up much of the day in factories and tenements? What practices and institutions could revive the spirit of working-class girls and boys? For while the atrophying effect of rote mechanical movements of modern industry worried reformers, their concern extended to the larger effect of monotony on the spirit of the race. And, to be sure, many reformers deemed these twined concerns of bodily and moral degeneration to be critical matters for all—young and old, native and immigrant—at a time when British and American business tycoons were justifying imperial roles by holding themselves aloft as beacons of "civilization." But the imperial vision found the domestic imperial subject—the working class—an equally vexing source for the fin-de-siècle degeneration. Some Progressive reformers focused on providing immigrants with skills to increase their opportunities; others worried more about their attraction to radical politics; for yet some others, the two concerns overlapped. Whether they were a domestic colonial subject or the subject of paternal reform, migrants and immigrants, recognized as usually coming from rural and peasant backgrounds, needed to be instilled with democratic lessons of citizenship, respectability, and cooperation.

Ironically, the rural and "peasant" pasts were both a problem and a solution. At the same time as reformers organized to teach these urban newcomers how to make budgets, adjust to factory rhythms, and behave like burghers, reformers (sometimes the same reformers) came to believe these newcomers had a vibrant, curative "peasant" past in their blood that only had to be awakened. A new cadre of folklorists, the new profession committed to the revival of a "peasant" past, had emerged in the past decade, and reformers now turned to them in the hope they could help revitalize the urban and national spirit with the curative "essence" of the American and English "race" embodied in English Country Dance.

The Folk Revival: Folklore and Song

Folklore as a scholarly discipline arose as one answer to increasing elite and middling anxieties about the immigrant industrial city. Folklorists and anthropologists—among the emergent social sciences—set out for the countryside to find, recover, and preserve what they imagined to be solutions to the maladies of urban-industrial life in the vital cultural remnants of a simple and pure peasantry. For the folk revival at the turn of the century was a phenomenon of the urban, industrial city. Moreover, it centered in the cosmopolitan capitals of England and the United States—London and New York—where social and cultural doyens were in place to try to ameliorate, as they understood it, the more intense transformations of daily life. To be sure, in the United States, Boston, which had historically been the center of Brahmin culture, played an important role in English Country Dance as well. But metropolises such as London and New York were logical places for these efforts to take root. These cities overwhelmed in scale and population other cities in each country, especially as New York was poised in 1898 to absorb Brooklyn, then the fourth-largest city in the United States. Each metropolis was a cultural and financial capital—the media center of the nation and home to its economic engine. As such, each stood as a national symbol of the urban transformation of the nation, and with their large immigrant populations, they provided a visible basis on which national identity was imagined, represented, and constructed.

The revivals also took place in the North Atlantic world. This is not to minimize the role of the colonial Atlantic in fueling the revival imagination. The heyday of imperialism in the United States and the United Kingdom, where the Anglo-American folk tradition on which we focus was rooted, shaped the revival in two ways: the imperial project demanded a virile race, often encapsulated in the idea of muscular Christianity, to "civilize" heathen others; and the creation of a Anglo-American identity, as in the case of all identity formation, required an other against which it could be advanced. Poor and black Caribbean and African peoples were seen as an uncivilized primitive other without a usable past or tradition. Thus, the folk revival that swept northern Europe and the United States at the end of the nineteenth and the beginning of the twentieth centuries was a fundamentally nationalist movement.

This movement also reflected European and Anglo-American imperial ambitions and, as such, had a colonial cast: against the backdrop of the immigrant city, the folk celebrated were white northern Europeans; Swedish, Danish, and British dances constituted most of the repertoire. Imperialists moved into India, Africa, the Caribbean, and Asia, but folklorists, whose racist, imperial vision could only imagine the folk as European peasants, never ventured far from home.[37] In the case of English Country Dance, a group of reformers mobilized English folk song and dance as expressions of Anglo-Americanism—what they saw as essential native American culture embedded in and privileging the nation's English heritage as white—in order to inculcate the "spirit of the race" in immigrant working girls and boys. It was many decades before folklorists seriously broadened their conception to encompass dances from Africa, Asia, or the Caribbean.

In England, the Folklore Society organized in 1878 and published the first issue of its journal, *Folk-lore Record,* the same year. A decade later, the *Journal of American Folklore* published its first issue (1888). Although the role of the collector in the early folk dance collecting is unclear, as early as the seventeenth century, music publishers such as John Playford provided important source material for later folklorists. It should be noted, however, that most early folklore study focused on song, not dance. In that regard, folklorists generally traced the origins of the field to the collecting work of Johann Gottfried von Herder (1744–1803), who worked a century after Playford. Herder pioneered studies of the *Volk* (folk) and published in 1778 a collection of song lyrics he had collected in the then German town of Riga (in present-day Latvia) using a new term of the day, *volksleider* (folk songs).[38] Less iconic but no less significant work parallel to Herder's collecting folk songs took place in England and Scotland at almost the same time. Thirteen years earlier, in 1765, Thomas Percy (1768–1808), an English clergyman, published a collection of broadsides, *Reliques of English Poetry,* which fueled the imagination of many Romantic poets. Joseph Ritson's (1752–1803) *A Selected Collection of English Songs* followed soon after in 1783. And in 1802, the Scotsman Sir Walter Scott (1771–1832) published his ballad collection, *Minstrelsy of the Scottish Border.*

Folkloric interest in folk songs took off in the nineteenth century, however, and on both sides of the Atlantic.[39] Increasingly seeing urban culture as rowdy, sordid, and vulgar in music halls, some people began to celebrate folk song as the unsophisticated, primitive, genuine, simple beauty of common emotion. The rise of the Chartists in the 1830s and 1840s stimulated the need for a unifying national culture in England, and well-to-do gentry pursued "folklore" as a "genteel hobby"; at the same time, as philanthropists, they developed "rational recreation." John Broadwood (1798–1864), for instance, who in 1843 published *Old English Songs, as now Sung by the Peasantry of the Weald of Surrey and Sussex,* was the grandson of pianoforte manufacturers and squire of a family estate on the Sussex-Surrey border.[40]

By the end of the century, a small band of enthusiasts-antiquarians had emerged to satisfy the growing interest in folk songs. In England, the gentry industry in folk song collecting took off in the late 1880s, in the decade before Cecil Sharp's Boxing Day epiphany with morris dance. Twenty-seven song collections between 1888 and 1925 used "folk" in their title, most with simple piano arrangements easily used in schools. The most prominent of these collectors were Sabine Baring-Gould (1834–1924) and Lucy Broadwood

(1858–1929). Sabine Baring-Gould was the niece of John Baring-Gould, a Church of England clergyman who was squire of Lew Trenchard, Devon. A prolific writer of religious books, and most famous as the author of the hymn "Onward Christian Soldiers," he moved on in 1888 to collecting folk songs. The historian Stefan Szczelkun has noted how, assisted by the German émigré Carl Engel, Baring-Gould emphasized folk music to advance the national rather than the popular interest. Publishing "Songs of the West" between 1888 and 1891, he was in his later years one of the few collectors to develop a working relationship with Sharp.[41]

The other major folk song collector of the era was Lucy Broadwood, a gifted singer and pianist who had been inspired by her uncle John. Traveling about the countryside, she collected folk songs from old-timers in rural villages. In 1893, she published with a relative, the music critic John Maitland (1856–1936), the influential collection *English Country Song*. In 1898, she was one of the 110 members at the founding meeting in Mayfair of the Folksong Society, a group that included major musical figures of the day such as Antonín Dvořák (1841–1904), Edward Elgar (1857–1934), Edvard Grieg (1843–1907), and Ralph Vaughan Williams (1872–1958). In tribute to the esteem with which members held her work—and consistent with hierarchical gender stereotypes—the society in 1904 made her its honorary secretary.[42]

The development of folk song studies in the United States followed a similar trajectory. Although it initially took a more academic turn than its British cousin, the Americans, too, focused on British folk song. In part, this was because the early folklorists were Anglophiles and themselves of British origin; increasingly though, the British ballad became implicitly recognized as part of an Anglo-American folk tradition. Two Harvard Shakespeare scholars steeped in the lore of "Merrie England"—Francis James Child (1825–1896) and his successor, George Lyman Kittredge (1860–1941)—trained and inspired the first generations of American folklorists, giving the early work a Brahmin academic cast. Having a passion for British ballads, Child published a renowned ten-volume collection, *The English and Scottish Ballads*, between 1882 and 1898. The books had a modest 305 titles but provided in meticulous detail every known textual variation—over thirteen hundred in all.[43]

The research methods and idea of the "authentic" folk ballad that Child deployed established important but not unproblematic standards for song collectors of his and subsequent generations. First, Child worked primarily as a literary researcher, rather than as a field collector. Considering ballads "narrative song," he treated folk song as popular poetry and analyzed songs as texts, largely dismissing the music. Second, Child believed commercial and aristocratic taste had corrupted songs produced after the emergence of the printing press; he was only interested in "uncorrupted" ballads from before 1475 that were distinguished not as Literature (with a capital L) but as "low art." With this perspective, Child's ballad "collecting" required travel no further than Harvard's Widener Library. Third, Child, ever the scholar, established new standards for folk song scholarship based on meticulous editing and research. However, he was also ever the eminent Victorian and not so different from many of his contemporaries. While he moralistically cited his own work as a model against the work of others who "altered" and "edited," he himself omitted stanzas he found tasteless or too bawdy.[44]

Child himself did not collect in the field, but his research was appreciated by others who moved to do so in the 1890s. In 1888, Child was elected the first president of the American Folklore Society. That same year, the society's journal began to publish the work of the new breed of folklorists; some of the first songs collected by Lila W. Edwards in the mountains of North Carolina appeared in 1893.[45]

In the following decade, although the settlement movement remained an urban phenomenon, rural settlements began to be established in the mountains, and word of "mountain ballads" began to spread. Berea College in Berea, Kentucky, was established in 1855, and the Log Cabin Settlement in Asheville, North Carolina, in 1895. Recognizing rural needs for organized recreation and social services, in May 1899, the Progressive journalist John P. Gavit urged the formal development of rural settlements that could, among their services, provide clubs and traveling libraries and teach cooperative farming and dairying. That same month, the Kentucky Federation of Women's Clubs met and heard a report from its traveling-library committee of the need for programs to teach mountain women sewing, cooking, and other domestic skills. A year later, in 1900, six of these well-heeled women, including Katherine Petit and May Stone, pitched tents in Hindman, Kentucky, with supplies for social programming. Well received by the locals, in 1902, Petit and Stone established the Hindman Settlement School, and the movement for rural settlements was under way.[46]

Southern mountain settlements such as Hindman Settlement proved to be vital repositories for folk collectors. Cecil Sharp, for instance, made what he considered his major American folk dance discovery at the Pine Mountain Settlement, which was organized in 1913. But the Hindman Settlement was the site of an equally important epiphany, that of Olive Dame Campbell (1882–1954). Olive Dame Campbell visited Hindman late in 1907 while accompanying her husband, John C. Campbell, on his Russell Sage Foundation–sponsored research in the mountains documenting social conditions. While there, she heard one of the students, Ada Smith, singing "Barbara Allen." Transfixed by the haunting tune of the British ballad that was "old as the hills," Campbell, then only a twenty-five-year-old recent bride, decided to become what a 2001 Hollywood movie based (unevenly) on her experience called a "song-catcher." In the next few years, she traveled throughout Kentucky, Georgia, and Tennessee collecting folk songs from old-timers, an experience for which she developed a passion that in time found her visiting folk schools in Denmark and that subsequently took her to England, Sweden, and Scotland.[47]

In tracing this history of folk song collectors, it is important to remember that these people were as much creating as discovering a tradition. This was an "imagined folk," a "peasant" folk as seen through the class perspective of an elite, as most historians have come to appreciate.[48] Thus, Ritson's 1783 collection excluded songs he felt were offensive or misrepresented the culture. Ritson, seeing the culture of the common folk as debased, corrected grammar and "senselessness" in order to preserve "authenticity." Baring-Gould modified song lyrics he found "too much" for Victorian taste. Child, as I have noted, elided stanzas he found "tasteless." Cecil Sharp omitted playful kisses from dances he reconstructed and famously changed the name of "Cuckolds All A Row" (Playford's title for what Samuel Pepys in his diary, in 1662, called "Cockolds All Awry") to "Hey, Boys, Up Go We," never realizing that the new name was a potentially indelicate political reference to hanging.[49]

Sharp's "invention" also involved what dances were authorized as part of the tradition and in what manner. Thus, as the historian Georgina Boyes has noted, Sharp omitted step dancing and clogging from his repertoire and dismissed the Lancashire morris tradition carried forth by factory hands as "modern" and inauthentic.[50] And notably, as pointed out by Douglas Kennedy, Sharp's student and subsequent leader of the English Folk Dance and Song Society, William Kimber, the concertina player whom Sharp (and others) claimed as the authority on morris dancing—to assert his own authority in turn—had a very particular style. Kimber taught the Headington tradition as he knew it, but "he enforced a military precision which he prized as a result of his own army experience. The result was that our [Kennedy's morris side] interpretation of the Headington tradition was very four square and measured."[51]

The Revival Expands

Appreciation for the recuperative power of folk traditions rose as industrial capitalism intensified and concerns about its effects mounted. Even in its first stages, the folk revival in both England and the United States was part of the "immense transnational traffic in reform ideas, policies, and legislative devices," as described by the historian Daniel Rodgers, for the United States to address "the problems and miseries of 'great city' life, the insecurities of wage work, the social backwardness of the countryside, or the instabilities of the market itself."[52]

Americans and the English looked to northern European celebrations of the folk—to Germany and Scandinavia in particular. Jacob (1785–1863) and Wilhelm (1786–1859) Grimm published their first collection of children's folk tales in 1812. Scandinavian folk song, children's games, and folk schools especially attracted the attention of Anglo-American folklorists, who, in turn, learned from one another as well. As Rodgers has noted, as early as the 1880s, Danish folk schools in particular infatuated some American reformers as an answer to southern rural poverty. As important, they saw renovated rural traditions—both of a revived Danish folk and, then, the hoped-for revival of the American folk in the highlands—as the basis of a vital national culture that could invigorate the urban immigrant city. U.S. Commissioner of Education Philander P. Claxton chanced upon a Danish folk school in 1896 and actively promoted them in the American South. A few years later, perhaps as early as 1904, Elizabeth Burchenal traveled to Denmark and soon after published the first of her many folk collections, two-thirds of which were Danish folk songs and games to be taught in playgrounds in settlement houses across urban America.[53] In point of fact, as Rodgers notes, Danish schools were *Folkehøjskoler*, which actually translates as "people's high schools" but was falsely translated as "folk schools" and bore the anthropological burden of the era.[54] Not surprisingly, most of the first books published of folk dances primarily consisted of dances from other lands—not of dances collected from the home country. Two volumes published in 1908 and 1909 featured dances and "singing games" from Scandinavian countries; they were followed by two 1915 books on the dances of Finland and Denmark.[55]

Much of the spirit, mission, and curriculum of the folk schools and that of the broader folk revival itself was expressed, however, in the Arts and Crafts Movement popular in England and the United States. It, too, spurred a renewed transatlantic appreciation of simple artisan craftsmanship and an enthusiasm for going "back to the land." Working in the second half of the nineteenth century, the Pre-Raphaelite English painters, often considered the first avant-garde movement in art, rejected what they saw as mechanistic approaches. The art and social critic John Ruskin (1819–1900) applied their critique to industrial labor for its dehumanizing impact on workers. As manufacturers raced to replace (expensive) skilled manual labor with machines, workers were turned into machines, routinized and lifeless: in Ruskin's words, "You must either make a tool of the creature, or a man of him. You cannot make both." Noting the integration of art with craftwork in Gothic architecture, Ruskin urged manufacturers to renew artisanal work as a way of bringing creativity and pleasure back into labor.[56]

The designer, poet, and visionary socialist William Morris (1831–1896) transformed Ruskin's belief in the redemptive potential of craftsmanship into what became the basis of a movement: the Arts and Crafts Movement. Morris was not a Luddite: machinery should "be used freely for releasing people from the more mechanical and repulsive part of necessary labor," not to "cheapen labor." But for a "healthy body," the worker "can not be continually chained to one dull round of mechanical work." Despairing that the capitalists' drive for profit would never permit a renewal of work and art, Morris and some friends started a decorative-arts firm that drew on the belief that there was an inherent joy in labor, especially in handiwork. Seeing beauty in simple labor evidenced in nature, he drew inspiration for his designs from the leaves of trees or the fruits and flowers of gardens. Reviving hand weaving, for instance, he rose at dawn to take advantage of natural light when working at his loom. By the 1880s, Morris's appreciation of the value of artisan labor had become a celebration of the value of labor itself, as informed by Marxism, and he became a revolutionary socialist. Coauthor of the Socialist League manifesto in 1884, Morris took to the streets on behalf of workers' rights. At the same time, arts and crafts societies sprang up across England and Scotland. When the first exhibition of the Arts and Crafts Exhibition Society was held in 1888, Morris's work was prominently on display. He attended as well, lecturing on tapestry weaving. More a form of sentimental than revolutionary socialism, the Arts and Crafts Movement, in expressing the dignity and aesthetic value of handcraft work, took its inspiration rather than its leadership from Morris. As such, the movement was consonant with Fabian socialism and the emerging liberal reform sensibility associated with Progressivism.[57]

Even as the Arts and Crafts Movement enjoyed wide appeal in England, it thrived especially in Scandinavia and the United States. Ruskin's criticism on art and architecture and Morris's poetry, criticism, and lectures on decorative arts were not published in the United States for decades, but news and versions of them quickly appeared in American athenaeums and libraries. At one point Ruskin was more popular in the United States than at home. Oscar Wilde's American tour in 1882 championed the work of Morris and the

Pre-Raphaelites and gave a wide audience to the Arts and Crafts Movement. Soon after, a veritable cottage industry of artisans and workshops began producing designs for wallpaper, carpets, and architecture modeled on or in the style of Morris's work. The extraordinary impact of the movement on U.S. design and architecture is reflected in the development of mission oak furniture by Gustave Stickley, the Prairie School of architecture led by Frank Lloyd Wright, and the popularity of both the bungalow house and the neo-Colonial home.[58]

The folklorist David Whisnant has described the Arts and Crafts Movement as primarily an urban phenomenon. In London, this was particularly the case: the architect and designer C. R. Ashbee (1863–1942) opened his Guild and School of Handicraft in 1888, and that same year artists rejected by the Royal Academy created the aforementioned Arts and Crafts Exhibition Society. London settlements also early on incorporated into their curricula theories and programs ideas put forth by Ruskin, Morris, and their contemporaries that a revival of handcraft could counter the dehumanizing effects of the industrial revolution. In the United States, the impact was more diverse, however. Reformers saw rural depopulation and decline as a problem in both countries, but the American problem had a distinguishing scale and name—Appalachia—and no redeeming legacy of the village idyll on which to draw. The United States also had a distinct counterlegacy of slavery. Not surprisingly, then, American reformers and craftspeople mobilized elements of the Arts and Crafts Movement to meet all these rural challenges in a variety of southern and rural institutions. Mountain folk settlements everywhere began to introduce new programs incorporating craft work. Vassar graduate Susan Chester's Log Cabin Settlement opened in Asheville, North Carolina, in 1895, and Berea College started its "fireside industries" craft program the same year. In the following decade, Fireside Industries, workshops based on the craft revival, spread to half a dozen settlements in the southern Appalachians, from the Berry School in Rome Georgia (1903) and the Pi Beta Phi School in Gatlinburg, Tennessee (1912), to the Hindman (1901) and Pine Mountain settlements in Kentucky (1913). Finally, in a similar commitment to the educative value of the "industrial arts," Booker T. Washington opened the Tuskegee Normal and Industrial Institute in 1881 to teach craft skills to former African American slaves.[59]

In the United States, the Arts and Crafts Movement was no less important in informing the curriculum in some northern urban settlements. Settlement workers shared the movement's foundational beliefs in the enervating character of industrial labor and bustling urban life and the redemptive role of artisanal handcraft. Accordingly, settlement curricula often embraced the Arts and Crafts Movement, from running Ruskin study clubs for members to emulating the clean decorative lines in their furnishing and décor. Tomko notes that the movement won especially strong support from Chicago's Hull House, where Ellen Gates Starr "opened a bookbinding workshop upon her return from study in England with T. J. Cobden-Sanderson." There was, of course, a paternalist cast to settlement workers' use of such "redemptive" work and craft skills in that the homespun prepared immigrant women more for domestic work or the needle trades than for entry into the more remunerative "semi"-professions such as social work, nursing, and teaching or new clerical trades.[60]

The settlements' embrace of folk crafts and ballads met reformers' desire to instill in immigrants and urbanites generally the lost values, attitudes, and spirit of the rural idyll and the pioneer. This spirit also needed to be embodied, both in space and in demeanor. Thus, girls and boys had to be taken out of the compromising moral morass of the music hall and given an alternative to the jazz or "animal" or "rough" dances in which unchaperoned "spieling" girls and boys, pivoting wildly—a move that required intimate physical contact—experienced vertigo, the giddy dizziness of being "out of control," out of one's "senses." Playgrounds, settlements, and schoolyards sanctioned competitive team sports in various gymnastics systems and sport as one set of alternatives, especially for boys.[61]

Yet, as Henry Curtis reminded reformers, it was not boys but "girls [who] are our great national problem." At the turn of the century, as the fear of the dance halls and "tango craze" escalated, the general answer for Curtis was "play and physical activity for girls, especially during the period below puberty."[62] Gendered attitudes, however, were also classed. Thus, more affluent parents encouraged "refined" daughters to choose Delsarte movements, and modern dance reformers sought an alternative for immigrant working girls who had neither the leisure time nor, it was thought, the predilection for the aesthetic dancing. The more specific solution, however, came from Luther Gulick, and it promised to combine the strengths of "peasant" folk traditions with the need for appropriate movement: folk dance.

Gulick understood the problem to be the dance hall, not dancing. "Dancing is in itself not only innocent, but good exercise. Its surroundings are often bad." Dancing is "language, particularly of the feelings," "the most universal of the arts." But in the United States, its "deeper possibilities" have been reduced to "a man and a woman holding each other and performing an exceedingly simply whirling movement to music set in four-four or three-four time" (i.e., the two-step and the waltz). Its "abuses" in rough dancing were legion; rather, one had to focus on its "uses" as "excellent exercise." Dancing schools for modern and ballroom dance teach "good posture of the body and grace of movement," but for Gulick, "dancing as a bodily discipline" is evident in "the old folk-dancing."[63]

No less significantly, for Gulick, body discipline also provided a lesson in democracy. Democracy requires the sand box for small children, the playground for youths, and "folk-dancing and social ceremonial life for the boy and girl in their teens," for "development of that self-control which is related to . . . the corporate conscience that is rendered necessary by the complex interdependence of modern life." Folk dances express the ties of the individual to a community, so they are important for immigrant children to know of their roots; at the same time, the dances express "mass feeling" and bring about a "consciousness of the whole."[64]

These were lessons especially important in the new immigrant city. National and folk dances, Gulick continued, traditionally existed to celebrate holidays and special events in older and rural societies. The United States at that time had occasions such as Thanksgiving and the Fourth of July that demanded celebration, but the country had no traditional form of group expression other than passively watching fireworks: the country has, he complained, a "poverty" of traditions or "social forms in which to express our common emotions." Immigrant children of so many diverse backgrounds can share only the simplest folk dances and lore that are common to all. Thus, "the great folk-dances and folk festivals are gone," and we need play leaders as "tradition carriers . . . capable of transmitting the social and moral traditions of the race."[65]

But who was to teach folk dance, and who was to train the "tradition carriers" to "transmit" the "traditions"? Contrary to conventional accounts, the answer did not come from Cecil Sharp: his encounter with William Kimber and the Headington Morrismen translated into an immediate fascination with song; he put dance on a back burner. Instead, a North London settlement worker, Mary Neal, and a New York folk dance aficionado and collector, Elizabeth Burchenal, initiated the study and teaching of the old rural and village dances. But as important, they renewed interest in a particular form of folk dance that expressed "gay simplicity" in a contained, respectable body thought to embody national civic values. This dance form, English Country Dance, they came to see as having special value for their urban subjects in particular and for the English and American nations in general.

2

Orderly Bodies: Dancing New York, 1900–1914

Bodies never lie.
—George Graham, to his daughter Martha[1]

Folk-dancing offers . . . possibilities as a Democratic Socializing Agent, and . . . value as a form of *real* Americanization.
—Elizabeth Burchenal, 1920[2]

Anglo-American exchanges in the decade before World War I, both of Americans traveling to the United Kingdom and of the British visitors to the United States, shaped awakenings of a folk revival in both New York and London. But, of course, English Country Dance was not new to America then; transatlantic crossings had brought country dance to the British colonies in the eighteenth century. At issue is how that past was remembered and the role of that past in the present.

Colonial Americans danced, and as a British colony, they inherited English dance traditions; historians are only beginning to unravel the regional, class, and ethnic variations of their dance experiences. Elites favored the minuets and the country dances historians have associated with the gentry, although the category had varied meanings and porous boundaries and the country dance appears to have engaged more plebian sorts as well. In the last quarter of the eighteenth century, New England and middle-Atlantic colonies tended to prefer the English dances, whereas the southern colonies, which maintained stronger allegiances to France, were more loyal to the minuet favored by their French allies. As important, English country dance traditions were reshaped by their encounter with ethnic American cultures, both religious and secular. Thus, the historian Rhys Isaac notes how "New Light" revivalists forced dancing underground in late-eighteenth-century Virginia and how African American dance culture informed the lively jigs. Isaac quotes the Virginian Andrew Burnaby, who found plebian country folk in 1759–60 challenging one another with jigs, "a practice originally borrowed," Burnaby was informed, "from the Negroes." Thus, both a young Virginian and Jack Tar, the archetypical Revolutionary War–era sailor, might on any given evening have kicked up their heels at a local dockyard tavern or a rural schoolyard with a jig or hornpipe (the two were not distinguished in the eighteenth century). Improvising with exuberant steps, each would show off his skill and would strut his manliness to the assembled crowd.[3] Meanwhile, across town or elsewhere in the county, in a plantation ballroom or one of the assembly rooms, George Washington—well known for his fancy footwork and grace—might have been opening the evening ball by dancing a minuet with the ball's hostess. The minuet, an elegant showpiece ceremonial dance with steps characteristic of the Baroque period, was developed for the French court in the 1660s. It had complex and precise stepping with formal upright carriage and was performed by couples for the assemblage, each in descending rank taking a turn.[4]

It was English Country Dance, however, the dance tradition colonists shared with the mother county, that dominated most venues, whether it was the village taverns or the assembly halls of the growing metropolises, and most especially in the middle-Atlantic and northern regions. The jig was a solo dance, and the minuet required well-rehearsed training and skill for a couple dancing alone; in contrast, the country dance was a social dance for the assemblage and more easily accessible, demanding relatively little practice. As in England, by the eighteenth century, as the dances moved from the village green to the ballroom and upstairs into more elite quarters, set dances for three and four couples and rounds fell out of favor, and longways dances "for as many as will" predominated. These were typically *triple minors*, in which the top three couples danced together, and after a turn of the dance, the first couple progressed down the set one place to activate another couple. The dance would continue until all couples in the line were dancing. Moreover, English Country Dance, as dance historians Kitty Keller and Charles Hendrickson describe, was not wild and unstructured: "Despite the informal-sounding name, country dances were not undisciplined romps."[5] Eighteenth-century ECD in America was formal, celebrated composure and "complaisance" with a graceful elegance of carriage, and honored society's local hierarchies.

The dance also had its American inflections, much as folk traditions would often adopt local village characteristics. For instance, "Sir Roger de Cloverly" simply took on an American name, "The Virginia Reel." Local choreographers wrote tens if not hundreds of dances to celebrate American events and historic sites, dances with names such as "Vernon Forever," "Washington's Reel," "Liberty," "Burgoyne's' Defeat," and "Saw You My Hero,

George" (which was also known as "Lady Washington"). Historians have counted over twenty-five thousand longways English Country Dances published just in England between 1700 and 1830, and Keller and Henrickson have counted over twenty-eight hundred published on the American continent within that period.[6] Dancers favored triple minor longways dances for three couples because they offered the couple dancing the third-couple role, which stood out a round, the opportunity to socialize. (Many of these dances were rechoreographed as longways duple minors "for as many as will" in the late twentieth century for "modern" dancers who had other opportunities to socialize and little patience for standing idle, valuing instead as much movement as possible throughout the dance.)[7]

But although English Country Dance was a vital part of colonial America, other country dance forms emerged in the late eighteenth century as the new country began to establish its own identity, dances that came to shape a diverse Anglo-American country dance tradition in the United States. Not surprisingly, the new nation looked with an admiring eye to its French allies. The court of Louis XIV had developed intricate couple dances, *danses à deux* like the minuet, as entertainment and for displays of status. As courtiers moved about, they brought dance vogues and status aspirations as baggage, and the minuet soon became popular also in the restoration court of Charles II in England. Indeed, the minuet remained a popular courtly dance of elites through the eighteenth century on both sides of the Atlantic.[8]

But the transmission process went both ways. The minuet crossed the channel northward, while the longways dances of the English gentry moved across the channel southward to be taken up by the French. The French called their dance *contredanse*, perhaps because partners stood in long lines across from one another, and gave them a French esprit. Over the course of the next century, *contredanse* morphed into a lively, less fussy sibling of the English Country Dance in ways little understood—perhaps as a variant of a *danse à deux*, the gigue. In colonial America, the dance assumed the Anglicized name, contra dance. One historian sees the minuet emerging as the favorite of the Virginian court, while the English dances, many of which Playford had published, predominated in the northern colonies.[9] But social class may have been as important a determinant of popularity as geography: minuets were the dance of the elites, English longways dances (the Playford dances) were the dances of the gentry or middling classes, and everyone did contra dances. Thus, when the French encamped for the winter of 1780 in Newport, a contemporary observer noted that they built a "French Hall" and "had their minuets and *contredanses*."[10] At the Newport ball that same year, however, when General Washington danced with Miss Margaret Chamberlain and asked her to "call the tune," they danced "A Successful Campaign," the popular country dance of the day.[11]

New American dance forms reflected the locals' appreciation of their French allies. By the end of the century, in the new nation, both young and old could increasingly be found celebrating weddings, barn raisings, or harvests by dancing vigorously to reels, hornpipes, and jigs. Many were zesty fiddle tunes from England—"Money Musk," "The White Cockade," and "Speed the Plow"—but increasingly others were new tunes that celebrated local places and events, dances such as "Portland's Fancy," "Jefferson and Liberty," and "Hull's Victory."[12] The infatuation with things French could be seen in the 1799 publication of new longways country dances called the "Spirit of France" and "Lafayette."[13]

In the last half of the eighteenth century, a new square form of the *contredanse*, called the *cotillon* (and soon Anglicized as the cotillion), quickly became all the rage, first in the French court and by the 1770s in the American colonies. The cotillion, a nonprogressive dance for four couples, dominated the urban American ballrooms from 1780 to 1810. Constructed with established patterns of different figures that alternated with repeated choruses, the cotillion was the direct ancestor of both the ballroom quadrille and the modern square dance. In the United States, the baroque steps of the French *cotillon* gave way to simpler, livelier steps of the quadrille (which also moved from France to England and the United States) in the early-nineteenth-century American ballroom.

By the second quarter of the nineteenth century, new exciting couple dances such as the waltz, the schottische, and soon after, the polka, each of which allowed for greater physical intimacy and the exciting vertigo of spinning, displaced the quadrilles and longways country dances in the ballrooms of the metropolis. It was the longways dances derived from the historical publications that revivalists largely sought to resurrect a century later as part of an Anglo-American political project to invigorate "the race." But although country dance disappeared from the urban dance floor, it continued as a vital part of rural American culture, albeit in two distinct variants. With the social upheaval following the French Revolution, out-of-work French dancing masters traveled to the New World, bringing quadrilles to French settlements such as that in New Orleans. At the same time, immigrants in the early National period took the four-couple dances with them into the West, where they evolved (and persisted)—enlivened by Cajun, Scotch Irish, and African American influences—as the square dance of rural America. Mean-

Orderly Bodies: Dancing New York, 1900–1914 | 45

while, longways contra dance, which had thrived in the Northeast, where settlers long had ties to Britain, evolved as a distinct dance tradition of rural New England, where it continued to flourish as well.[14] By the late nineteenth century, French Canadians, Cape Breton Scots, and Irish immigrants who settled in New England mill towns had given New England longways contra dance its own unique musical character. In one folklorist's evocative words, the local ethnic communities added "Celtic and French Canadian bowing and fingering techniques, as well as tunes, to the Yankee dance bag."[15]

In England, villagers outside London continued to do traditional jigs, hornpipes, and reels. Recall that Sharp, before moving on to transcribing Playford dances from the seventeenth and eighteenth centuries, began his collecting by recording traditional dances that were a living tradition in West Country villages. But for the American story, it is important to note that country dance continued as well, especially outside the cities in New England, the West, and the southern mountains. Urban sailors and immigrant workers might still rise in a local tavern or neighborhood club to do a jig, and some of these steps probably continued in the shadows of urban nightlife in minstrelsy and "low-life" culture.[16] But the country dances that persisted and flourished in these backwoods areas—variants that have come to be known as square and contra dance—have roots in seventeenth-century English Country Dance and helped constitute (with ECD) the modern Anglo-American dance tradition represented today in the Country Dance and Song Society of America (CDSS). The origins of contra and square dance may be only partially understood, but it is clear that salient elements of these forms are an important part of the American country dance story.

Ritual dances such as the morris, which began the folk revival on both sides of the Atlantic, also existed in the United States and right up to the moment of the revival. Morris dance enthusiasts and historians Rhett Krause and James C. Brickwedde suggest the possibility that morris dancing was done by Sir Humphrey Gilbert's settlers in Newfoundland as early as 1589. More convincing is evidence that at least three morris tunes were written by Americans in the mid-nineteenth century and that a New Hampshire May Day celebration as recently as 1898 included a morris dance, although these were more likely to have been music-hall performance groups than recreational village sides.[17] Morris dance was not a social country dance; limited "teams" or "sides" practiced the various ritual and ceremonial dances as performance dances.

In any case, the morris revivalists of an English dance tradition also did not understand the transnational and heterodox influence of the American minstrelsy tradition on the morris, most particularly in the use of blackface by the

Puckish character who usually danced playfully around the side. To be sure, the conventional historical view has been that blackface has primitive origins in efforts to disguise one's identity; but Krause notes the inconclusiveness of this evidence, and he seems quite right to suggest that "the American minstrel shows, if not the actual origin of black face among some morris dancers, at least contributed to its popularity." As he notes, minstrel shows were extremely popular in England from 1843 through the early twentieth century, and morris was part of a New York City minstrelsy show in early 1861.[18]

English Country Dance as the basis of an American national identity, then, belies the complicated transnational exchanges of cultural forms that informed dance in England and early America. French and Italian dancing masters traveled to London to introduce dances such as "Jacob Hall's Jig" into the local repertoire. Renaissance dance from the Continent also influenced the basic forms ("Up a Double," "Siding," and "Arming")[19] of the earliest Playford dances. And the process of transmission traveled back and forth among the nobility, for much as they fought, they also intermarried and danced together. Over the course of the nineteenth century, square and contra dances further developed and flourished, taking on their own style and meter. Local variants emerged as well, shaped by French Canadian music in New England and by Scotch Irish, Cajun, and African American music in the West and southern mountains. Finally, reels owed much to Scottish dance, and vernacular jigs such as the eighteenth-century "Negro Jig" probably had African American influences if not roots.[20]

Oral traditions and a fragmentary record of dance as experienced by people have passed on the little that is now known of these histories, but there are two important facts that must be recognized. First, different but rich contra and square traditions existed throughout the nineteenth century and drew on the diversity of American immigrant and migrant cultures. Second, the Anglo-American folk dance tradition moved between English Country Dance and contra and square dance, making the broad range of country dances that came to fall under the umbrella of ECD in the twentieth century as much a native as an imported dance.

The Revival Imperative

Chapter 1 detailed how in the late nineteenth century, confining and alienating urban life, rural depopulation and decline, and foreign immigrant cultures threatened cities, the nation, and the healthy body and animated the search for vital physical-culture regimes to relieve anxieties. Leaders of the American folk revival knew of the colonial prehistory of ECD, but their redemptive project did not appreciate, understand, or find its heterogeneous origins useful to the new political and social imperatives of the age. Rather, as Progressivism piggy-backed on the imperial ventures that justified acquisition or dominion over places such as Cuba and the Philippines as Christian mission to "little black brothers," so did ECD, as imagined with roots in a "pure" Anglo-Saxon white peasantry, serve as a domestic colonial mission to the immigrant other. In the new century, the pace, intensity, and dimension of these changes, rather than easing, quickened and similarly accelerated the embrace of folk dance as a rehabilitative technology of the body. And as the industrial city became the wartime city, the fear of bodies at risk intensified.

Cecil Sharp's initial voyage to New York in late December 1914 on the SS *Lusitania* was prophetic of the dangerous times; no less so was his return to England four months later. As war fever heated up, Sharp set sail for England on the SS *Adriatic* on April 21, 1915. The last day of the voyage, April 29, in the "danger zone," men paced the deck all night, and he described everyone as "rather tense and excited." Indeed, friends had convinced him not to delay his return a week and to return on the supposedly faster and safer *Lusitania*. The decision to sail early, of course, saved his life and, in turn, ironically, gave life to the American Country Dance movement. Home in Uxbridge, Sharp learned on May 7 of the sinking of the *Lusitania*.[21]

Many others, including some prominent young male dancers, were not so fortunate. The war decimated Sharp's demonstration team, much as it did the young male population of the British Isles, the United States, and the Continent. Four of the seven male members of Sharp's demonstration morris side (six danced at a time; one was a spare)—Perceval Lucas, George Wilkinson, George Butterworth, and Reginald Tiddy—were killed at the Battle of the Somme in August 1916; Sharp's own son, Charles, was seriously wounded, although he did recover.[22]

The horrors of trench and gas warfare in World War I brought home to many families, in the most personal way, the physical dangers to men's bodies. But Americans had only to look at their own cities during the half decade in which Sharp and his protégés established ECD on American soil to feel that the body politic was as much under siege on the domestic front as on the foreign one—and women's bodies as much as men's.

Immigrant Bodies and Respectable Bodies

The history of the folk revival directly engages bodily comportment, but the context for that discussion again requires weaving together several of the threads—themes—of the story: the imperatives of Progressive reform, the politics of the folk, the political culture of liberalism, and what we might call "reluctant modernism."[23] The combination of these themes shows how in patrolling the boundaries of popular culture, the revival story engages broader aspects of American culture that are often treated, if at all, as distinct.

First, the disruptions of urban industrial life generated anxieties about bodily expression and control. Three sets of related transformations at the turn of the century—in social relations of production and consumption, in the cultural fabric of the city, and in the organization of urban space—came together like a triple witching hour on the stock market to heighten social fears of establishment citizens that disorderly bodies would undermine the new American empire and the promise of industrial progress. Changes in work and social relations undermined familiar workplace traditions and hard-won trade-union prerogatives at the same time as they opened up uncertain possibilities in new labor sectors. In earlier stages of capitalism, owners had focused on economies of production—of scale, wages, hours, and the like. But continued profit squeezes made owners seek new efficiencies in production and new markets—both abroad and, through advertising and sales, at home. The latter saw manufacturers increasingly shift resources into selling rather than making goods.

The capitalist quest for new markets coincided with the rise of new technologies to create leisure industries for dance. New technologies of electricity and petrochemicals put in place a "second industrial revolution" with new industrial sectors such as auto, film, and radio. But music halls, dance halls, playgrounds, and ballrooms—all venues in which social and folk dance could be done for fun and profit—were a central part of this new leisure world. In these industries, people who every day struggled to work under demands of capital for greater productivity had to learn to play for capital as well.

The leisure industries were as much testimony to the rise of a new white-collar labor force as to a site—a social space—where white-collar workers' bodily identities as respectable citizens were molded. Managing workers and selling products and services became essential adjuncts to the production of goods, but these new trades also became the core of a "new middle class" that sought to distinguish itself from the immigrant working class. Good workers also had to be taught to be good consumers. But the challenge for manufacturers, and the managers, advertisers, and industrial-relations experts hired by them, was to naturalize these new relations of production and consumption in a new immigrant labor force. The folk dance revival (and other forms of social dance in cabarets) were part of this project. Folk dance was a part of the new leisure industry, and immigrant workers and Progressive reformers were the subjects and agents, respectively, of its mobilization.

Dancing bodies, then, were a political project of and for Progressive reformers in the new middle class. The working class (or its "peasant" progenitors), however, was both the object and subject of their project. The culture of containment and the culture of liberalism were embedded in Progressives' political culture—in their concern with respectable bodies in space and in motion, whether in streets, factories, or dance halls. The reformers' focus on immigrant workers and concern with space came together in folk dance, where the immigrant "problem" was to be solved in the celebration of immigrant culture. English Country Dance in the United States, like other folk dances, was celebrated by revivalists as an expression of the pure folk traditions of a simpler past that peasant peoples had left behind, which could now be revived to build an inclusive American identity. Jane Addams caught the essentially conservative spirit of this urban liberalism in her 1909 volume *Spirit of Youth and City Streets*: "These old forms of dancing, which have been worked out in many lands and through long experiences, safeguard unwary and dangerous expression and yet afford a vehicle through which the gaiety of youth may flow. Their forms are indeed those which lie at the basis of all good breeding, forms which at once express and restrain, urge forward and set limits."[24]

Thus, economic and social transformations animated reformers' concerns with the body, both personal and political. Immigrant worker bodies called on to make the industrial machine work could be disruptive and dangerously unhealthy. Against them, these elites celebrated the "respectable" body. It would be orderly, disciplined, and genteel, albeit with gendered distinctions. Respectable female bodies would be nurturing and express refined grace and elegance of movement and demeanor. The respectable body would also not agitate or vote Socialist. And in contrast to both the swarthy southern and eastern European immigrants and the poor African Americans migrating north to cities such as New York, respectable bodies would be white.

New York's Body Impolitic

New York, the city in which Cecil Sharp arrived to advance his cause, was the belly of the industrial beast. By the turn of the century, the United States had displaced Great Britain as the world's leading producer. New York, quickly emerging as the manufacturing and corporate capital of the new economy, was transformed in kind. One in every eight Americans dwelt in the city at both the beginning and end of this period, but the population

Socialist women delivering *The Call*. Photographer unknown. (UNITE Archives, Kheel Center, Cornell University, Ithaca, NY 14853-3901)

mushroomed exponentially. Over 4.75 million people filled streets that had accommodated less than 1.9 million in 1880, a gain of 255 percent. The city, which had been consolidated into its present five boroughs in 1898, was in 1880 still a mercantile city; by 1910, it had been transformed, in the words of the historian David Hammack, into a corporate city "more extensively involved in management of American industry than in the Atlantic trade."[25]

The new industrial machine was directed by a new corporate bureaucracy, the backbone of the expanding professional white-collar class. Immigrants did the physical labor in the city's factories, ran its printing plants and its transport and construction industries, increasingly made up the low-paid clerical and service sector, and, in due course, became the subject of the revivalists' crusade.

The largest share of the newcomers consisted of Italians, eastern European Jews, and African Americans. Two-thirds of the African American population of the city lived in Manhattan, and new migrants from the South more than doubled their numbers there between 1890 and 1910 to 60,534. The number of New York City's foreign-born population grew at a comparable rate. Their percentage tripled between 1880 and 1910, coming to comprise nearly two million of the city's population. Of that number, 340,770 were born in Italy, 445,625 in Russia, and 242,545 in the Austro-Hungarian Empire. A handful from each country had been in the city thirty years before, but the social profile and culture of newcomers was often very different from that of landsmen who had preceded them. For example, German Jews, often wealthy and urbane, made up about 5 percent of the city's 1880 population; by 1920, Jews, now predominantly working-class eastern Europeans from small shtetls, constituted an astonishing 29.2 percent of the city. In contrast, Irish and German-born populations remained fairly constant between 1880 and 1910, with about a quarter million recorded at each census.[26]

These new immigrants and migrants reinvigorated nativism, which had never been far from the surface in American politics. The story of the Jim Crow South is familiar; less so is that of the reracialized northern cities, where infamous race riots that erupted in St. Louis and Chicago in 1919 only dramatized more pervasive discrimination and violence against urban blacks across the North. Moreover, old-timers racialized immigrants from eastern and southern Europe, often swarthy or Mediterranean, as a debased caste that was "not quite white." Indeed, many of them spoke strange languages and appeared alien. Some wore unusual clothing or had a custom of long beards or sideburns; some practiced Judaism or Catholicism. Fearful of what they did not understand, many old-timers thought these immigrants seemed content to live in crowded and unsanitary conditions.

In *How the Other Half Lives* (1890), the journalist Jacob Riis constructed in word and picture what became for contemporaries the paradigmatic image of squalid tenement life—that of the Lower East Side in New York City. A conservative reformer who believed in self-help, Riis exaggerated poverty and drew on ethnic stereotypes of his subjects. Nonetheless, his images thrived well into the twentieth century, too, shaping urban social policy wherever immigrant workers lived. The density of the Lower East Side was infamous: over half a million people crowded into its 2.3 square miles. Seeing the city in contrasting images of dark shadow and bright lights, Riis averred that "the tenements to-day are New York, harboring three-quarters of its population," and if some lived in elegant Fifth Avenue mansions, more than half lived in tenements that were dark, foul, and disease ridden.[27]

The Lower East Side was not just disease ridden; it was filled with immigrants—and the two were inseparable in many people's eyes. Indeed, in 1901, only 14,014 of its half a million residents had American-born parents.[28] But the sickly bodies of these newcomers were isolated, stigmatized, and contained from the moment they set foot on American soil, as the historian Daniel Bender has so graphically detailed. Inspectors, in a "performance" of medical pathology, quarantined one in five immigrants who passed through Ellis Island at the turn of the century. Thousands more were denied entrance entirely. Settling in, the stigmas of class, ethnicity, religion, race, and gender continued to be inscribed on their bodies. Thus, in November 1914, just as Cecil Sharp prepared to disembark in the city, the U.S. Public Health Service (PHS) completed its nine-month study of the industrial hygiene and health of two thousand male and one hundred female garment workers in New York's garment industry. The PHS discovered 4.36 defects or diseases per worker, with the largest threat coming from tuberculosis. And while such diseases set "respectable" minds imagining far worse, workers organized their own response to the problem, and they recognized the same relationship between health and play that reformers came to champion. Francis Cohn, who helped design a health plan for the New York local of the International Ladies Garment Workers' Union (ILGWU), recalled, "We considered play as important . . . for health." Also like the reformers, the ILGWU understood disease as gendered, affecting women differently than men. The union pioneered then in establishing gynecological clinics for women workers, if only to help them return home to fulfill what the male trade unionists (and many women leaders too) saw as their primary roles as wives and mothers. The union led the way as well, however, in creating family resorts such as Unity House, where workers' families could recuperate (with International Folk Dance) in the clean, country air upstate. The union motto was "Playing, Thinking, Acting."[29]

To reformers, however, "playing" was one thing; "acting," especially if it came in the form of trade-union agitation, could be quite another. In that sense, for many bourgeois New Yorkers, emaciated, tubercular bodies were but the physical display of the more pervasive and insidious infections of the body politic threatened by radical immigrant workers. The United Hebrew Trades represented the unions dominated by Jewish employees in the garment industry as early as 1888. By the end of 1910, when English morris dance teachers Mary Neal and Florence Warren arrived in New York, Jewish garment workers, with their Italian trade-union brothers and sisters, had already initiated a series of the largest and most dramatic strikes in the city's and nation's young history. A year earlier, on November 23, 1909, twenty thousand women from Local 25 of the ILGWU had walked out for a 20 percent wage increase and fifty-two-hour work week. The "Uprising of the Twenty Thousand" lasted three months. The strike resulted in a major union victory, notably after suf-

Orderly Bodies: Dancing New York, 1900–1914 | 53

Young woman victim of the Triangle Shirtwaist fire lying dead on the ground. From the *New York Evening Journal*. (UNITE Archives, Kheel Center, Cornell University, Ithaca, NY 14853-3901)

fragists (a movement that also plays a role in the folk dance story) joined the fray. Large manufacturers led by the owners of the Triangle Shirtwaist Factory conceded only after receiving adverse publicity when prominent wealthy suffragists such as Alva Belmont (first wife of William Vanderbilt) and Anne Morgan (the daughter of J. P. Morgan) joined the women garment workers' cause. Later in 1910, over one hundred thousand male cloakmakers were back out on the street to win improved conditions in their branch of the trade. And finally, just around the time Neal and Warren were returning to London, a terrible fire swept through the Triangle Factory, sending 146 of 500 mostly young immigrant Jewish and Italian girls employed there to their death when the fire ladders could not reach them. Management on the floor above them escaped down the stairwells, but to the outrage of the city, the girls had been locked in to prevent their taking work breaks.[30]

Two additional well-publicized labor protests led by the radical syndicalists of the Industrial Workers of the World (IWW) followed soon after, furthering the climate of urban disorder and upheaval, and of women's (and men's) bodies at risk. In 1911, a train brought starving children of Lawrence, Massachusetts, strikers to the city, and in 1913, the "Paterson Pageant" at Madison Square Garden celebrated IWW Paterson strikers in 1913. None of the labor protests was violent, and indeed, the major group victimized was the immigrant working girls at the Triangle Factory. But business leaders and the mainstream press painted a very different picture of the United States on the brink of insurrection.

The Modernist Historical Crisis

The dislocations and culture of protest associated with Progressivism triggered what historians have called a "modernist historical crisis," "the yearning for orderly, scientific solutions" to the chaos of industrial protest and disorderly bodies.[31] In this regard, although folk dances looked back to "peasant" origins and are easy to pigeonhole as antimodern,[32] folk dance enthusiasts embraced folk dancing as a critical element in educational reform and as integral to the development of physical culture for building the race.

Greenwich Village, where Sharp often went to teach—and where the Country Dance and Song Society was based until 1986—was precisely the kind of liminal modernist cauldron in which folk dance could thrive. The Village brought working-class activists cheek to jowl with bohemian, radical, middle-class intellectuals. Christine Stansell has described the emergence of the cultural dominance of leftists in the Village at this time and notes how they informed a culture of modernism. But modernism, as Stansell notes, is about more than machines; it is about "the pressures of democracy and the claims of women"—that is, about new "modern" social roles associated with demands for broadened opportunity and the emergence of the New Woman. For Stansell, the dancing figure of the New Woman is represented by Isadora Duncan, the pioneering modern dancer.[33] But the New Woman could become the Rebel Girl like radical labor organizer Elizabeth Gurley Flynn or evolve into the comfortably bourgeois flapper. And likewise, folk dance offered opportunities with complicated social meanings: it afforded many young women the opportunity to express their bodies in respectable public spaces. It also gave public roles to many women folk dance teachers, even as they taught dances that expressed traditional gender hierarchies.

The road to modernism, then, had many twists and turns. Missionaries and many corporate leaders and politicians saw the United States' new role as global, imperial power as the future for the Christian West. Dancing bodies could be an opportunity to build muscular Christianity to achieve the imperial mission and meet the needs of the "race"—or they could be threats to disorder. Women's bodies were as much at risk as men's, as the mothers of America's future, and their plight drew particular concern from Progressive reformers. The danger was evident everywhere—from unsupervised fraternizing on the street and in the libidinous social spaces of dance halls and cabarets to the dangers of lecherous bosses in workplaces.

Differently Dancing Bodies

Dance, as the rise of modern dance and gymnastics suggests, took many forms in the opening decades of twentieth-century urban America. Nowhere was it more varied and richer—and for the growing bourgeoisie, more worrisome—than in New York. "Respectable" elites preparing for society balls could go to the fashionable Dodworth Dancing Academy on Fifth Avenue. Allen Dodworth, whose family was known for founding the New York Philharmonic Society, had written the leading book of the time on social dance, *Dancing and Its Relation to Education and Social Life, with a New Method of Instruction, Including a Complete Guide to the Cotillion (German) with 250 Figures* (1885). His nephew, T. George Dodworth, who took over the academy in 1887, continued to teach the Dodworth Method that had been the bible for New York society since the 1830s—a series of measured steps that emphasized discipline for stately dances such as the pavane, the court quadrille, the minuet, and the polonaise.[34]

The rise of the two-step in the Gay Nineties gave a new spring to the national dance step, leading society matrons, according to one dance historian, to "smart hotel and drawing room classes."[35] But when it came to dancing the new rhythms of urban dance, the children of these matrons began to cross or blur the class boundaries of the venues. In this regard, the story is again transnational—both New York and London theatrical impresarios negotiated censors' concerns with scanty dress as part of the new commercialized leisure industry by importing exotic barefoot dancers back and forth across the Channel and the Atlantic. Americans such as Maud Allen, Ruth St. Denis, and Isadora Duncan, for instance, transformed the erotic into the aesthetic as "modern" dancers in both cities.[36]

The new nightclubs of the urban metropolis epitomized these liminal social dance spaces. In New York, "The Follies of 1907" inaugurated twentyone revues over the next quarter century. Produced by Florenz Ziegfeld— along the lines of the *Folies Bergère* in Paris—Ziegfeld's follies displayed Parisian cosmopolitan wickedness in scantily clad young, svelte women for bourgeois audiences, not as working-class vice.[37] A dance craze—not as performance but as participation—took hold of New York between 1911 and 1916, and the cabarets removed the boundaries of the theater, encouraging the audience to participate. The dance floor became a staging area in the new cabarets and lobster palaces that seemed to spring up overnight. By accounts, there were over five hundred dance halls in the city in 1910, and another one hundred academies enrolled over one hundred thousand students. Jesse Lasky observes that dancing in public was "still scandalous" in 1911, but such stigma only seemed to add to the allure and excitement of all who flocked to these places. The liberal use of alcohol added to the breakdown of inhibitions, and dances, contests, and drink made for public sociability at the cabaret. During the next two years, the number of nightclubs and cabarets mushroomed, and many of them installed dance floors.[38]

To be sure, as Lasky's observation suggests, "respectable" New York had already in the first decade of the century consigned dance halls—and the working boys and girls who flocked to them—to a place in hell.[39] The historian Kathy Peiss has recounted the complaints of wild dance-hall "spieling," in which dancers seemed to lose their sense of balance and propriety. The dance, which may have migrated from the German beer hall to the broader immigrant dance hall, was probably a version of the zweifacher, a fast turning dance in which a couple has to be glued together to execute alternating pivot and waltz steps.[40]

New dances arose to scandalize New York in the second decade of the century, most infamously, the tango. The "tango craze" inaugurated a popular dance mania that came to include a host of animal and jazz dances that swept the nation and attracted participants across social lines as perhaps never before. First danced in Europe around 1910, the tango's introduction in the United States has been credited to Joseph Smith, a ballet master, and the American dance teacher Maurice Mouvet has been credited with popularizing it. Mouvet brought it from Paris to New York in 1911, and he and a partner opened a studio and offered tango lessons for twenty-five dollars per hour.[41]

In 1912, cafés inaugurated *dansants,* or tango teas, with enticements for working people. The cafés had low admission fees (or perhaps a one-drink cover charge), and unescorted women could dance with men hired by management. At the same time, "respectable" women could thrill to a dance in the afternoon or evening with immigrant Jews or Italians, scandalizing their parents and putting their reputation on the line. As the historian Lewis Erenberg has observed, cabaret was a "direct challenge to the cult of domesticity," with close physical contact, suggestive bodily display and movement, and "risky" cross-class interactions in a "dangerous" space where "tango pirates" were seen as using drugs (cocaine) to force women into sexual wantonness. The dance won the additional cachet of being banned in Boston from 1911 to 1919.[42]

The tango craze had already ebbed by 1914, but the craze of animal and ragtime dancing continued in its place. Notably, in dances such as the black bottom (early 1900s), fox-trot (1912–14), cakewalk (1915), and Charleston, the craze borrowed from African American dance, not from more formal European steps. Ragtime also stimulated a lot of new dances as Irving Berlin popularized the music with publication of "Alexander's Ragtime Band" in 1911. The major emphasis of these dances was rhythm, not steps—moving the body in tune to the music. The one-step (1911), also known as the turkey trot, with 2/4 or 4/4 meter and a step for each lively beat, was the first ragtime dance of 1911. Others followed: the grizzly bear (1910), the monkey (1911), the crab (1911; in 1916, it became the American crab, a 4/4 ragtime dance), the camel walk (1912; similar to the stroll of the mid-1950s), the Texas tommy (a fast pivoting fox-trot, with the woman hanging on the man, as in the grizzly bear), and the lame duck (a 1915 ragtime waltz). There were also novelty line ragtime animal dances: the gabby glide (1911), the bunny hug (1912), ballin' the jack (1913), the funky butt (n.d.), the chicken scratch (1915), and a simple two-step, the snake dip (1915).[43]

Some reforming dance teachers, rather than flee from these cabaret dances as dangerous and wanton, sought to domesticate the dances and the spaces in which they were performed. In 1914, Flora Voorhis, who taught at the Hotel McAlpin, and Dodworth formed the New York Society of Teachers of Dance to try to systemize society dance teaching. They had little success, and Dodworth closed his school in 1920, convinced that "cutting in, bad manners, and vulgar dancing were apparently here to stay."[44] Two of the stars of the cabaret, Irene and Vernon Castle, both of New York, tried instead to work within the new dance forms, but to refine them. Reflecting the new use of the dance floor, they began their performance of social dance by coming out of the audience. The Castles had returned to New York in 1912 from the Paris musical stage, where they had developed a café dance act doing new animal dances that they heard were the rage in New York. After dancing to success at Louis Martins's café, they opened a string of their own cafés and established a national reputation, soon producing their own instructional dance films. A well-groomed, married couple, they came to represent respectability and became known as "society dancers" (later, "café society") because of their ties to the upper class.

The Castles' refined air legitimized the social dance by easing the concerns over its lower-class, sensual origins.[45] Irene Castle demonstrated how the couple, even as they created a "safe" alternative cabaret space for society, did so in the modern spirit. She was the first woman to bob her hair (albeit for surgery), and her look, the "Castle clip," became the flapper style of feminine independence, a New Woman who could flaunt her sexuality as boyish androgyny.[46] The couple also soon added a mix of European, Latin, and waltz dances to their repertoire. The fox-trot, introduced in 1914, became their leading dance, although they gradually replaced it with the one-step. In 1913, they entered a dance of their own devise into the craze, the Castle walk.[47] Finally, as Erenberg has noted, they made "black dances" over into respectable "white" dances, obscuring their origins. Irene Castle said of the shimmy, "We get our new dances from the Barbary Coast. Of course, they reach New York in a very primitive condition, and have to be considerably toned down before they can be used in the drawing room. There is one just arrived now—it is still very crude—and it is called 'Shaking the Shimmy.' It's a nigger dance, of course, and it appears to be a slow walk with a frequent twitching of the shoulders."[48]

The Folk Alternatives

Café society was neither affordable not necessarily attractive to the immigrant working class and its children, yet reformers who ran the settlement houses and playgrounds agreed that people had a "legitimate desire" for drama, music, and dance. Needing merely to find an alternative to the "exploitative" form of "commercialized amusements," they looked to play and gymnastics.[49]

Pageants and festivals, most notably popular annual May Day celebrations organized around the maypole dance, quickly became a staple of the settlements, playgrounds, schools, and colleges of the United States. Quoting the dance critic Joan Acocella to the effect that modern dance arose from primitivist impulse to "heal the split the modern world was thought to have created between nature and the human soul," the dance historian and critic Janice Ross notes that the fêtes "illuminate a pervasive primitivist yearning at the time."[50] Thought to originate in medieval England, these May Day festivities contrasted with the parades of working-class solidarity that had marched through the city every May 1 since the Haymarket Massacre in 1886, parades in which, perhaps not coincidentally, parents of many of the children would have participated.

In contrast, the folklore May Day began with excursions to woodlands so that girls could pick flowers for garlands and boys could find sticks for bows and arrows. The children, attired in white frocks or slacks, then marched to city parks for folk games, songs, and dances. The day culminated in crowning the Queen of the May and the maypole dance, a serpentine dance with ribbons around the pole. Little is known of the first event, but the second annual Folk Dance Festival for Manhattan and Bronx took place in 1900 and found twenty-five hundred girls dancing the "May Pole Dance" in Van Cortlandt Park on May 29. (In this case, their parents could have brought them to the May Day parade earlier that month!)[51] By 1909, only three years after the founding of the Playground Association, tens of thousands of city children across the United States were participating in the dances: over twenty-five thousand spectators were reported to have watched twelve thousand children dance and frolic in Pittsburgh's Schenley Park in 1909, and New York's Central Park hosted equally impressive numbers each year. In 1914, for instance, a *New York Times* article entitled "Schoolgirls Seen in Folk Dancing" reported Burchenal's efforts to have the 22,915 girls who were enrolled in the Girls' Branch of the Public Schools Athletic League learn and do folk dances in Brooklyn's Prospect Park and New York's Central Park. And on June 8 that year, the Sheep Meadow in Central Park saw between seven and eight thousand children—including some who were blind and deaf—entertain fifteen thousand spectators with their dance around one hundred maypoles. The event concluded with the girls singing the "Star-Spangled Banner" and cheering their head teacher, "Miss Burchenal," who was joined at the reviewing stand by the French and Danish consuls, the chair of the Norwegian Woman's Suffrage Society, and ladies and gentlemen from society who supported the physical-education movement.[52] Indeed, the country dance historian Allison Thompson has catalogued annual May fêtes, with young women in layers of white, ankle-length loose gowns, in cities and at eighty women's colleges and land-grant universities across the country, most beginning early in the century. Undoubtedly, women physical-education teachers, such as Wisconsin's Margaret H'Doubler, initiated many of these activities, and in turn, the dance events fed into the emerging development of dance education in the nation's new schools of education.[53]

The maypole dance was the staple of the early Progressive Era folk dance diet. Dance educators valued it as a democratic experience in that it required teamwork, fostered harmony, and had no "star" performer. But dance educators and teachers felt the need to fill out the diet with dances that reflected the immigrant cultures of their students. They did have a few publications to which they could turn, but the pickings were slim and emphasized some of the European couple dances that had made their way into the ballroom repertoire—the waltz and the polka, for instance—and rural American dances. A Brooklyn-based aficionado who went by the name of C. H. Rivers had published two volumes of reels, squares, contras, polkas, and waltzes that he (mis)titled *Modern Dances* (1885) and *New Dances* (1891). A book of

Girls of the Public School Athletic league folk dance in Central Park at the turn of the century. (George Grantham Bain Collection, Library of Congress)

quadrille (square dance) calls, *The American National Call Book*, was also published in 1893.⁵⁴

Along with the formation of the Playground Association, Luther Gulick's appointment of Elizabeth Burchenal to be executive director of the Girls' Branch of the Public Schools Athletic League in 1906 was a foundational moment in the development of the American folk dance movement. Burchenal's background was not unlike that of those who developed and led the dance revival on both sides of the Atlantic: she had the privileges of a college education, was reared in a progressive tradition, and had a particular interest in dance and the body.

Elizabeth Burchenal was born in 1876 in Richmond, Indiana, the second of six children to Judge Charles Burchenal and his wife, Mary. She had a close relationship to at least two of her sisters, Emma and Ruth, both of whom collaborated with her later in life when they all seem to have moved to New York. Elizabeth attended Richmond's Earlham College, a Quaker liberal arts college with traditional progressive commitments to equality and peace studies. Earlham was the first accredited college to have a May Day celebration in 1875 and sometime soon after introduced the maypole dance—according to Thompson, "performed to a sedate march suitable for Quaker maidens."⁵⁵ She graduated with a bachelor's degree in English literature in 1896, but having developed a passion for the healthy bodily movement, she promptly enrolled in the day's most well known program in physical education and dance, the Sargent Normal School of Physical Education (later affiliated with Boston University). By 1889, she had earned an advanced degree in

Elizabeth Burchenal in folkloric costume that reflected her commitment to the importance of all forms of folk dance. This photo originally appeared in the *Cincinnati Enquirer* (March 1929). (From the Burchenal Collection, Howard Gottlieb Archival Research Center at Boston University)

physical education and, after a brief interlude teaching (presumably physical education) in Chicago, moved to New York, where she studied at the Gilbert School of Dance. By 1903, she had won a post teaching physical education at the Horace Mann School, a premier preparatory school experiment run by Teachers College of Columbia University. Horace Mann catered to the children of wealthy New York, undoubtedly many of whom had English roots, but it also had a pool of scholarship students, many of them Jewish, drawn from the city's immigrant population.[56] Believing that the spirit embodied in folk dance was exactly what her young women needed to be teaching urban girls, Burchenal set out to Europe to develop a curriculum of international and English folk dance.

In organizing the curriculum of the Girls' Branch, Burchenal drew heavily on the Danish and Swedish folk songs and games, as well as the English maypole dances, she had seen. Her reliance on Scandinavian folk traditions was in a venerable American folklorist tradition: she was replicating both the itinerary and programs created by highland and southern mountain settlement reformers based on Danish folk schools; after all when Mary Wood Hinman sought folk dances to teach Chicago's immigrant girls, she also started in Scandinavia in 1907. Burchenal's *Folk-Dances and Singing Games* (1909) was the initial publication of the American Folk Dance Society, which Gulick and Burchenal collaborated in founding in 1906 and of which Burchenal served as president and director. The publisher's blurb for the 1938 reprint credits Burchenal for having "inaugurated" the folk dance movement "in the City of New York," and she certainly merits at least a shared credit (with Hinman) for its national beginnings.[57]

Burchenal began teaching folk dance at Horace Mann around 1905, and the next two years, 1906 and 1907, were seminal years that saw the development of an American folk dance movement. Gulick had invited the former ballet master of the Odessa Government Theatre, Louis H. Chalif (1877–1948), to start his Normal School of Dance in New York in 1904. Gulick then in 1906 hired Chalif to teach folk dance at the New York University Summer School, where he was introduced to many local folk enthusiasts. Chalif subsequently taught folk dance at Felix Adler's Ethical Culture Society of New York. He directed the Grand Harvest Festival of All Nations at Van Cortlandt Park in September 1908, an event sponsored by the Playground Association. And he taught at settlements, including Henry Street, whose head, Lillian Wald, testified to his "wonderful folk dancing." Chalif years later published three volumes of European folk dances, some of which are actually stylized classical dances drawing on folkloric traditions (character dances).[58]

The years 1906 and 1907 also witnessed a significant set of Atlantic crossings. Twelve dancers and two fiddlers from Sweden, the Skansen Dancers, self-organized a tour of the United States. Arriving in New York in January 1906, the group parlayed successful visits to Chicago and Minneapolis into a fifty-seven-city tour of the country and a return trip the next winter.[59]

Fledgling American dance researchers made return visits to Europe. A volume called *Swedish Folk Dances*, translated by a Swedish American physical-education instructor in the Staten Island public schools, appeared in 1906, but it seems to have only whetted the appetite for more dances. The next year, two intrepid and pioneering American folk dance researchers took off for Europe.[60] Dance historians believe that Mary Wood Hinman took a research trip to several European countries, including Sweden, in 1907 and based her four-volume *Gymnastics and Folk Dances* (1923) on it. That same year found Elizabeth Burchenal in England in quest of morris dances.[61] Burchenal's first collection of twenty-six songs and dances consisted predominantly of material from Sweden and Denmark. The one English dance included was the "May-Pole Dance."[62]

Dance leaders across the country seemed to have moved quickly to incorporate folk dances "from many lands," although, in fact the dances were primarily from northern Europe. An interesting exception was the 1907 May Day program at the University of Wisconsin; it presented German, French, Danish, Norwegian, Swedish, Russian, Irish, and Spanish dances, but the day also included "Negro" and American dances.[63]

University dance programs served a relatively elite young constituency, however, for whom "peasant" folk dance was gendered recreation and exercise through exposure to the culture of "others." Urban settlement and playground workers were equally eager to build on the modest early work to build folk dance programs, but their programs carried an additional moral and missionary class valence with political meaning. Chicago's Hinman introduced folk dance at Hull House in 1897 and, shortly after, at the Dewey School, where John Dewey actively supported the program. Writing twelve years later, Hinman waxed about how folk dance had had two major results: "The men gained the American attitude of respect for women, which they knew nothing of in the other country; and second, they learned the value of self-respect." Young people, she noted, "lose the desire to go elsewhere"—presumably the music hall. And she was surprised to note that many of them, having learned to be more "reliable," get job promotions. By 1909, folk dance had become a part of the regular curriculum at all the leading Chicago settlements and for girls at four Chicago elementary schools, including the Latin School for Girls and the University School for Girls. Dance programs were concentrated in girls' schools, but they were also introduced for both boys and girls at University of Chicago Elementary School and High School, where fourth graders learned their first folk dance: the sailors' hornpipe from England.[64]

Efforts in Baltimore and Boston were more modest, but local program directors offered no less glowing reports of the impact of folk dance on children. Mary B. Stewart, supervisor of the Children's Playground Association of Baltimore, wrote of the "beneficial" effects of the dance on the children's "poise, [and] lightness of step." She noted also its social and moral benefits: it "broadened their interest in each other" and made them happier, kinder, and "less selfish."[65] Boston's Helen Storrow, a wealthy grande dame who came to play a leading role in the American movement, was equally effusive. The classes at her Boston dance academy had taught both aesthetic and folk dance, but they had begun to stress the latter, "as it encourages sociability."[66]

New York, where Elizabeth Burchenal was based, had the largest dance program. Burchenal used her organizational roles in both the Public

Schools Athletic League and the Playground Association to good advantage. By 1907, 253 New York City teachers were teaching folk dances, virtually all of northern European origin, to 8,219 girls in 128 city schools.[67] A 1909 letter to Gulick from Margaret Knox, principal of PS 15 on Fifth Avenue in Manhattan, testified to the impact Burchenal had on her school alone. Burchenal had directed folk dance classes at the school in 1907, and the fifth-grade girls had since formed a folk dance club, the Burchenal Athletic Club. Forty of the sixty girls in the club took part in folk songs and games, and the "healthy, happy girls" performed fifteen of the dances. All the dances originated in northern Europe, and most were British or Scandinavian.[68]

Folk dance was more than exercise, however, and it was the political import of the practice that impassioned reformer-educators such as Gulick and Burchenal and gave them their sense of mission. This was especially the case as the second decade of the century unfolded and labor struggles heated up in the immigrant city. The enthusiasm in the nineteen-teens for "Americanization" drove reformers' desires to impart roots of American nationalism that could both redeem and transform foreigners into Americans, albeit hyphenated ones. Folk dance was social dance, but it was also an orderly form of sociability. Unlike the tango, for which there was no single tune and people improvised as a couple within a set of moves to the beat, every English Country Dance had a name and a particular piece of music (or in some cases, a couple of tunes) associated with it. Each dance also had an ordered set of figures, each with taught embodiments that constituted a turn of the dance. Dancers were not free to move about the floor at will, but as a couple and within the unit of the set. ECD was an ordered and orderly *communal* dance event. Indeed, beyond its sense of decorum, both Gulick and Burchenal believed folk dance taught a cooperative spirit that spoke to core American democratic values. Diversity of immigrant cultures risked dividing urban peoples, thought Gulick. In folk festivals, children dance national dances, but at the same time they are "uniting with other citizens in a spirit of civic unity." Folk dances, he argued, express the ties of the individual to a community. It is important for immigrant children to know of their roots; at the same time, the dances express "mass feeling" and bring about a "consciousness of the whole." Democracy, then, requires a sand box for small children, a playground for youths, and "folk-dancing and social ceremonial life for the boy and girl in their teens" for "development of that self-control which is related to . . . the corporate conscience that is rendered necessary by the complex interdependence of modern life."[69]

Elizabeth Burchenal was even more pointed in establishing the connections between folk dance, democracy, and Americanization. In their countries of origin, folk dances, she wrote, "*are the traditional rural community recreation of the people*, and contain the very essence of *social group play*." They have "universal appeal . . . as an innocent, wholesome, happy form of relaxation and social enjoyment." She particularly wanted to "emphasize the large opportunities, as yet not generally realized, which folk-dancing offers as Recreation for Adults, its possibilities as a Democratic Socializing Agent, and its value as a form of *real* Americanization." In this sense, folk dance, for Burchenal, is no less than a path to citizenship: it familiarizes people with other peoples, establishes a common ground, broadens their education and culture, and most importantly allows immigrants to "appreciate the spirit of cooperation and good fellowship engendered by this social contact in play." Burchenal understood these lessons of cooperation as not just for foreigners but to teach all "folks" how to "develop citizenship . . . in a friendly and democratic way." That, she noted, would be "*real* Americanization."[70]

The infusion of the Americanization project gave new purpose and direction to Atlantic crossings. English Country Dance could do double duty as expression of the folk and of Anglo-American national culture. In the second decade of the twentieth century, then, England rather than Scandinavia became the new destination of choice for a growing cadre of Anglophiles and folk dance enthusiasts.

Anglo-American "Roots" as Revival and Invention

In traveling to Europe, and especially to England, early U.S. revivalists, ironically, for the most part imagined their revivalist project, especially in dance and in the urban context, as primarily the reinvigoration of a European tradition, not that of a longstanding American activity. This was as true for those who worked in rural America in what came to be known as "Appalachia"—both American folklorists and, famously, Cecil Sharp—as it was for those who labored in northern urban settlements. As noted earlier, early folklore collecting focused on highland ballads of English origin and generally ignored the complicated origin stories and multinational, transnational, and urban histories of dance in the United States that had roots in colonial America.[71] Thus, when folklorists such as Elizabeth Burchenal focused on Scandinavia and England for American settlers' roots, the "revival" they helped lead was partially a process of historical amnesia. Burchenal's fifth book, *American Country-Dances* (1917), focused on the contra dances of New England, which she acknowledged were "slightly reminiscent" of English country dances but were "the products of . . . one of the old, most truly American sections of the country, where many generations have grown up undisturbed by foreign influences."[72]

But Burchenal also embraced and welcomed Cecil Sharp to the United States as the fount of "genuine" folk dance for the United States and, at least initially, welcomed and promoted his teaching of English dance. And in doing so, American folk revivalists generally forgot America's historical experience with English Country Dance, and they underappreciated the polyglot cousin forms that flourished in the American countryside, if they did not discount them entirely, and scurried off instead to find and experience their English folk "roots."

3

Orderly Bodies:
Dancing London, 1900–1914

> I'll try anything once, except incest and morris dancing.
> —Linzi Drew, a British stripper (also attributed to Oscar Wilde, Sir Arnold Bax, Sir Thomas Beecham, and George Bernard Shaw, among others)[1]

Elizabeth Burchenal seems to have been the first twentieth-century American to voyage to London in search of folk dance roots, going perhaps as early as 1903. Around 1903 or 1904, she traveled from village to village in Denmark, Norway, Germany, Sweden, France, Ireland, and Spain collecting folk dances that she subsequently published in New York. She then visited England to see morris dancing at Bampton and Bidford, which Cecil Sharp had only recently collected and published.[2]

Burchenal was, though, but the first of a cadre of American pilgrims of English origin in search of a usable folk past—both of their own roots and of an Anglo-American tradition that they could, in the most benevolent construction, "share" with newcomers. The roster of visitors illustrates the elite character of the revival project as progressive reform, but it also illustrates the larger tensions in this gender- and social-class-inflected Progressive-Edwardian-era project between social (and socialist) reform and paternalist if not imperial (and imperious) social control. Pittsburgh's Mrs. James Dawson Callery's husband was president of Baragua Sugar Company and chairman of the board of the Philadelphia Company, the Duquense Light Company, and the Pittsburgh Railway Company. Helen Osborne Storrow's husband, James Jackson Storrow of Boston (he and his wife lived on an estate in neighboring Lincoln), was an investment banker and social reformer, and he and his wife were major philanthropists to heritage, environmental, and Girl Scouts projects.[3]

Few of the pilgrims may have been as wealthy as Mrs. Callery or Helen Storrow, and most worked for a living as part of the growing (semi)professional class made up of people such as teachers and social workers, but they were all sufficiently wealthy and privileged to afford to travel to Europe on holiday and to do so first class. Mary Wood Hinman, for instance, was a leading settlement house worker from Chicago's Hull House. In the years before World War I, and before leaving to try her hand at acting in Los Angeles, she ran pageants and programs of folk and interpretative dance at the progressive Francis Parker School, where one of her young protégés was the distinguished modern dancer Doris Humphrey.[4]

Not surprisingly, the largest contingent of American devotees of English Country Dance came from the city prized for its Anglophile elites with English heritage: Boston. In addition to Storrow, they included Harvard professor of dramatic literature George P. Baker and two adventuresome enthusiasts who were introduced to ECD on the Storrow lawn in Lincoln in 1913 or 1914, Louise Chapin and Dorothy Bolles. These four Bostonians later took on major institutional roles as ECD organizers and dance teachers in the United States.[5]

Americans visiting England to learn country dance encountered an exciting movement, but they remained largely oblivious to an underlying fractiousness that swirled about Sharp. In fact, the Americans were sometimes unwittingly the subject of disputes, but in truth, sometimes they appeared deliberately to aggravate the conflict. The most profound and earliest dispute involved the two people who took the lead in the revival in England, Mary Neal and Cecil Sharp. Their relationship began at about the same time as Burchenal would have arrived in their midst, although there is no evidence she met with either of them until a few years later.

Mary Neal

The English folk dance revival may properly be said to have begun with Mary Neal, a woman every bit as imposing and outspoken as Sharp. Sharp had put his experience with the Headington Morrismen behind him and moved on to collecting folk song. It was Neal's success with folk dance that reawakened his interest in dance in 1905.

Born on June 5, 1860, and christened Sophia Clara, Mary Neal was the daughter of a well-to-do Birmingham button manufacturer. Tall, curly haired, and, according to her lifelong close friend, the suffragette Emmeline Pethick-Lawrence, "extremely emaciated," Neal's "vivid blue eyes" lit up a room. "She brought into the atmosphere the sparkle of a clear, frosty, winter day." She was also a woman with strong opinions and a sharp tongue (no pun intended) that made her quite Sharp's equal when it came, as it did, to trading barbs.[6] But that lay in the future.

Mary Neal. (Reproduced courtesy of EFDSS)

As a young woman, Neal read of the horrid conditions of the London poor in Andrew Mearns's pamphlet "The Bitter Cry of Outcast London" and resolved to do something about it. She moved to London in 1888 to join the Methodist West London Mission as a "Sister of the Poor" (later, after reading a biography of St. Francis of Assisi, she described her work as in his tradition) and took the name Sister Mary.[7] She was joined in this work in 1891 by Emmeline Pethick (who married Frederick Lawrence in October of that year). Together, committed to the gospel of socialism and the labor movement, they established the Espérance Club and Social Guild for girls in 1895 (*espérance* being French for "hopefulness"), a social settlement based in Cumberland Market, St. Pancreas. The club attracted the working girls of Soho and Marylebone—seamstresses and tailoresses—and Neal and Pethick-Lawrence set up an adjunct commercial tailoring establishment, Maison Espérance. A socialist model shop, it had wages nearly double the norm, regular year-round employment, and a forty-five-hour work week. To ensure that her working girls also experienced regular holidays, Neal also purchased (jointly with a Jewish girls' club) a house in Littlehampton that she named "The Green Lady Hostel."[8]

Throughout her life, Neal's vocation in social work on behalf of the dispossessed—poor working girls, in particular—was her passion and her mission, and she embraced song and dance to enliven the girls. As seamstresses, the girls of the club were "mostly employed in sedentary work," as Neal saw it, and so "made dancing, singing and acting as chief occupations." Pethick-Lawrence, as the club's musical director, introduced Scottish song and dance at the Christmas party in 1903. When Emmeline left her position shortly thereafter to turn her attention full-time to woman's suffrage, at the suggestion of the new musical director, Herbert MacIlwaine, the club moved on to Irish song and dance the next year.[9]

But by 1905, Neal had a problem. Espérance girls seemed bored of the songs they traditionally sang at the Christmas party, and she needed an alternative. They had tried Scottish and Irish; what were they to do next? Then on July 29, 1905, MacIlwaine read in the *Morning Post* of Cecil Sharp collecting songs by "unlettered folks in remote country villages . . . which had been traditionally handed down from singer to singer." Enticed, MacIlwaine proposed to Neal that such songs would be ideal for the "unlettered members of their singing class," who "would probably take to these songs as to no others, [as] . . . they were the natural inheritance of the country folks."[10]

Neal "longed for some life-giving wind" to "lessen the weariness" of her girls and resolved to go see Sharp a few days later. Sharp, who at the time was in a dispute with the managers of the Hampstead Conservatory of Music about his use of the facilities, was threatening to leave his position as director. (He continued to be music master at Ludgrove, the preparatory school for Eton, to which he commuted.) Conflict over authority often swirled about Sharp, but at this point it worked to his favor: he was ready to move in new directions. Hearing Neal's request for "unlettered" songs for her girls, Sharp was "enchanted." He visited the club a few weeks later and was delighted at their singing. But as the Christmas season neared, Neal asked Sharp if there happened to be any country dances "in harmony with their [songs'] spirits?" He told her of his encounter with Headington dancers almost seven years previous and gave her Kimber's contact information.

Sharp's referral set Neal and the dance revival into motion. Neal traveled to Oxford and met with Kimber. Two morris dancers subsequently went to London and taught the Espérance girls dances that had traditionally been done only by men. So, ironically, given the rancorous debates over authenticity in the dance form that were soon to erupt, the first dance of the folk dance revival consisted of half a dozen morris dances such as "Bean Setting," "Constant Billy," "Blue-Eyed Stranger," and "Shepherd's Hey" that were danced by a girls' club.[11] Neal and the Espérance girls had begun the dance revival with a gender inversion.

When Neal contacted Sharp about folk song and dance in 1905, however, she awakened an old interest in him that had lain dormant. Until then, Sharp's focus had been on folk song. Sharp had had Kimber teach him morris dances shortly after the Boxing Day performance, but an encounter in 1903 with a Somerset gardener with the apocryphal name of John England had redirected him to folk song. Sharp had overheard the gardener singing "The Seeds of Love" and got England to give him the words to transcribe. That evening, in formal dress, Sharp had his vocalist Mattie Kay sing it to his accompaniment at a choir supper: The irony of dressing up the occasion was not lost on the gardener: "John was proud, but doubtful about the 'evening dress' [worn by Sharp and Kay]; there had been no piano to his song."[12]

The experience with John England transformed Sharp, and he turned to collecting folk songs. He published his first book of folk songs in 1902, *A Book of British Song for Home and School*, and by 1907 he had collected more than fifteen hundred tunes. By the end of 1903, he had begun to lecture on folk song, and one such occasion was the event that MacIlwaine read about in the newspaper. By 1904, Sharp had established himself as the emerging authority on English folklore, crowding out earlier collectors such as Sabine Baring-Gould and Lucy Broadwood. Sharp was that year elected to the committee of the Folk-Song Society, an organization that had been floundering since its founding in 1898.[13]

Just as Sharp had begun to establish himself as a folk song authority, the wondrous 1905 Christmas party performance of the Espérance girls moved folk dance onto Sharp's agenda. He later described seeing the Espérance girls sing and dance as the "turning point of his life" (although he had described seeing the Headington Morrismen in 1899 the same way). The audience's response to the girls was similarly electric. Recounting the experience nearly two decades later, Neal waxed poetic. Having become by this point a committed theosophist, Neal combined an almost religious reverence with a paean to supposedly primeval virtues revived by the dance. She wrote in her memoir, "And that night there awoke, after generations of sleep, a little stir of an older life, an older rhythm, an older force, in tune with a simpler life, a sweeter music, . . . [with] vibrations . . . and rhythms of an older world, a world untouched by machinery and mechanized power but responsive to the vibrant rhythm of sea and wind, earth and stone." Laurence Hausman, one of the writers among the audience of two hundred (which evidently included the labor leader Kier Hardie), prophesied a great revival, telling Neal that she "must not keep such a national possession in the narrow area of a Girls' Club."[14]

Neal picked up the challenge and took the girls on the road. For social elites, they performed their identity as the folk, giving the first performance of folk dance and song and singing games at the Queen's Hall in London on April 3, 1906; they similarly performed in concert for well-heeled young men (and presumably their women guests) at Fellows' Lawn at Trinity College, Cambridge, and at Eton College. They also, however, brought the dance to village and working-class youth, dancing in villages, schools, training colleges, and factories from Norfolk to Devon. "Everywhere," according to Neal, these "boys and girls . . . welcomed these songs and dances as if some ancestral meaning, some instinctual knowledge recognized them and loved them."[15]

Transformed by the girls' initial Christmas performance, Sharp inaugurated a collaboration with Neal (and with MacIlwaine). For the two years following the Christmas gala, the three of them worked, in Neal's words, "in perfect harmony." In fact, though profound differences between Neal and Sharp ultimately severed their relationship, the two shared much in common. Both were children of the commercial elite: he was the son of a slate manufacturer, and she was the daughter of a button manufacturer; Sharp was a Fabian socialist, and Neal was a Christian socialist; and both developed a relationship, as many others of their background did, to theosophy—though Sharp more flirted with it, whereas Neal embraced it. Unfortunately, the two also shared a personal trait that strained their ability to work together: both were strong willed and sharp tongued.[16]

Their differences, which to a contemporary observer might seem small, finally undercut their ability to work together. To begin, the two had different temperaments and conflicting personal ambitions. Sharp, who disappointed his family by choosing a musical over a commercial career, was never happy with what he saw as his "modest" position. He came to see folk song and dance as allowing him to follow his musical passion but always worried that it did not afford him the status and livelihood he deserved. Driven to make his way and prove himself, he was continually in disputes with supervisors and those he saw as competitors. For instance, Sharp committed himself to the Folk-Song Society's growth but promptly found himself embroiled in a dispute with its other leaders. The society supported the board of education's new curriculum that mixed music-hall and other popular songs, and Sharp was appalled that the curriculum did not distinguish "pure folk songs."[17] Sharp's famous 1906 lecture at Queen's Hall emphasized the political stakes he saw in the board's proposed folk song and dance curriculum, and Sharp actively led a successful fight to have the 1907 Education Act include fifty "pure" English songs and dances, "to refine and strengthen the national character. . . . The Introduction of English folk-songs into our schools will . . . arouse that love of country and pride of race, the absence of which we now deplore." As he explained, "Let [the board of education] introduce the genuine traditional song into the schools and I prophesy that within the year the slums of London and other large cities will be flooded with beautiful melodies, before which the rancorous, unlovely and vulgarizing music hall will flee as flees the night mist before the rays of the morning sun."[18]

Sharp's cantankerous nature and anxious personal strivings shaped both his career and personal relations, but when he combined them with the political and moral passion he invested in folk song and dance, he became a force to be reckoned with. His letters, which sometimes read like account books, are full of his social and financial anxieties and petty jealousies. At the same time, his ability to extract songs from countless village and backwoods women and men with whom he shared little but a passion for song demonstrates the mixture of charm, awe, and respect he clearly won.

We know less about Neal. Although she was enterprising and socially engaged, her political passion and critical edge seem to have been tempered by her theosophy and spiritualism. Pethick-Lawrence, in a sympathetic portrait, acknowledged her "unexpected remarks and criticisms" and observed that a "spice of malice in her speech" meant that "meals were never dull if she was at the table." Her friend added, however, that on balance, Neal—quite unlike Sharp—was "incapable of doing her worst enemy . . . a bad turn." Indeed, Neal's unpublished autobiography fairly gushes with theosophy and overheated poetic turns, and she reluctantly, if at all, strikes a discordant note. Unlike Sharp, the revival never seemed Neal's "career" as much as a vehicle for her feminist socialism. Indeed, Neal had developed another passion during these years—for suffrage—and that divided them as much as their views of folk dance, and their division over the former seemed to complicate any rapprochement over the latter.

Ironically, Neal discovered suffrage just as she was mobilizing on behalf of folk dance. She took the minutes at the inaugural meeting of the Women's Social and Political Union (WSPU) in 1906, and suffrage and socialism quickly became the twin pillars of her life's work, including how she thought of her Espérance girls and their dance. Her closest friends, the Pethick-Lawrences—their decision to hyphenate a shared last name reflecting their radical social politics—were the center of the suffragist movement. The WSPU was based at their home, and they published *Votes for Women*, the militants' paper, for which Neal contributed occasional pieces. And although Mary Neal never was arrested in suffragette protests—possibly because arrest would have taken her from her social-work responsibility toward the settlement girls—she actively supported those who were, including Emmeline, who was imprisoned six times, and Evelyn Sharp, Cecil's sister, who was arrested twice.[19]

The historian Georgina Boyes concludes that suffrage was the one area of disagreement between Sharp and Neal that could not be bridged, a view that Neal came to share by the end of her life. Mary Neal regularly had the Espérance club perform at suffragette events. In contrast, Cecil Sharp, the self-described "conservative socialist," barely kept in touch with his sister Evelyn during her prison travails, and he blanched at the thought of working with folk dancers who were suffragists. As noted earlier, "Evie" was the one who reached out to him. When she was released from Holloway prison in August 1913, in one of the few letters they seem to have exchanged, she urged that they stop "quarreling" simply because they "differ on Woman Suffrage."[20]

Neal, noting in her autobiography that the beginning of the revival and the "militant suffrage movement" were coincident and that Sharp "violently opposed" the latter, concluded, "I am now [writing in 1935] convinced that the controversy between us [over suffrage] was, at the bottom, of a much deeper significance than I had any idea of then."[21] But, reflecting back, Neal struck a balanced and appreciative view of Sharp that seems to catch the many qualities of the man that made him both revered and difficult. He was, she wrote, "a curious mixture, as probably we all are, sometimes quite charming and helpful and then again very obstructive and unkind."[22] Unfortunately for Neal, she experienced both of Sharp's sides in the next few years.

In 1906–7, while Sharp fought with the board of education, he also worked collaboratively with Neal and MacIlwaine to establish English folk dance. At the same time, he was slowly allowing himself to begin to imagine making a career as an expert in folk song and dance. He had left the Conservatory of Music, most likely in 1905, and the diminishing appeal of the long commute and job at Ludgrove made the prospect of earning a living as what came to be called a "folklorist" more attractive. But there were no precedents, no established job trajectories, to such a career. Sharp's worries about his ability to provide "properly" for his family grew more shrill as time passed, and he came to see his career in folk dance as tied to his authority as "expert."

Still, during the next two years, Sharp, Neal, and MacIlwaine proceeded to work together equitably. In 1907, after the school board took notice of their work, Sharp and MacIlwaine coauthored *The Morris Book*, a history of morris dancing that included a description of eleven morris dances that could be taught in schools. Neal described in her memoir their working relationship in completing that book. Neal invited a group of "traditional dancers" to London to teach the girls and, in turn, teach others. Sharp notated the music while MacIlwaine provided the dance-step notations by copying the footwork of one of the Espérance girls, Florrie Warren. Warren, a poor girl from the East End who had been orphaned at a young age, had been taken under wing by Emmeline Pethick-Lawrence. Twenty years old in 1907, Warren was the leading Espérance dancer and was quickly emerging as the group's instructor as well.[23] The two men, fully acknowledging Warren's contribution in their introduction, dedicated the book to the Espérance Morris, the dance for which the club had gained renown. Neal's description of the challenges of the work was telling, for it foreshadowed a debate she and Sharp would engage about the complicated ability to ascribe authenticity to any rendition of the dance: "it is not easy to describe the actual steps and figures . . . for no two sides of dancers did a particular dance in precisely the same way. No two men in the side did the step in the same way, and no one danced it in exactly the same way on two separate occasions."[24] "Set to Music," a pamphlet Neal published in late summer 1907, expressed the promise they all felt in their joint project. Neal dedicated the volume to Cecil Sharp, who continued to recommend her to others and give introductory lectures to performances by the girls.[25]

Even as Sharp and Neal worked together, however, they began individual research projects. Both went into the countryside to collect new dances. Neal and Clive Carey, a young musician-scholar (he later became a distinguished opera baritone and director), collected new dances that she could teach her working girls. Carey had replaced MacIlwaine, who, though he pleaded poor health, had in fact resigned as musical director of the Espérance club because of the club's association with suffragette militancy. MacIlwaine and Neal remained friends, however, and upon his death, she adopted his son Anthony.[26] Meanwhile, Sharp uncovered eighteen traditional dances then being done in West Country villages, which he published in 1909 as *The Country Dance Book*. Completing the work for this volume, Sharp discovered, however, that he did not have to leave London to recover English country dance. Nellie Chaplin, a journalistic researcher, had recently uncovered the Playford volumes of historical country dances from the seventeenth and eighteenth centuries in the British Library, and Sharp now turned his attention to them.

Playford aimed his collections of social country dances at the gentlemen of the Inns of Court and their ladies; they were for both sexes and were simple and very charming. Sharp mistakenly imagined the heterogeneous origins of these dances as "peasant," but to his credit, he recognized that 1651, when Playford began to publish, was a complicated transitional moment in the dances' history. Originally of the "village green, farmhouses and dancing booths of the annual fairs," he wrote, the country dances slowly invaded the "parlours and drawing-rooms of the wealthy" and were "subjected to an enervating influence which . . . ultimately led to its corruption."[27] According to Karpeles, Sharp recognized that the "conscious manipulations" by seventeenth- and eighteenth-century dancing masters of most of the dances Playford published, especially those that appeared in the latter volumes, meant they were "not pure folk dances." Still, he thought them beautiful and that they could be "said to rest on a traditional basis." So, enamored of their basic "gay simplicity," Sharp devised a notation system and transcribed the dances. In the five additional volumes of *The Country Dance Book* that he published between 1912 and 1922, Sharp described the way he imagined the figures to 158 Playford dances were done.[28] But in 1907, Sharp's transcriptions of the Playford manuscripts still lay in the future.

By the end of 1907, the potential for a folk dance movement was increasingly apparent to people such as Sharp and Neal. So, too, however, was the potential for conflict. As noted earlier, for Sharp the stakes were partially personal, as he increasingly saw that folk arts—both song and dance—held the promise of a career for him. But as important, both saw great moral and political import in the revival. In the grammar of the age, folklore collectors such as Neal and Sharp imagined English Country Dance as having a vital role to play in the revitalization of the "race."[29] As the *Daily Telegraph* reported a decade later, in 1917, "These old dances, with their quaint names, belong to an age that knew not the depravities of the turkey-trot, and the glide and the pseudo-tango."[30]

Against the "depravities" of the music hall and dance hall, both Neal and Sharp romanticized these "simple" folk. Neal imagined that folk song and dance resonated with her "unlettered" girls' "natural inheritance of the country folk"; Sharp saw folk song and dance as the English "race's" salvation from "coarse music hall songs" and the working-class sinfulness it symbolized. "Flood the streets . . . with folk tunes," wrote Sharp in 1907, and it will cleanse the thoroughfares of "those who now vulgarize themselves . . . and do incalculable good in civilizing the masses."[31]

Both Neal and Sharp embraced the "purity" of the "simple" folk, but they did so in fundamentally different, and in what they came to feel were irreconcilable, ways. Sharp, the Fabian socialist, claimed a paternalistic responsibility as "expert" to capture their simplicity and translate it to others. He wanted the dances standardized for teaching in schools (with him overseeing the standard). Neal, the radical feminist socialist (and theosophist), assumed that the "uplifting" quality of the folk would emerge as an evolutionary process from the intrinsic, almost magical essence of the folk themselves. She believed that the essence of the dance was expressed in the bodies of her working girls and that a standard was neither possible nor appropriate. Thus, while both agreed on the "peasant" origins of the dance, they disagreed on how it was understood and conveyed—"taught"—to others.

The raised stakes of the inflated rhetoric only raised the temperature of disagreements, such as that which broke out with the appearance of a cartoon by Bernard Partridge in *Punch* in November 1907. Entitled "Merrie England Once More," the cartoon, which depicts three male and three female dancers led by Punch, accompanied a short paragraph about the dance revival and a notice for a conference to be held at a local gallery the next evening. Neal, delighted with the publicity, took it "straight to Mr. Sharp" and "saw a blind come down over his face." Sharp saw the invocation of "Merrie England" as precisely the saccharine view that the revival needed to correct. He could not abide by what he saw as the cartoon's ridicule and fundamental misunderstanding of the meaning and power in past traditions. It was, for him, the wrong sort of publicity, and the conference, he believed, was premature. Petulantly, Sharp announced that he was not going to the conference.

The conference was "well attended," and Sharp did appear, though clearly as a reluctant participant. The attendees initially agreed to form a permanent association "for the collecting and practicing of folk dances." According to Neal, Sharp advocated a "strict constitution" so that it "would be possible to control it [the association] in a way impossible with the simple constitution of the Folk Dance Society," with which Sharp was still embattled. Sharp's view was that the group should not be in the business of "collecting"; that needed to be done by "experts," presumably by people like him. So although the group met several more times, the only thing it could agree on was to disband. Neal got a few friends together and the next year started a "small association," the Association for the Revival and Practice of Folk Music, to move the movement outside the Espérance club. Neal demurred that the association would not be in the business of collecting folk music, because that was "being done so admirably by experts such as Cecil Sharp." Still, despite her effort to stay clear of his turf, she remembered Sharp as "bitterly attack[ing]" her from that day on.[32]

The feud between the two remained relatively muted for the next couple of years, staying out of the press until 1910. Meanwhile, each went about

"Merrie England Once More," *Punch*, November 1907, cover. Cartoon by Bernard Partridge. (Fales Library, New York University)

teaching folk dance and developing his or her own reputation in the field. In May 1909, the two even sat on the same panel to adjudicate a children's folk dance competition held in conjunction with the Shakespeare Festival at Stratford-on-Avon. But if Sharp remained polite in public, he bristled in private. He increasingly chose to distance himself from the Espérance girls' performances and in a March 7, 1909, letter to Neal made the breach formal, chastising her for incorporating stories he had told her about folk singers into her programs. Not to put too fine a point on their difference and the import—moral, financial, institutional, and authorial—it carried for him, he concluded, "So that it comes to this: if you wish to pose as an expert and authority you must not ask me to support you."[33]

Sharp had at this juncture already established himself as an authority on folk song; he had some way to go, however, to establish his bona fides in dance. He now expeditiously and with deliberation moved to do so. The board of education's official approval of morris dance as part of its revised 1909 school syllabus was just the opportunity he needed. The new syllabus increased the demand for folk dance teachers and offered Sharp a new opportunity that would enhance his investment in developing a career in English folk dance. Neal, however, also rose to meet the challenge, writing publicly to the board in letters to the *Morning Post* and *Westminster Gazette* that teachers from her association were already instructing youth across the country.[34]

The Education Department's new syllabus gave cash value to the mantle of folk dance authority, which both Sharp and Neal rushed to claim. In public, both remained polite. In May 1909, Neal, MacIlwaine, Sharp, and Edward Burrows, inspector of schools for Portsmouth and West Sussex, sat together as judges at the Stratford Festival of Folk Song and Dance. But the politesse masked little. Increasingly vitriolic, bitter exchanges accompanied the publication of Sharp's *The Morris Book, Part II*, in August, and they quickly became, in public, as much enemies as opponents. The historian Roy Judge, in a splendid essay on Mary Neal, describes this exchange in detail. The trigger for the open conflict was Sharp's decision to rewrite the introduction to the first volume, which probably had been written by MacIlwaine. In Sharp's version, he pressed his own view of "authentic" morris dance style, a view that was a thinly veiled critique of Neal and the Espérance girls. In his rewrite, Sharp deleted a well-known reference in the first volume to the dance as more about vigor than grace, pointedly warning readers to avoid tendencies "to be over-strenuous." Then, adding insult to injury, he deleted all references to the Espérance girls (to whom the first volume had been dedicated) and to Florrie Warren, the demonstration dancer for the authors.[35]

Neal claimed to be content simply to disagree with Sharp's position about style, but she could not abide his dismissal of Warren. The bitter exchange between the two only clarified the depth of their disagreement and hostility. Neal wrote that she was "done with the farce of expecting fair play" and would from then on focus on the "interests" of the "movement at large" and her "Club in particular."[36] Sharp, in response, ignored her interest in the movement and alleged that her problem was that "from the beginning" she has only cared for her club. The greater problem, continued Sharp, was that Neal's club advanced a low artistic standard of the morris as "a graceless, undignified and uncouth dance quite unfitted for educational uses." Striking a note that probably unintentionally signaled the personal financial import that winning this struggle held for him, Sharp concluded that he was "not going to stand idly by any longer and allow [Neal] to make or mar the fortunes of the movement."[37]

By 1910, for both Sharp and Neal, the stakes were clear, the differences between them plain, the personal animosity manifest. And both moved to consolidate their position. Neal had superior organizational talents and significant institutional bases in her association, her Espérance girls, and in her relationship with the Stratford-on-Avon Summer School for which the Espérance girls had performed. She also had the personal and social advantages of being a daughter of privilege. Sharp had a leading reputation in folk song, a professional standing in music as a teacher and scholar, and equal privileges of class. He had two other less tangible but no less important advantages, however: he was male and a "professional." Indeed, practitioners of Neal's vocation, social work, worried about their ability to win "professional" standing because of their putative lack of an "expert" specialized knowledge base. (It was another decade before the occupation began to claim casework and, after that, Freudian theory as bases.) Moreover, professionalism traditionally celebrated "objectivity," an attribute conventionally thought to be uniquely male, so to that extent, any claim by a woman such as Neal to professional expert standing was suspect. At a moment when reformers on both sides of the Atlantic—in both Edwardian England and Progressive Era America—celebrated the "expert," Sharp had the decided advantage. The furor surrounding the rising voices of militant suffragette women only strengthened traditional male bonds to Sharp's advantage.[38]

One key to success was to win the mantle of teacher-trainer, and as each side mobilized, two prominent men lined up behind Sharp. In July 1909, in the midst of the vitriolic exchange of letters between Sharp and Neal over the introduction to the second morris book, Burrows, who had previously worked with the two adversaries, appears to have become inclined toward Sharp. He arranged an advantageous meeting for Sharp with E. G. A. Holmes, the chief inspector for elementary school, two months *before* the board of education announced its new syllabus.[39] Sharp had already begun instructing teachers at the Chelsea College of Physical Education that March, but with the support of Holmes and following the publication of the new syllabus, the college established a School of Morris Dance in September 1909 with Sharp as director. Two sisters who attended the dance competition, Maud and Helen Karpeles, were "enchanted" by the dance and returned to London and joined Sharp's classes at the Chelsea school. By April 1910, the sisters and some of their friends had formed the Folk-Dance Club, rented the Portman Rooms in Baker Street, and organized performances of country dances, for which Sharp played the piano. Little is known about the composition of the audience of five hundred that the club attracted, but the address of the venue and the leading role of the affluent Karpeles sisters (their grandfather was a banker and their father was a merchant and stockbroker) suggests that those who attended

Orderly Bodies: Dancing London, 1900–1914 | 81

were well-heeled men and women of the emerging white-collar professional class or were from society. In any case, what is clear is that country dance had become an urban phenomenon and that Sharp had become its leader.[40]

However, by the spring of 1910, Mary Neal had also moved to train teachers. Neal had been bringing her girls to her "hostel" in Littlehampton for a decade and by 1909 had initiated a "vacation school" there for teaching folk dance. The school came to the attention of the Stratford-on-Avon governors, and at their request, she agreed to move the school there under her direction. As part of the arrangement, the governors invited Neal's newly formed Espérance Guild of Morris Dancers (formerly the Association for the Revival and Practice of Folk Music) to participate. The governors intended the school to be an annual event, but the question that almost immediately arose was who would run it: Cecil Sharp or Mary Neal?[41]

The public emergence of the Sharp-Neal feud in the *Morning Post* in the spring of 1910 over style and authority made the governors' choice one of more than personality. Sharp, as he had said earlier, argued that the dance should be only taught by experts, by "accredited teachers," who he presumably would train. Neal responded that the dance is "communal in origin," "from the heart of the unlettered folk," and "should also be left in the hands of the simple-minded and of those unlettered and ignorant of all technique." Debunking the need for the "expert," Neal averred that any "average person of intelligence" can teach a morris dance. She derided the debate with Sharp as simply the "age-long" difference "between the pedant and those in touch with actual life itself"—to which Sharp rejoined with a critique of the Espérance girls' own technique, complaining that they "were raising their thighs and legs up and down too violently."[42]

As the governors debated their choice, Neal fought back on what Sharp claimed as his own terrain: research. She published *The Espérance Morris Book*, her own authoritative volume on the dance. Then, accompanied by Clive Carey and others, she went to Headington and did her own research on Kimber's "authenticity." Addressing Sharp's critique of her Espérance team, on whether the free leg in the morris should be straight or bent, she discovered from her interviews with dancers that Kimber was himself a revival dancer. There was no one "proper" leg position, she announced—a view of the socially constructed character of the dance with which subsequently historians and folklorists have generally agreed (including Douglas Kennedy, a member of Sharp's original demonstration team who followed him as president of the dance society). In a letter to Archibald Flower, the Stratford director, Neal quipped bemusedly, "We have indubitably proved that the whole basis of Mr. Sharp's contentions as *an expert* are entirely unfounded. . . . It is all extremely funny from one point of view, after the fuss he has made about expert knowledge."[43]

Sharp was not amused, and the role of the (male) expert was not so easily debunked in this era, especially by a woman. So whether her work was discounted as that of a woman amateur, and therefore inconclusive or irrelevant, is not known. She forwarded her "data" to Sharp and the governors but to no avail.[44]

With the governors' decision pending, an invitation to Mary Neal to visit the United States intervened. During the summer of 1909, Emily M. Burbank, a New York writer, arrived in London to lecture on the folk song and dance that she had just been studying in eastern Europe. Invited by Adeline Genee, a Danish-born ballerina and star of the London ballet, to a fundraising exhibition by the Espérance girls, Burbank felt compelled to invite Neal to visit the United States and demonstrate the morris.[45] Neal agreed on the condition that she could bring Florrie Warren to help her illustrate the dance, and in December 1910, the two set out for New York.

Apparently confident that her status at Stratford was secure, Neal traveled in part as an ambassador for the Stratford program. She was still advertised as the presiding instructor and took many announcements of the vacation school with her to try to drum up business from Americans. However, when she returned from America in the early spring of 1911, she discovered that she had lost whatever advantages she had had with the Stratford governors.

Sharp had not been idle during Neal's absence, although personal setbacks had left him increasingly discouraged. Determined to make a living as a folklorist, after eighteen years, he had finally resigned his post at Ludgrove. But his eldest daughter, Dorothea, was seriously ill; his own asthma was worsening; the commute to work was debilitating; and he had too little money. Prospects in England seemed dismal, and he talked of emigrating to Australia, where he had first developed his music career after university. But during Neal's absence, Sharp's fortunes changed. While Neal made her mark in New York and Boston, the governors of the Shakespeare festival, although acknowledging that Neal had better organizational skills, chose Sharp, as the "authority," to direct future Stratford summer schools. Male bonds and paternalism would have merely cemented the draw of the cult of expertise that Sharp cultivated and represented, and Sharp's privileged entrée to the two men who were key to the teaching program, Edward Burrows and E. G. A. Holmes, undoubtedly helped his cause.[46] For otherwise, Sharp and Neal were both well connected; it was just that for the purposes of song and dance, Sharp's connections were

Orderly Bodies: Dancing London, 1900–1914 | 83

more relevant. Neal's ties were more to the bohemian and radical Left—and to the controversial suffragettes; Sharp's personal coterie was the musical and intellectual elite of North London. His friends and associates, for example, comprised a roster of the leading British composers of the day: as early as 1907, he provided English folk tunes that Gustav Holst used in his *Somerset Rhapsody*, an orchestral piece dedicated to Sharp; Vaughan Williams, who also used folk tunes in his compositions, was a close friend and devotee of the dance movement; and George Butterworth, the young composer, was one of the original members of Sharp's demonstration side.[47]

Soon after the governors' decision was made public, Sharp's personal life also took a turn for the better. In May 1911, the family moved to Uxbridge, where the country air improved his daughter's health and his asthma. In July, the government awarded him a civil list pension of one hundred pounds in recognition of his pathbreaking work collecting and preserving English folk song. He also found himself with a growing and profitable schedule of lectures and performances of morris, jigs, and country dances, most notably at the Crystal Palace, and he illustrated the dances with performances by his Chelsea students.[48]

When the summer school resumed at Stratford-on-Avon for four weeks in August 1911, Sharp was at its head, as he was for the rest of the decade. Neal resigned as honorary secretary of the Festival Association, and Sharp substituted his own program for her 1911 school syllabus. The Stratford position gave Sharp an important base for training a coterie of teachers who remained indebted and devoted to him. But as important, the venue introduced Sharp (and members of his demonstration team) to influential American student-visitors and transatlantic possibilities for both the revival movement and his career. In his diary, Sharp recalls that "Miss Hall and Miss Lauman, women who do the Dalcroze [sic] stuff at the Francis Parker School," attended the 1912 session. Harvard's George Baker attended the same year, and 1913 brought Helen Storrow and Mary Wood Hinman to the summer school.[49]

Neal did not retire quietly from the dance scene upon her return from the States. She remained active in folk dance until the war, though she remained highly involved with the suffrage campaign as well. She published two volumes on morris dance in 1910 and 1912, *The Espérance Morris Book*, and three years later, with Frank Kidson (1855–1926), another accomplished folk song collector, published *English Folk-Song and Dance* (1915). Vestiges of the acrimony between Sharp and Neal accompanied the books and filtered into the reviews: the reviewer for the *Musical Times*, for instance, dismissed Neal's contribution on dance in the 1915 volume as "an object lesson in uncritical method [that] is difficult to take seriously." The reviewer acknowledged, however, Neal's critique (which the reviewer rejected) of those who distort folk dance by "obsessing" with "technical knowledge [and] academic restrictions." Of course, no reader needed to be told who "those" were.[50]

Neal continued to direct the Espérance Guild in performances until the war. By 1913, she was back at Littlehampton running her own vacation school at the Green Lady Hotel with the help of Clive Carey and the Espérance Girls' Club dancers. Two school activities merit particular mention: even as she debunked Sharp as the academic pedant, and in turn was dismissed as not scholarly herself, Neal lectured on the history of folk dance and the revival based on her research in the British Library; and on another occasion, Grace Cleveland Porter, an American "authority on negro songs," gave a lecture on "old negro plantation stories and 'spiritual'" accompanied by a demonstration of "negro folk singing games . . . by the Espérance Guild of Morris Dancers."[51]

Little is known of the success or fate of the Littlehampton school, although a 1913 account notes that there were "many teachers" in attendance. With the coming of the war, and the clear ascendance of Sharp, Neal disappeared from the folk scene by the end of 1914. Sharp made a gesture to Neal in 1921, inviting her to a folk dance festival. She was "unable" to attend, and they reportedly exchanged cordial notes. In 1937, Mary Neal was appointed Commander of the Order of the British Empire (CBE) for her role in folk song and dance collecting. It was a long-overdue and bittersweet award. Still, reading Neal's memoir suggests that any formal politeness in her exchanges with Sharp masked a legacy of sorrow, if not anger.[52] The English Folk Dance Society eventually awarded her a gold badge for her role in the movement, but toward the end of her life she reportedly walked into the EFDSS headquarters and returned it to them, saying in effect, "Thank you very much. I've enjoyed having this, but I think it really belongs here."[53]

Sharp Consolidates His Position

By the end of 1911, Sharp had also moved to solidify his organizational base. With Sharp taking the initiative, on December 6, the English Folk Dance Society (EFDS) formed. (It united with the Folk-Song Society to form EFDSS in 1932.) Sharp was made honorary director at the meeting and later became the society's first director. His desire for a prestigious figure as president was filled when Lady Mary Trefusis, the eldest daughter of the sixth Earl Beauchamp and Woman of the Bedchamber to Queen Mary, agreed in 1913 to serve. Lady Trefusis, whom Sharp's biographer describes as herself a "first-rate player of the dances," was an important bridge to society and a source of capital for EFDSS in years to come.[54]

Under Sharp's leadership, EFDS quickly established the first of its branches—in Liverpool, Oxford, and Cirencester—where former supporters of Mary Neal were realigning with Sharp.[55] With Sharp now in control of both Stratford and the new society, one of EFDS's first activities was to organize a 1911 Christmas Vacation School at Stratford-on-Avon. According to Karpeles, eighty students attended, "of which a good many were men" who did jigs and sword dancing, but there continued to be no men's morris, as men were still struggling to learn in the beginner's class. Interestingly, a nonwhite international researcher for whom the English were a quaint "other" was distinguished for his dancing as much as for his race: "Among them was a very interesting Japanese scholar, who did everything with the greatest facility and was very much envied by the other men."[56]

Sharp's men's morris side became his exhibition team, and the men were paired with his women dancers to demonstrate couple country dances. Two of the men came from the Chelsea Polytechnic: A. Claud Wright and A. J. Paterson. The others were part of Sharp's intellectual-musical world: Douglas Kennedy, who upon Sharp's death became EFDSS director; the writer Perceval Lucas, who went on to edit the first volumes of the *Journal of the English Folk Dance Society*; the professional musician George Wilkinson, who succeeded Sharp at Ludgrove; and the brilliant young composer George Butterworth. The Oxford literary scholar Reginald Tiddy was the "spare" dancer. The women included Marjory Sinclair, Olive Lett, Maggie Muller, Helen Kennedy (Douglas's sister), and the two Karpeles sisters, Maud and Helen.[57]

On February 22, 1912, EFDS hosted its first "at home" for "a large number of influential people," at which the men's morris team made its debut. Soon after, it and the women teams were out and about the country demonstrating morris dance nearly every weekend. Women dancers included a young Scarborough teacher trained by Sharp, Lily Conant, who came to assume a major role in the history of ECD in the United States, and the two Karpeles sisters, among others.[58]

In the next few years, Sharp and his demonstration dancers began to establish an international reputation. In June 1913, they performed the Playford dance "Black Nag" in Paris, and the next summer they danced the "Old Mole," another Playford classic, in Brussels before a "large and fashionable audience" attending a fashion show. Among the many performances, however, it was a Savoy Theatre performance on December 2, 1912, that helped propel Sharp to the United States. The avant-garde director Granville Barker lent EFDS the use of the theater for a matinee (he was staging Shakespeare's *Twelfth Night* then), and the sold-out performance excited Barker's interest in incorporating country dance into one of his plays. Soon after, Barker staged *A Midsummer Night's Dream* and asked Sharp to arrange music and dance for the production. The fairies danced two country dances—"Sprig of Thyme" and "Sellenger's Round"—and Barker invited Sharp to repeat his work for the New York production to follow.[59]

By the time Sharp prepared to debark for the United States in December 1914, he had consolidated his hold on the English folk dance movement. EFDS had blossomed; it had grown to nearly five hundred members spread over twenty-one regional branches. Sharp had cemented his role as the English folk dance authority as well and had institutionalized it with a certificate program whereby he taught, evaluated, and then "certified" dance proficiency in formal examinations. By 1914, Sharp had awarded 169 certificates. Each certified the "authenticity" of the English country dancer and served as an active representation of Sharp's authority in English Country Dance.[60]

Conclusion

For the English folk revivalists and their American visitors, the revival was as much a project for the renovation of the revivalists themselves as for their immigrant subjects, either in the settlement houses and playgrounds or in the "depravities" of the music halls of the city. Of course, the immigrant and working-class girls and boys who were taught (and, at times, assigned) to learn the dances in the schools and playgrounds were quite different from adults such as Sharp, Neal, and their friends, who chose to do it recreationally and as a social mission. The experience of Florence Warren was an exception, not the rule. The men and women who started, led, and joined EFDS and its soon-to-be-organized American branch were as a rule cut from different class and ethnic cloth than the settlement youth. They were white, Protestant elites of Anglo-American or northern European background who identified with ECD and Anglo-American culture as the core of national identity. All the major protagonists in this story—notably, Neal, Sharp, and Wright in England and Burchenal, Storrow, Baker, and Hinman in the United States—shared an elite or affluent middle-class Anglo-Saxon social identity. A notable exception was the Karpeles sisters, who were of German-Jewish descent. They, too, however, were thoroughly Anglophile, and in their letters and writing never represented themselves as other than English. Maud, for example, was baptized into the Anglican Church at the age of fifty-three, and she had converted to Christianity at the age of fourteen.[61]

Sharp's determinate role in dictating the spirit of the dance, however, was advanced by a tight coterie of supporters with whom he surrounded himself. The English leaders were a close-knit social "family" devoted to its patriarch. The Kennedys and Karpeles were at the center of this group of devotees. Helen Karpeles, who became the society's secretary, married Kennedy, and her sister, Maud, became Sharp's confidant, travel companion, collaborator, and personal secretary. In the context of the heated debate within the movement, it was only a matter of time before one wag would uncharitably dub the group the "Sharpeles."

The ascendance of Sharp and disappearance of Neal, however, had consequences for the character of English Country Dance as it emerged on both sides of the Atlantic. Both could agree on the central missionary project of the folk revival that Neal had described in 1910: "This revival of our English folk music is . . . part of a great national revival, a going back from the town to the country, a reaction against all that is demoralizing in city life. It is a re-awakening of that part of our nation's consciousness which makes for the wholeness, saneness and healthy merriment."[62] Accordingly, both could also accept the doctoring (what was, in fact, censoring) of dances to remove elements they thought unseemly—whether it be to delete a kiss (really more a peck) from a folk dance, as Neal had suggested (and Sharp enacted), or to change a dance title, as Sharp had done in retitling "Cuckolds All A Row" as "Hey, Boys, Up Go We."

Neal and Sharp also had significant class- and gender-inflected differences that had a bearing on the history of the dance movement, most especially in the style and spirit of the dance. In both cases, Sharp proceeded as the dance patriarch. Karpeles, Sharp's devoted helpmate, even as she blurs the line between hagiography and biography, acknowledges that he was "dogmatic" and that his polemics "were often vehement and were occasionally enlivened with a kind of schoolboyish invective."[63] In truth, Neal's and Sharp's class backgrounds were not very different, but their class politics were, and Neal's departure from the movement had profound implications for the spirit—the style—of the country dance over the next quarter century. Rather than a movement rooted in the working class and led by a militant socialist suffragette, under Sharp's leadership EFDS expressed the more restrained and elite bodies of the bourgeoisie who put the dances of village folk, both literally and figuratively, into more formal attire. Ironically, although Sharp recognized the deterioration of Playford as it moved into the drawing rooms, he enacted the same process. He might learn a dance or song from a gardener such as John England—or later from a backwoods highlander in the United States—but he would return to the city, put on his black tie and starched shirt, and "dress up" the dance or song for urban bourgeois consumption or for the remaking of the urban proletariat. Ostensibly, the conflict between Neal and Sharp was over the proper character of the dance—"authenticity"—and their different positions on authenticity mirrored the ambivalence and contradictions in their views as a "conservative socialist" and radical socialist-suffragist, respectively. They divided on how much they identified with the working class, but together they located a politics of the folk on a progressive-socialist continuum.

But there were larger personal and political differences that also divided the two. In retrospect, the *Punch* cartoon and 1907 conference triggered Sharp's anxieties about any challenge to his authorial role. Basically, Sharp assumed one of the hallmarks of Progressive reform, the role of the expert, but he did so as the Folk-Song Society patriarch. Neal essentialized the working-class authenticity of her seamstresses, believing they expressed the natural enthusiasm of the dance. Sharp complained that the Espérance girls, with their "violent" leg movements, ignored the historical form that he thought the dance teacher—an expert such as himself—had to teach. Neal's views conformed to her militant suffragist and active socialist engagements. Sharp's Fabian socialism was a more restrained and elite stripe. Never comfortable with competition, Sharp seemed to tolerate it least from strong women who were suffragettes. Folk dance attracted women dance teachers, of course, and Sharp did surround himself with women. But Sharp's women teachers were cut from a different cloth than Neal—they were not suffragettes, to be sure, but more to the point, as Sharp assumed control of the new folk dance movement, they accepted him as the ECD authority and were devoted to him.[64]

Sharp's assumption of the ECD throne in England did not necessarily translate into authority in the United States, however. For that, he had to wage additional struggles. And in the United States, his hegemony came ultimately to rely on his reservoir of young female teachers, acolytes, and devotees.

4

Planting a Colony in America

> Miss Burchenal and all that crowd know what poor stuff they are passing off as folk-dance and they know that if I come & see it I shall have to show them—and those they have taught—how wrong they all are and so queer their pitch.
> —Cecil Sharp to Maud Karpeles, January 8, 1915, New York City

On December 23, 1914, the SS *Lusitania* docked in New York Harbor bearing renowned folklorist Cecil Sharp, chair of the English Folk Dance Society. The man cut an impressive figure. Sharp's square-jawed visage, firm posture, and formal dress belied his fifty-four years and the chronic asthma that left him often weakened and sick. Mrs. May Eliot Hobbes's description of him in 1911 when he entered a drawing room captured the imposing sense of the man: "the piercing blue eyes—falcon-like—the strong nose, the firm set of the head on the shoulders, the superb carriage, which he retained even when more bent with increasing age. There was a controlled suppleness in the whole body, loosely knit without being wobbly and this is what made his dancing unique in its grace and ease. It might be summed up in two words—'line and carriage.'"[1]

Sharp was not, however, the first English dancing master to visit Progressive Era America. His arrival had been preceded by visits from three other teacher-performers who were at once his protégés and competitors, and they embodied different expressions for the dance. Sharp prevailed, and his victory enshrined a particularly constrained bodily expression for English Country Dance that had a lasting impact on the shape and form of the dance in the United States. As important, though, Sharp put in place a leadership that embodied the nascent country dance movement with traditional gender roles and as white, Anglo-Saxon, and elite.

Cecil Sharp. (Reproduced courtesy of EFDSS)

Mary Neal and Florence Warren

The first two English folk dance teachers who went to America preceded Sharp by four years. On December 3, 1910, the SS *Arabic* set sail from Liverpool with Mary Neal, the fifty-year-old leader of the Espérance Girls' Club, and the group's leading dancer, the twenty-four-year-old Florence Warren. The girls had developed a remarkable performance morris side, and Warren had joined Neal on the trip to help demonstrate the dance. In the next three months, Neal led a triumphant tour of New York and Boston, awakening new interest in the old English dances among public-school educators and Anglophile reformers. The timing of their visit and practical considerations made morris dance rather than country dance Neal's focus, though the one quickened later American interest in the other. Kimber and the more flamboyant and showy morris dance had excited the early interest in English folk dance, and in 1910 the Playford repertoire remained largely unknown. Equally to the point, morris could be demonstrated by individual dancers; unlike the country dances, it did not require a set of at least four and often several more dancers.

Eight days after departing from Liverpool, the two women arrived in New York to a rude awakening: Neal's feud with Sharp had preceded them, and all their engagements had been canceled. Neal was told that a friend of Cecil Sharp's in New York had gone to all the societies and educators in New York and told them that the education authorities in the United Kingdom had "thrown [them] over." Sharp's "friend" appears to have been Elizabeth Burchenal. As early as September 1908, Sharp's publications and public presence had attracted Burchenal's attention, and she had written him while collecting dances in England. "Especially" desiring to "see some of the morris men dancers in the country" during her time in Oxfordshire, Burchenal had sought Sharp's help in winning her access to Kimber.[2] Nothing more is known of their exchange at the time, but she had probably returned the favor. Burchenal returned to England in 1910 (though it is not clear that she attended the summer school) and concluded that Sharp and not Neal best represented the English tradition. As she wrote Sharp a year later, "It was a great thorn in my side to have Miss Neal here last winter representing herself as the morris dance authority and I feel that many people knew no better than to accept her as such."[3]

Discouraged, one part of Neal was ready to take the next boat back to London; another part, however, was determined to stay and fight Sharp. A feature article in the *New York Tribune* four days after the women's arrival heralding their visit undoubtedly helped convince her to stay on and fight back. In the *New York Times,* in a barely disguised attack on Sharp, she described the dance as "an eminently democratic thing." "The introduction of pedantry"— her charge against Sharp—"of sophisticated art, would utterly kill the movement." In a few weeks, she and Warren managed to rebook their dates, and by her account, their demonstration of morris dancing soon captured the hearts of both New York and Boston. Neal, in what was to prove a premature forecast of her triumph in a letter back to Clive Carey in London, trumpeted, "Cecil Sharp has done his best to poison people's minds over here. But we are here and he is not! . . . Nor do I think he will ever come now."[4]

Thought to be a surviving pre-Christian ritual, Neal and Warren's triumphant performance—with its exuberant leaps, twirling handkerchiefs, and the rhythmic jangling of the bells tied to their calves—was heralded by the *New York Times* as a refreshing example of the folk revival under way in England. Lost on the reporter was the transformed or "invented" quality of the women's morris "revival" of a dance traditionally performed by men.[5] For the

Times, ECD held the promise of reawakening what the reporter bemoaned as the repressed spirit of the Anglo-American race.[6]

Having agreed to press on with their tour, Warren promptly assumed responsibility for teaching three different sides of morris dancers (in an intense nine days) for the MacDowell Club's Christmas Festival at the Plaza Hotel. Described in the *New York Times* as "one of the season's brilliant events," the affair reflected the city elite's fascination with English heritage dance. But the two women's experience also reflected the burgeoning interest in folk dance for schoolchildren, native-born and immigrant. The two women taught morris dance to New York City schoolteachers, which Burchenal, who had led the teaching of folk dance to the city's teachers, must have found personally galling. They then traveled to New Haven and Boston, where their dances were soon incorporated into the emerging folk repertoire. Neal lectured on the morris at Boston's prestigious Twentieth Century Club, and by late April 1911, the Women's Athletic Association of Boston, under Helen Storrow's leadership, included three morris dances as part of its International Folk Dance exhibition.[7]

Neal returned to London sometime in the early spring 1911. She had managed to rescue the tour, and she was probably fortunate that it was the modest success that the dance historian Roy Judge considers it to have been. Florence Warren stayed on to spread the morris gospel, and her experience proved as much a success for her personally as for the morris dance movement. One highlight of Warren's tour occurred in early May when Adeline Genee, in an extraordinary offer, invited her and her new American morris side to take the stage with her and share the billing for Genee's Carnegie Hall dance concert. The Boston papers gave the morris dancers mixed reviews, but *The Times* of London, in its humorous delight in the event, inadvertently caught the class ironies (and appeal) of morris dance at Carnegie Hall: "We may yet hear of a 'side' of American Morris-men, multi-millionaires every one, dancing the Processional Morris down Wall Street."[8]

Warren followed her New York success with teaching and demonstration classes in Hartford, Connecticut, and Albany, New York. Again, the upper-class Anglo-American constituency for the dance was apparent. The Hartford performance took place at the home of Archibald Welch, a wealthy insurance executive who later became president of Phoenix Mutual. In Albany, Warren's appeal was such that she was kept on for six weeks, teaching upward of two hundred schoolchildren and teachers. The numbers suggest that her Albany classes attracted students with a broader social background, but a local newspaper's comment indicates the continuing elite appeal of the English dance: "several families" decided to delay their "summer home plans" so that their children could participate.⁹

Little more is known of Warren's dancing career. Rhett Krause, in his history of the tour, suggests that she taught in Chicago in 1915 and later coauthored a children's book. She does not appear to have returned to England, however, until 1937, and then she did not travel alone. Warren had found good personal reasons to remain in the States: just before the scheduled return to London in March 1911, she had met a Yale law student, Arthur H. Brown, at a dinner in conjunction with a morris demonstration in New Haven. Brown tells a romantic story of his impetuously leaving a golf game and racing to New York Harbor to propose marriage to a delighted Warren just as her boat was about to sail. On Valentine's Day 1912, they married—at the home of the New York writer, lecturer, and folk collector Emily Burbank. In 1937, on their twenty-fifth wedding anniversary, the Browns visited London, where Florrie Warren and Neal had a reunion with the Espérance girls.¹⁰

A. Claud Wright

One of Sharp's protégés was the other teacher-dancer to precede him to America, and their conflict may have been as important for the history of English Country Dance in the United States as had been that between Sharp and Neal. A. Claud Wright (1888–1977) was one of the original six male dancers from Sharp's own morris demonstration side.¹¹ George P. Baker, Harvard University professor of dramatic literature, attended the Stratford Summer School in 1912 and was captivated by the bold athleticism of Wright's dancing. Upon Baker's return to the United States, he inaugurated a folk dance class in 1913. The group, which consisted of fifty-six members, often used the open-air theater at Chocorua, New Hampshire, at George Baker's summer camp 130 miles north of Boston, and Baker's hope was that Wright would teach them morris dance. Subsequently, at Baker's invitation, Wright visited New England on two occasions, in the summers of 1913 and 1914.¹²

Wright's verticality and energy contrasted with Sharp's more forward-moving, fluid, but composed style. As James C. Brickwedde has concluded in his careful study of Wright's American visits, "Claud Wright took the base created by Cecil Sharp and added strength, height, and power to the movement."¹³ The difference was probably lost on most Americans, who knew of Sharp at most by reputation and were thrilled by the dramatic character of Wright's bold leaps. A growing community of folk dance enthusiasts in the New World embraced Wright during his visits. But Wright's success, of course,

A. Claud Wright displaying his verticality while morris dancing. (Used by permission of the Country Dance and Song Society Archives, www.cdss.org; Milne Special Collections and Archives Department, University of New Hampshire Library, Durham, NH)

threatened to undermine any aspirations Sharp had about his own prospects in the United States. To the extent these ambitions animated him, Sharp kept them at bay; to speak of financial ambition was unseemly, if not unprofessional. Instead, Sharp expressed his dispute with Wright as one of style: he found his protégé's athleticism (Wright had a background in gymnastics) incompatible with what he considered authentic country dance style.

Wright's visit in the summer of 1913 came at the high point in his folk dance career and won him an enthusiastic following in the United States.[14] After two weeks at Chocorua, he spent what appears to have been a hectic and extraordinary week in Lincoln at Helen Storrow's grand country home teaching and demonstrating morris, sword, and country dance. He was, he chortled in a letter to "My Dear Baker," "the sole specimen of masculinity amid a crowd of 14 maids. You can imagine my confusion (?) better than I can describe it."[15]

The visit also won Wright impressive moneyed connections. The Storrow house was "a wonder"; he observed that he had the third floor all to himself. He marveled at the breakfasts and banquets of food. The earnings—all his expenses and fifty pounds—were not insignificant either, especially to a person of relatively modest means. In contrast to Sharp and most of his group, who were a similarly well-heeled part of the intellectual-artistic elite, Wright's father was a skilled cabinet maker. Wright contrasted his own situation by noting, "we are not money folk and what little comfort we have has been gained through long years of striving."[16] Unlike others in the performance troupe, Wright lived entirely on his teaching income and continued to support his parents. The teaching offered potentially significant financial benefits, especially for Wright. Hinman, with whom he had also established contact for projected teaching in Chicago, assured him that "the financial end [of the American teaching] will be alright."[17] Wright and his American hosts also had begun to talk of a return visit, and soon after his return to London, Wright wrote Baker, "I must simply get in another visit to the land of freedom—if the dances become popular and my friends wish me to come."[18]

Unfortunately for Wright, jealous English compatriots had begun to wish otherwise for him. Although coincidence is not necessarily causation, Sharp's reservations about Wright coincided with increasing pressures from Americans attending the August 1913 Summer School for Sharp to consider his own visit. The previous year, when Baker first raised the prospect of an ECD "export to America," Wright had found Sharp "quite bucked" by the idea, thinking Sharp "very pleased" with his "work and success." But upon his return from America, Wright picked up negative vibrations. Sharp, he noted, "had a curious air of complaisance." Wright worried that the source of Sharp's displeasure was a mistaken belief afoot that he was an agent of EFDS and a personal ambassador for Sharp, and he pleaded with Baker to let Storrow know that he was not "sent out by the Society" and that he preferred "to be known as a free agent and [Baker's] guest."[19]

Sharp's opposition to Wright was more rooted in his concerns about Wright's style and increasing role in the United States—both concerns Sharp could not disentangle from his own ambitions abroad—and there was little Wright could do to counter the growing hostility to him on the English side of the Atlantic. Sharp had initially agreed that he would "not stand in the way" of Wright's teaching abroad, but by the fall 1913, Wright found Sharp's response and that from other members of his group noticeably cooler. Wright understood the hostility as veiled jealousy, but it was complicated by his sense of himself as an outsider in a tight little club, the "Sharpeles":

What the matter is with Sharp & his band I know is jealousy—that I might forestall. . . . This is where I see the shoes pinching—Wilkinson & Kennedy [two of the dancers] through the Karpeles (Kennedy and Miss Helen [Karpeles] are more than friends—all the world may see) hold Sharp close. See thus, Helen Karpeles is Secretary for the Society. Maud [Karpeles] is Sharp's Private Secretary, so that no correspondence reaches Sharp without one or the other knows it. Hence at Stratford I was amused by a perfect stranger referring to them as the Sharpeles.[20]

In fact, Sharp's own financial ambitions probably added to his disquiet with Wright's success. In the fall and winter of 1913, as Wright contemplated his return, he also became increasingly aware that Sharp had his own plans for the United States, and they did not include Wright. Wright, who at the time was twenty-five years old, complained to Baker that Sharp spoke of sending a "Mrs. Hobbes" as his representative, who "can neither dance nor teach" and was "about forty-five years of age."[21]

Wright could do little about the animosities he felt but soldier on. In the next months, while his own teaching flourished, conflict between the two remained below the surface. "The jealousy is still out there," wrote Wright, "but disguised or recognized so plainly that we are all much happier." At the same time, Wright, perhaps aware that Sharp thought his style problematic, wrote triumphantly to Baker of glowing evaluations he had won from the board of education inspector. The inspector had "no advice or criticism to give him" and, rather, brought the head inspector to see his teaching. Meanwhile, his classes at Stratford, "always overcrowded," were "pleasingly successful." In contrast, he evinced sadness about what he thought to be Sharp's "joyless" teaching and style. With comments similar to those voiced by Neal, Wright described Sharp's style to Baker: "You know what the dances mean to me, & when I see the hand cutting here and pacing there—throwing out all joy of the dances & making of them far too much of a business, I am grieved." One suspects that the "business" of the dance referred to fussiness about style, but it inadvertently bespoke larger financial concerns of Sharp's that also shaped his views of "proper" country dance and his role in authorizing them.[22]

By May 1914, plans for Wright's return had formalized, and Sharp, at least publicly, expressed his support for the trip. Sharp outwardly blessed the trip, sharing with Wright a letter he had received from Storrow asking for Wright's revisit. Sharp could even appreciate that Wright's trip could be to the advantage of the movement. Wright's return would further establish ECD in the United States and keep a wealthy patron such as Storrow happy. But Sharp's

Planting a Colony in America | 97

subsequent complaints and own ambitions suggest that he did continue to harbor reservations about Wright. Sharp was explicit about his concerns with Wright's "athletic style": "So far I have found it easier to make dancers out of those who have not been trained and have done little or no athletics. Nearly all physically trained people and athletes suffer from stiff or inflexible joints, and muscles that have been developed beyond their power of control. What faults Wright has, may all be traced to his early physical training. The *ideal* physically trained person . . . is far more likely to be the product of the dancing master than of the gymnast."[23]

Sharp's reservations did not dissuade Storrow, however, and with Baker's support, Wright embarked on a two-month return visit between July and September 1914. Wright's second American visit was, at least by his own account, another success, although the outbreak of war had distracted some potential dance students. Wright bracketed his trip, teaching for two weeks again at Chocorua and, at the end, for two weeks in Lincoln on the Storrow lawn. Wright described the two weeks at Lincoln as "tremendously successful," although the session attracted but twenty-two students, and only seven for the fortnight. Still, being paid $1.25 an hour to teach—a day's work for a garment worker then—he did rather well, netting $629.25, less $58 for the pianist.[24]

The month between the teaching at Chocorua and at Lincoln foreshadowed both the widening impact Wright was having in the United States and his plans to expand his reach in the future. Wright spent the interval visiting in York Harbour, Maine, and teaching at Lanier Camp in Elliot, Maine. He followed those assignments with classes at the MacDowell Artists' Colony in Peterborough, New Hampshire, where one of his students was Doris Humphrey, later to be one of the pioneering American modern dance choreographers. Moreover, even as he completed this trip, Mary Wood Hinman and Percival Chubb (the English-born Fabian leader of the St. Louis Ethical [Culture] Society) were planning for Wright to teach in Chicago and St. Louis later that fall.[25]

Baker organized what was to be one last but extensive four-month visit for Wright in early 1915. A tour was to take him to Chicago, St. Louis, Pittsburgh, and Madison, Wisconsin (presumably mostly to venues where he could teach young women and men in physical education and settlement house and playground programs), as well as through New England. Ultimately, the trip never took place, but it was neither jealousy from the Sharpeles nor Sharp's personal agenda that deterred Wright; rather, it was the coming of the war that did, and in ways that were personal and ugly.

As the war engulfed England in 1914 and young men enlisted, Wright was conflicted. All the other members of Sharp's demonstration team enlisted. Wright's brother and James Paterson, a friend and fellow dancer in Sharp's troupe who boarded with his family, also enlisted, and Claud was now the only support for his parents. "Were I to enlist," he wrote Baker, "I do not know what would happen to my people [his parents]— they would almost be destitute."[26] His commission was unlikely to come through for another few months, and he could assume it after earning some money in the United States with which to provide for his parents. Seeking advice from Baker, he explained that he had no intention of going abroad "if it damages his reputation with him [Baker] or his American friends." At the same time, Wright acknowledged that his larger ambitions for himself in the United States did influence him: "I do not want anyone else to step in the place I, with your help, have made. That's why I want to come!"[27]

As late as December 27, with Sharp already in New York for two days with his own folk dance agenda, Wright still hoped to fulfill his planned tour. He had been busily taking on all the work he could in England, teaching classes at various folk dance centers and organizing public dances for the military effort. The efforts, according to Brickwedde, had allowed him to put aside some extra money for his family. In any case, it was increasingly apparent to Wright that many Americans might look askance at an Englishman traveling to America while England was at war. And Sharp was particularly clear and vocal about his feelings: patriots enlisted. But as the war escalated, Sharp's views were increasingly echoed by others, and dance organizers in New Haven and elsewhere soon also voiced their reservations about Wright's pending visit. Baker's explanations about Wright's family situation settled some concerns, but organizers wrote Baker that they could not guarantee attendance while the war raged.

Ultimately, the pressure on Wright to cancel his trip was too great. On January 1, 1915, Wright received a telegram from Baker suggesting he come for a shortened tour. The telegram tipped the balance for an obviously ambivalent Wright; later that day, he cabled to cancel his tour, explaining that his commission in the Royal Flying Corps had materialized. Wright's withdrawal could not have been made easier by the fact that Sharp had told him less than a month earlier—only three days before Sharp's departure—that he was going to the United States. In Wright's absence, Sharp would have free rein to "step in the place" that Wright had made for himself.[28]

Cecil Sharp's First Visit to America

Cecil Sharp arrived in the New World in December 1914 with a full agenda, both personal and political, and the one shaped the other. He had immediate personal needs to make enough money to allow him to live in the comfortable manner he thought appropriate to his station. His larger cultural and political project was to establish English Country Dance in America. As the director of the English Folk Dance Society, where better to spread the folk revival gospel than in the former American colony, where so many kinfolk had settled. And as the leading teacher and collector of folk song and dance in England, who better to lead this mission than himself. Yet to do so required him to establish his authority in the United States, where Mary Neal and, especially, A. Claud Wright had already made names for themselves.

Upon his arrival in New York, Sharp's financial and professional anxieties set the tone for his trials and tribulations. He had traveled first class—as indeed he always did—and settled in the Algonquin Hotel on West 44th Street. But he could scarcely contain his disappointment at the accommodations. It is "a fairly comfortable but distinctly 2nd class hotel," he wrote in a letter, penned on Christmas Day 1914, to Maud Karpeles on hotel stationery.[29] The disparity between his second-class circumstances and the high style in which he sought to travel reflected the genteel poverty of his privileged intellectual class. The class pretensions and anxieties of the bourgeoisie, of course, lay at the heart of the liberal problematic: they celebrated the "natural" culture of those "below," accepted their own social privilege as an extension of their moral and intellectual superiority, and worried all the time about the fragility of their status. These tensions, in fact, shaped Sharp's attitudes toward other Americans and the occasional ruthlessness into which he lapsed toward those he viewed as competitors for the folk dance mantle.

Sharp always worried about money, and not without cause. The Cambridge-educated son of a London slate merchant, he had been bred for the comfortable life. But his tenure as music master at Ludgrove from 1893 to 1910 had given him modest prospects. The 1911 government award of a civil list pension of one hundred pounds in recognition of his services collecting and preserving folk songs gave him a cushion that permitted him to embark on a career teaching folk dance. Indeed, the addition of his wife Constance's one hundred pounds a year gave him an annual income of five hundred pounds (approximately twenty-five hundred dollars, at a time when a schoolteacher earned about fifteen hundred dollars per annum). Now, just prior to arriving in New York, he and his wife had purchased a new home at 27 Church Row in the fashionable North London suburb of Hampstead. They moved there in October 1915, when Sharp was back in London.[30]

Sharp wittily dated the Church Row house as "about the time of the sixth edition of Playford."[31] A rather simple red-paneled house dating from the late seventeenth century, its neighborhood was anything but simple. Charles Booth's London social map paints the street red—"Middle Class. Well-to-Do"—and it is surrounded by streets in "upper class" gold. On a walk about the village in 1898, Booth's investigator, George Duckworth, was more impressed: "the Row itself [is] almost the most picturesque street in London with its quaint old Georgian red/sash brick houses. Yellow."[32]

Sharp's financial position improved after the end of the war. With the return of some measure of social stability after the war, EFDS was able to pay him an annual salary as director of four hundred pounds; before then, the post had been honorary. As his biographers note, the salary "did not make him a wealthy man, but it did relieve him of financial anxiety."[33] As his book royalties also rose, three years later, in 1922, Sharp relinquished his civil service pension, feeling that his "instinct" told him that he "had no longer a right to it."[34] Sadly, after developing heart trouble from a bout with scarlet fever in the early summer of 1915, Constance was often housebound, a semi-invalid for the rest of her life. Still, with Sharp's finances improved, the family was able to move into a more commodious four-story brick semidetached Victorian with a garden about half a mile away, at 4 Maresfield Gardens, Hampstead. Ironically, Sharp's final home was originally half of Westfield College, an institution with precisely the kind of women whom Sharp targeted as his folk dance teachers. It, too, was a quality address, and in the next decade, Sigmund and Anna Freud moved in eight doors up the block.[35]

But in New York in the winter of 1914–15, these better days were in the distant future and difficult for Sharp to envision. His financial problems were also more immediate. It was unseemly for the well-to-do to complain about money, and even as he acted the part, his own financial obsession, about which he was keenly aware, made him uncomfortable. Still, he could not escape it, and it shaped his attitudes and responses to life daily. The same Christmas Day that Sharp complained about the Algonquin to Karpeles, he wrote worryingly to his wife, Constance: "I only hope I may bring back a little money to pay for the move and to make our house a little more decent than Dragonfield [their prior home in Uxbridge, a northwest London suburb]. It has been on my mind—as I think you know—that my inability to make money has pressed so hard on you and the children."[36]

Sharp continued to stay at the Algonquin whenever he visited New York. It was fashionable among the artistic set, and Sharp found it convenient to dine there or at the nearby Players' Club. His modest, by his count, income and his initial impressions of New York made him at times an unhappy camper. In the United States only forty-eight hours, he vented in a Christmas letter to Maud Karpeles: "What I have seen of NY and the people I do not like overmuch." Finding the combination of central heating and arctic conditions "overbearing," he returned to his usual theme, his obsession with money. With no sense of the irony of his critiquing American materialism, he castigates his hosts:

Everything is money and everything hideously expensive. The only thing one cares for is dollars. Their quest of which is conducted nakedly and unashamedly! The degree of efficiency in ordinary matters conceiving material living is amazing, but there it stops—and I prefer my own country and my own countrymen. The Americans are foreigners. Their city does not talk English nor do they behave like English people. I fancy the predominant element outside the Anglo Saxon is German and the two make an abominable mixture.[37]

Sharp's comments prefigured more than his financial anxieties: his negative view of Germans reflected the hostilities that had already erupted in Europe, conflict that profoundly influenced his ability to move back and forth between England and the United States. In addition, Sharp's appreciation of American "efficiency" became one basis for a growing appreciation that he came to have for the United States. Not that his view of the United States ever seemed far removed from the money question, though. Upon his arrival in New York City, he also made a quick visit to H. W. Gray of Gray and Novello, his publisher, who "seemed very impressed with the number of books he [Sharp] sold," a judgment that encouraged Sharp immediately to speculate on lecture possibilities.[38]

Sharp's days were filled with rehearsals for Granville Barker's staging of *A Midsummer Night's Dream*, but he quickly moved to explore his lecture prospects. Folk song, for which his collecting in England had begun to win him international acclaim, seemed the logical best bet, so to illustrate his lectures, Sharp sent to England for Mattie Kay to sing to his piano accompaniment. But the decision proved both costly and unwise. Sharp had to assume Kay's costs in America, and folk song proved unremunerative. The first public lecture at the Plaza Hotel "went very nicely," according to Sharp, but the quality of the reception was insufficient if it did not meet his expenses—which it did not: it was a "good audience but not a paying one."[39]

Until he found his moorings, Sharp's first month in New York found him vacillating between hope and despair about ever establishing himself as a lecturer. Dinner with the Burchenals on the evening of January 7 led him to conclude, "They won't be able to help me much. They were full of plans for me to speak here and there for nothing but dried up when I asked about fees." Word from Hinman led him to fear that the same was true of Chicago. Sharp understood the problem, however, as less about their access to money than about their status as folk dance teachers, which he would surely undermine, as he was quite convinced that "that crowd know[s] what poor stuff they are passing off as folk-dance." Any intervention on his part would require a balancing act: he would have to show them "how wrong they all are and so queer their pitch," but he would have to do so "without showing them up."[40]

Yet, when the prospect of both lecture and dance classes improved, Sharp's spirits rose, and so did his attitude toward his hosts. After spending a week in which he got to know Burchenal better, his criticism of her softened. He concluded, "She has the right idea about folk-dancing & is painfully impressed with the necessity of accuracy, etc. but of course her knowledge is painfully small."[41] The lecture she arranged for him at the Colony Club was not a success, however, and sent Sharp's emotional roller-coaster downhill again. Ninety percent of the crowd, he complained, was not the least interested in hearing him talk about dance. A noisy, "social crowd," it was a "terrible ordeal" that left him "feeling very depressed." With a flair for the melodramatic, he added to an always sympathetic Karpeles, "So I must be philosophical and resigned to my lot, and to dying a poor man! After all the work I have done is far more important than a mere means of making a living."[42]

A dance class soon after, however, convinced Sharp that he had a future—it was just not to be as a lecturer. Burchenal had arranged for Sharp to teach a class at Susan Gilman's fashionable dance studio, and to his delight, Sharp found it surprisingly easy. Despite a slippery floor, and the fact that the twenty students had only ballet training, he taught them two country dances that he had reconstructed, both with roots in the "peasant" past: the circle dance "Gathering Peascods" and the two-couple dance "Hey, Boys, Up Go We."[43] As important as the success of the class, in Gilman, Sharp discovered a dancer who met his standards, a person who became one of his disciples, giving up all her other work, according to Karpeles, to teach ECD in New York.[44]

The success at Gilman's studio got Sharp's mind racing. He began to envision sources of income in awarding dance certificates, attracting Americans

Planting a Colony in America | 103

to Stratford, and selling back issues of the *Folk Dance Journal*. "There is heaps of talk here of folk dance but absolutely no knowledge whatsoever and if I do no more than expose their lack of information I shall have done a lot." Now, for the first time, he began publicly to express the hope of establishing a permanent presence for the English Folk Dance Society in the United States. Writing to Karpeles, he said he wished she were there to team in the dance with him: "if you were here, one demonstration would do the trick!" Meanwhile, he would try "to work Miss Ferris for all she is worth." Locals seemed reasonably content with "the magic word 'folk-dancing'" and with Ferris as the teacher, but Sharp thought this more a commentary on their infatuation with "anything so long as it can be called by that name." He obviously thought Ferris's ability limited. So while his dream of establishing a branch of EFDS in the United States appeared increasingly plausible, Sharp realized that someone other than himself had "to take general command of the folk dancing in N.Y." His thoughts immediately turned to his cadre of dancers in England and initially to Maud's sister, Helen Karpeles Kennedy.[45]

A full-time paid teacher from England would need an organization and dance community for support, and Sharp set out to build both. At the time, he was still preoccupied with rehearsals for *A Midsummer Night's Dream*, on top of which Barker had induced him to arrange some songs and dances for a production of Anatole France's *The Man Who Married a Dumb Wife*.[46] Nonetheless, an indefatigable enthusiast on a mission, Sharp filled his free days and nights teaching folk dance and planning for his American branch.[47] Focusing on the early dances, such as "Mage on a Cree," "Rufty Tufty," and "Sellenger's Round," his commentary on the attendees' dancing, while alternatively acerbic and conciliatory, teasing and direct, gives a sense of his candid (or, to some, brutal) teaching style: "They were quick to learn but their style was simply awful—dreadfully affected. . . . But I chaffed them mercilessly and imitated their air & graces & recommended them to look at themselves in the looking glass when they were doing their movements, etc.! By the time we got to Mage they were dancing more or less like human beings."[48]

Buoyed by the responses of audiences, Sharp's agent, Miss Wick, suggested he set up a course of six country dance classes that would allow students to earn an EFDS certificate. Sharp, delighted with the prospect, immediately wrote Karpeles to send him twenty-five certificates signed by the secretary as soon as possible. Sharp envisioned a fee of fifteen dollars for the course of six lessons and the examination. He realized, however, that he had to tailor his program to his American audience. EFDS had developed a graded certificate scheme, but Sharp was convinced that ambitious and status-conscious

Americans would not be interested in an "Elementary" certificate. Instead, he asked that "Associate" certificates be sent, conceding that a bonus might be additional business from Americans who would then decide to attend the Stratford-on-Avon Summer School.[49]

While awaiting the certificates and with plans for a course in development, Sharp set out to drum up more business in New York and elsewhere. The planning for Sharp's lectures, however, both for those scheduled for New York and the prospective tour, had disappointed him, and Sharp was quick to blame his agent, Miss Wick, railing against her gender. Sharp needed someone who could negotiate among what he reported to be three competing folk dance organizations—possibly Burchenal's Athletic League or the dance studios run by Beiderhaze, Cass, and Gilman. He found them "all very jealous of each other & more or less antagonistic." He conceded that Wicks worked "very hard to get [him] arrangements," but as we have seen, Sharp's rather traditional views on gender roles undermined his ability to work easily with women as equals. As he concluded in a letter to Karpeles about Wicks, "Business women are a mistake.... She works... with people she likes but is very abject with those she objects to." "She makes the whole thing a purely personal matter and it is impossible to do business with her as one would with a man! I can't speak straight to her without her making a flare up—she takes umbrage very quickly, and the result is I do not know how my affairs stand.... She is going to have a baby soon and I dare say she is in consequence not quite compo [mentis]—another argument against a woman-agent!" Having vented, though, Sharp seemed to recognize the irony of his having written what could be read as a misogynist diatribe to a woman (Karpeles), and in an era of intense suffrage agitation. Accordingly, he closed his rant to Karpeles with a conciliatory coda: "I am not railing against her [Wick's] sex so much as against her. Some woman might do her job all right—but she can't and I am suffering from her hubris."[50]

After firing Wicks, Sharp did, in fact, look to hire a female replacement, but a wholly compliant and devoted one with whom he could complain and rail with impunity. A woman named Lellah offered to be his secretary, but his preference was the diminutive and loyal Maud Karpeles, who he affectionately addressed as "little minimus." In his usual manner, he teased her as he held out the prospect that she would take charge of his arrangements: "I like someone rather smaller & merrier—if not so beautiful—upon whom I can sit when I want and upon whose good-nature & generosity I can always count. That I think is one of my typical compliments: 'Hot ice and wondrous strange snow,' and should amuse Joan [his daughter] even if it angers you."[51]

Planting a Colony in America | 105

Sharp now moved to consolidate the rest of his financial obligations and recommitted himself to a career as a teacher of folk dance, not as a performer of folk song. Two months after having summoned Mattie Kay to New York, he sent her back to England. With his expenses now substantially reduced and his prospects brighter, he crowed, "I could coin money out here," set up a "swagger studio," and charge high fees to society people. He appreciated that to do so would go "against the grain," but high costs would make it justifiable nonetheless. All told, he admitted to "a sneaking satisfaction" at his sudden ability, for the first time in his life, to make a good deal of money.[52]

Sharp's energies now focused on establishing himself as a folk dance teacher. The logical places to do so were New York and Boston, the two centers where Mary Neal and Claud Wright had helped to establish ECD. But, again, for Sharp to succeed politically and financially, he had to supplant them both as the recognized leader of the ECD movement. Neal had helped establish an Anglo-American network of settlement house dance teachers in New York, Boston, and London, but her focus on morris dance, with its performance sides of six to eight dancers, meant that she had not left an appreciable following of dancers in her wake. Moreover, Florrie Warren had settled into her new marriage and retired from teaching dance.

Elizabeth Burchenal now smoothed Sharp's reception in New York City. Burchenal had concluded that Sharp and not Neal best represented the English tradition. "Many [other] people knew no better than to accept her [Neal] . . . as the Morris Dances authority," she had written Sharp late that year, but she reassured him, "You may be sure that all of my circle know you as the authority."[53] She had, of course, established a relationship with Sharp over the course of the past decade during her regular trips to England and attendance at the Stratford summer schools. She now knew him as the director of the English Folk Dance Society and represented him as the undisputed leader of the country dance community there. And her friends counted: she was head of the Girls' Branch of the Public Schools Athletic League and close friends of Luther Halsey Gulick, Professor Farnsworth of Columbia University's Teachers College, and Dr. Richard Cabot, of the Boston Brahmin Cabot family and renowned pioneer at Boston Psychiatric Hospital in psychiatric social work. So with all the advantages of Burchenal's social and financial connections in both New York and Boston, Neal had been supplanted well before Sharp disembarked in New York Harbor.

Harvard professor George P. Baker's personal commitment to Wright was not so easily surmounted. Sharp never really won over Baker, but they remained on good terms; by way of contrast, he forged a strong relationship with Helen Storrow, and within a week of his arrival in New York, he was off to Boston to take up Storrow's invitation to visit her in Lincoln. He hoped a lecture he had been promised there would cover his expenses and admitted that he hoped it would "perhaps till the soil for another & and more profitable visit later." The larger gain, though, was the close and long-term relationship Sharp forged with Storrow. The tie that bound the two gave Sharp a Boston counterweight to Baker, but more to the point, it forever shaped both Sharp's personal fortunes as well as those of English Country Dance in the United States.[54]

From Sharp's account, he and Helen Storrow hit it off right away. For instance, whereas his letters during his first week in America complained endlessly about his lack of money and his loneliness, after visiting Lincoln, his letter home for the first time struck a positive, albeit oxymoronic, note: "I had an awfully nice time in Lincoln." He and Storrow did "not see eye to eye about dances because she is primarily interested in physical education rather than dancing for its own sake," but Sharp could recognize her type. Storrow's wealth and demeanor made him feel quite at home. She was decidedly not a suffragist, and he found her "quite charming" with a "great kindliness." Years later, a devoted family friend described her as a "super patriot" devoted to the Girl Scouts and physical culture. In that regard, however, she shared a family resemblance to the generation of physical-cultural devotees who were familiar to Sharp and had shaped the growth of gymnastics, the playground movement, and physical education in both countries. In England, these were the people associated with groups such as the Boy Scouts and with Sharp's own dance group from the Chelsea physical-training college. Much the way teaching a folk song and dance would further English (and Anglo-American) culture, the physical-culture movement sought to preserve "the race" through the careful training of young men's and women's bodies.[55]

By mid-March 1915, Storrow had committed herself to traveling to New York to take one of Sharp's classes, and Sharp had come to consider her the chief supporter of his teaching, "thoroughly capable in every direction, straight as a die and transparently sincere."[56] He did have a problem with her dancing, however. Sharp believed Storrow first had to learn to appreciate that the value of folk dance extended beyond physical culture to the realm of moral uplift and "racial" naturalness. Then Sharp saw his primary task as ridding her of aesthetic dance training associated with ballet and the new "modern" barefoot dancers.

Sharp might appreciate aesthetic dance in its own place, but he certainly did not see its place in folk dance. Truth be told, though, he was less than enthusiastic about aesthetic dancing elsewhere either. Early in his New York

Planting a Colony in America | 107

visit, he attended a private performance of Isadora Duncan at her studio. He found the heavily draped studio oppressive and complained that the troupe "wore the scantiest of clothing." Observing "scarcely a rhythmical moment" in any of the dances, he found that "the whole thing left a nasty taste in [his] mouth." Nonetheless, the next day they had tea together.[57] But Isadora Duncan and the "barefoot" or "aesthetic" dancers had broad influences on many of Sharp's potential students at the time. Sharp complained that "nearly all" the young women in his classes had "been taught 'aesthetic dancing,' which is a bowdlerized form of the so-called classic ballet. This form of dancing, God Save the Queen, has overrun this country. Even Mrs. Storrow," he noted, "has qualified in it and had taught it before I counseled her of its artificiality and general badness. My chief technical difficulty is to get them to do the running step."[58] Before the month was out, Sharp had succeeded, at least to his satisfaction, in raising the quality of some students to an acceptable and appropriate standard. Storrow and four of her teachers, presumably all young women training to teach folk dance, received certificates from EFDS attesting to their basic proficiency in ECD.[59]

In Storrow, Sharp had trained a local teacher, established a friendship, and won himself a powerful patron. Helen Storrow was an ally to whom he could relate socially both as a person and as a dancer—and the two went hand in glove, shaping the politics of his dance world. Noting to Maud Karpeles how "thoroughly capable" Storrow was in comparison to Mrs. Dawson Callery of Pittsburgh (who was "a little deaf, poor thing, younger [and pettier] but not so capable"), Sharp returned to some of the underlying obsessions in his narrative—money, class, gender, and an apparent reference to suffrage: "Both are well off. They are the only women I have met here whom I should call *ladies*, except perhaps Mrs. Huntington, and *you* know what I mean by that."[60]

Sharp found displacing Claud Wright both easier and more difficult than winning over Storrow. It was easier in that when Wright's commission in the Royal Air Force came through, he had enlisted and canceled his own planned tour just as Sharp arrived in America. Wright would be unavailable for a return visit any time soon. But displacing Wright was more difficult in that Wright and Baker had hit it off rather well and formed an alliance of sorts, a relationship that could be an alternative to Sharp-Storrow leadership of any new folk dance movement, either nationally or in the Boston area. This remains pure speculation, however. Yet two things became increasingly apparent to some of the concerned parties: Sharp's opposition to Wright's athletic style had grown more personal, and at issue was the leadership of the English Folk Dance Society in the United States. In a meeting at the Harvard Club in late February, Baker told Sharp that he and those who Wright had taught were "very keen" to have Wright as their teacher if and when a permanent appointment was made to run an American branch of EFDS. In response, Sharp pressed Baker for an alternative who he thought would be better "from the dance point of view," someone who "carried beautifully." Sharp lamented, "But [for Baker] it was W[right] or nothing."[61]

In retrospect, Maud Karpeles seemed to know that Sharp's (and her own) hostility toward Wright was bad form, for in editing her letters from Sharp (for the archives), she on two occasions crossed out critical references to Wright, and in the first instance to Baker as well. In the first instance, Karpeles tried to delete Sharp's outraged response to Wright's hiring Baker as his agent (for 10 percent of Wright's earnings), an arrangement that Sharp believed would undercut the financial health of any new American branch.[62] In the second instance, Karpeles censored Sharp's criticism of Wright's supposed reluctance to go to war, crossing out "What you [Karpeles] wrote about Wright is very amusing but very deplorable too. I think he told Prof. Baker that he was training to go to the front but that his duty to his parents made it quite impractical. He showed himself apparently in his true colours when he wrote to Mrs. H. about his American honours. He's a poop stick."[63] In any case, Wright was drafted, and the question of his appointment as permanent teacher in the States was moot. Not that Baker was pleased. Storrow found him "cutting up rather rough about Wright," and Sharp, ever mindful of the need to sustain a working relationship with Baker, had to craft a "very careful reply" to a "rather nasty letter" from him.

Baker continued to play a role in the new society during the next few years, but in the interim, Sharp surrounded himself with his own team of players. Though there was the occasional male leader, his "team" consisted mostly of female devotees: young "ladies"—not suffragists!—who were wealthy patrons like Helen Storrow and relatively well-off young women from England who he had trained personally.[64] As significantly, in rejecting both Wright's athleticism and Storrow's aestheticism as inappropriate English Country Dance styles, by subtraction Sharp emphasized the forward movement and restrained gestures of the running step that he authorized as an enduring legacy of his reign.

An American Branch

As an authority, Sharp now needed to construct the dominion over which to rule: an American branch of EFDS. He began by assessing the state of folk dance in the New World on two fronts, one national, one local.

New York City was the logical place to base his movement. The city, home to the Russell Sage and Carnegie foundations, record and book publishers, and many wealthy society leaders, offered the prospect of patronage and funding for Sharp's efforts. It also had Burchenal's legions of dance teachers in the schools and a host of folk dance enthusiasts in the teachers colleges.

Boston, where a small but influential group of enthusiasts congregated, was the other logical place to establish an ECD colony. Storrow, who was an obvious well of patronage, lived in the suburb of Lincoln but had her dancing school in the city. Baker and Dr. Charles Peabody were secretary and president of the American Folk Lore Society, which was based in the Boston area and had hosted Wright's earlier visits and classes. According to the *Boston Herald*, many of the other early ECD enthusiasts were "Harvard faculty and their families."[65] Still others seemed to congregate around Wellesley College. For although Wellesley placed Sharp in the middle of the suffrage movement, the institution, like many women's colleges and land-grant universities, had several spring folk pageants: a Tree Day pageant and a May Day celebration. A woman, Mrs. Shaw, who represented the college's leadership, was also herself taken with ECD. The college was, then, a prospective jumping-off point from which Sharp could try to replicate his Stratford Summer School program in the United States.[66] But that lay in the future.

The meeting to establish an American branch of the English Folk Dance Society occurred in the midst of a whirlwind three-week national tour on which Sharp embarked in early March to demonstrate, teach, and spread the ECD gospel.[67] The trip, which he found enormously encouraging, took him to Boston and Pittsfield, Massachusetts, and to Pittsburgh, Pennsylvania. Surveying the whole of his tour, he reflected that he "could make a heap of money" in the United States, and he acknowledged in letters home to increasingly thinking about return trips.[68] But in the middle of his tour, flush with the success of his receptions, word reached Sharp that supporters had agreed to meet in New York to consider the creation of an American branch of the English Folk Dance Society.

On March 19, 1915, a select group of ECD enthusiasts gathered with Sharp at lunch at a Miss Ware's home to discuss the possibilities. The major account of the meeting is from Sharp's letter soon after to Maud Karpeles. In addition to the host, who seems to have been the sister-in-law of a local dancer, it appears to have been a relatively intimate group. Storrow, Baker, and "several others," presumably representing New York, were there. Prominently in attendance as well was Mrs. Morris, representing Wellesley College.[69]

Sharp was particularly concerned to have a representative of his own choosing direct the American branch, a person who, in his words, could function "as a central authority with respect to English folk-dancing." Sharp had learned his lessons from previous battles with Mary Neal over control of an English style that was taught and sustained according to his criteria. Moreover, as regards "authentic" style in the dance, he did not need to look far to see present dangers: he worried about the impact of "artificial" aesthetic dancing, the lack of grace in the muscular physical-training tradition, and the "commercially-minded teachers" who cared more about keeping clients happy than teaching "good" (as he authorized it) style.

Sharp's concerns about teaching "authentic" style focused his desire for control of the American branch. He also believed in the importance of a national American movement and was concerned to oversee local teachers in far-flung reaches of the country. The situation in Chicago was a case in point. He had heard rumors that in Chicago Mary Ward Hinman was altering dances to make them easier for schoolchildren to learn.[70] Hinman, like Burchenal, had pioneered the introduction of folk dance into New York and Chicago settlement houses and public schools, from which it was fast expanding into physical-education programs of East Coast and Midwest teachers colleges. These programs made efforts to teach the folk dances of many lands, many of which Burchenal had helped collect and disseminate in her published collections. In this context, Sharp saw the American branch as having what he believed to be its deservingly leading role in sustaining the hegemony of Anglo-American national culture.

Sharp's campaign envisioned an American branch that would provide a model and legacy for the future: an "authentic" and ennobling folk dance tradition of supple but controlled Edwardian bodies in "gay" but decorous motion. Sharp's authorized ECD was an alternative to the dance halls, but it also avoided the excesses of aesthetic dance, gymnastics, and other folk traditions. The American branch was to be specific to English folk dance but also a model for other, albeit what he considered inferior, folk dance traditions. People dancing in other traditions should set up parallel organizations (for example, for Russian dance and the like). Such a scheme, he believed, would develop good folk dancing in the country. He said this, though, "knowing" it would "mean the complete domination of English folk-dancing over all other forms, for ours," and here Sharp was at his most nationalistic and chauvinistic, "is probably the best and certainly, technically, the most accurate and definite."[71]

For Sharp, then, the appointment of one of EFDS's senior certified teachers for a year to run the American branch—someone of his choosing—was of paramount importance for English Country Dance in the United States, for Anglo-American culture, and for folk dance more generally. Indeed, an appointee of his choosing was a condition for any affiliation with EFDS. Sharp recognized that this position put him up against Baker's interest in appointing Wright. Admitting that this was a "difficult matter to engineer," Sharp noted that he had to "think straight & and walk warily" if he was "to pull it off."[72]

Also troubling Sharp was the question of whether to base the branch in New York or Boston. Sharp's initial preference was for an autonomous organization based in Boston, with Storrow as secretary and treasurer and Baker as president. Whereas Sharp had early established a personal connection with Storrow, he never exuded any personal warmth toward Burchenal, and in coming months he was, in fact, to grow increasingly wary of her ambition and strong will. Storrow, perhaps trying to help Sharp negotiate the groups from each city, proposed instead that the branch become a subcommittee of the New York–based Playground Association. But Sharp did want to subordinate his organization to anyone, much less an organization such as the Playground Association led by Elizabeth Burchenal. In addition to his growing reservations about her personally, he thought that her Athletic League Society, which was tied to the Playground Association, "produces no results in the way of folk-dancing because no one knows any!" Thus, the proposal to form an autonomous New York–based branch led by Baker and Storrow may have been a compromise to assuage both Burchenal and Baker. In any case, at a subsequent meeting that evening at the Colony Club, it was determined that New York would be the base of the American branch and that Baker and Storrow would be its president and secretary, respectively.[73]

The surprise of these organization meetings for Sharp, however, was a subsequent decision to mount a "Summer School this coming June!!!!!!" which the Americans wanted Sharp to teach. This opportunity was, in turn, doubled with an offer from the Wellesley representative. The college had an annual summer pageant—actually it was their Tree Day/May Day festival—and it was the president's recommendation that it have a demonstration of English folk dances, songs, and games that year.[74]

Sharp was delighted with all the possibilities, but he remained concerned about how they would be financed. His immediate response was to contain costs, albeit not at the expense of his own income; rather, he volunteered the labor of his female teachers, holding out the prospect of future income from a stable program. Thus, he dismissed Storrow's suggestion that the college pay a teacher from England to run the summer program. All that was needed, according to Sharp, was expenses; he would find someone "happy for the holiday." He had in mind a woman such as Helen Kennedy and, as a backup, a young teacher recently installed as the head of his Scarborough branch, Lily Roberts. Immediately writing Maud Karpeles, he instructed her to offer the director's post to each of them, in that order, and to invite each to assist at the summer school as well. He also insisted that Karpeles would have to join him at the summer school—and then stay on as his assistant—though he warned her that she would have "to risk some money," as the organizers could only guarantee his expenses. In fact, Karpeles, who came from a wealthy family and was herself a woman of independent means, was committed to Sharp's mission and could handle the risk; Sharp envisioned the teacher—either Helen Kennedy or Lily Roberts—staying on after the summer school and becoming the "Branch Teacher at 500 or rather 300 pounds a year." The former, approximately Sharp's own annual income, was about twenty-five hundred dollars, roughly the salary of a university professor or a school principal. Sharp's only condition was a guarantee of one hundred entrants, a condition that no one seemed to question.[75]

A meeting at the Colony Club on March 23 put the finishing touches on what, for Sharp, had to be a successful American trip that augured well for the future. The New York meeting established the American Branch of the English Folk Dance Society, with "Centres in New York, Boston, Chicago and Pittsburgh." (In fact, the only bona fide "centres" that year were in New York and, later, Boston; the other locales hosted small groups that struggled to attract enough dancers to sustain longways sets.) During the next month, Sharp made additional trips to Pittsburgh and Chicago to consolidate his agenda and help build these groups.[76]

On April 21, 1915, Sharp set sail for home on the SS *Adriatic*. He could take pride and comfort in knowing that he had left behind a group of trained dancers and teachers in New York, Boston, Chicago, Pittsburgh, and Pittsfield to carry on his work. Most notably, in New York, the city with arguably the largest potential dance community, he had two disciples in whom he had confidence. Charles Rabold, a musician and piano teacher, had become, according to Karpeles, "one of Sharp's most ardent followers." In the past two months, Rabold had grown into Sharp's favorite male dancer, a man he regularly came to rely on to help him demonstrate couples dances. In years to come, Sharp increasingly entrusted him to teach ECD.[77]

Meanwhile, Susan Gilman had transformed her Studio of Dance into a center for ECD in New York. So while at sea, Sharp could pace the deck worrying about U-boats, but he could do so with a great anticipation and full pockets. The pageant and the summer school were to bring him back to America in two months. Meanwhile, the profits from his lecturing and teaching—each expense and income carefully detailed in his diary—had in four months pocketed a net $1,748.53, an amount his biographers estimated as over four hundred pounds.[78]

Conclusion

By 1915, Sharp and his coterie had established hegemony over the country dance movement, broadly understood as an Anglo-American tradition that in its celebration of white, Anglo-Saxon culture spoke as much to an essential Americanness as to Englishness. The war also became the occasion for the "Sharpeles" to establish a dance style that gave women teachers a public voice, but in traditional coupled patterns. In the settlements, public schools, and playgrounds, reforming dance teachers taught "democratic" lessons to young men and, in particular, to women in how to have respectable bodies. In teachers colleges and ECD groups themselves, far from the madding immigrant crowd, highly educated, white, Protestant elites embodied these lessons for themselves.

The women and men supporting the revival in both the United States and England also had a class distance from their immigrant and "peasant" subjects. The revival dance community constituted a well-heeled coterie of people, most of whom had independent means or relatively high-status professional careers. And while folk song and dance may have had to be imposed on the immigrant working class in the school curriculum, the English aristocracy and their bourgeois idolizers—and their American cousins—embraced its heritage: New York society, for instance, could delight in reading in the *New York Times* of holiday pageant dinners in the Swiss Alps resorts attended by rich Americans such as the Duchess of Marlboro (the Brooklyn-born mother of Lord Ivor Spencer Churchill), who had married into English society. The highlight of the banquet, served by men and women in Tudor dress, was schoolchildren singing folk songs and performing morris dances.[79] And while Lady Spencer danced in swanky Swiss resorts, her scions folk danced in hoity-toity New York hotels. "Society Women in Folk Costumes" headlined the *New York Times*, noting in particular the presence of Mrs. T. J. Rhinelander, Mrs. Lorillard Spencer Jr., and Mrs. Frank Phipps dancing the "Fjallnaspolka" at the Waldorf-Astoria Hotel gala for the benefit of the Girls' Branch of the New York Public Schools Athletic League.[80]

The leadership of the ECD movement likewise shared privileged class positions. As noted, Neal and Sharp had similar class backgrounds. The class difference between Sharp and Wright was also small, but it was greater than that between Sharp and Neal, and it undoubtedly complicated the men's relationship. Wright, for instance, felt that his more modest social background and economic position did not quite "fit in" with that of the other members of the demonstration team. Neal came to believe that gender politics (notably, suffrage) was the basis for her conflict with Sharp, and there is much evidence that Sharp had difficulty dealing with strong women.

Ultimately, Sharp's conflict with both antagonists seems to have been rooted in serious differences that each invested with considerable moral and social import over the "authentic" style in the dance and who was to authorize it. Sharp's victory over Neal in this struggle had implications for the politics of the body and its "respectable," "authentic" expression: the spirit of the dance would be codified by "experts" rather than given more free-form expression by the Espérance working girls. So would there be a price for Sharp's victory over Wright's "aestheticism": the dance would be more restrained and contained, more horizontal than vertical.

Wright had his own critique of Sharp, albeit one that was less well articulated. A glimpse of his concern about Sharp suggests that it mirrored Neal's belief in a certain "spontaneity" in the dance. In a letter to Baker in late 1914, a few months before Wright enlisted and Sharp arrived to take the American movement in hand, Wright worried that Sharp was "not well" and was "aging." Both observations were true, although Sharp's indefatigable energy continued to carry him through brilliantly. More to the point, Wright complained that Sharp's personal interests and formality were misrepresenting the accuracy of the figures and style of the dance: "He is altering the dances in places, without authority it seems to me—so they lack now the old spontaneity that I loved."[81]

Sharp's victory over Neal and Wright, then, came with a price: Neal's alternative socialist-feminist embodiment of the dance in the exuberant, idiosyncratic expressions of her working girls and Wright's athletic physicality and love of "spontaneity" gave way to Sharp's more highly stylized bodily expression. Wright thought Sharp had lost the "joy" in the dance; for Neal, the "pedant" in Sharp had a similarly stultifying effect on the dance. Sharp's contained dancing bodies were, however, precisely the liberal body he and other "professional" Progressive Era experts valorized. Much like efforts at sanitation, lighting, and municipal reform, Sharp's dancing body—"gay simplicity" with authorized "style" rather than "vitality"—meant to bring order to the "disorder" that he and others of his social class saw all around them, whether it was radical anarcho-syndicalists and suffragettes in the streets or unchaperoned young toughs in the dance halls. As "experts," men such as Cecil Sharp expressed conventional patriarchal and benighted class attitudes of the day. They did so not to demean but to uplift, to transform urban newcomers from worrisome immigrants into respectable Anglo-American citizens with an infusion of what they saw as the vital spirit of the race that they believed to be innate in "simple" rural peoples. ECD was, then, the flowering of the liberal conscience of the day and the bodily expression of its social mission.

Neal and Wright were in the past, and Sharp put the exuberance and anti-elitism they embodied in the past with them—at least for a while. The war that soon enveloped both the United States and England was a transitional era for the English Country Dance community and the politics of the folk it embodied. The Progressive Era looked outward with a social mission to the immigrant poor. During the war and the decade that followed, these imperatives receded, and the conservative caste of liberal culture—the elitism of the cult of expertise and the celebration of the ordered and disciplined body in graceful balance—took a turn inward. An Anglo-American Anglophilia of a national folk identity increasingly characterized its recreational participants. This nationalism became vulnerable to the growing political currents of fascism on both sides of the Atlantic, currents in which Henry Ford's nationalist version of folk dance and the Nazis' invocation of the *volk* were an extreme caricature. For some folk dance enthusiasts, however, this worrisome national turn led toward an emerging International Folk Dance movement, a dance form that increasingly came to stand as an alternative political and cultural style of dance against which ECD stood.[82]

5

The American Branch

> No country in the world can be gay in the simple, fresh way that England can—it is our contribution to civilization.
> —Cecil Sharp, 1916, on his "Interlude" for the New York celebration of Shakespeare's tercentenary winning first prize

> [The English] . . . songs and dances are not foreign importations, but a vital part of the *traditional culture of America*.
> —Maud Karpeles, February 2, 1928[1]

In the years between 1915 and 1918, Cecil Sharp put his stamp on the American Branch of the EFDSS as an authoritative outpost of Englishness as he imagined it. During three extended collecting trips in the southern Appalachian Mountains, he also advanced the belief that native American song and dance was an extension of Englishness—a pure representation of an English tradition that had been lost in the mother country but preserved in the backwoods by generations of English settlers. Sharp did not pioneer this view, however. Only a few years earlier in 1911, a Transylvania University professor had published an article in the *Sewanee Review* documenting what he called "British ballads" in the Cumberland Mountains and noting a veritable cottage industry of newly organized Southern State Folklore Societies, and English professors had followed his lead. By the time Sharp began his collecting trips, over a dozen articles on southern mountain ballads had already been published in the *Journal of American Folklore*. Rather then pioneering or "discovering" the Appalachian ballads, then, Sharp's contribution consisted of the sheer volume of songs and variations he collected and "in his ability to crystallize and extend trends," most especially in building a folk song and dance movement around them.[2] Moreover, working to build an English Country Dance community in the States and staff it with trusted English women he had trained, he increasingly came to understand himself as establishing an Anglo-American transatlantic dance tradition that could revitalize the "race" on both sides of the ocean.

In the next two decades, as Sharp's American followers took on his mission, they increasingly worried about ensuring a leading role for English Country Dance in the folk revival. They realized the American Branch of EFDS was but one of many ethnic urban folk centers among a wide range of immigrant cultures with folk dance traditions. One person in particular—and again it was a strong woman—embodied the alternative vision of an International Folk Dance of the peoples of many lands, and she found herself as the center of conflict with the American Branch, and most especially with Sharp: Elizabeth Burchenal.

By 1915, Burchenal had already been transcribing and publishing dances "from people of many lands and immigrants for the past 12 summers," had introduced dances from all these lands into the public schools, and had pioneered International Folk Dance programs that expressed the shared vitality of folk dance traditions. She wrote to Sharp then of her deep respect for him as "the only person" besides herself "whose life is devoted to folk dancing . . . and whose feeling is the same" as hers about it. But while Sharp applauded English folk dancing as "probably the best and certainly, technically, the most accurate and definite" folk dance tradition and expected it would dominate over other forms, Elizabeth Burchenal averred to him that "all things *good* in dancing are in the folk traditions of all countries."[3] So almost a year after the formation of the American Branch, in February 1916, she announced the organization in New York of the American Folkdance Society, with herself as president. Then, two years later, just as Sharp was completing his pathbreaking field work in Appalachia, she published a volume of twenty-eight American contra dances. In the volume's introduction, acknowledging that her society's actual work would not begin until after the war, she staked out her leadership role in the collection and preservation of American "folk-dances and music at their original sources" with the development of an Archive of American Folk-Dance.[4] Burchenal had thrown down the folk gauntlet.

Differences between Sharp and Burchenal emerged in a series of conflicts in the next years, over everything from copyrights to the leadership of the New York dance community. But the American Branch's growth and, more so, its claim to a leading position in folk dance in the United States became a struggle with greater stakes. For Sharp and his devoted followers, who believed in the superior cultural value of the English folk dance tradition, at stake was the larger Anglo-American civilizing project of folk dance.

The Missing Link: Sharp in Appalachia

Sharp returned to the United States in early June 1915 for six weeks, primarily to run the first American ECD summer school. While preparing for the summer school, however, he became bedridden with excruciating back pains. Diagnosed with lumbago and confined to bed in the Storrow home, the rest proved recuperative and came with an unexpected bonus: a visit from Olive Dame Campbell and her husband, John C. Campbell, the director of the Highland Division of the Russell Sage Foundation.[5] The Sage Foundation's William Chauncey Langdon had heard one of Cecil Sharp's former students, Rosalind Fuller, and her brother-sister quartet of folk singers, the Fullers, then touring the United States, sing some English ballads. Their songs reminded him of the southern mountain ballads that Olive Campbell had collected while accompanying her husband on his research trips. The Campbells, Langdon told Fuller, "were inclined to think [these ballads] . . . were purer and older, many of them, then their [the Fullers'] own Dorset and Somerset versions." Intrigued, Fuller sent Sharp some of the ballads Olive had collected. In turn, Sharp invited Olive Dame Campbell to visit him.[6]

Olive Dame Campbell and Sharp shared much in common and developed a good working relationship. Campbell's commitment to helping her husband develop an Appalachian school system did not afford her time to accompany Sharp back to the mountains on a collecting trip, but as she wrote Sharp, she was committed to seeing her work furthered by him as "the person most competent to do it." Appreciating the pioneering work she had done—and surely aware of her connections in both Appalachia and the foundation world—Sharp was "anxious not to do anything discourteous to her nor to queer her pitch in any way." Fortunately, her decision to cede the field to Sharp eliminated the competition (especially with women) that had so often plagued Sharp's personal relationships, and they had the kind of collaboration on which Sharp thrived: she simply handed over the mountain project to him. To his credit, he carefully always credited her prior work in the mountains, and the book of folk songs ultimately published of southern mountain songs was coauthored by Sharp and Campbell.[7]

The Campbells together provided the plan for Sharp's initial fieldwork in the Southern Appalachians the next summer, and that trip laid the groundwork for a series of collecting explorations. In total, Sharp spent twelve months of the next three years visiting seventy to eighty small towns and settlements in the mountains of North Carolina, Virginia, Kentucky, and

Tennessee (and a few days in West Virginia). Forty-six weeks were dedicated primarily to collecting folk songs. John Glenn of Russell Sage gave Sharp $50 to defray an initial trip in the spring of 1916 to Asheville, North Carolina, to see the Campbells and transcribe the songs Olive had collected. But Sharp's primary benefactor for these trips was Helen Storrow, and her gift of $650 funded the first of his collecting trips. Returning from that trip with a rich trove of nearly four hundred ballad tunes, Sharp hoped it would encourage foundation support for the rest of his research. Giving a lecture to "a large number of 'Foundation' people" at the Washington Square Park home of a Russell Sage vice president, Robert W. de Forest, Sharp felt that Russell Sage support was "likely." But his hope of foundation support was, to his great disappointment, soon dashed. Nothing was forthcoming either from Russell Sage or the Carnegie Foundation. Fortunately, Sharp still had $350 left from the money Storrow had given him for the first trip. That money and other earnings from his lectures helped fund further trips.[8]

Sharp did not travel alone, however. Although historians have credited his exploratory trips, they have underappreciated the central role of his companion, Maud Karpeles. Often described as his amanuensis, she nominally served as his secretary, agent, and confidant. Karpeles was, however, equally his collaborator, even if she was never formally credited as such. She was never far from his side, and they presented an odd couple: tall, erect, and formal, Sharp towered over his diminutive and much younger companion. In 1916, Maude was thirty-one years old, and Sharp, twenty-six years her senior, was fifty-seven. During the next three years, they in practice worked together as a team, trekking literally through hill and dale in the heat of summer collecting folk songs. When not collecting in the mountains, they moved from city to city to teach dance, often staying no more than a week in any one place. Asthma constantly left Sharp short of breath, but he was often ill with other ailments as well. In addition to the lumbago attack that had kept him bedridden in Lincoln, he was repeatedly confined on his collecting trips with what Karpeles recalled as "fever" and what, on one occasion, a local doctor diagnosed as "probably typhoid." Often left extremely weak, exhausted, and depressed, he periodically required bed rest for two or three days at a time. Sickness even required them to cut short one of the 1917 collecting trips. So in addition to all her other duties, Karpeles often served as Sharp's nurse.[9] And although their intimate travels have led some scholars to speculate about their relationship, there is no evidence of sexual impropriety. Karpeles never married, and Sharp, to whom she was devoted, may have been the love of her life. For his part, Sharp was deeply attached to Karpeles, but in a fatherly way. Upon his death, she was the executor of his estate, his biographer, and a steadfast protector of his legacy.[10]

Sharp and Karpeles's collecting trips in Appalachia during the summers of 1916, 1917, and 1918 were extraordinary personal achievements that had far-reaching consequences on both sides of the Atlantic for the development of an Anglo-American folk movement in both song and dance. According to Karpeles, Sharp "collected from 281 different singers a total of 1,612 songs, including variants, representing about 500 different songs and ballads."[11] Sharp's best respondent was a woman whose stories continue to entertain English folk dancers some ninety years later. In August 1916, Sharp collected seventy songs from Mrs. Jane Gentry on eight separate visits to her home in Hot Springs; her great-granddaughter, Daron Douglas, a renowned ECD fiddle player from New Orleans, continues in the new millennium to sing these songs as she recounts Gentry's stories of "when the Englishman came."[12]

As remarkable as the number of songs Sharp and Karpeles recovered, though, were the conditions under which they did so. A few excerpts from their diaries begin to give a sense of the difficult circumstances under which they worked.

Sharp, August 1917:

On Sunday we trudged 13 miles, Monday 7, Tuesday 9, Wednesday 16 and Thursday (today) 8, all over the worst and most uneven roads.... At the present moment I can scarcely look at food, as I suspect anything contains hog's grease or something diabolical.

Karpeles, May 5, 1918, in Natural Bridge, Pennsylvania:

Walked 4 miles. Called on several people who knew about the songs & had sung them, but dropped them for one reason or another. The Hazletts who lived at the terminus of the 4 miles might have been of some use, but would not sing as they were Baptists.

Karpeles, September 16, 1918:

Started off directly after breakfast from Bolden's Creek [near Burnsville, North Carolina] taking lunch with us. Made a great many calls—10 in all, I believe. Got some good songs from Mrs. Ida Banks and a few from Mrs. Calloway, but feel that we have pretty well done the Creek & that there is not much more to be got here. People all delightfully friendly. Zeb Fox, who has a great reputation as a singer was out unfortunately, but his wife says we can see him at the P. Office tomorrow. Got home about 6. Hot sun, but it has been a lovely day.

Karpeles, September 17, 1918:

> C♯ saw Jeb Fox but he maintains he does not know any songs & so it is useless to proceed any further with him. So started off on Green Mountain Rd. Called on several members of the Fox family, but can get nothing out of them. Most of them are rather above singing love songs having learned note singing. Finally called on old Noah Styles. His wife was out, which was fortunate as she sings only "good" songs, so we had a chance to pump the girl who lives with them—Laurel Jones, who gave us some beautiful tunes. She is a nice girl with a tragic history, which she told me. We got let in for dinner there—afterwards got stuck up on account of thunder, so consequently did not get home till abt. 5:30.[13]

Beyond the great labor involved in these trips, both Karpeles's and Sharp's diaries exude the admiration tinged with paternalism that characterized their interactions with and responses to the southern mountain people. Yet, while the songs they collected constituted a significant documentation of folk traditions in the southern Appalachian Mountains, as important for the history and spirit of the folk revival that Sharp and his followers imparted—both in dance and song—was the Englishness and "peasant" meaning they attributed to these songs and the people who sang them. In Ashville, in July 1916, early in Sharp's first trip to the mountains, he wrote in his diary, "I notice the type of people I saw was very decidedly English and different from anything I have seen in other parts." But more than seeing them as merely English, by the next month he had come to see them as a pristine version of the English peasantry—a new and improved form that was even "freer than the English peasant [sic]." He attributed the change to their owning their own land for the last three generations, "so there is none of the servility which, unhappily is one of the characteristics of the English peasant." Rather, "the people are just English of the eighteenth or nineteenth century. They speak English, look English, and their manners are old-fashioned English. With that praise, I should say they are just exactly what the English peasant was one hundred or more years ago."[14]

Sharp, of course, much as he romanticized English village life and wrongly characterized it as peasant, little appreciated the heterodox influences on mountain song. He collected only what he wanted to hear on both sides of the Atlantic, ignoring Negro spirituals and songs, Lancashire morris, and urban vernacular music-hall song and dance. His "discoveries" in the southern mountains emphasized a continuous Anglo-American tradition understood as a "peasant" expression that formed a "simple," "pure" basis for

Cecil Sharp and Polly Patrick, Harts Creek, Manchester, Clay County, Kentucky, August 1917. (Reproduced courtesy of EFDSS)

the revitalization of the "race." Sharp believed, in Karpeles's words, that the songs he collected constituted an "expression of the innate musical culture of a homogenous community," with "racial attributes." Sharp, she notes, felt these songs were "immune from that continuous, grinding, mental pressure due to the attempt to make a living, from which nearly all of us in this modern world suffer."[15]

Historians have observed that urban degeneration and the romanticizing of "peasants" and mountain folk went hand in hand with views of racial degeneration, and Sharp evidenced the third part of the trilogy as well. The Anglicizing and Americanizing of immigrant children in schools, playgrounds, and settlements through these songs and dances (by Sharp and by some of his American counterparts) often expressed more than a kernel of racialist attitudes. Sharp shared these views and on at least a couple of occasions in his diary exposed his prejudice directly. Visiting Winston-Salem, North Carolina, for instance, he described it as "a noisy place and the air impregnated with tobacco, molasses and nigger." When challenged by his hosts for "dubbing the negro as of a lower order," he rejected their views and ascribed them to "a mere lack of education, etc."[16] To be sure, Sharp's racial views were usual for the time (or too often, since), but as the historian Benjamin Filene has poignantly observed, they illustrate again "the racial undertone beneath the earliest self-conscious efforts to define American [and British] folk song [and dance] heritage."[17]

It was a "discovery" in dance among the "white" mountain folk that most transported Sharp and confirmed his interpretation of the Anglo-American character of English Country Dance. One evening "after dark," in early September 1917, while visiting the Pine Mountain Settlement School in Harlan County, Kentucky, "the air seemed literally to pulsate." "One dim lantern" and the moon lit up a wondrous sight of whirling dancers moving to "only the stamping and clapping of the onlookers" and the "falsetto tones of the Caller."[18] Sharp had seen the "Kentucky Running Set," a "most wonderful," "strenuous," "circular country dance" for four couples unlike anything he had ever seen in England or knew of from his research.[19]

Sharp quickly came to believe that in Kentucky he had "found" a critical missing piece in the history of English Country Dance. English immigrants to America who had settled in the backwoods, he averred, had preserved intact in the "Running Set" a "lineal descendant of the May-day Round, a pagan quasi-religious ceremonial of which the May-pole is, perhaps the typical example." The speed of the turns, the "unconventional" comportment of the dancers—presumably their almost boisterous high energy and informality—differentiated the "Running Set" for him from the Playford dances and "all other known form of English country-dances." Years later, Karpeles described the dance as "an unsophisticated form of the now popular American Square Dance."[20] But at the time, Sharp proclaimed the dance to be no less than "the sole survival" of a dance that had "preceded the Playford dance" and once "flourished in other parts of England and Scotland." Thus, the dance was for Sharp a key "stage in the development of the Country-dance" that bridged the gap between the older "peasant" circular dances that dominated Playford's first volume in 1651 and the more stylized longways gentry dances of the eighteenth century.[21]

Sharp, according to Karpeles, regarded his Appalachian finds as "the crowning point" of his collecting career. The dissemination of these songs and dances in the United States was a logical follow-up to his revival work in England. Reflecting on the significance of their work in a 1923 article in the *EFDS News*, Karpeles emphasized the "vigour, spontaneity and simplicity of expression" that the American dances expressed as part of the "traditional culture ... common to both countries."[22] In its dance and song, the mountain community, Sharp wrote, expressed the "supreme cultural value of an inherited tradition, ... the many graces of life that are theirs."[23] He contrasted these songs, for instance, to the cowboy songs collected at the time by the American folklorist Alan Lomax, songs that he dismissed as "divorce[d] from tradition" and "nothing but the dregs of literature & the garbage of musical phrase."[24]

In retrospect, it is easy to debunk Sharp's foundational story of the "Running Set" and inherited peasant traditions as naive inventions, to dismiss his occasional cattiness and financial obsessions as the petty jealousies of a grasping bourgeois-intellectual, and to disparage his paternalistic Anglophilia as elite snobbery. These traits tainted Sharp's work and too often troubled his personal interactions, but they stand alongside a record of enormous accomplishment. This driven but sickly man and the young, proper Edwardian woman at his side completed extraordinary collecting under remarkably difficult physical circumstances. Strangers in a strange land, "the Englishman," as Jane Gentry remembered him, managed to win the cooperation—and admiration—of backwoods men and women. As important, with the "discovery" of the "Running Set," he helped create the rationale for a national Anglo-American country dance tradition on both sides of the Atlantic as white, Anglo-Saxon, and "pure." In the United States, this formulation in time brought English Country Dance and Englishness and American Country Dance and Americanness under one roof. But that organization was a few years from flowering. First, the EFDS Branch had to take root.

Teacher-Disciples (Sharp-Shooters)

Sharp needed someone of his choosing to carry on his work in the States. He had a family in London, and given that he was often laid up with illness and already fifty-seven years old, the appropriate person would be someone younger than he with more of a future in the movement. She or he would of course also be someone he had certified. Helen Kennedy (née Karpeles) was not prepared to leave England in the spring of 1915, and so Sharp chose as the new teacher Lily Roberts (1887–1973), who had been the teacher of the Scarborough group in Yorkshire.

Born in 1887 in Bradford, England, Roberts had caught the folk revival bug and been trained by Sharp at Stratford-on-Avon. Certified, she had gone on to teach English Country Dance in public and private schools in and around Scarborough before being appointed teacher of the EFDS Scarborough Branch. Now in her twenty-eighth year, she was ready for a fresh challenge and responded enthusiastically to Sharp's invitation to move to the States. Her voyage, like many during the war, was eventful and telling. Her original May 6 reservation on the *Tuscania* was canceled when the Cunard line heard of the threat to the *Lusitania*. Traveling a few days later on the *New York*, her boat became known as the "funeral boat" for its cargo of bodies being returned to New York from the *Lusitania*'s sinking. Then, finding her cabin lodged at the end of a dark corridor in the steerage section of the boat, she chose to spend the first night on the deck instead. The next day, the purser took pity on her and moved her to what she clearly thought more appropriate, if only somewhat more respectable, quarters: a "better room" shared with a trapeze actress. In retrospect, she made light of the experience as "an entertaining education."[25]

Roberts had been in Lincoln a month when Sharp arrived. She and Storrow had already begun to establish a friendship that lasted a lifetime, and both women helped Sharp navigate the suffragist currents then swirling about Wellesley. Storrow, it will be recalled, had warned Sharp about what he called "the maniacs of that persuasion." Roberts, who also objected to being "political," was an ideal partner for Sharp at Wellesley, and the college's spring Tree Day dance pageant, the college's version of a May Day fête, went off without incident.[26] The summer school was a similar success, and Sharp returned to England after six weeks, convinced he had left the American Branch in good hands. "I do not think there is anyone," he wrote Roberts from his ship, "who has taken in and understands our E.F.D.S. aims better than you or who will propagate them more wisely." He reassured Lily's mother that her daughter's tasks, as his official representative in the United States, were straightforward and her livelihood secure: her chief duty, he explained, was "to inspect the classes at the different Centers, to teach them when required and to found other Centers elsewhere." There was to be no minimum salary, but Sharp trusted that her teaching should provide a "very good income." If not, he assured Mrs. Roberts that "Mrs. Storrow has personally undertaken to look after" her welfare.[27]

Lily Roberts directed the American Branch for the next decade, but personal circumstances demanded that she do so from a base in Boston and that others help out. In October 1915, Lily taught a country dance on the Storrow lawn to accompany a Harvest Festival and Barbeque to aid the National Allied Relief Fund; one of the young men trying the dance was Richard Conant, a social-work educator. Smitten with each other, Lily and Richard married two years later. Sharp, who had arrived for his fourth and last visit to America in February 1917, gave the bride away at a ceremony in the Storrow parlor on December 15, 1917.[28]

The staff at the 1915 summer school in Eliot, Maine. Left to right: Nora Jervis, Cecil Sharp, Maud Karpeles, Lily Roberts. (Used by permission of the Country Dance and Song Society Archives, www.cdss.org; Milne Special Collections and Archives Department, University of New Hampshire Library, Durham, NH)

In the years immediately following the marriage, Lily Roberts Conant continued to direct the American Branch, often traveling to visit the New York Centre or to help establish groups in Cincinnati, Pittsburgh, Chicago, Buffalo, and Toronto. She found that family life increasingly conflicted with the demands of the job, however, especially after the birth of her first child, Betty, in December 1921. Fortunately, there were strong and well-heeled supporters in each place, notably women, who could take on some of her responsibilities.[29]

By early 1922, Helen Storrow had come to believe that Conant's need for help could no longer be deferred, and she intervened with Sharp. Storrow pleaded for him to send someone to help Conant. It was one of their last exchanges before his death. Sharp could not think of anyone to suggest and encouraged the American organization to become "self-sufficient" and develop in its own way, in a manner that would be "fitted" to the country's unique "environment."[30] Fortunately for Conant, by 1926, when she had herself concluded that family responsibilities did not allow her to continue, help was available. Sharp died in 1924, and EFDS was then directed by someone from his tight-knit group of

May Gadd in 1963. (Photo by Stan Levy; used by permission of the Country Dance and Song Society Archives, www.cdss.org; Milne Special Collections and Archives Department, University of New Hampshire Library, Durham, NH)

loyal followers, Douglas Kennedy. One of the few male dancers from Sharp's original Chelsea demonstration team who did not die in the war, Kennedy's wife, Helen, was Maud's sister. Moreover, Kennedy's elevation to the directorship continued a family folklore tradition: his aunt Marjorie Kennedy-Fraser was a song collector and author of *Song of the Hebrides* and his grandfather, David Kennedy, was a famous Scottish singer. Not surprisingly, then, Kennedy now sent over another woman teacher from one of the regional branches who had been personally trained by Sharp: Marjorie Barnett.[31]

Relatively little is known of Barnett. She had taught English dance in the west of England and was a member of Sharp's demonstration team at the 1915 summer school at Stratford. That same year, Sharp had himself proposed sending her to help a struggling Pittsburgh group. But a decade later, in 1926, and after only a year in New York, she took the opportunity to join the faculty of the Eastman School of Music in Rochester. The American Branch abruptly found itself once again needing a national director and head teacher.[32] Soon after, the third English woman to lead the American Branch within a decade arrived to take Barnett's place: the indomitable May Gadd.[33]

May Gadd (1889–1979) arrived in New York in 1927 to assume the mantle of national director of the EFDS American Branch and head teacher of the New York Centre. She had been transported in 1914 by a performance of a Playford dance, the "Old Mole," probably at one of the Savoy Theatre performances that Sharp agreed to do for Granville Barker. The performance convinced her to focus on teaching dance, and she went to Stratford the next summer to learn from Sharp. While working as a physical-education and dance instructor at St. Mary's College in Newcastle-on-Tyne, she then directed the EFDS Northumberland Branch. Aged thirty-seven in 1927, starting a new life and new challenge in New York must have been inviting. Gadd's boyfriend, and the love of her life, had been killed in the war, and she had never married. Instead, like many women who made a lifetime commitment to charity work in the nineteenth century, and like others in subsequent generations who followed them into social service, the American Branch and what was to become CDSS became her extended family.[34] Although relatively small in stature, for the next forty-five years (until 1972) Gadd cast a large shadow over every aspect of the American movement. Trained by Sharp, devoted to his revival project, and indefatigable, she made the American Branch and its successor organization in Sharp's image and kept careful watch that it remained so.[35]

Building a Movement in the United States

The women Sharp trained and appointed as national directors of the American Branch worked tirelessly and faithfully as his surrogates, but he labored equally hard to put an infrastructure in place to support them. Sharp returned to America in June 1915, less than two months after he had left, to begin the work of movement building. He had planned to have Karpeles accompany him on his voyage, but she had to delay her trip a week. With other members of the Sharp family, Karpeles had contracted scarlet fever. So, on June 7, 1915, Sharp was met by Charles Rabold and Helen Storrow. In addition to being Sharp's patron, Storrow was now certified as a dancer and was his trusted point person in Boston; Rabold, a local piano and singing teacher, was a new convert to English dance whom Sharp had already begun to use for demonstrations at the end of his first trip. The meeting with Olive Dame Campbell had been an unexpected bonus.

The visit in the summer of 1915 was for only six weeks, and Sharp's activity was largely confined to planning and running the summer school. He did, however, use the time to organize a longer trip for the next year, both to begin his Appalachian collecting and to build the American Branch. Upon his return to England, he learned that his wife had developed heart trouble after her bout with scarlet fever. A semi-invalid for the rest of her life, Sharp moved his family to more comfortable (and fashionable) surroundings in Hampstead.[36] Sharp was not to be deterred from his American projects though, and his work and the war kept him in the States for most of the next three years.[37]

Sharp returned to the States in February 1916 and quickly found himself consumed with classes and lectures in New York and other cities. In fact, the strain of travel and lecturing was such that Mrs. Callery convinced him after six weeks to send for Maud Karpeles to assist and care for him. Karpeles and Sharp remained the rest of the year, even as tragic war news constantly discouraged them. In late August, while in the mountains, they received the particularly devastating news that three members of Sharp's demonstration team had been killed at the Battle of the Somme: Perceval Lewis, Reginald Tiddy, and George Butterworth. They later learned that a fourth dancer, George Wilkinson, had also been killed there. Then, in September, Sharp received a cable from his wife that their son Charles had been seriously wounded as well. Charles eventually recovered, but in the interim, the paucity of hard news left Sharp anxious to return home immediately. He did not, however, and Karpeles's explanation speaks to his priorities: they had many speaking and teaching commitments, and "he could not afford to do so."[38] They did finally return to London in December 1916, but it was for a two-month hiatus before continuing their American work. They returned to the States in February 1917, and German U-boat threats against neutral shipping kept them in America until the Armistice in November 1918.

Between February 1916 and November 1918, when Sharp were not running a summer school or collecting songs in Appalachia, he, usually with Karpeles's assistance, traveled across the country to establish English Country Dance. There were folk centers in the mountains, some of which remained active sites for English folk dance well into the twentieth century. One that was particularly important to Sharp was the Pine Mountain Settlement, where English and American folk song and dance flourished. Sharp visited a second site during one of his trips, Berea College in Kentucky, which taught mountain students, and he subsequently published a book of folk tunes he collected there. A third important site in folklore studies, the John C. Campbell School in Brasstown, North Carolina, organized in 1925, nearly a decade after Sharp's southern sojourns.[39]

The American Branch was a decidedly *urban* revivalist project, however. English Country Dance was meant both to quicken the spirit of latent Englishness among those of English ancestry and to bring the "civilizing" effects of Englishness (and Americanness) to the immigrant city. So Sharp and Karpeles focused on major metropolitan areas to which he had invitations, most usually from wealthy or well-connected Anglophile women such as New York's Elizabeth Burchenal, Boston's Helen Storrow, Pittsburgh's Mrs. Callery, and Chicago's Mary Wood Hinman. As we have seen, such women had visited Stratford and been introduced to English dance. Of course, these cities, and others such as Cleveland, Cincinnati, St. Louis, and Toronto, were also relatively likely to have a critical mass of people of English origin. And finally, these cities also had settlement houses and playgrounds where immigrant children learned folk dance and thousands more participated in annual maypole fêtes in urban parks.

The other promising site for dance was the college or university, most especially those with music or physical-education programs. Many of the fifty-six members of Baker's Chocorua dance group, for instance, were Harvard faculty and students. In New York, Columbia University faculty regularly invited Sharp to lecture. Kalamazoo College was another frequent stop. Chicago, where Sharp developed ECD at the Normal Physical School, was his base for the winter of 1917–18 and several other shorter trips.[40] And, of course, Sharp had directed the 1915 pageant at Wellesley College. Indeed, scores of women's colleges and coeducational land-grant universities held annual May Day celebrations and pageants, and English Country Dance was a logical extension of these programs, an opportunity to build on the "gay simplicity" of the maypole festivities.[41] Thus, in the spring and fall, when Sharp and Karpeles were not in the southern mountains, virtually every week found them in another city, teaching by alternatively cajoling and enticing.

Sharp's May 1916 visit to St. Louis illustrated how his forthright manner could alienate prospects. His invitation to St. Louis had followed his triumphant direction of an English "Interlude" as part of a Shakespeare tercentennial celebration in New York. Winning first prize over contributions from other countries fueled Sharp's chauvinism, and he crowed, "No country in the world can be gay in the simple, fresh way that England can—it is our contribution to civilization."[42] Moreover, the prize came with offers from other cities—one being St. Louis—to tour his work for their celebrations. A woman named Mrs. Hardcastle invited Sharp to direct a dance interlude with her St. Louis dance class in *As You Like It* as part of the St. Louis festivities. Sharp's imperious and snobby manner, however—"he looked so cross . . . he talked so loud . . . [and he] smoked . . . gold-tipped cigarettes" in the ballroom—did not sit well with many participants, especially since at least some of them undoubtedly were quite used to throwing their own weight around. Dancers, a local newspaper noted, included J. C. Kendall, president of the Kendall Motor Company, and M. C. Dolph of Judge and Dolph.[43] Sharp, however, was appalled at what he saw and heard at rehearsal and, as was his manner, could not resist saying so. The local newspapers had a field day with the response from his dancers. "'As You Like It' Pageant Dancing Class On Strike," announced the bemused *St. Louis Post-Dispatch* headline. Grabbing the pianist by the shoulders and shaking him, Sharp had screamed, "Play it right. You're murdering it. That's beautiful music. I wrote it myself." Then he announced to Hardcastle that ten of the forty dancers had to go. Ironically, after all the uproar, the St. Louis pageant was canceled for bad weather,[44] but not before, with those ten dancers in tears, all forty voted to go on strike.[45]

Fortunately for Sharp, the St. Louis contretemps was not typical. To be sure, his career had been punctuated by conflict. But Sharp's gruffness, rigidity, and formal manner were but one side of the man. He could also be a loyal friend and an appreciative audience for a song or dance he loved. He confined many of his snider comments to his letters, and Karpeles, ever the loyal protector of his legacy, recalled that his "rhetorical tirades" "rarely gave offence," as "they were always tinged with good-humour."[46] Indeed, traveling about, he and Maud could often rely on the goodwill of old friends and patrons.

One result of their work and, ultimately, perhaps testimony to Sharp's abiding appeal, was their success in spreading the American Branch. By 1915–16, the American Branch had established groups in at least four cities, and maybe in as many as seven: in New York, Boston, Chicago, and Pittsburgh and perhaps in Cincinnati, St. Louis, and Rochester. There is little reliable membership information until 1924, but outside of New York and Boston it seems that most regional groups largely consisted of a handful of committed devotees. For most of the next two decades, New York and Boston maintained the only substantial groups. The Boston Centre claimed a membership of two hundred in 1915–16 and sponsored six parties that year, attended by an average of eighty people. The annual membership was two dollars, a considerable sum at the time for a working girl but not beyond the means of the young professionals who attended.[47] The New York Centre, by comparison, was robust: it reported that 1923 was the "most successful year the Branch has ever had," and its membership, which in 1924 stood at 382 (161 of whom were new) enjoyed fifteen country dance parties.[48]

Membership in the American Branch continued to be centered in its New York and Boston groups until the mid-1930s. Membership in Boston remained fairly constant, but in New York it vacillated. By 1931, New York's membership had swelled, however, to 655 people in fifteen local groups spread through the city and into some of New Jersey's and Westchester's more prestigious suburbs: Glen Ridge, Montclair, and South Orange, New Jersey, and Larchmont, New York.[49]

Then, in 1934, the American Branch suddenly expanded. With the country mired in the Great Depression, folk dance must have seemed a welcome and relatively inexpensive diversion for its relatively well-heeled devotees. There were four U.S. centres that year, but the movement had become truly national with groups in San Francisco and Palo Alto, California, where Stanford University was based.[50] In the years that followed, although the number of members did not change appreciably, the number of centres grew dramatically, to five in 1935, eight in 1936, ten in 1937, and seventeen in 1938.[51]

The growth in the movement encouraged some of the leaders to rethink their organization. The branches generally functioned as autonomous groups, but in December 1928, representatives from the New York, Boston, and Rochester branches (Barnett had begun what was to be a short-lived group there) moved to create a stronger, central organization: the Federation of American Branches of the English Folk Dance Society. The group chose Storrow and Gilman to serve as president and secretary, respectively. Each branch continued individually to affiliate with the English centre in London as well as with the federation, but the new central organization initiated a move toward an independent American identity for their movement.[52] In 1933, the federation itself agreed to affiliate with the English Society as a central organization but, at the same time, changed its name to the English Country Dance Society of America. Three decades later, as had happened in England, "Song" was added to the title.[53]

The change in name mirrored the functional independence of the ECD dance community in the United States. It may have signaled an increasing awareness of the broader Anglo-American provenance of the dance tradition, as more dancers became familiar with square and contra dance as well. The new name, however, did not translate into less local identification or operations. Beyond helping to build a national audience for the summer schools, each branch continued to operate as an autonomous group. According to May Gadd, the New York Centre, where Sharp began his work and had organized the American Branch, functioned mostly as "a bureau of information" and primarily organized the summer school.[54] In sum, despite the name changes, English Country Dance in the United States in the era of the American Branch existed through largely autonomous branches that were affiliates of the EFDS, and principally in New York and Boston.

The New York and Boston Centres

From the outset, the New York Centre of the American Branch had the largest membership of any American group, a distinction it seems to hold still almost a century later. Two hundred people reportedly attended a dance in March 1916 and thirty-five new members joined the group, and in the first decade of its existence, the New York Centre's membership fluctuated between approximately 250 and 400.[55] Sharp's two strong local followers in New York provided dependable leadership. Susan M. Gilman had turned her dance studio into a venue exclusively for English dance, and Charles Rabold had given up his music career and dedicated himself to teaching the dance. Even so, late in 1916, Sharp confided that he felt "very depressed" about the New York Centre "falling into the hands of the public school and professional element"—presumably, Burchenal and her followers.[56] Indeed, Sharp's view of the outlook for English dance in New York and the United States in general waxed and waned (often in rhythm with his view of his financial prospects). In December 1915, he was optimistic, writing Storrow, "if the dances are to be firmly rooted anywhere in my life time, it will be in America rather than England."[57] But after the poor attendance of the 1918 summer school, he bemoaned what he foresaw as a poor prognosis for ECD in the United States: "there will never be more than a few people in America who will ever give the necessary time to become proficient. In this country they like change and quick results and it will be a long time before this attitude will alter, and until it does alter English folk dancing will not be popular here."[58]

Hoping to see English folk dancing become a daily passion for all people, Sharp had reason to be pessimistic. In the interwar years, the community of English dancers in New York and Boston remained a small and a relatively elite slice of the city's society and professional class. Still, they were a committed and passionate few united by some strong, talented leaders and wealthy patrons.

In New York, Rabold had Sharp's confidence and ran most of the classes, though he occasionally called on Lily Conant to make a guest appearance. Sharp felt that Rabold's "musical knowledge and feeling" made him "remarkably quick in picking up these dances and in understanding their inward meaning."[59] Gadd recalled that Rabold "did much to arouse enthusiasm by filling teaching engagements about the country." Rabold himself described the dancing in New York in 1920 as of a "low" level, but with "first class spirit." He nonetheless worked enthusiastically to maintain the quality of his own dancing and to build a base of local teachers. In 1920, he ran a class for teachers, which although "small," he thought of "first-class quality"; in 1922, he was one of seven Americans at Stratford attending the summer school.[60]

Rabold's efforts were rewarded by the development of a strong team of New York teachers. In the 1920s, and until Rabold's tragic death in an airplane crash in 1931, which had shortly followed Gadd's arrival and ascendance, men dominated the New York teaching scene.[61] Notably, Elizabeth Burchenal mostly disappeared from the English scene, having moved on to her Folk-Dance Society and her own research in international European and American folk dance. With her absence, the prominence of men was striking, although the elite social profile of the group was not: the home addresses and achievements of these early teachers demonstrated that the New York dance community drew from a familiar well-heeled and professional class.[62] Conforming to gender stereotypes, the branch secretary was usually a woman, though David Morland, who lived in the affluent Westchester suburb of Larchmont, held the post in 1931. Members of the new suburban groups were similarly well-off. Most prominent was the painter Kathleen Townsend, who was regularly in New Jersey society news. She gave up her painting career when she wed Robert Higer so that the two of them could marry their shared passion for ECD, and they soon became fixtures as dancers and teachers in the local and national scene.[63] However, men such as Rabold, until his death, did much of the teaching. Moreover, the sword and morris dances were taught as traditional all-male performances. The best known of the men, Milton Smith, typified their musical background, English ancestry, and professional standing. One of the four Smith brothers to dance in the United States, Milton Smith taught at the Horace Mann School for Boys and went on to a distinguished career at Columbia University in the drama department, which he eventually chaired.[64]

In contrast to New York, women ran the Boston Centre from the start.[65] Helen Storrow assumed the presidency of the American Branch in 1916 and remained its leading officer until her death in 1944. As noted earlier, Lily Conant, Sharp's personal ambassador, settled in Boston and ran the American Branch from there. She continued to teach after she married and remained a major presence in the dance community, but Louise Chapin became Boston's head teacher, a position she held through midcentury. Two other local

Boston women, Emma Wright Gibbs and Dorothy Bolles, also took on major roles in the local and national dance movement.[66] A third woman, Evelyn Wells, came out of the Boston community to work at the Pine Mountain Settlement School and teach English dance around the country.[67]

No English community could thrive, however, without a strong male component, and Boston was no exception. Men were needed both to make up the sword and morris teams and to partner the women in the country dances. Thus, men such as Richard Conant and Charles Peabody, the secretary of the American Folk-Lore Society, joined their wives, Lily Conant and Trixie Peabody, on the dance floor. And in both New York and Boston, major roles were played by the Smith brothers. Writing in 1974, May Gadd recalled Everett Smith, "of the [four] famous Smith brothers, who were wonderful dancers and did much of the early teaching."[68] That said, the roster of Boston teachers in 1930–31 was an all-woman team: Lily Conant and Louise Chapin were the director and head teacher of the staff, respectively; the other teachers were Dorothy Bolles and Constance Conant (Lily's sister-in-law), while, notably, Mary E. Longley taught the Girl Scouts classes.[69]

The appointment of a teacher for the Boston-area Girl Scouts merits analysis, for the presence of the Girl Scouts in the ECD movement was not unique but was politically significant. Karpeles notes that ECD was "used to a great extent by the Girls' Scouts Association."[70] In New York, for instance, folk dance, but "especially Country Dance," had become very popular, noted an August 1928 article in the *Dance Magazine,* where in addition to Marjorie Barnett's class, five hundred dancers gathered at the Manhattan Trade School on 22nd Street. A May festival of the New York EFDS Branch at International House included (male) students from Princeton and Columbia universities, who were presumably paired with girls from the Girl Scouts of Manhattan and the New York League of Girls' Clubs.[71]

The symbiotic relationship between the Girl Scouts and ECD also provides a window into the complex politics of English dance and, more specifically, into the more conservative cast both to gender politics and the culture of liberalism in the dance community. ECD provided mixed messages for young women about their appropriate roles and bodily carriage. It is notable that dance attracted suffragettes such as Mary Neal and had some appeal at women's colleges such as Vassar and Wellesley, though the conservative Storrow undoubtedly exaggerated the latter as a "hotbed" of women's suffrage.[72] As feminist historians such as Linda Tomko have astutely noted, ECD offered women a preeminent place as teachers and leaders of the dance community. But these women reinforced traditional gender roles on the dance floor and in the dance community and are more aptly described as matriarchs than feminists.

Moreover, the Girl Scouts' relationship to ECD echoes a more complicated story, heard earlier in concerns voiced by people as varied as Cecil Sharp and Jane Addams about "civilizing" slum streets and dance halls. Juliette Low may have created the American Girl Scouts movement as an act of resistance to Baden-Powell's refusal to open the Boy Scouts to girls and to give girls lessons in independence and outdoor survival. But the organization's messages were overwhelmingly nationalistic and hyperpatriotic and celebrated domestic femininity. In this regard, ECD helped to instill American girlhood with traditional ideals of femininity. Girl Scouts learned homemaking, nursing, and mothering skills and then danced the "pure" country dances of the "peasant" folk who, they imagined, had tamed the wilderness before them.[73]

By offering "respectable" healthy activity of a controlled body, ECD advanced a traditional bodily regime that the Girl Scouts could recognize. A constrained woman's body danced in a traditional coupled form; men invited women to dance, initiated moves, and performed the more athletic and "masculine" morris leaps. But these bodily messages also accompanied socially conservative political messages about the value of a national culture for civilizing and Americanizing. Thus, as Sharp and his acolytes built the American Branch, they sought to enforce a uniform "style" that would embody literally and figuratively traditional modes of being in "independent" women and "manly" men. ECD mattered to many people, then: it was an important source of recreational pleasure, to be sure; but for the dance community it also carried greater, if often understated, political weight.

Setting "Standards"

Sharp wanted the American Branch to function "as a central authority with respect to English folk-dancing."[74] He was convinced that the "success" of the U.S. movement required a "different standard of efficiency" than Americans had hitherto experienced, a standard that would require grading, examining, and inspecting. He also knew that some Americans, notably Elizabeth Burchenal, had very different ideas about that standard. Echoing Neal a decade earlier, Burchenal seems to have been more sympathetic to the "authority" and variety of expressions of a dance of the folk themselves, rather than that of those who collected and spoke for them, such as Sharp.[75] As an International Folk Dance collector, she seems to have found Sharp overly chauvinistic.[76] Sharp and his followers for their part believed it was essential that they put in place a series of women trained and certified by Sharp himself to ensure continuity with "proper" EFDS dancing. Ironically, conformity to Sharp's protocols may have been enforced more in the United States than in England. But the key is that Sharp put people in place in the American Branch to teach his standard; moreover, he and his followers also established a regime of vacation schools, certificate programs, and standardized music to ensure that the ECD dancing body would be uniform across the nation.

At Stratford-on-Avon, for instance, Sharp implemented a certificate program for sword, morris, and country dance, as well as for singing games and folk singing. Each area had between six and nine grades, and Sharp rigorously enforced who would be allowed to teach and certify in both England and the United States. Classes "must be very carefully graded," he explained to Storrow. But since the United States had "scarcely anyone who could qualify for the intermediate grades"—not to speak of the advanced levels—Sharp determined that Americans could "manage with four grades." More practically, he worried that impatient Americans would not continue dancing without an easier reward system.[77] Nonetheless, teachers in the United States, both in his lifetime and after, took even the watered-down version of grading that Sharp had put in place "very seriously." Students took ECD seriously as well, as a five-lesson course in 1925 in New York either in morris dancing, grade 1 or 2, or country dancing, grade 1 or 4, cost the not inconsiderable sum of fifty cents a lesson.[78] Indeed, graded teaching and dancing remained an integral part of the ECD movement through the 1980s. The New York group, CD*NY, for instance, until 1992, did not permit dancers to join the "experienced" first part of the regular Tuesday-evening dance until the teachers had determined that they met the grade.[79] Certificates reflected competence and knowledge of a syllabus of required dances in the Playford and ritual dance corpus. Each level consisted of an additional series of five to ten dances. Of course, dancers also had to dance well—"airs & graces, the head-wagging and toe-pointing" were not to be tolerated; rather, teachers looked to see simple, graceful, and contained forward movement on the balls of the foot in the running step, and so forth.[80]

A remarkable number of dances quickly became a part of the American repertoire. A 1919 event billed as the "Annual Ball of the English Folk Dance Society of New York" demonstrated the range of dances that participants were expected to know. The evening began with an alternative to the Grand March, the "Tideswell Processional Dance," which the program told attendees was "really a Morris Dance" from Derbyshire. The evening program proper then opened with eight country dances. Beginning with "Sellenger's Round" and "Rufty Tufty," most were fairly easy dances from the early Playford volumes, but the first half of the program included the more challenging three-couple longways set dance "Picking Up Sticks." The last half of the dance program was quite similar. Mostly easier dances, the Ball Committee also programmed one of the more difficult dances in the repertoire, a complex dance for four couples called "Newcastle" that did not repeat any figures.

Interestingly, however, teachers and leading dancers used the intermission to demonstrate the full range of dance and song in the English folk tradition—and to document its Anglo-American connection as well. First, a team of six men, led by Rabold, did a sword dance, "The Captains Song." Program notes explained that the dance, a rapper dance, was a "survival of some primitive religious rite" and that Sharp had collected it in Northumberland. The team danced in a close-knit circle with short swords that had hilts at both ends. Each member held the hilt of his own sword in his left hand, placing the sword against his right shoulder so that the dancer behind him could hold the other hilt with his right hand. In this formation, the dances kept up a rapid two-fourths step while turning the swords under and over one another in a series of moves that culminated in a traditional "nut" climax. In the "nut," which uniquely is formed six times in this particular dance, the dancers interlock the six swords together into a six-pointed star, which the leader then lifts triumphantly aloft.

The interval entertainment then continued with the performances of folk songs and more demonstration dancing. After Miss Marjorie Kilborn sang three of the folk songs collected by Sharp in the southern Appalachian Mountains, another team of men, four of whom had performed the sword dance, demonstrated two morris dances: a handkerchief dance from Ilmington, Warwickshire, called "Shepherd's Hey," and a stick dance from Badby, Northamptonshire, entitled "Beaux of London City." Again, the program notes described the "rustic" origins of the bells and how swords from other ritual dances had given way to handkerchiefs and sticks and suggested that the use of blackface in the dance more likely reflected a customary use of facial smudges for luck than any "Moorish" origins as some folklorists had speculated. The interlude proceeded with Kenneth Wheeler singing three folk songs that Sharp had collected in England. Wheeler, one of the branch's teachers who had also participated on the sword and morris teams, then joined Rabold in a jig from Oxfordshire, "Princess Royal." And finally, the entertainment's grand finale was the four-couple dance Sharp had noted in the United States, the "Running Set." Indicating the American provenance of the dance and that it was "probably in form the oldest of any dance to be done this evening," the program notes concluded with a pregnant air: "Its value is thus apparent."[81]

New Moon Sword Team. Brooklyn Promenade, May 30, 2006. (Photo courtesy of Jeffrey Bary)

The 1919 New York Ball demonstrated the breadth of dance and song already established in the New York repertoire within four years of Sharp's founding of the American Branch. The Boston Centre showed a similar breadth. After that, however, opportunities to learn and practice diminished substantially. Local groups in New York and Boston ran weekly dancing for its members; small regional affiliates had neither sufficient numbers to support regular dances nor the trained teachers to lead it, much less to develop advanced levels and quality of dancing. Often a local community lacked musicians to play for it as well. The certificate program and its repertoire-syllabi established a "standard," but that was not sufficient, either for Sharp and his followers who led the branch or for those in local communities who wanted to learn more and achieve at a higher level. Thus, both those who produced the standards and those who consumed them could agree on the need for institutions to advance that standard on a national level. One premier institution was the summer school.

Summer Schools

Cecil Sharp recognized the important role the Stratford-on-Avon Summer School played in the growth of EFDS on both sides of the Atlantic. He had struggled with Mary Neal for control of the venue, as much to enforce his standard of dance as for the opportunity to train followers who could spread his message. In fact, almost all the dance teachers in both countries visited Stratford at one time or another. Not surprisingly, Sharp leapt at the chance to direct a summer school in the United States in the July following the formation of the American Branch.

English folk dancing in the United States as part of a summer retreat preceded the formation of the American Branch, however. In both 1913 and 1914, Claud Wright had taught morris, sword, and country dancing to some fifty or more adults and children in the Theater-in-the-Woods in Chocorua. Baker also taught at the MacDowell Colony in Peterborough, New Hampshire, as well as on the Storrow lawn and at her Red Barn in Lincoln, Massachusetts.[82]

The three-week summer school that Sharp directed in July 1915 intended to advance the summer programs on a more structured and professional level.[83] Any national ambitions for the camp would have been premature. The summer school met at a camp site in Eliot, Maine, on the banks of the Piscataqua River. Everyone slept in wooden shacks and danced on wooden floors under two specially built large marquees (enclosed tents), which a violent rain storm subsequently flooded and blew down with one week still remaining. The school decamped for a nearby hotel and conference center, and while everyone carried on with the program, the experience undoubtedly convinced organizers to seek another venue for the future.[84] The summer school moved the next year to the Massachusetts Agricultural College in Amherst, although the location meant that it more easily served Boston Centre members. At Amherst, Sharp, Karpeles, and Roberts did the teaching, probably with the help of Rabold, who provided a much-needed male body. And Sharp was generally pleased with the results. Attendance in 1916 was comparable to the first year, and the school experience "dissipated" his "chief fear" that the average American student would "not take the trouble to acquire the complicated techniques" of English dance. At the conclusion of the session, all eleven dancers who took the exam for certification passed—which Sharp noted was "a very unusual result"—and he awarded six Elementary Certificates and five "C.D. Certificates," the latter presumably an intermediary level.[85]

Attendance at the 1917 Amherst summer school augured less well for the future. Only twenty students appeared the first week, and Sharp thought the "prospects . . . very gloomy." School went well, but the classes were "feeble." By the second week, however, the number of students had grown to thirty, a number that Sharp thought "fairly respectable." Sharp attributed the decline to a combination of things: the war, the fact that Storrow had "spread rumours of [Sharp's] illness abroad," and "no advertising." Regardless, by the end of the school, he took considerable pleasure in being able to award seven of the American students advanced certificates, an award given only to those who passed the EFDS's most exacting final tests. Three of the seven—Louise Chapin, Charles Rabold, and Dorothy Bolles—went on to teach and lead the American Branch for the next generation.[86]

Of course, American involvement in the war made summer frivolity unseemly, if not impractical, and organizers canceled the summer school at Amherst for 1918.[87] Instead, Sharp and Karpeles began the first of what became annual visits by the EFDS staff from the Boston Centre to a site a few miles east of Cape Cod on the shore of two ponds, where Helen Storrow had established her Girl Scouts Camp and had a family settlement. Sharp and Roberts had visited the camp in 1917 to teach the girls about folk traditions and folk "songs and dances." In mid-July 1918, after plans for Amherst collapsed, they spent most of a week teaching country dances to the girls. They agreed that the girls were "a particularly clumsy inartistic lot," which Karpeles thought was "accentuated by their awful costumes—blouses & bloomers." Sharp found the classes "unsatisfactory," but he carried on. Undoubtedly happy to please his patron, Sharp merely reconciled himself to making little effort to teach good dance form.[88] For Storrow, however, Sharp's appearance at her camp had wed her two passions: the Girl Scouts and English Country Dance. After Sharp's visits, English Country Dance became a regular part of Girl Scouts Camp, and for a few years at least, the Girl Scouts had their own morris team.[89]

The Boston Centre was also not idle during these summers, although less is known of its program. Baker evidently continued to sponsor English dance at his summer camp in Chocorua, though these were not EFDS-sponsored programs. In 1925 and 1926, though, the Boston Centre took advantage of Storrow's generosity and ran its own summer school at the site on Long Pond. Ed Wilfert, the camp's historian, writes that the dance pavilion was built during those years and "named 'C#' in honor of the newly deceased mentor of the English Dance movement." He adds that, in keeping with the tenor of the facilities as Girl Scouts camps, these summer schools were attended mostly by women.[90]

During this period, the New York Centre also sponsored summer camps, "resuming" its summer dance school in 1924. Following the Eliot, Maine, and Amherst models, the Centre opened a two-week camp in the town of Becket in the Berkshire Mountains of western Massachusetts. The next two years, it moved a few miles away to East Otis, Massachusetts, renting the Camp Bonnie Brae facility in late August after the children's season had ended. Milton Smith, whose day job now had him at Columbia's Teachers College, directed the camp. Enrollment was limited to seventy-five, but they also had to be people with some disposable income, as the fee and train fare was forty-two dollars.[91]

By 1927, leaders of the American Branch had come to believe that the relative autonomy of the Boston and New York centres was not good for the national growth of the American Branch or its summer programs and moved to reestablish the summer school at Amherst for dancers from across the nation. It was in this context that, with the initiative of Charles Rabold and some of the musicians in both dance communities, the Boston and New York centres cooperated to renew the summer schools at Amherst in 1927 at the Massachusetts Agricultural College. Douglas Kennedy, the new leader of EFDS in London, came over with his wife Helen (née Karpeles) to lead a star-studded cast of EFDS teachers trained by Sharp that included Gadd, Barnett, Chapin, Conant, and others. A resounding success, the lively dancing and enthusiasm was recorded on eight-millimeter tape for posterity, apparently by Helen Storrow using the new technology of the day.[92]

The summer school continued at Amherst for the next six years, until a wonderful and familiar alternative site became available. Storrow offered the American Branch her upgraded camp facility as a permanent home for the summer school. From 1933 on, and for the next generation, Lily Conant oversaw the camp, and May Gadd directed it, together working to ensure that Sharp's legacy was carried forth and embodied in the character of the dancing. The Girl Scouts had called their Long Pond camp "Pine Tree Camp"; in 1935, Lily Conant and Helen Storrow renamed it "Pinewoods Camp."[93] Although until considerably later in the century the camp drew most of its attendees from the Northeast and in particular from the large Boston and New York centres, Pinewoods drew enthusiasts from across the country and visits from EFDS leaders from Britain as well. Sharp-trained teachers ran Pinewoods with a firm hand, with a legacy that shaped the dance community for the next half century. The Pinewoods experience knit together a national cadre of ECD enthusiasts with Sharp's authorized dance style and his sense of propriety in the dance, and participants took these lessons back to their local dance communities as the core values of a national dance culture.

Music and Dance:
The Gramophone Revolution and the Politics of Copyright

Crucial to the embodiment of the dance was the music. For Sharp, ensuring that the dance was understood—both in the mind and the body—entailed twin foci: the creation of a record archive of the songs and dances

Staff at the 1927 summer school at Massachusetts Agricultural College, Amherst. Left to right: top, Douglas Kennedy, unknown, unknown, Lily Conant, M. (Milton or Melville) Smith, Al or Everett Smith (?), Charles Rabold; middle, Dorothy Bolles, Louise Chapin, unknown, Marjorie Barnett, Peggy Kettlewell; bottom, Helen Kennedy, Maud Karpeles, May Gadd, M. (Milton or Melville) Smith, Elsie Avril. One of the unknown men in the top row is probably the fourth Smith brother, either Al or Everitt. (Used by permission of the Country Dance and Song Society Archives, www.cdss.org; Milne Special Collections and Archives Department, University of New Hampshire Library, Durham, NH)

he had collected and notated, and the copyright of all his work, including his increasingly impressive collection of authored books.

In crossing the Atlantic and then seeking to secure the copyright of his books in the United States, Sharp entered an alien legal culture. The United States had not signed the Berne Convention, which recognized international copyright among the signatory sovereign nations in 1887, and it did not do so until 1988. Moreover, under Berne, copyright was automatically granted without the author formally registering it. In contrast, American copyright law applied only to American publications, so European authors could not profit from the sale of U.S. editions of their books in the United States. Both Berne and U.S. copyright law were amended, in 1908 and 1909, respectively, to include protection for the products of new sound and visual technologies, and new provisions set the terms of protection at fifty years after the author's death abroad and at twenty-eight years in the United States.[94] But American copyright law, even with the new provisions, continued to operate with no international protections; its provisions continued to apply only to creative works published in the United States. How much laypeople knew of these provisions and their local provenance is unclear, but copyright issues became the occasion for Sharp's further split with Burchenal.

From the start of his American sojourns, Sharp moved to meet with the new recording-industry moguls to create a living corpus of his work. At the same time, he met with publishers, record producers, his agent, and lawyers to protect the copyright on his books and music. Sharp had reason to be concerned: some of the music he had notated and published had begun to appear in the United States, where it was now fair game. What he saw as problems of copyright infringement both undermined his income and threatened his vision of the dance. He moved quickly to meet with publishers and the new record companies, in both cases quickly finding himself in conflict with his erstwhile friend and increasingly frequent competitor: Elizabeth Burchenal. Of course, the abiding irony in Sharp's copyright assertions was that he never addressed or gave voice to the rights of people such as William Kimber or John England or his countless other village informants. The case of Olive Dame Campbell was a noticeable exception: he trod carefully and respectfully, giving her a coauthorship of his first collection of songs from the southern Appalachian Mountains. With Burchenal he was less flexible.

Burchenal and Sharp's differences may have been as much about personal and political style and authority in the folk dance world as anything else. Indeed, Burchenal tended to be more egalitarian about the value of all folk dance traditions, and one way to read her dispute with Sharp is that she was more democratically inclined and less enamored with elite patrons than Sharp was.[95] Indeed, Burchenal, it will be recalled, had early been a strong supporter of Sharp. She had tried to undermine Mary Neal's 1909–10 visit, had encouraged Sharp's initial trip to the United States, and had introduced him to the playground and settlement crowd. Yet within a fortnight of Sharp's arrival in New York, he wrote a salutary note to Maud Karpeles that projected the split to come. Sharp, whose penchant for forthrightness often bordered on tactlessness when he was challenged by strong women, thought little of Americans' knowledge of folk dance. Yet depending on both their financial and political support, he faced an impossible dilemma. Sharp had to establish his preeminent authority without undermining that of his hosts and possible patrons: "[Hinman] and Miss Burchenal and all that crowd know what poor stuff they are passing off as folk-dance and know that if I come & see it I shall have to show them—and those they have taught—how wrong they all are and so queer their pitch. . . . The problem is to put them right without showing them up and this is not easy of solution."[96]

Burchenal and Sharp sustained a working relationship in the spring of 1915 during Sharp's maiden visit to the United States; they were seen dining and dancing together on several occasions. But this eliminated neither their differences nor Sharp's skepticism about Burchenal. Hearing from Rabold that Burchenal was trying to "crab" plans for the first summer school, Sharp reportedly "let out full broadsides at poor Miss Burchenal. He says she has no brains, is a very jealous person, wants to be cock of the walk (that doesn't sound quite right!). And loves money almost as much as herself."[97] Confiding to Storrow that it would "be a thousand pities" if Burchenal "were able to influence the [American EFDS] committee," Burchenal was notably the one major participant in the founding of the American Branch not to end up in a leadership position.[98]

The most serious source of the rift between the two, however, was a copyright conflict. This division occurred in the midst of the larger controversy over Burchenal's role in the American Branch and was probably overdetermined by the broader conflict between the two individuals. Details of the copyright conflict are unclear, but it appears that Burchenal had proposed to Sharp that he agree to allow her to publish some of the songs and dances that he had previously published in England. She felt the arrangement resembled one that Sharp had earlier made with a woman named Miss Brower for a similar work. Moreover, she assured Sharp that Gray, his publisher, was "enthusiastic" about the idea as good business for him, good advertising for Sharp, and a favor to her.[99]

Sharp begged "to differ." He knew of no instance in which an author in the United States had agreed to the kind of arrangement she proposed. Brower had published her book of morris tunes without his permission, as the American copyright did not cover his British publication. He wrote Burchenal of his hope that they could work "amicably together," but in private, he was less optimistic. Meeting with her for five hours, he felt that she "feigned complete ignorance of the law of copyright, etc., and promised not to offend again." He had concluded, though, that she "is a very difficult & rather crooked young woman who will require delicate handling." As was his manner, he then told her indelicately "of the enormities she had been guilty of with regard to [his] books and tunes."[100]

Sharp made it clear that he did not trust Burchenal or her promises, and when their competition spread to the record industry, he moved quickly to shut her out. Sharp had a growing interest in producing records of his dance music—and equally important, the record companies had an interest in getting him to record dance music for them. Technical improvements in recording on disks instead of on cylinders encouraged the Victor and Columbia gramophone companies to seek new markets for their products. As early as 1904, Victor began to market recordings of the famous opera tenor Enrico Caruso. By 1915, the quality of sound had been substantially improved, and companies raced to sign up other artists who could help them reach additional "ethnic" markets. A Victor agent, for instance, proposed recording a Creole trumpeter that year, but the arrangement fell through when the company insulted the man by asking him to audition to test the sound. In 1917, a recording by an all-white Original Dixieland Band, playing the New Orleans sound, sold two million copies, more than Caruso or recordings by the bandleader John Philip Sousa.[101]

The Dixieland sound initiated the marketing of "race music" in the 1920s, but its success suggested the potential market that both companies and Sharp could envision when they met in 1915. To begin, the record companies and Sharp had a mutual need for product. For Sharp, recordings offered a legacy of dance sound he could authorize, as well as a welcome and steady source of income. Until World War II, although ritual morris and sword dances were accompanied by a concertina or accordion player or a fiddler, most local English Country Dance venues had only a pianist.[102] Sharp played piano, and many of the women and men who taught ECD had musical backgrounds: Rabold played the piano, Gilman and Gibbs ran dance studios that relied on a pianist, Melville Smith had a distinguished career as an organist, and so forth. But live music was not always available when small groups of dance aficionados gathered at someone's home or at a local studio outside a metropolis. Recordings made by the dancing master—Sharp—had a vital role to play even when musicians were on hand: they preserved his sense of the timing, cadence, rhythm, meter, and energy in the dance. Thus, with the emergence of the gramophone (and its American sister pioneered by the Victor Company, the Victrola), gramophones and recordings became highly desirable commodities for ECD groups. Moreover, the record player also facilitated the teaching of ECD dance in schools. As early as 1915, schools in over 3,000 American cities and towns reported owning Victrolas; by 1925, their presence had spread to more than four times the number: 12,313 localities.[103]

Records of folk dance preceded Sharp's arrival in New York, however, and it gave him cause for concern. He had discovered that four records had been produced by the Victor Company that included Swedish folk dances, a polka and a schottische, and a May Day processional "ribbon dance." One of the records drew on Sharp's 1911 publication of morris dances and had "Shepherd's Hey" on the B-side; the other side was a rendition of the (Swedish?) "Gotlands Quadrille." Victor credited Sharp as "composer" but seemed to have recorded the track without his permission, simply ignoring British copyright. Moreover, the poor quality of the recording undoubtedly gave Sharp additional reason to intervene with the record companies as soon as possible: the brass band played the same tune with little verve and without the slightest variation.[104]

Within two months of Sharp's arrival in New York, he had both Victor and Columbia competing to get him to sign a contract. He vowed to "pit them against one another," because he had learned that Burchenal had gotten five hundred dollars (about one hundred pounds) "for the right to reproduce 25 of her wretched tunes."[105] A month later, he signed a contract with Victor to make twenty records, each with two short country dances or one long one. With "fear & trembling" he asked for one hundred pounds, which "they accepted with such alacrity" that he concluded they must have "expected him to ask for a great deal more."[106]

Sharp recorded with the Victor Gramophone Company at its Camden, New Jersey, studio in the spring of 1915. Directing the Victor Military Band, he recorded twenty-four records with a total of twenty-nine tunes. The first recordings seem to have been of "Gathering Peascods" and "Sellinger's Round," both early dances in the round for "as many as will" that Playford had published in his first volume and that Sharp often taught to new dancers. Later recordings included several sword dances and the "Tideswell Processional Dance," but Sharp continued to concentrate on country dances. Recording one dance to a side, by the spring 1916 he had produced a corpus that could sustain a dance group.[107]

Sharp was not completely satisfied with the Victor arrangement, however. The Columbia Gramophone Company was not, to his mind, as "strong a company," but it was willing to give him "a free hand" in the choice of instruments and direction of the band. That said, he offered to make morris dance records for Columbia for five pounds per record.[108] So July and October found him recording as many as ten additional records for Columbia, though he did not conduct them; rather, they were recorded by the Prince's Band, under Columbia's musical director, Charles Prince. The Columbia recordings offered listeners twenty-four dance tunes, twelve of which had not been previously recorded. Among them were some dances from Sharp's book, giving Columbia a market advantage in that regard. Sharp may have leveraged his choice of companies though, since he did conduct the Black Diamonds Band in six recordings he made under the Victor label.[109]

Even with his obvious delight with the contracts, Sharp remained anxious about both his publisher's response to his negotiations and his American copyrights. He understood his position to be weak, as the songs he collected did not have American copyright. He reluctantly agreed to a U.S. copyright for the publication of his Appalachian Mountain song books, because they could otherwise be published without his permission anyway. He also feared that the books could otherwise be published in England without his permission. Royalties were to be split, with the publisher, Novello & Company, getting 25 percent, an arrangement that seemed to suit all parties.[110]

One person not party to the deals, however, was Elizabeth Burchenal. Burchenal had also recorded English folk dance tunes and now sought to record more. Her close association with the wife of the representative of the Victor Recording Company meant to Sharp that she was "dangerous opposition." He now learned that she had recently recorded half a dozen more records, but as they were "only half-ones" (recorded on only one-side), it was a simple matter for Sharp to have them rejected by Victor in favor of his recordings. Sharp took some delight in writing Karpeles that he was able to, as he shamelessly gloated, "settle Miss Burchenal's fate quite completely, so far as the records go."[111]

By mid-1916, Sharp had gained a monopoly on the recording of English folk dance, and the music bore his imprint, both in copyright and in style. By the time of his death in 1924, he had produced a record archive that served as a base for dance groups on both sides of the Atlantic. (The U.S. recordings were released in England only after the war, in 1922 and 1923, and subsequent recordings for the next two decades came mostly from England.) The repertoire of the early recordings replicated Sharp's dependence on Playford dances published in the seventeenth and eighteenth centuries, rather than traditional dances then being done in the pubs and on the greens of English country villages. The sound provided by the military and brass bands, however, was more suited to the early twentieth century. This instrumentation did not mirror the sole sound of the piano one heard at dance classes; nor did additional English recordings in the late 1920s, by orchestras such as the Folk Dance Band and Folk Dance Orchestra, led by musician-dancers (and distinguished composers) from the community such as Vaughan Williams or Imogen Holst.[112]

Most important in the dances recorded was the tempo, the meter and energy that the music conveyed to listener-dancers, a pace that they, in turn, were expected to embody. Tempo was also critical for maintaining a standard for dancing.[113] In this regard, the recordings were vital to the establishment and maintenance of a consistent, national, even transnational, Anglo-American dance style that Sharp could conduct, even from the grave. And the recordings preserved all this information on tape for succeeding generations. The tempi in these early recordings were more than 25 percent faster—typically 136 beats per minute—than those used in the last quarter of the twentieth century. The tempo for "Rufty Tufty," for instance, which the Victor Military Band recorded for Sharp in March 1916, varied between 136 and 138. In contrast, Sharp's 1911 publication of his notation for the dance tune suggested it be played at 124, and the 2006 recording by Bare Necessities, the internationally influential home band for the Boston Centre, played the tune at 108, the standard tempo for Playford-style dances at the end of the twentieth century.[114]

The 1916 orchestration with brass bands enhanced the driving sense of the earlier, faster tempi. For instance, the Victor Military Band's performance of "Rufty Tufty," with a trumpet, clarinet, flute, tuba, and perhaps a euphonia, helped drive dancers, encouraging verticality and forward movement; in contrast, Bare Necessities' more mellifluous version, played by a piano, two violins, and a pennywhistle, encouraged a sprightly but more restrained carriage. Indeed, the music in its orchestration and tempo helps to explain the forward-leaning style seen in photographs and the eight-millimeter film footage from Amherst in 1927. The "running step," in which one danced on the ball of the foot in a well-paced, forward-moving energy, became less frequent in the postwar era; it was a common part of Sharp's reconstruction of these dances and was clearly a usual part of the movement then.

In sum, by the mid-1920s, Sharp and his generally well-heeled acolytes directed the American Branch in New York and Boston and looked outward to further growth across the nation. Whatever pretensions ECD enthusiasts had of their dances' peasant origins, either in England or in Kentucky, groups met in fairly elite urban and suburban (but always urbane) social places inaccessible socially and financially to the working class of the city. They cared deeply about the movement, both as source of their own pleasure and for its larger nationalist role as the embodiment of civilizing values. They also had in place a training program with certificates, summer schools, classes, and their own music to ensure the development of an Anglo-American tradition rooted in "proper" English Country Dance.

The 1927 summer school in Amherst, Massachusetts. Visiting EFDS leadership from London demonstrates the Sharp style of the running step. (Used by permission of the Country Dance and Song Society Archives, www.cdss.org; Milne Special Collections and Archives Department, University of New Hampshire Library, Durham, NH)

To be sure, the movement was relatively small in numbers, but in the years between the wars, it flourished as an Anglo-American transnational folk idiom, though largely as an activity of the more privileged in society. Titled aristocrats presided over twenty-five of the thirty-seven branches in England, and most members were remembered as "leading lights" of a locality. Indeed, Douglas Kennedy recalled that Lady Trevelyan hosted folk dance classes at her Smith Square, Westminster, townhouse.[115] In 1930s New York, the average dancer was of course not titled, nor was she or he as rich as Helen Storrow, but she or he was typically a well-established professional or artist, indeed not so different from Sharp. Gadd described members in 1942 as "photographers, nurses, social workers, artists, musicians, editors . . . , the majority . . . from the professional groups."[116] In fact, the social profile of the typical ECD dancer remained remarkably unchanged through the interwar era in significant other ways as well: in contrast to the heterogeneous ethnic character of the immigrant city, she or he was also white and Anglo-Saxon. In addition, in an era when radical socialist and communist politics punctuated daily life of the metropolis in the Great Depression, the movement, reflecting the conservative liberalism of Sharp, was a nationalist tradition with paternalist/maternalist sentiments at best.

The American Branch

Two incidents were symptomatic of the elite and paternalistic character of the movement in which the folk were a "hobby," not a way of life or political commitment to the downtrodden. In the first case, Cecil Sharp responded to a neighbor who observed him taking down songs from a washerwoman in the Appalachian Mountains around 1917. "You be going to make a deal o' money 'o this, sir?" the neighbor asked. Embarrassed, Sharp was relieved to hear the washerwoman reply, "Oh! It's only 'is 'obby."[117] The second case, from a decade later, involved a complaint from a group of New York Centre members in 1928 that the local branch was not run in a democratic manner. In lieu of making any changes, the response of the branch secretary, Mrs. Blanchard, was to invite disgruntled members to her house for tea.[118]

But the self-conscious upper-class social position of these women and men was only one element of their politics; their ambivalent gender attitudes were another. Roberts, according to her son, "objected to being political," and this was a legacy that ECD carried with it for much of the century. Of course, there was a politics to presuming to be "nonpolitical," and the dance community expressed "a very strong, maternalistic effort" that was an equally important part of its legacy. Roberts was a pacifist and Storrow a "super patriot," but both women were devoted to the Girl Scouts and shared a set of elite, maternalistic class perspectives. Roberts's son described how the influence of philanthropy "shaped the dancing [as] it was emanating from a place in society that . . . directed it towards the upper-class group, or the aspiring upper-class group, and it didn't reach the populace . . . except in a sense when there was a jamboree, or a very large fair." Not surprisingly perhaps, given Sharp's own antipathy, both Storrow and Roberts kept a distance from any suffrage movement that swirled about Wellesley College. Still, the central role accorded to women such as Storrow and Roberts—and notably Louise Chapin and Evelyn Wells from Wellesley—meant that the Boston group functioned in what Ricky Conant described in 1991 (using presentist language informed by second-wave feminism) as "a very woman-centered, women's lib group."[119]

The Times They Are A-Changin'

In 1931, a most interesting and unnoticed harbinger of change occurred inside the ECD movement and, notably, in the musical arena that embodied the traditional spirit of the dance. In 1930, a young thirteen-year-old dancer who had been reared in the Sharp tradition, Patrick (Pat) Noel Shuldham-Shaw (1917–1977), wrote an English Country Dance in the "historical style."

The dance, "Monica's Delight," deployed Playford stepping, choreography, and period music.

But writing a new historical dance directly challenged the meaning and rationale for the revival, which had been based on reconstructing old dances that could instill the spirit of peasant life into modern urban, industrial peoples. Of course, as Georgina Boyes has reminded us, this "peasant" tradition downplayed step-dancing, clogging, Lancashire morris, and much village "traditional" dance to focus on Playford dances.[120] Few if any people at the time, though, understood ECD as an "invented" tradition, and the idea of making one up was audacious if not presumptuous, both to ECD revivalists and to traditional folklorists. Shaw could still presume to capture or "revive" the spirit of the old dance era, but "Monica's Delight" was not a revived dance. The work of this talented and precocious if not presumptuous dancer challenged the idea of folk dance—indeed, were these dances not those of a contemporary dancing folk? And what if dancers enjoyed the new dance, what then? Indeed, many did, and Shaw's work implicitly prefigured an expanded idea of the folk as anyone—not merely peasants—that remained contested in folklore studies for the rest of the century. Shaw's composing also in time stimulated generations of new "modern" ECD choreographers who came to revolutionize ECD as practiced in the twentieth century. Despite Shaw's being born in ECD royalty—his mother, Winifred Holloway Shuldham Shaw, was honorary secretary of the Cecil Sharp Memorial Fund that had raised thirty thousand pounds to build what opened in 1930 as Cecil Sharp House,[121] the EFDS headquarters in London—most of Shaw's dances were published only after his death, by Marjorie Fennessey in the 1980s. In 1931, the idea of writing a modern folk dance in the historical style was an oxymoron and a revolutionary idea whose time had not come. It was, however, a hint of the future.

Other controversial hints of changing times came from outside the ECD movement as well, and from political forces of both the Left and the Right. The American Branch grew and consolidated through the 1930s, but at the same time it became an increasingly narrow social movement of a national dance tradition. The celebration of the folk could invoke the *volk* and support fascism, as it did, for instance, in Nazi Germany. Indeed, a few people in the United States and the United Kingdom took the Anglo-American national projects of Sharp and his American followers into strident nationalist directions. These hypernationalists may have been a distinct minority, but several were important personages in the country dance movement on both sides of the Atlantic. Henry Ford, for instance, extolled the fascist Protocols of Zion, at the same time as he was publishing and teaching "American" country dance in his pioneer "model American" museum at Greenfield Village in Michigan. Meanwhile, in Britain, the iconoclastic English revivalist, folk dance collector, and leader Rolf Gardiner joined Brown Shirts in a Morris Ring celebrating white Anglo culture. Large numbers did not flock to his side, but even if Boyes overstates the case, his views did find a "ready echo" within some of the EFDS community, including for a time with Douglas Kennedy.[122]

Many English Country Dancers were, however, more ecumenical and tolerant of other ethnic cultures, although they often still sustained and privileged ECD as part of what Sharp had unabashedly bragged of as a "superior" national tradition. The investment in this tradition was illustrated, for example, in a public kafuffle around the "Running Set," in which once again Elizabeth Burchenal was at the center. An article in the *Herald Tribune*, provocatively entitled "Two Folk Dance Societies Claim Kentucky Mountain Territory," summarized a passionate exchange that had appeared on its editorial pages. The American Branch highlighted the "Running Set" every year in its annual festival as an "authentic" English Country Dance. In a letter to the editor, Burchenal, who had been the American delegate to the inaugural International Committee on Folk Arts in 1927 and wrote as the president of the American Folk Dance Society, noted that its assertion ignored the Scotch-Irish and German background of many of the settlers. In response, Helen Storrow reclaimed the Englishness of the dance, invoking Sharp as the folk dance authority.[123]

More was at stake in this controversy for the American Branch than the provenance of one dance. Storrow's intervention and persistence may be understood in part as her loyalty to her client and former leader, Cecil Sharp. In a letter a week later, Leonard Elsmith, the president of the American Branch, tried to make peace, offering that each side take "a share in set-running."[124] It was a position that allowed EFDS's American Branch to sustain its paternity claim and the Anglo-American nexus as representative of not just English but also Anglo-American dance. Thus, ECD in the 1930s settled in as a national folk dance tradition with its leaders maintaining, passionately if need be, the foundational story of its Anglo-American peasant origins.

However, during this era an alternative international folk tradition also emerged, and it constituted a different challenge to EFDS's American Branch. The prewar focus on creating "healthy" alternatives for youth in playgrounds and settlements ceased to animate some local ECD leaders; moreover, school and university physical-education teachers interested in teaching English folk dance to their students found that such dances were a distinct minority in the leading texts, only one of many folk dance traditions from which they could draw. Sharp may have dominated record production, but it was Elizabeth Burchenal who published the many highly readable and well-illustrated collections of folk dances from across northern and eastern Europe on which school teachers drew.[125] Emil Rath's 1939 teacher-training textbook offered a typical selection of dances: it contained a handful of English Country Dances and a couple of morris dances, but they were offered alongside fifteen "American" squares and contras, four Indian dances, and over eighty others. Almost half the others were from Scandinavia, but there were multiple offerings from Spain, Mexico, Bohemia, Russia, Hungary, Poland, Germany, Italy, France, Scotland, and Ireland as well.[126]

The international provenance of the dances in these books was not happenstance; rather, it was symptomatic of changing times, coming from broader internationalist challenges inside and outside the folk movement. Folk dances from other countries were not generally part of the repertoire or recreational pastime of English folk dancers, but Sharp, it will be recalled, believed that other ethnic groups needed to set up parallel organizations for other forms of folk dancing, even as he remained convinced such a development would "mean the complete domination by English folk-dancing over all other forms."[127] In the late 1920s, though, Fabians and other artist-intellectuals who were increasingly drawn to the League of Nations and an international peace movement began also to embrace the internationalist culture. Among them were a couple of ECD stalwarts who were to play a leading role in helping to inaugurate a new revival based in international folk traditions.

In 1928, Maud Karpeles led a British delegation to the Congress of Popular Arts that met in Prague under the auspices of the League of Nations. (Burchenal was the American representative.) Never offered a leadership position in EFDSS, Karpeles turned her considerable energies to advancing research in international folk traditions. The inaugural International Folk Dance Festival at Cecil Sharp House that she organized in 1935 compelled EFDSS leaders to rethink the character of its dance. In 1947, an offshoot of the festival emerged as the International Folk Music Conference, an organization for which Karpeles served as honorary secretary or president for the next twenty-odd years.[128]

In the United States, May Gadd, as national director of the American Branch, lent her name to comparable efforts to advance dances from around the world. But whereas EFDSS sponsored the London Folk Festival, in New York, ECD and the international alternative competed for billing. In the spring of 1932, for instance, the New York Centre invited all to its Sixth

Annual Festival at the Park Avenue Seventh Regiment Armory. The Honorary Committee for the event included the British ambassador, Helen Storrow, Mary Simkovitch, Lillian Wald, and Eleanor Roosevelt, among notable others. But three weeks later, folk dance enthusiasts had another folk event to attend: a "Springtime" program sponsored by the twenty-four nationalities who made up the newly formed Folk Festival Council. That evening saw performances of Swedish, Italian, Danish, Bulgarian, Polish, Ukrainian, Hungarian, Estonian, Norwegian, and Czech dances alongside an English maypole demonstration at Broadway's Chanin Theater.[129]

The partial list of patrons for the Folk Council Festival was no less prestigious than that for the ECD program, but it included some notable additions. Governor and Mrs. Franklin D. Roosevelt were joined on the list by pioneering modern dancers Ruth St. Denis, Doris Humphrey, and Martha Graham. These women, though they did not take part in the emerging revolutionary modern dance groups led by women such as Sophie Maslow, Helen Tamaris, or Edith Segal, reflected a new emerging international folk tradition that was at the center of growing left-wing enthusiasm for folk dance. The embrace of International Folk Dance as an affirmation of liberal diversity continued, but special attention must be paid to the Russian revolution's fueling of a more self-consciously left-wing embrace of the folk as a celebration of proletarian internationalism. This movement transformed country dance in the United States and England. In the search for "socially relevant" dance during the Great Depression, these modern dancers began to adopt the "folk" as a metonym for the "worker," in time marrying "bourgeois" and "revolutionary" modern dance.[130]

The presence of these women bespoke the beginnings of a second folk revival in the United States that was to transform "dances from around the world" into "International Folk Dance," a social movement whose internationalism gave it a distinctly liberal or even left-wing political orientation. In the course of the next thirty years, this second revival and its celebration of international folk traditions transformed the history of country dance on both sides of the Atlantic, albeit in quite different ways that set each country's movement on its own trajectory.

The 1937 decision by the leaders of the American Branch to end their formal tie to England and organize as an independent American group was, then, in part a response to their sense that changing times demanded new strategies if they were grow. Leaders such as May Gadd periodically reminded would-be participants that "English folk dancing is by no means limited to those of British descent."[131] Indeed, people of British origin represented a decreasing fraction of the American population, particularly in the groups' urban catchments. Recognizing that any substantial future growth had to look to those who imagined themselves as "Americans" and wanted to invest in the identity—even if a hyphenated one—in 1940 the federation dropped its singular identity as an English dance movement and renamed itself the Country Dance Society (CDS). War was on the horizon, and Americans were increasingly anxious to distinguish their national identity as more inclusive than that of the fascist Axis powers. American and English country dance under one umbrella positioned CDS to appeal to a larger dance community that increasingly had other folk dance options in the city. Elizabeth Burchenal's objections to the American Branch's claims had been ignored; the impact of social movements such as International Folk Dance and the Cold War were not so easy to dismiss.

Part II

Liberalism and Folk Reimaginings

6

The Second Folk Revival

> In this country, English Country Dancing in the '30s and '40s and '50s was definitely an American upper-class snooty activity. It was done at the Metropolitan Club in New York, things like that. . . . It did loosen up in '60s, as many other things did.
> —Gene Murrow, ECD caller and musician, 2000[1]

> I guess we came at it from folk singing actually. We were products of the folk revival of the '60s. . . . We ultimately opened a folk club, and one of the people . . . got interested in this strange ritual called morris dancing. . . . And then we decided to do some country dances. . . . And it's been downhill ever since.
> —Tom Seiss, past president of CDSS, 1999[2]

"Freaks" are destroying conditions in Washington Square Park, wrote Newbold Morris, the New York City commissioner of parks, in March 1961, denying a renewal of the permit to folk sing in the park. "I want to emphasize I am not opposed to the wonderful symphony concerts, bands, quartets or chamber music"; rather, he opposed the "fellows that come from miles away to display the most terrible costumes, haircuts, etc. and who play bongo drums and other weird instruments attracting a weird public."[3] But from the rise of a bohemia in the teens to the beatniks of the fifties, cultural and political radicals had long congregated in the Village and its main park on Washington Square to socialize, organize, and rally; Morris's polemical response to the folk singers reflected something new: a growing culture clash between affluent, middle-class, Anglo-Saxon whites and the young, ethnic denizens of the park. Thus, when a "Right to Sing" protest movement led by Alan Lomax and a new young Village politician, Edward I. Koch (who himself sang in the park and later served the city as its 105th mayor for three terms from 1978 to 1989), held a mass protest demonstration in the park, police met passive resistance with billyclubs in what the press (mis)characterized as a "riot." Although a committee that was formed to protest Morris's denial of their permit to sing in the park won a reversal from Mayor Robert F. Wagner Jr. several months later, notably absent from the controversy was a neighborhood organization with an aligned set of interests, the Country Dance Society of America.[4] May Gadd, national director of CDS, lived only three blocks east of the park, and the society's weekly dance events were held a few blocks further north in the West Village, at Metropolitan-Duane Church at the corner of West 13th Street and Seventh Avenue.

The folk singers and CDS did share some characteristics that distinguished them all from the new migrants to the city from the South and Puerto Rico. Both groups were relatively well-off and mostly "white"—though the folk singers, as white ethnics, had won that identity only as they became more affluent second- and third-generation immigrant Americans. But the two groups were divided by political world views, class, and ethnicity. The folk music spoke to and for a growing political movement committed to social action on civil rights and for nuclear disarmament. With roots in the beatniks and bluegrass, though, the new movement had cultural as well as political dimensions.

In truth, both Newbold Morris and CDS dancers could view the park folkies as "freaks." Morris's social profile and disposition resembled that of the folk dancers at Duane Hall—mostly well-to-do Anglo-American elites—rather than the scruffy folk singers in the park, many of whom were middle-income secular Jews.[5] Morris was a Yale-educated descendant of a wealthy colonial family (the Bronx area of Morrisania was their original fiefdom). CDS's social profile and the outlook of its members were not so different. In 1961, in Boston (where the countercultural scene around Harvard Square mirrored developments in Washington Square Park) and New York—still the two main centers—CDS remained a socially conservative, elite group.[6] Like Morris, the members were liberal on social issues such as race—Morris had taken progressive public positions on controversial civil rights issues—but they remained socially conservative. As important, both Morris and CDS members lived in the shadow of the Cold War, in which association with "reds" was suspect if not dangerous. In addition, to social conservatives, long-haired, "disheveled" New Left radicals and hippies, many of them ethnic Americans, lacked proper social manners.

However, ironically, the social distance between CDS and the folk "freaks" could mask cultural affinities, for they shared interests in country musical idioms. At the same time as folkies in the park sparked the urban development of modern bluegrass, they helped nourish a revival of what the folklorist John Bealle valorizes as "authentic," "old-time" (and antimodern) traditional southern Appalachian music dear to CDS: the music for the "Kentucky Running Set" that Sharp that had "discovered" in 1917 and American contra and squares.[7] Indeed, a decade after the Washington Square Park "riot," some children of the folk participants (and others from similar folkie haunts) migrated into CDS, unleashing a culture conflict within the organization itself and a fundamental shift in its character. But in the United States in 1961, the two movements remained apart. The folkies in the park represented an intermediate moment in the second folk revival that only later came to have an impact on the American Country Dance movement in schooling a generation of young people who moved laterally into ECD in the seventies from a late-sixties contra revival. Significantly, the second revival had an earlier and more direct impact on the Americans' English brethren. The reasons for the difference illustrate once again both the transatlantic character of the twentieth-century folk revivals and how the Cold War and the local political culture of EFDSS and CDS/CDSS took each organization into very different directions.

The twentieth century witnessed two folk revivals, and the markedly different political and social meaning of each for the folk dance movement divides this study. In the second half of the century, the English Country Dance movement took on a new geographical reach and political valence. Geographically, the movement, which had been largely rooted in New York and Boston, became truly transcontinental. As important, though, a new young generation of dancers that was shaped by the postwar folk song and dance revival entered ECD and broadened the ethnic and class base of the community into the professional, white-collar strata. In turn, this series of political and cultural transformations offers a metacommentary on the history of left-liberal political culture at the end of the twentieth century. So while this chapter contrasts the histories of the second revival in both countries, it does so with an eye to the larger focus on ECD and the politics of the folk in the United States.

The two twentieth-century folk revivals were Atlantic World experiences involving the transnational flow of ideas and peoples, but they differed in some fundamental ways. The earlier revival at the turn of the century traveled from the Old World to the New; the second reversed the flow. Originating in the United States, the second revival moved eastward to Britain. But while both revivals established roots in urban dance venues, they did so with different political valences. In the first, revivalists often sought to renovate city life by "educating" immigrants or teaching them to respect their parents' culture and tradition; in the second, revivalists promoted a multidimensional and ever-changing left-liberal "popular" political culture as an alternative to what they saw as a hegemonic, hierarchical, and materialist bourgeois culture.[8]

The second folk revival, which occurred in midcentury, unlike the first, has largely been studied as a music revival, but it transformed dance as well as song.[9] Moreover, it did so with surprisingly different effects on English Country Dance on each side of the Atlantic. Indeed, by the end of the twentieth century, commentary on the distinct styles and trajectories of the country dance on either side of the Atlantic had become commonplace in public dance forums and within each community. In England, people came to English dances as couples and danced with a certain British reserve. American dance etiquette required that dancers regularly change partners, and the style urged eye contact. Most interesting, by the end of the century, many well-traveled and knowledgeable dancers on both sides of the Atlantic came to see Playford-style historical dances as thriving in the United States and languishing in England. This chapter examines the origins of this ironic history in the overlapping but distinct sounds, styles, repertoires, and legacies that emerged out of the differing experience of the second revival in England and the United States.

Folk Song and the Origins of the Second Folk Revival

Historians and folklorists have tended to date the second revival to the late 1950s, when the Newport Folk Festival began and hints of a counterculture emerged in the mobilization of folk music by the civil rights and anti-nuclear-bomb movements.[10] The second revival has a longer history, however, with at least two distinct phases: beginning in the 1930s, the first phase ends in the late 1950s or early 1960s; the second phase, associated with "the Sixties," extends into the early 1970s, although recent historians of folk song carry the revival into what could be considered a third phase during the next decades: a national turn focuses on discovering "roots" in the 1970s (i.e., Celtic, Israeli, Balkan, and other roots) and then on World Music of the 1980s.[11] Regardless of the precise dating, the key is that the Cold War complicates this genealogy, especially in the United States. The second revival transformed the English Country Dance movement in England as early as the mid-1930s, but its effects on ECD were more muted in the United States because of the virulence of the Cold War here. Only when the United States finally emerged from outside the oppressive shadow of the Cold War in the closing years of the second phase did the revival transform English Country Dance in the United States.

The roots of the second revival lie in the interwar years, when radical political culture and new commercial interests in ethnic radio and "race" records combined to stimulate and spread an increased love affair with "common folk."[12] The historian Benjamin Filene's work on prewar "roots music" demonstrates the seminal place of the three Lomaxes—John Lomax and his two sons, John Jr. and Alan—in the awakening of new voices and conceptions of the folk during the Great Depression. In the preceding decade, record companies increasingly popularized vernacular music—cowboy songs collected by the senior Lomax, "hillbilly" music, Negro spirituals, and jazz—and some of the music, especially the jazz, found enthusiastic but select urban audiences in both the American North (the Harlem Renaissance) and London's Soho nightclubs. These infatuations won audiences, but on the whole, the "myth of the British ballad" remained well entrenched as the main repository of "folk" culture.[13]

With the outbreak of the Depression, the stage was set for a renewed interest in the folk with new emphases, and the American folk were at the center of this new revival. In publishing *The American Songbag* in 1926, the renowned poet and biographer Carl Sandburg gave credence to the idea that there was an indigenous American music tradition, and two years later, the appointment of Robert Winslow Gordon as the inaugural director of the Archive of American Folk-Song in the Library of Congress institutionalized this belief in the country's national library. But as important as the American roots of this revival was the reinvigorated cult of authenticity it promoted. To be sure, in Cecil Sharp's debates with Mary Neal and others, each side had advanced its own vision of the "authentic" dancer and referenced or challenged the authority of a dancer-source such as William Kimber. The second revival, however, gave much greater voice to the source than just to the collector. Unlike in Sharp's days, folklorists such as the Lomaxes continued the troubling practice of claiming copyright of songs they "collected," even as they shared the stage with native singers such as Muddy Waters, Jean Ritchie, or "Lead Belly" (Huddie Ledbetter).[14]

The "roots" music and collecting during the 1920s constituted an important prehistory of the second folk revival, but as Filene points out, the cross-country collecting trip of the three Lomaxes in 1933 laid its "groundwork."[15] The Lomaxes' trip, funded in part by both the American Council of Learned Societies and the Library of Congress's Folk-Song Archive, pioneered the use of electronic recording machines in collecting, giving the collectors considerable authority and power in the dissemination of their findings. Ironically, their collecting strategy replicated Sharp's belief in how the Anglo origins of the "Running Set" had been "preserved" in pristine "backwoods" settlements. On the assumption that prisoners' isolation from corrupting commercial pressures would have helped "preserve" their music, the Lomaxes focused on recording black singers in prisons. This belief took them to Louisiana's Angola Prison, where they "discovered" the man who was to shape the American folk music revival: Lead Belly. Lead Belly became the best known of the coterie of "authentic" folk singers given voice by collectors such as the Lomaxes and Woody Guthrie. Subsequently, folk singers such as Pete Seeger and the groups for which he was a lead singer, the Almanac Singers and the Weavers, popularized their songs (such as Lead Belly's "Goodnight, Irene") and inspire a generation of urban folk singers.[16]

The revival sound was characterized by its music, both in the twang and down-home intonations of singers and in the instrumentation and rhythms. Folk music was the umbrella term for a series of musical traditions with southern, western, and mountain country roots that came together in a folk-jazz-blues triad. The music incorporated aspects of earlier jazz music with ballads, folk songs of social significance, cowboy songs, blues music (e.g., Muddy Waters), and the gospel songs that accompanied civil rights protest. In contrast to the "authentic" music sung by native singers, bluegrass was a high-energy, modern ensemble form that gained enormous popularity during the 1950s with five- and six-member bands accompanying songs on acoustic guitars, mandolins, banjos, and dulcimers or autoharps. Bluegrass instrumentation and tunes bore a family resemblance to southern mountain music, but the band gave the music its own character, and like many of the folk songs of this era, bluegrass musicians freely wrote new "folk" tunes. Categorized by record stores as Country/Western Music until 1960, bluegrass and "old-time" music coexisted uneasily in the next decade as two strains in a second revival phase and fueled new interest from the counterculture in country music and dance. "Folk" in this new revival became a modern idiom based on an imagined past with a rural or country tradition, and the city folkies became the folk.[17]

The folk music movement—collectors, singers, musicians, and enthusiasts—in pressing the "authenticity" of its sources, romanticized and exoticized singers from the mountains, as Filene and others have pointed out. But how folklorists, "folkies," performers, and commercial producers of records and concerts constructed and patrolled definitions of "the folk" always riddled folk revival controversies, and continued do so. More important to the particular character of the second revival folk project than its "authenticity" were its left-liberal politics, the political values of a spectrum of groups that spanned liberalism and radicalism with different permutations and connections at different times.

Among the most distinguishing characteristics of the revival's politics was its "internationalism." Revival events featured international folk singing or dancing—that is, though songs and dances had national origins, they were sung, danced, or performed as part of international events, where they shared the stage or floor with dances or songs "from many lands." In fact, the audience as a nonnational conglomerate was crucial: people sang *other people's* songs, and significantly, in doing so the song became transnational or international, a song of the "common man [sic]."

The roots of the left-wing core of the second revival lay in the interwar years. Radicals, who had looked to Russia ever since the Russian Revolution of 1917 for alternatives to capitalist culture, saw the international proletarianism of folk cultures as an inspiration and source for nurturing "Socialist Man [sic]." Folk song and dance became an integral part of a radical alternative socialist culture. By day, left-wing socialists and communists organized and protested, whether in cotton fields and mills of the South or in the steel, auto, or garment factories of the industrial city; at night, they took inspiration from, built unity with, and relaxed listening to the records of folklorists such as Alan Lomax and Woody Guthrie, or they sang along with the songs of "the people," of the same rural and urban working class for whom they fought by day. The coming of the Great Depression only quickened radical Americans' commitments to the "common man," a person who bore a family resemblance to the figure at the heart to the New Deal imaginary, FDR's "forgotten man."

The midcentury folk revival that emerged in both Britain and the United States in response to the Great Depression was, then, the cultural side of socialist and communist social and political movements. In contrast to the first revival, it included a fundamental left-wing celebration in song and dance (and other cultural forms) of the dispossessed or, in more orthodox terms, of the proletariat. Much like the first revival, it gave voice and body to the cultural legacy of peasant traditions as pristine and uncorrupted by the materialism and decadence associated with urban life. (Of course, this idea had long fueled a nationalist context for celebration of the folk as carriers of national heritage, for which Nazi National Socialist claims of the purity of *volk* were an alternative to the communists' internationalist celebration of the same songs and dances.) In the United States, folk singers such as Pete Seeger and the Weavers, Lead Belly, Woody Guthrie, Burl Ives, and the Almanac Singers all spawned a new revival of what Seeger tellingly called "songs of social significance." Published in *The People's Songbook* and monthly editions of *Sing Out!* a few were the old English ballads that the folklorist and Harvard professor Francis James Child had first "discovered" in archives in the 1880s; others were Wobblie labor songs written by Joe Hill and others in the opening decades of the century and now recycled for a new Congress of Industrial Organizations (CIO) labor movement; others still were spirituals, "hillbilly" songs from the mountains (and not British ballads), and "common people's" songs of work, protest, love, struggle, and survival. And still others were new songs of protest written for ongoing social movements for peace, civil rights, and social justice. The songs, then, were more than clarion calls for the labor movement: they were the revivalist spirit for the cultural critic Michael Denning's "cultural front," a left-liberal social movement that extended, for instance, to summer camps, hootenannies, and in time, to the civil rights and antiwar peace movements of the 1950s and 1960s.[18]

Of course, much of the second revival did not fit so neatly into either radical or liberal camps, and many revival groups were more equivocal and expressed a contradictory hybrid of a left-liberalism. The International Folk Music Council, for instance, an offshoot of the League of Nations, was a social-democratic forum that attracted, on the one hand, people such as May Gadd, Elizabeth Burchenal, and Maud Karpeles, who avoided taking public political positions and were quite conservative socially, and on the other hand, activist folksingers such as Pete Seeger and Burl Ives and folklorists such as Charles Seeger and Alan Lomax. The groups' annual meetings radiated a Fabian socialism that spoke more of peace, friendship, and understanding than of anticapitalist economic restructuring.[19] The cultural production of the Popular Front in the late 1930s occupied a similarly anomalous left-liberal political space.[20] Folk song and dance at the left-wing overnight camps was unequivocally internationalist, but other cultural expressions—murals sponsored by the Works Progress Administration or "Left" modern dance based on folk motifs—could be polemical political statements, more moderate gestures in alternative forms, or national celebrations.

Composers such as Ralph Vaughan Williams in England and Charles Ives, Aaron Copland, and Ira Gershwin in the United States turned to folk song to inform the spirit of classical music (e.g., in *Appalachian Spring, Ode to the Common Man,* and *Porgy and Bess*). Similarly, in modern dance, choreographers reflected the gamut of possible political invocations of the folk. At one end of the spectrum were radical dancers such as Edith Segal, who the historian Victoria Geduld notes "was inspired by the CPUSA agitprop department in the 1920s." Segal had several troupes, and the more professional dancers did agit-prop "modern" dance (workers at work and in struggle), while folk dancers met in other dance groups. Other choreographers, such as Sophie Maslow and Helen Tamaris, also used the folk to express political protest but ultimately paid for their choice in the next decade: they were blacklisted (Maslow from mainstream television) or kept from any government funding opportunities (e.g., postwar State Department tours discussed later in this chapter). Their experience contrasted with that of the "queens of using folk in high modernist/theatrical forms": Agnes de Mille and Martha Graham. They used highly trained professional bodies to perform highly abstract folk themes (as in *Rodeo* and *Appalachian Spring*) to celebrate the nation. While Maslow and Segal were debunked, ignored, or persecuted in the Cold War, Graham was awarded the Presidential Medal of Honor, and de Mille was tapped to be a cultural ambassador for the State Department.[21] In sum, while some cultural expressions were radical and oppositional, others were reformist and, like Earl Robinson's modern folk cantata "Ballad for Americans," could be a uniquely alternative form of American nationalism.[22]

The International Folk Dance movement also varied and, significantly, tended to be more liberal and less unequivocally populist and internationalist than the folk song movement, although the commodified form of the revival that moved forward from the late 1960s encompassed liberalism in folk song as well. However, in the United States during the Cold War—and in contrast to the British experience—the liberal version of internationalism that characterized much of the dance revival movement had special resonance, for it often served a nationalist agenda that the left-wing version eschewed. Liberal revival groups or individuals, often claiming to be nonpartisan or nonpolitical, celebrated the diversity of song and dance they performed as a testimony to uniquely American pluralism and democracy—a version of American exceptionalism that was popularly advanced by anticommunist liberal cold warriors. In the Cold War climate of the postwar United States, those trying to distance themselves from the radical side of the second revival, which had strong communist and left-wing socialist affinities, welcomed this liberal safe haven.[23]

In the United States, ECD was one such safe haven until the late 1960s. Only then did newcomers come out of the folk dance revival and into country dance, and in doing so, they reshaped the social profile, values, and traditions in the ECD community. The legacy of International Folk Dance, then, bears special attention, both for the impact it came to have and for the fact that in the immediate postwar era, International Folk Dance was the path that English Country Dancers in the United States, as part of a national dance tradition, for the most part *did not take*.

International Folk Dance

While the internationalism of the second revival was, for the most part, populist and left-wing in song, it had both liberal and radical political expressions in dance that had historical precedents. Through the mid-1930s, the dances that were to become the International Folk Dance repertoire were taught and performed as "character" or ethnic dance. Folk dance teachers such as Louis Chalif, Elizabeth Burchenal, and Mary Wood Hinman (who left Chicago for New York in the 1930s to take a leading role in teaching folk dances "of many lands" in settlements) did not present these dances as international expressions of a common peasant or "common people's" experience so much as windows into rich national cultures, much in the mode of the International Folk Music Council. The New York City Board of Education recommended Chalif's four 1914 dance texts, and Burchenal and Hinman organized folk festivals with dances from many lands across the country during the first third of the century.[24] The New York Folk Festival Council—the 1931 brainchild of Elba Gursay, an Italian folk dancer, and the Foreign Language Information Council—was also not an "International Dance" per se, as each group performed dances from only its "own" land; it was an international *occasion* in that different ethnic dance groups from across the city came together and demonstrated their dances to one another. Indeed, audience complaints that they wanted to dance rather than just to observe transformed the occasion in the next years. Audiences began to dance "other people's" dances, and the event became fundamentally an "International Dance."[25] The coming of the Depression and the rise of the "cultural front" enhanced this new meaning of the dances as an expression of "international proletarianism." And in the shift of both practice and meaning, International Folk Dance became the dance centerpiece of a second folk revival.

The International Folk Dance movement emerged in three different urban centers across the United States in the 1930s—San Francisco, Chicago, and New York—to become the dance core of a social movement. The ethnomusicologist Mirjana Lausevic has described the leading roles played by three men, two immigrants and an immigrant son, in developing the American International Folk Dance movement. All three men experienced discrimination in their lives, and the movement they built was characterized as both participatory and inclusive, both of dancers and national dance traditions. In Chicago, the movement was led by Vytrutus ("Vyts") Beliajus (1908–1994), a Lithuanian American who immigrated to the United States in 1923. Beliajus seems to have been introduced to international dance at Chicago's settlement houses, but it was New Deal programs that spurred his programmatic work. Hired by the city's Park District to teach folk dance in 1936, he edited the folk dance magazine *Lore* as a WPA project. The years between 1937 and 1940 found him touring and teaching International Folk Dance at over two hundred universities, colleges, and institutions, establishing the base for a national and regional International Folk Dance movement.[26]

In San Francisco, where the movement took root in California, the leading figure was Song Chang, who the local folk dance journal as early as 1944 described as "the father of the folk dance movement in the west." Chang, who may have been introduced to folk dancing on a boat traveling from Germany to France around 1930, came by internationalism naturally: a Chinese immigrant who had lived in Europe, his wife, Harriet, about whom little else is known, was Scandinavian. Settling in San Francisco in the 1930s, he hooked up with a Swedish group, and after an enthusiastic reception greeted his teaching a range of Scandinavian dances on his honeymoon voyage to China, he resolved to start a recreational group in the city. International dances had long been taught in area schools, colleges, and community centers—the legacy of folk dance as a missionary activity—and he felt the need to create a "public" site where all people could come together to dance voluntarily as a recreational and social experience. As important, in the spirit of the era, he wanted to break down the national barriers in ethnic dance (indeed, ethnic groups constantly worried that international dance groups would butcher their dances) and organize on a "true democratic basis." In contrast to the insular and narrow social profile of the ECD communities on both sides of the Atlantic at the time, and inspired by the efforts of the New York Folk Council, Chang wanted to create a "democratic" public dance venue.[27]

Chang's International Folk Dancers began in 1938 with a small group of writers, artists, and artisans. The Treasure Island World's Fair in 1939 stimulated further interest in International Folk Dance and jump-started what became a West Coast social movement. By 1942, the Folk Dance Federation of California had formed with an "authoritative" repertoire, dance camps, training sessions, and new groups scattered throughout the Bay Area, and Chang's dance group remained a major focus for northern California International Folk Dance until the mid-1960s.[28]

Beliajus and Chang played major regional roles in the development of a nationwide International Folk Dance movement, but the "father" of this movement in the United States was New York's Michael Herman. Born in Cleveland in 1910 of Ukrainian parents, Herman was reared on ethnic dance. Herman and his wife, Mary Ann, with whom he spearheaded International

The Second Folk Revival | 171

Folk Dance in New York, were both active in the New York Ukrainian community and in the late 1930s began to join other ethnic dance groups, notably Danish and French, to learn their repertoire. Together they built a movement: they created and taught a repertoire, they brought an enthusiasm and standard of excellence to the practice, and they institutionalized the dancing at their Folk Dance House.

Much as the World's Fair in San Francisco had helped kindle International Folk Dance on the West Coast, the New York World's Fair of 1939 stimulated international dance for Herman on the East Coast. Herman's reputation as a folk dance leader won him an invitation in 1940 from a Folk Festival Council leader to teach folk dance on the "American 'Common.'" The space was dedicated to "nationality days"—the liberal nationalist idea—but Herman took the opportunity to introduce International Dance sessions and, significantly, as participatory events, not performances. Building on the momentum from the dances, in which Herman estimated over five thousand people took part, he rented a room in the Ukrainian National Hall on East 6th Street on the Lower East Side and on October 15, 1941, held the inaugural session of his Community Folk Dance Center. That year, adopting the model of the EFDS summer schools, the Hermans also held the first International Folk Dance camp in West Virginia, and in March 1941, they began the publication of *The Folk Dancer*. (Chang's magazine with the same title had begun a month earlier, but the two coasts were worlds apart then.) The camp later moved to Maine, where the Hermans continued to run it for the next four decades, and in 1951, they opened on Sixth Avenue and 16th Street what American enthusiasts came to view as the citadel of International Folk Dance in the United States: Folk Dance House.[29]

Thus, the folk dance movement that emerged in the wartime and postwar eras was a complex folk village with many houses. The *New York Times* listing of "folk dance events" in New York for a week in November 1941 is illustrative. It announces sixteen different sessions, with decidedly different venues and, presumably, audiences. The listings for Monday, Friday, and Saturday suggest that the social geography of the dance community had class boundaries. On Monday, Italian folk dancers met at the YWCA on East 17th Street, while two blocks away on East 15th Street another group met to do "general folk dancing." A third group, led by Gene Gowing, inaugurated a new series of weekly ECD and American squares in Rockefeller Center's Rainbow Room. On Friday, Michael Herman's group met at Arlington Hall on St. Mark's Place in the Village, while May Gadd's CDS group offered an evening of American squares called by Adrian Hall at Steinway Hall on West

International Folk Dancing, ca. 1950. A line dance snakes around the room (a gymnasium). The "authentic" costuming was Balkan, though the dance could have been Greek or Balkan. (Used by permission of the Country Dance and Song Society Archives, www.cdss.org; Milne Special Collections and Archives Department, University of New Hampshire Library, Durham, NH)

57th Street. The Scottish Country Dance Society met two blocks to the north on 59th Street. Finally, on Saturday there were four sessions for beginners and more advanced international or "general" folk dancers, ranging from Elizabeth Burchenal's session at the Folk Arts Center in Midtown at 650 Fifth Avenue to those at the YWCA and Steinway Hall. CDS held sessions of "mostly English Dances" on Saturday as well, at a hall in the Russell Sage Foundation building on East 22nd Street.[30]

The many venues for International Folk Dance meant that there was an evening that might appeal to almost anyone's particular social or political inclination, whether it was liberal, radical, or some hybrid formation. The variation and possible political overlaps could, for instance, be seen in the contradictory messages involved in Herman's World's Fair dances. As Lausevic has noted in her study of the roots of International Folk Dance, Herman's celebration of internationalism at a time of world disunity held great irony: "the American Common was created by the Soviet Union's withdrawal from the Fair with the outbreak of the Second World War, and as an ideological Cold War paean to 'democracy' against totalitarianism." One did ethnic dances, Lausevic points out, as Americans.[31] Thus, the celebration of diversity (what a later generation called multiculturalism) and nationalism underpinned the appeal of International Dance to both liberal and conservative participants.

But, of course, the New York World's Fair experience was not the whole story. Lausevic has described the significant local and regional differences: California's movement was more oriented toward teaching and performance than the New York or Chicago groups, for instance. The East and Midwest cities also drew on larger white ethnic communities, and New York had a strong left-wing community with roots in Left secular Jewish culture. It is important, though, not to allow the domestic nationalism of the Cold War International Folk Dance movement to obscure the more left-liberal meaning of International Folk Dance for many of its proponents, especially in East Coast cities such as New York, where ECD was also headquartered. Although some dancers belonged to more than one group, those in the wartime and postwar eras for whom International Folk Dance became a passion chose it rather than join an ethnic national group. International Folk Dance was populist, although dancers could be liberal or radical or Popular Front or communist or social democratic. Herman's appreciation that "all walks of life" and "every nationality and race was represented" at the World's Fair dances was a radical commentary on class and racial inclusion, even if it was somewhat overstated.[32]

Chang's Chinese heritage testifies to the diversity of the movement, and it did encourage ethnic inclusiveness, but photographs, oral history, and available data suggest that the racial and class social profile of the movement was, with some important differences, remarkably similar to that of the ECD community. First, although both communities had few if any dancers of African American, Hispanic, or Asian background, the "whiteness" of the international community was "colored" by the presence of large numbers of white ethnics, who only more recently had "become" white.[33] Second, a 1946 survey conducted among 117 California Federation dancers attending a folk festival found the occupations of dancers to be white-collar workers and predominantly professionals and semiprofessionals. The surveyor did suggest that the questionnaire may have had a bias because semiunskilled and unskilled workers known to be in the dance community may have chosen not to respond. Of those responding, clerks, engineers, teachers and professors, chemists, and secretaries constituted the largest number, although the crowd also included students, housewives, students, and three carpenters.[34] By 1950–51, the California Federation reported that it had forty to fifty thousand members—a number that included ethnic and international dancers—suggesting that the social base of the American folk dance community during this pre-1960s era was generally broader and more democratic than the ECD community. No folk dance group seemed to have many industrial workers, but the second folk revival also increasingly brought people from the growing middle class into its ranks.[35] Thus, while International Folk Dance was a more varied political expression than folk song in this first half of the second revival, it provided an alternative racial, class, and transnational experience to that of the dominant American political culture. Henry Glass, the first president of the Folk Dance Federation of California, captured the fundamental populist spirit of the dance community: International Folk Dance was a "chance to live brotherhood."[36]

Populist sentiment was the broadest expression of the International Folk Dancers, but their ranks also included a significant left-wing cadre with more formal political affiliations and programmatic interests. Left-wing groups of International Folk Dancers, many made up of communist and left-socialist sympathizers, if not party members, constituted a vital core of the International Dance community. The left-wing community was not without its contradictions, however. Committed to social justice, ideals of world peace, and brotherhood, their identification with the peasantry as a socially redemptive force meant that the cult of authenticity in the International Folk Dance community led to frequent obsessions with costumes and styling. And as was so often the case among those transmitting folk traditions across time and generations, the imagined folk bore a less precise relationship to the peasantry than acknowledged. Moreover, while the left-wing dance community also spoke of equality and cooperation, the dance floor was a competitive and hierarchical space where leaders and "experts" held and expected to be given pride of place.[37]

Still, left-wing International Folk Dance groups offered a distinct alternative vision of social relations and political engagement to that proffered by either the dominant Cold War culture or the more elite ECD community. By day, International Folk Dancers organized trade unions, led rent strikes, and dreamed of socialism as they imagined it was being built in the Soviet Union; at night, they joined together at one another's homes or in left-wing resorts in the Catskill Mountain region such as Camp Unity, Camp Nitge

Daiget ("I Don't Worry"), Chester's, Crystal Lake, Arrowhead Lodge, Camp Kinderland, White Lake Lodge, and Nature Friends to sing "songs of social significance" and do International Folk Dance.[38] And in the summer, they sent their children to radical overnight camps where Pete Seeger and other left-wing folksingers would lead them in song one evening, and counselors would bring them together to folk dance another. In this way, the "romance of American communism" was embedded in the romance of the folk and the romance of International Folk Dance.[39] These groups celebrated in their dances the shared struggle of the oppressed and dispossessed—the common man—as, to borrow the title of a film that they admired at the time, the "salt of the earth." Surviving and struggling outside mainstream culture during the Cold War, folk dance events drew left-wing partisans together in a supportive alternative culture that, in welding them together for the fight for social justice, was also oppositional.[40]

A select few country dances, including some English dances, were part of the International repertoire, of course. Most children learned "Turkey in the Straw" and "The Virginia Reel" in school, and International Folk Dance leaders frequently also programmed the Scottish dance "Road to the Isles," the longways English dance from 1696, "The Hole in the Wall," and the traditional couples dance done in a circle, "St. Bernard's Waltz."[41] Beyond those, little English dance was done. The fact of the matter is that International Dance and the politics of "brotherhood" and internationalism was the path *not* taken by ECD participants on either side of the Atlantic. EFDS and CDS members were decidedly more conservative socially and politically than those attracted to International Folk Dance. The more apolitical public stances of ECD dance leaders inoculated them from the very public anticommunist attacks and persecutions suffered by folk song icons such as Paul Robeson and Pete Seeger, but the chilling effect of the Cold War still made any association with the International Folk Dance community suspect. Indeed, folk dancers per se were not persecuted and blacklisted, but folk dance venues—clubs, resorts, camps, and union halls, many of which in the United States were forced to close during the McCarthy era—were frequented by folk dancers and their friends who were attacked and persecuted.[42] In this context, EFDS and CDS dance halls were "safe spaces," and both groups stuck with their national tradition through most of the second revival.

The second revival in dance did play a role in shaping ECD, however. The impact was made, though, as much by the revival of another dance movement that had a tangential relation to the second folk revival—square dancing—as by International Dance. Square dancing as it revived in the late 1930s and took off in the next two decades shared little of the Left political spirit at the heart of the second folk revival; it was a nationalist movement in keeping with the patriotic temper of the war and Cold War eras. In any case, though it blossomed on both sides of the Atlantic, it altered the ECD dancing body and repertoire quite differently in England and in the United States.

The Second Folk Dance Revival in England

In England, American square dance transformed the postwar country dance scene, but not before International Folk Dance had left its mark. The expressive difference between ECD and other nations' dances was quickly apparent at the inaugural International Folk Festival in 1935 at Cecil Sharp House, to one important observer in particular. Douglas Kennedy, the director of EFDSS, was enthralled by the liveliness of European "peasant" dances. There was a "fire" in the folk dance performances from abroad that Kennedy recalled "set fire to the ambition of the English dancers." Part of the problem with the less energetic British style he attributed to British "reserve": "a wonderful economy and dignified reserve hid the latent fire" in English dance, although he acknowledged that "latent fire" was more prominent in sword and morris dance. Kennedy understood and appreciated Sharp's responsibility for what had emerged as the English "style" as part of his "educational mission," his concern with propriety and "dressing up the dance" for his Edwardian middle-class market and classroom.[43] But, in 1964, writing twenty years after the event, Kennedy concluded that the International Folk Festival had a transformative effect. "Everyone," he noted, had a new picture of an English dance form and of the linkage with folk customs of a vast antiquity."[44] Indeed, in the years to come, Kennedy drew on the "new picture" he had from the festival to reshape the content and spirit of ECD in England in unique ways that distinguished it from the sound and spirit of its American cousins for the rest of the century.

The reshaping of ECD did little, however, to reconstitute the social profile of the EFDSS dance community. As noted in the previous chapter, the dance community in England remained liberal, at most; some of its leading members, such as Kennedy, were in fact quite conservative, and in the case of Gardiner even reactionary. On the whole, EFDSS was elitist and professional, its leadership patriarchal, and its exclusiveness de facto continued to make it inhospitable to the working class.[45] As important, the dance movement in particular was nationalistic and patriotic. Scottish and Irish balladeers and folk singers such as the Clancy Brothers and Tommy Makem could share the stage with English balladeers in the late 1950s and 1960s, but "Englishness" had little appeal to the Irish or Scottish dancers who had developed their own separate dance movements.[46] Thus, the International Folk Dance Festivals in the 1950s reshaped the spirit and vision of the dance tradition and the dancing body, but it did not internationalize or democratize EFDSS political culture. In addition, while Cecil Sharp House became the center of all folk dance in England and hosted ethnic dance groups and vernacular dance sessions (tango, flamenco, Cajun, etc.), as the home of the national cultural dance tradition, English Country Dance retained pride of place in its programming and publicity.

Square Dancing

The class and political profile of the British dance community did not change dramatically in the wake of the International Folk Dance festivals, but the introduction of square dancing did enhance the role of community dance in the wartime and postwar eras. As important, community and square dance fundamentally changed what EFDSS came to understand by English Country Dance in England. At the same time, Kennedy introduced new policies about gender balance at dances that had a profound impact on gender relations in the British dance community and, in years to come, on the age and marital composition of the dance community as well.

As Kennedy moved to light his "fire" under English Country Dance, the social impact of World War II on EFDSS complicated his task. The catastrophic loss of young men in World War I had been a profound shock to the fledgling English folk dance movement, decimating Sharp's demonstration team, for example. The impact of World War II on EFDSS was equally difficult, although it less affected the leadership of the movement than the reconstitution of the dance community. The deaths of many young men in World War II again left the English dance community with a dramatic gender imbalance, a serious problem for a coupled dance form in a heteronormative society. The shortage of men was an unintended boon for some women who rose to positions of leadership in the dance communities on both sides of the Atlantic (although as noted earlier, there is little evidence that female leadership made the dance community more populist or gender-neutral). But the persistence of a traditional gender ideology in EFDSS that privileged men (as directors and morris dancers, for example)[47] limited women's ascendance into the dance leadership, especially after World War II. Kennedy's response to the gender imbalance further complicated women's gains.

Through most of the twentieth century, many British women may have been reluctant to go to a dance on their own; others interested in finding a male partner, whether for the evening or for life, would have been disappointed. Kennedy was not concerned with their emotional life, however; rather, the imbalance occasioned by the lack of men undermined his traditional view of couple dancing. Attendance had steadily declined over the course of the 1930s, even with the amalgamation of the English dance and song societies, and he worried that the specific decline in the presence of men, which quickened with the war, threatened the future of the country dance movement. Accordingly, in 1944, Kennedy instituted a "couples only" policy for social dance; he was quite content to have ceremonial morris or sword dance be all male. With Kennedy's new policy in effect, ECD in Great Britain increasingly became a coupled evening, with a problematic legacy for the future of the dance community.[48]

The attendance problem was more than a gender issue, however, and Kennedy looked to make other changes in the character of the dance that might excite new members. In this regard, Atlantic crossings of the second folk revival, this time with a tilt eastward from the United States to England, played a major part both in reviving the British folk scene and, ultimately, in addressing further "the men problem."

One set of crossings came from the American military, which brought another aspect of the revival with it: square dance. Douglas and Helen Kennedy, returning from a dance tour in the United States, had introduced square dancing in England in 1938, but the presence of as many as two million American soldiers on British soil during the war created a new audience and demand for square dance.[49] The American military sponsored square dances for its soldiers stationed in England, events that required a regular pool of English girls and the military men, and square dancing made a lasting impression on many villages. "[A] number of villages have been attached to certain forms of the square dance," noted May Gadd during her annual visits back home, "because their particular soldiers called them that way."[50] The energetic pace of the square dance, its relative lack of precise styling beyond footwork, and its pulsating music met Kennedy's new enthusiasm for dances with "fire." So, at the same time as he introduced the couples-only policy in 1944, Kennedy inaugurated a series of Saturday-night square dances at Cecil Sharp House. To make the music more "alive," Kennedy formed a quartet with his wife, Helen, and a Hampstead couple, the Fleming-Williamses. Kennedy played the side drum, Helen played the concertina, and the couple played a guitar and fiddle. And for the next twenty years—with Kennedy, in the American style, "calling" the dances—the band became a regular presence at Sharp House dances.[51]

With the end of the war, EFDSS imported American callers and musicians to spread the square dance message. In another irony, the American caller who arrived every spring for most of a decade starting in 1947 was no less than New York's May Gadd, Sharp's English-born protégé. Teaming with New York's country dance music leader, Phil Merrill, Gadd taught square dancing throughout West Surrey and Sussex as well as in London as part of an EFDSS "experimental scheme" to attract new dancers and more men. Two local leaders from the North East Hants area were "keen" that the "new revival should be in the name of Square Dancing—as any reference to a Folk Dance course would keep away just the people [they] most wanted."[52] The report by the field agents for the "experiment," Kathleen Church-Bliss (later Atkins) and Elsie Whiteman, was more explicit: the events were advertised simply as "Dances," "without any mention of the word 'Folk,'" acknowledging that "a certain number of people are put off by the word."[53]

The "experimental scheme" met with halting success. Equal numbers of men and women were allowed into the dances, but that did not avoid embarrassing events such as the evening in March 1950 when a Sandhurst Group session attracted a full hall of one hundred women paired with only "three men and two boys." "We seemed to have slipped back 20 years," bemoaned Church-Bliss and Whiteman.

Shortly after the Sandburg embarrassment, however, a dramatic piece of news arrived from Ottawa, Canada, that hastened the flow of men as well as women into square dancing. As part of an official 1951 state visit, Government House in Ottawa arranged a Canadian Square Dance Party for Princess Elizabeth and Prince Philip. The next day, a newspaper photograph appeared throughout the British press of an obviously delighted princess and prince. The photo and the dance boom that followed brought people—including men—back to Cecil Sharp House in droves, with "people queuing up down the road to get into dances, to do square dances at Cecil Sharp House." According to Nicolas Broadbridge, an English choreographer, musician, and dancing master living in Scotland, whose family played a leading role in British ECD for most of the century, the photograph "determined" the tenor of English Country Dancing for some time to come. He also notes the prominence of London in shaping the tradition:

> That [photograph] really determined which way the society was going to go for a little while after the square dance boom, and everybody wanted

to perform those kind of dances and do those kind of dances. Cecil Sharp House, at the time, was the only place really. Since the '50's there's been a burgeoning of folk clubs and places to dance all over the country. But in London, really, this was the place to come, and there would be queues all down the road. If you didn't get to Cecil Sharp House an hour before a dance began you may not get in, which is quite something actually.[54]

The new prominence of London was not coincidental and bespoke an evolving sense of Englishness. The wartime blitz had given London and the everyday soldier a new place in the British imaginary as a symbol for the English "fighting spirit." Thus, while square dancing in England took on the characteristics of the imagined English village, the crowds lining up to get into Cecil Sharp House in London gave a new geographic and class resonance to Englishness.

The Royal Barn Dance. The Duke of Edinburgh square dancing with Princess Elizabeth at Ottawa House, October 17, 1951. (Photographer: Keystone; used by permission, Hulton Archive, Getty Images)

The Second Folk Revival

Moreover, in the folk tradition of evolving forms, British square dancers developed their own English variant of an American dance. Thus, a Canadian girl who had done square dancing with American soldiers during the war commented that, dancing for the first time at a local dance in Sussex, she found the "English tempo . . . slower and dancing less intense."[55] American squares and contras were danced with U.S. and U.K. inflections on each side of the Atlantic, and in time, these variants became part of the larger difference in the way English Country Dance came to be understood and experienced differently in the latter half of the twentieth century on either side of the Atlantic.[56]

Community ("Traditional") Dance

In Kennedy's drive to add "fire" to English Country Dancing, he made a second decision that equally reshaped the English Country Dance: he determined that British evenings should place less emphasis on the more fussy Playford style and more on kick-up-your-heels village reels, jigs, and hornpipes. While the desire to infuse more energy into the dancing undoubtedly motivated his policy, the action also afforded Kennedy, long in Sharp's shadow, an opportunity to put his own stamp on the history of English folk dance. Personal motives aside, Kennedy believed that "traditional" English dance—jigs, hornpipes, and reels still (or more recently) being done in the countryside—could do the same double duty as American squares in instilling "fire" in the English Country Dance scene and attracting men to ECD. Ironically, of course, Sharp had begun by collecting traditional dances being danced in the West Country at the turn of the century. His decision to focus on deciphering, notating, and publishing the old "historic" dances from the Playford volumes was a second move. By the early 1940s, Kennedy had come to believe that EFDSS, following Sharp, had placed undue emphasis on the historical dances, many of which he thought reflected eighteenth-century gentry formalism and were too elaborate, uniform, overstudied, and stylized. To Kennedy, the Playford dances expressed little of the spirit that Sharp imagined as "peasant." So, just as the BBC and EFDSS began to promote renewed collecting and archiving of indigenous village dances, Kennedy pushed EFDSS to focus on traditional dance. Thus, down-playing Playford historical dances, Kennedy remade the typical country dance evening and with it the British ECD tradition. And to make it all possible he produced the *Community Dance Manual* (*CDM*), seven edited volumes of traditional dances that include American contras, squares, mixers, and waltzes. To this day, the *CDM* remains the bible for those who teach community dance.

Kennedy's changes—the couples-only policy, the deemphasis on the older historical dances, and the new focus on American squares and community dances—had uneven results. The changes coincided with a modest 10 percent increase in membership in 1946; however, increased opportunity for leisure with the end of the war might well have accounted for the additional interest in recreational dance.[57] The photo of Princess Elizabeth dancing brought many new dancers into square dancing in the 1950s, but so did the quickening song and dance revival, which drew on the new community dance repertoire. Thus, although the 1950 Sandhurst dance with virtually all-women attendance may have been a disaster at gender balance, Church-Bliss and Whiteman took solace in the positive effect of the new dance curriculum. They noted that the quality of dancing improved over the course of the evening because the dance had been "infiltrated" by members of the Reading Group, "who are converted to the more rational modern style"—Kennedy's new emphasis on "traditional" rather than Playford-style dance.[58]

Kennedy's new policies left some longtime members disaffected, most likely especially some single women. One south county group's "fierce" opposition to Kennedy's policies is illustrative. As Church-Bliss reported to Kennedy, the group did not approve of "the Society's present policy and were sure Mr. Sharp wouldn't either." They objected to all the new dances, wanting a return to the older repertoire, and they "resented Couple Events." Writing a "fierce letter" to the head of the Reconstruction Fund for Cecil Sharp House, which had suffered a direct hit during the blitz, the group withdrew its financial support from EFDSS, refusing to subscribe to the fund. In truth, there is no clear picture of the depths of disaffection with Kennedy's policy, but many single women without partners and longtime dancers had reason to be angry. Kennedy, writing years later, acknowledged that "many were furious" with his couples policy and "hoped [his] heart would soften. But it never did, and soon there was no need."[59]

Ceilidhs

The end of the war quickened a second set of Atlantic crossings from America that were to inform the British folk revival. Earlier, during the interwar years, Soho nightclubs highlighted American jazz musicians and British jazz bands in the American tradition to an adoring British bohemia, although as Georgina Boyes has pointed out, this was a selective version of jazz racialized as black music.[60] Still, these bands were forerunners to a jazz-folk-blues revival in postwar Britain that changed the sound, social composition, and bodily carriage seen and heard on the folk dance floor. For with the end of the war and transatlantic travel again possible, American folk singers and folklorists quickly took the opportunity to visit England to share their music with those from the land that had brought them the British ballad. In 1950, Alan Lomax "came over to England and started banging on doors very loudly, especially at the BBC." In turn, as noted by Malcolm Taylor, librarian at the Vaughan Williams Memorial Library at Cecil Sharp House and himself an expert on the song revival, the British folk singer Ewan MacColl "started thumping tables and said, this is great stuff; what about the stuff here, the indigenous material here?"[61]

MacColl did not have long to complain. The Columbia Record Company and the BBC, both eager to find product, quickly saw the potential of indigenous folk music. Lomax's visit stimulated Maury Sloackum, the BBC music librarian, to team with Margaret Dean Smith, the EFDSS librarian, to begin new collecting projects of folk song, dance, and customs in Ireland and Britain. At approximately the same time, in 1952 and 1953, Alan Lomax enlisted Peter Kennedy, the son of the EFDSS president and himself an aspiring folklorist, to help him record folk song in England and western Europe for Columbia Records and persuaded the BBC to launch a systematic recording program.[62]

In mixing with their British counterparts, American folk revivalists created a British variant of the folk revival. The arrival in England of "authentic" folk such as Lead Belly and folk singers such as Pete Seeger and Woody Guthrie in the 1950s stimulated a new high-energy folk sound and democratic spirit.[63] The Almanac Singers, the Weavers, and, later, the Kingston Trio and burgeoning numbers of bluegrass bands sang "songs of social significance" in a hybrid folk-jazz-blues idiom to the accompaniment of exciting new instrumentation. In England, five-string banjos, twelve-string guitars, mandolins, and basses joined with more traditional fiddles and accordions to send feet a-tapping; as important, the revival encouraged people to believe that they could make their own music, whether from a fiddle or from a spoon or washboard.

In Britain, the folk-jazz-blues revival spawned in 1947 an indigenous folk music movement in that spirit with a family resemblance to bluegrass: skiffle. Skiffle—a band sound with a "chucking guitar, tea-chest bass and rattling washboard" accompaniments[64]—lasted only about a decade into the mid-1950s, but it had its transatlantic moment as well. In 1954, a Scottish banjo player in a skiffle band, Lonnie Donegan, recorded the first popular British song to crack the American "Top Ten," "The Rock Island Line."[65]

Malcolm Taylor remembers the role of Donegan in his own family:

Lonnie Donegan was part of the Ken Colyer jazz band. In the intervals between sets, he would get out with his guitar and they would play this very raucous, rough and ready kind of skiffle music. It's just guitar, bass, and voice largely, and snare drum maybe. There was a burgeoning—every family that had children, they had a skiffle band in their front room. My brother did it—an old keg and a piece of string and a scout staff and made a bass out of it, and guitars, whatever. It really introduced people in many ways to a kind of folk music, to the blues, rhythm and blues, coming out in America.[66]

Skiffle waned by the mid-1950s, but the movement, in the words of one contemporary, "awakened the consciousness of young people" to the folk revival. By the end of the decade, new converts to the music were flocking to folk clubs that had begun to appear in London and urban England as adjuncts to an emerging left-wing youth political culture increasingly drawn to a growing anti-nuclear-bomb movement.[67]

The folk clubs were places for song and music rather than dance, but they reshaped the British folk dance community more generally. To begin, in contrast to EFDSS, the folk clubs had a broader social base and democratic ethos that was expressed in both the political sympathies of the songs they sang and the spontaneity and informality of the music and instrumentation they accepted. Together, skiffle, the folk-jazz-blues revival, and the folk clubs generated the first large-scale recruitment into the folk music world since the formation of the Folk Dance Society forty years earlier. As important, the enthusiasts in these folk revival groups became the base for a new social folk dance program—ceilidh—that took off in the late 1960s in the heyday of a second and more popular phase of the second revival.

There are several origin stories for the introduction of ceilidh dancing in England. An Irish or Scottish word that originally referred to an evening of folk song, it came to denote an event that mixed dancing, singing, and instrumentation. The word first appeared in EFDSS publications in 1950 to describe "party" evenings that mixed set dances, reels, and squares with country dances and interspersed the dancing with folk singing. The rise of the ceilidh also coincided with the early beginnings of a Celtic revival (the School of Scottish Studies was launched at Edinburgh in 1951) that blossomed two decades later as the waning second revival took a nationalist turn.[68] But in the early 1950s, Peter Kennedy downplayed any Celtic origins, describing the dance as akin to a barn dance or American square dance and thus in service to "Englishness." In this era, however, as often as not, a ceilidh was used to describe an evening of song. Only by 1967 did its meaning as a dance event become established, and within a few years, a "Knees Up Ceilidh" became a regular fixture at Cecil Sharp House, drawing enthusiastic crowds of younger dancers to its "thumping" sound. For unlike Playford-style "historical" dances, ceilidh dances required little styling: emphasizing reels and jigs, the goal was to have fun getting from point A to point B, not to think about how you looked or held your body when doing so.[69] The high energy and informality of the English ceilidh meshed with Douglas Kennedy's efforts to have English folk dance reach a broader public. In doing so, though, it effected a basic shift in the repertoire, style, spirit, and social composition of an evening of English Country Dance in England in the last third of the twentieth century.

Enthusiasts for the older historical dance programs did not disappear from EFDSS, however, and continued to claim a prominent place in how the organization represented itself. Thus, the English caller Marjorie Fennessey developed her own performance troupe, Whirligig, a name taken from the classic Playford dance of that name. The group was dedicated to the classical repertoire, and participants demonstrated and promoted the older "standard" as official bearers of the EFDSS seal. During the mid-1960s, at the height of the second revival, Whirligig performed samplers of morris, sword, and coupled country dances at EFDSS's annual shows to packed audiences at London's Albert Hall. They danced "beautifully," remembered one person in attendance, but were "so precise" and "word-perfect" as to be lifeless, "like mannequins." This perspective echoed older controversies about style, of course, from Sharp's day to Kennedy's quest for more "fire," and it came from a person with a stake in her own position in the dance history: Fried de Metz Herman (known simply as "Fried").[70] Fried, a recent émigré from the Netherlands then rooming in Pat Shaw's Hampstead home in exchange for some light housekeeping, soon after emigrated to the United States, where she became one of the most acclaimed, influential, and prolific teachers and composers of inventive English Country Dances in the historical style. Like her mentor, Shaw, her dances were "modern" folk dances, often with figures of her own devising, and her critical perspective on Whirligig should be seen in the context of her own invested position in controversies over the ECD canon and style. Fried's perspective, however, illustrates how the ECD scene resisted easy characterization even as change swirled about it. A cadre of dancers dedicated to the older repertory remained a bulwark within EFDSS, but they represented the past in the movement, not its future.

Playford-style programming did continue, but as leading English callers such as Tom Cook and Pat Shaw produced new reconstructions of seventeenth- and eighteenth-century historical dances, they also began to play inventively with it within new choreography. The new choreography and the idea that folk dance could be modern and of the present shook the foundations of the historical Playford-style dance repertory in the last quarter of the century on both sides of the Atlantic but, ironically, in the United States in particular. For although all dances done in the Sharp style are "modern" reconstructions of how folklorists imagined seventeenth- and eighteenth-century dances, late-twentieth-century dances are distinguished as modern in two ways: the dance style and dancing body at the end of the century differed, and choreographers such as Shaw and Fried wrote dances for a contemporary folk. The development of this "modern" ECD genre is a story that unfolded most especially in the United States, but its origins could be seen around the edges of the London dance community of the 1960s.[71]

In the interim, Kennedy's postwar response to the second revival put in motion a decline of the historical dances in England as a centerpiece of country dance. Evenings of Playford-style dances continued, but their reliance on a partnered constituency that was institutionally inhospitable to new single dancers did not bode well for future growth. The barn dances, ceilidhs, or "beginners' nights" for country dancers at Cecil Sharp House drew on versions of the same mixed repertoire with relatively little opportunity for new dancers to learn the more intricate styling of Playford dances. Thus, under Kennedy's leadership, the second folk revival—both in the impact of International Folk Dance and American squares—remade English Country Dance in the United Kingdom but, ironically, set it on a path that by the latter quarter of the century made it quite distinct from ECD in the United States.

ECD and the Second Folk Revival in Wartime and Postwar America

The irony of ironies is that although the second folk revival originated in the United States and moved across the Atlantic to reshape ECD in England, it had a delayed and limited impact on ECD in the United States. In part, the difference was the chilling effect of the Cold War on American cultural and political discourse. As noted earlier, the virulence of the Cold War in the United States made any association with the left-liberal culture of the second folk revival suspicious if not dangerous. But other factors contributed to the difference as well. To begin, EFDSS, which had played a foundational role in the revival at the start of the century, remained the institutional home of folk song and dance in England. In addition, London served as a cultural and political capital in England, and the United States had no equivalent site. No one place in the United States duplicated the dominant role that London and Cecil Sharp

House had as the home for English folk dance and, as significantly, for all folk dance in England. From the outset, New York and Boston shared the stage as twin centers for the American Branch. Significant centers for ECD also flourished in the southern mountains, though, at the Pine Mountain Settlement, Berea College, and by the mid-1920s, the new John C. Campbell Folk School in Brasstown, North Carolina. Moreover, during the interwar years, dancers established groups elsewhere, most notably in Pittsburgh, Cleveland, and Chicago. And after World War II, groups started to spring up in urban centers across the country, and in the more affluent suburbs around them, albeit as much around square dance as historical English Country Dance. Finally, although Pinewoods Camp in Massachusetts served as a national beacon for the English dance community, it only operated in the summer and never as the center for folk dance in the United States. Thus, New York and Boston remained the centers of an eastern-centric English Country Dance movement in the United States until the last quarter of the twentieth century.

One additional factor helped account for the relative stagnation of ECD in the United States during the postwar revival: although the American Branch of EFDS claimed to represent an Anglo-American tradition, English Country Dance had at best a liminal role as the repository of a national "American" culture. For the extensive immigrant diversity of the twentieth-century American city always distinguished the United States from England. Neal's Espérance girls were children of the British poor, and the folk dance curriculum that Sharp pressed as part of the Educational Reform Act of 1907 dwelt on English dances rather than on those of "many lands." In contrast, the central place given to immigrant folk cultures early in the United States meant that "ethnic" dance had a strong claim as integral to a national folk dance legacy for Americans. Until midcentury, led by proponents such as Elizabeth Burchenal, American folk dance curriculum drew on the diversity of the country's immigrant population, not just on "American" dances. When American schools, like their British counterparts, taught folk dance, the American syllabi consisted of dances from the many countries represented in their classrooms. "Hyphenated" Americans from other than the British Isles and northern Europe had no reason to look to English Country Dance to affirm their American identity. Consequently, unlike in England, American public schools had no reason to teach exclusively English Country Dance and were not, by and large, feeders for American ECD groups. In urban city schools, children were as likely to learn the Russian comarinskaia as "Turkey in the Straw." So, in contrast to the establishment of Cecil Sharp House as the center for folk dance in England, cities such as New York witnessed the development of distinct centers for "ethnic" or "international" dance. In the 1920s and 1930s, Elizabeth Burchenal's Folk Arts Center served as home to ethnic or International Dance—not to a "national" folk dance, either American or Anglo-American. Similarly, when Martin Koenig, joined later by Ethel Raim, a "red diaper" baby, opened Ethnic Arts Center in New York in 1966, English or any country dance was virtually invisible.[72]

As noted in chapter 5, the greater competition in the United States from both ethnic and International dance groups for the hearts of folk dancers and the mantle of folk capital, if anything, had helped to mobilize the EFDS's American Branch in the 1930s to change its name to Country Dance Society of America and broaden its purview. The new name referenced its claim to be an Anglo-American tradition of country dance and to represent "America's dance." The new designation brought square and contra, or American Country Dance, under the CDS umbrella and May Gadd's authority.

Appointed national director of CDS in 1937, Gadd remained in that position for most of the next thirty-five years, only taking a two-year leave in 1943 to do war work. The local New York group created a new volunteer committee, the New York Dancers' Council, to run local affairs, and in 1951, the group moved its dance to the gym in the basement of Metropolitan-Duane Hall, the "reconciling church" in Greenwich Village, where it remained through 2008.[73] But while the Dancers' Council assumed responsibility for recruitment, local finances, and event planning, May Gadd remained the CDS éminence grise. Gadd oversaw details large and small, both in the local New York community and in the nation, although she had notable help from another English-trained dancer, Genevieve (Genny) Shimer (1913–1990), who arrived after the war. Shimer, like so many of her predecessors, had taught ECD to schoolchildren in England and for the next forty years became a leading CDS teacher in New York and at Pinewoods Camp. But until Gadd's retirement in 1972, Shimer and other leaders remained in her shadow.[74]

Gadd left an indelible mark on the organization, as great as that of Sharp. A fierce defender of Sharp's legacy, Gadd was at once an Edwardian woman and a Sharp devotee. Old-timers remembered her with both admiration and awe, as impressive and often intimidating. But the dance community was devoted to Gadd—as was she to it. Examinations were still required for acceptance as an experienced dancer, and Gadd, keeper of the Sharp flame, oversaw credentialing. Phil Merrill directed the musicians, but Gadd anointed new leaders and set the tone for the evening and weekend events in New York, Pinewoods, and as she traveled about the country as guest teacher, in the nation.[75] Dedicated to Sharp's legacy, Gadd knew the style and comportment

The Second Folk Revival | 189

that she wanted from dancers, and she was not shy about enforcing it on both the local New York and national levels. But at the same time as she brought great energy and creative public programming to her work, Gadd held and exercised the role of social arbiter both on and off the dance floor. During the 1960s, when young people from the counterculture began to appear at dance camps, she monitored social etiquette as readily as she dictated dance style. But those days were near the end of her reign, and in the preceding twenty-five years, Gadd's conservative personal style, apolitical disposition, and embrace of all forms of country dance—historical, "traditional" or community dance, and American square and contra—made her an ideal leader for a relatively conservative, elitist, and Anglophile dance community.

Gadd's hegemonic role in CDS was partially attributable to her strong personality and partially to the consent of a like-minded community. In the tempestuous English dance scene, Sharp had fought Neal, Wright, and Burchenal, and the Morris Ring and some women and old-timers had challenged Kennedy's authority. In contrast, Gadd had no real opposition. Helen Storrow did not teach and, in any case, died in 1944. In Boston, Gadd's counterparts—Conant and Chapin—were cast from similar social molds and were also devoted to Sharp's legacy. In fact, CDS prized its historical continuity with Sharp-Storrow and celebrated the Pinewoods legacy. Originally Storrow's Girl Scouts Camp, the facility was willed by Storrow to the Conants, who in turn sold it in 1974 to a consortium of users, among which CDSS always played a leading role.[76]

The Cold War Chills the Revival

Continuity, then, rather than change characterized the history of CDS in the postwar era. Although the second revival swirled about the English dance community, the cultural gap between the International Folk Dance and English Country Dance communities and the Cold War overdetermined the ECD community's limited interaction with the International dance community. A new generation of dancer leaders did begin to appear in CDS in the 1950s—most notably, Christine Helwig in New York and Arthur and Helene Cornelius in Boston—but the elite, insular character of the dance community persisted. In the 1950s, the English Country Dance movement in the United States had more in common with its preceding history than its history to follow.

May Gadd's social profile as a socially conservative woman from the solidly "middling" ranks reflected the CDS community she led. Most of Sharp's protégés who led the two major centers in New York and Boston were themselves immigrants from England. To be sure, many newer leaders in mid-century were born in the United States, but most of the grande dames of the mid- and late-twentieth-century ECD community—Christine Helwig, Fried de Metz, Sue Salmons, and Helene Cornelius—were either of English or northern European ancestry.[77]

The rank-and-file dancer looked little different from the leadership. There is no statistical profile of the American ECD community for early in the century, and evidence is mostly anecdotal, but period photographs from dance events, news stories about members, and oral histories tell the same story: the typical dancer may well have been American born, and the new curriculum increasingly integrated American dance into programs, but white, elite people of English ancestry remained a core constituency. Indeed, longtime dancers speak of the ECD community as having been anti-Semitic and elitist until the 1960s.[78] A few Italian and Jewish Americans joined the dance community, but they were a decided minority.[79] More typical was the remarkably similar social profile that characterized old-timers interviewed half a century later: most were immigrant English professionals. The Cambridge-educated philosopher John Bremer, the Oxford-trained physicist Richard Wilson, and the Lincolnshire-born social anthropologist Peter Fricke all joined the New York and Boston postwar dance communities (Bremer becoming a New York ECD teacher), where they found themselves at home with compatriots, most famously, with both longtime dance leaders such as Lily Conant and new leaders such as Genny Shimer.[80]

The conservative social cast of the organization shaped its efforts to broaden its base and attract new members. There was, however, ample competition for the folk dancer body: immigrant American cities hosted many alternative forms of folk dance and the exciting new International Folk Dance movement. Gadd's task as national director of her band of like-minded Anglophiles, then, was to give CDS a compelling public presence. And as she moved energetically to do so, the outbreak of war and the domestic Cold War that accompanied it shaped her efforts.

Gadd, unlike Kennedy, sought an alternative to International Folk Dance; she was not inspired by it. To advance ECD, she led the American EFDS group's participation in the 1939 World's Fair. She did not succeed in gaining the foothold for CDS that Michael Herman won at the American Common, but the experience did stimulate her to take up square dance and give it a heightened presence in CDS. The pioneering work of a Colorado teacher in the late 1930s, Lloyd Shaw, was then quickening a new revival of square dancing. The couples turning dances such as the polka and waltz, which had become popular in the mid-nineteenth century, and the new animal dances at the turn of the century had effectively buried square dancing as an urban social dance in the United States after 1890.[81] In 1925, Henry Ford, who had taken his nativist turn, published his dance collection, *Good Morning*, to extol squares as an alternative to the evils of jazz. But in the wake of the Dust Bowl and newfound concern for the plight of the "Okies," Shaw's decision in 1938 to teach his students "cowboy dances" and the publication the next year of his book *Cowboy Dances* inaugurated a popular enthusiasm for a highly stylized modern square dance movement called Western Squares and the quaint cowboy slang and twang of the calls that accompanied them. Shaw's classes then and in the postwar era were the training ground for many of those who developed the Western Squares movement. This square dance movement has provided the dominant image of square dancing to this day: women in multi-petticoated short skirts and men with string ties and long-sleeved shirts. It is important to note that the modern Western Square Dance movement and the country square dance communities in New England and the southern mountains remained quite distinct traditions with quite different constituencies: the former, with its uniforms and uniform style, has been popular among conservatives, evangelicals, and traditionalists; the latter programmed both contras and squares for local and countercultural communities who were more likely to dress in jeans and dance barefoot or wear sandals. The general postwar embrace of square dancing, however, led over thirty state legislatures in the subsequent years to declare square dancing the official state dance, and pending federal legislation would have made it the national dance.[82]

May Gadd's and CDS's adoption of square dancing, however, also differed from its embrace in England in one important way: unlike EFDSS, where the embrace of square dance was accompanied by new emphases on community dance, CDS did not reject historical Playford dances. In contrast to EFDSS, CDS incorporated square dancing into its mission as a way to broaden its definition and appeal as an Anglo-American tradition. Thus, the program for the Silver Jubilee Festival in 1940 celebrating the twenty-fifth anniversary of the EFDSS of America made clear that the new Country Dance Society of America intended to inaugurate a new era in Anglo-American dance as an American national tradition: "The dances and songs are as much the inheritance of Americans as the English language and include a number that were brought here by Americans as the settlers. Because of this common tradition the Society includes in its repertory many examples of the Square Dance and the New England Country dance that have been developed here." Held at the

Square dancing in the United States, ca. 1950, in "country" dress. (Used by permission of the Country Dance and Song Society Archives, www.cdss.org; Milne Special Collections and Archives Department, University of New Hampshire Library, Durham, NH)

Seventh Regiment Armory on fashionable Park Avenue at 66th Street, the event was to be the last of the Armory festivals, but it was the start of a new outreach. Five hundred attendees were treated to the complement of the new Anglo-American country dance repertoire: performances of half a dozen morris dances and several processional dances were intermixed with American squares and English Country Dances for all.[83] Indeed, *Cue* magazine reported that by 1941 the square dance craze had "swept the country"—a full decade before it brought crowds to Cecil Sharp House in London. Observing the "biggest" of the New Jersey groups in Montclair, led by Robert Hider of Glen Ridge, *Cue*'s reporter crowed, "No longer are folk dance fanatics viewed as with full supercilious tolerance, for the square and round cavortings have swept the country, penetrating urban and suburban communities alike."[84]

The impact of square dancing on the American ECD community is hard to measure. The caption for a photo that accompanied the *Cue* article, showing couples learning a "basic step" in "The Virginia Reel," told readers that the dance was "inspired by an old English country dance." Teachers of English Country Dance such as Gadd and Hider embraced square dancing in

The Second Folk Revival | 193

the New York area, and the callers Louise Winston and Ted Sannella led American dancing in Boston. Square dancing and contras were incorporated into the programming, but they seemed to have limited effect on the social composition of the community. Longtime dancers remember relatively few square dancers moving over to do English Country Dance, although Arthur and Helene Cornelius, who went on to become prominent leaders of the Boston dance community, were significant exceptions. As a rule, reminiscences by dancers suggest that the ECD scene remained quite staid and unchanged into the 1960s.[85] Gene Murrow, for instance, heard rumors of anti-Semitism in the dance community when he joined the community in the 1960s as a Jewish Columbia College student from Brooklyn. But at least as important as the ethnic bias of the community was its class bias: Murrow, for instance, went on to embed the restrictive climate in elite class attitudes: "In this country, English country dancing in the '30s and '40s and '50s was definitely an American upper class snooty activity. It was done at the Metropolitan Club in New York, things like that."[86]

Square dancing did become a central part of the CDS programming during the war, however, much as it had in England. The rationale was not quite the same, though. Rather than gender balance and the need to light a fire under the dance community, increased interest in American dance from new members coincided with CDS's desire to recast itself as an Anglo-American "national" tradition and serve the war effort by building morale among soldiers. Square dancing was by definition American dancing, and it was easier during wartime for a "national" dance organization to justify than something called "English" dance. So CDS branches in New York and Boston and ECD clubs elsewhere increasingly incorporated square dancing into wartime programming. Even the ECD stalwart Helen Storrow had attended a square dance before her death in 1944, and by the end of the war, Louise Chapin, Boston's head teacher, was teaching square dancing.[87]

In New York, highly visible public work of CDS national director May Gadd illustrated both the increased role of square dance and the patriotic impulse. With the war swirling about dancers, from 1941 to 1945, CDS took part in a weekly television broadcast on CBS-TV dedicated to square dancing. Led by Gadd, the programs incorporated other ethnic dances, including English Country Dancing, but featured squares. Then, in 1943, Gadd took a leave of absence from CDS to work for the USO in the war effort, leaving the leadership of the local dance community in the capable hands of Phil Merrill, the head of New York's musicians, and others. Gadd spent the next two years working as a "program consultant" to the army and navy and YMCA for the promotion of country dancing at USO clubs throughout the country, teaching American squares and rounds as what she called "defense recreation." Committed to realizing the "place of the arts in the defense effort," she reported back with enthusiasm to the dance community that "service men like Country Dancing!" Gadd prophesied that in addition to providing good recreational relief to soldiers, the dances "will result in thousands of new enthusiasts from every nook and cranny of the United States." And "lastly, though by no means . . . least important," she saw country dancing playing a vital political role in serving the war effort: "through participation in this most democratic, sociable, recreative activity," the morale of America's fighting men and women would be built up.[88]

Building military morale during the war served a unified domestic political agenda, but as the military struggle ended and a Cold War took its place, the work of patriotism could morph into something more partisan. This partisan political role was logical for ethnic eastern European folk groups made up of émigrés from Soviet states, but CDS existed in a more liminal national space. CDS was fundamentally transnational, but in the United States, as an Anglo-American tradition, it claimed a role as carrier of the nation's cultural heritage. Its vision of that heritage, however, remained a version of Anglo-Americanism rooted in the English village idyll. As custodians of that heritage, CDS members shared a role with highbrow elite cultural institutions that served people who looked like them and shared their aesthetic interests. Thus, the major public activities of CDS in the postwar era consisted of four performances of "An English Village May Day," by a seventy-dancer demonstration group, and a series of performances by a presumably smaller demonstration team for a United Nations Fiesta and for audiences at Carnegie Hall, the Metropolitan Museum of Art, the Brooklyn Museum, and, in the next decade, at Lincoln Center.[89]

The demonstration team's venues and programs reflected CDS's sense of its "cultured" audience and heritage. Not explicitly political, the activities reflected choices made by CDS and its leadership in the context of the 1950s political culture and alternative folk forms. As noted earlier, with the McCarthy Committee and the House Un-American Activities Committee casting a wide censorious net among folk singers and musicians, these CDS public activities were uncontroversial and safe. But other activities in which some groups and individuals associated with CDS took part told a more complicated story and gave the lie to Gadd's and CDS's claim to be apolitical. For despite CDS's avowed apolitical character, some of its members and others in the International Folk Dance movement found themselves servants of State

CDS morris dancing at the United Nations Fiesta at Rockefeller Plaza in 1947. Left side, back to front: Jack Langstaff, William Partington, Russell Loughton. Right side: Jack Shimer, Bob Guillard, Bob Hider. (Photo: Jack Shimer; courtesy of Joan Shimer and David Millstone)

Department Cold War projects to win the hearts and minds of peoples and administrations in strategic locales around the world.

The U.S. government mobilized folk dance, as Victoria Geduld has ironically noted, "deploying the Soviet tactic of using dance as propaganda to fight the Soviets." In that effort, the government operated on two levels, employing high-modernist ballet troupes using folk themes and, more modestly, recreational folk groups. In the immediate aftermath of the war, efforts included the participation of some left-wing and communist-affiliated dancers such as Sophie Maslow and Jerome Robbins, but the Cold War blacklists soon restricted opportunities to those such as Martha Graham and Agnes de Mille who could be "cleared" to perform uncompromising Americanness as the State Department understood it.[90]

In the mid-1950s, the CIA, which covertly funded the Congress for Cultural Freedom, worked hand in glove with the State Department to do the cultural work of Cold War diplomacy. As an adjunct of that project, the

National Cultural Center (NCC) mobilized folk dance groups to travel abroad to contrast American cultural "freedom" with Soviet "totalitarianism." In 1956, the State Department sent the Hermans, Ralph Page, Jane Farwell, and Nelda Drury to Japan for six weeks, where they taught forty-six dances from sixteen nations, successfully, according to Michael Herman, helping "to build the morale of Japanese young people."[91]

The NCC's dance panel rejected square dance caller Rickey Holden's offer to form a folk dance troupe because they wanted someone less oriented toward educational/recreational dance. The panel then considered asking Lloyd Shaw or Ralph Page. But, convinced a professional dancer would mount a more polished performance, they turned to Agnes de Mille. De Mille went so far as to form the Agnes de Mille Folk Dance Project, in which professional high-modern dancers deployed folk themes as a performance art in concert halls. The project was to be a traveling theatrical extravaganza, and de Mille proposed a performance that would "derive from our traditional inheritance—country and urban—the country dance, square dance, buck and wing, tap and jazz, the ballroom forms and the theatre heritage which can include ballet." De Mille added a comment that reflected her recognition perhaps that the American government wanted these Cold War projects to counter the racist image of the United States abroad. She added, "We will first develop the Anglo-Saxon and Negro forms and exclude the Indian."[92]

De Mille's project enticed the panel, but when State Department funding for it never materialized, the panel became less ambitious. A program evaluator recommended a group of young dancers from a school in the South as "charming, wholesome and sweet," the Berea College Folk Dance Group. More in line with their budget, on the heels of the Cuban Missile Crisis, the NCC funded sixteen dancers and four musicians from Berea to perform free programs of English Country Dance for thousands of students and middle-class audiences in Mexico, El Salvador, Guatemala, Honduras, Nicaragua, Costa Rica, Panama, Colombia, and Ecuador in 1962. The cultural affairs officer in Honduras described their performance in Tegucigalpa as "one of the highlights of the Cultural Exchange Program." Dancers concluded their performance by going into the audience and selecting "Honduran partners for an old-fashioned square dance." Returning to the States, the troupe encored its performance at the White House for President Kennedy.[93]

The State Department program did not typify daily life in the dance community, but left-wing international proletarianism was clearly the road not taken during the years of the revival. There were exceptions: Peter Fricke, who lived across the street from Gadd in Greenwich Village, was in the merchant

The Second Folk Revival

May Gadd and Berea dancers greeted by President Kennedy at the White House, 1963. (Photo: Stan Levy, Jack Shimer Collection, courtesy of Joan Shimer and David Millstone)

marine, one of the more radical trades with a deep history in the Communist Party.[94] But some of Gadd's own associations suggest a more complicated political subjectivity not so far removed from Sharp's Fabianism that more seemed to typify ECD liberalism. Gadd, it will be recalled, was a member of the International Folk Music Council, where she working alongside internationalist folk revival stalwarts Burl Ives and Pete Seeger, among others.[95] Moreover, among Gadd's friends was Priscilla (Prossy) Hiss, the wife of Alger Hiss, who had been convicted and jailed for espionage after a highly public and controversial trial. Prossy, an Anglophile, only danced occasionally, but her son Tony remembered how warm and welcome the whole family felt at parties at Gadd's apartment in the West Village. Young dancers often found Gadd imposing, but Prossy, a contemporary and fellow "bluestocking"—and most definitely not a "freak"—found Gadd wholly simpatico, even "privately sympathetic."[96]

In the penumbra of the Cold War, however, being liberal in private often translated into being "apolitical" and "respectable" in public. When internationalist or antiracist positions left one vulnerable to McCarthyism, dancers such as Peter Fricke recall that May Gadd made sure "politics" did not enter the ECD dance floor.[97] Gadd also demanded that dancers on the New York dance floor dress appropriately, although she probably had little to worry about on that score. The ECD dance community was socially conservative; "freaks" kept their distance. It was a decade later yet when a young dancer's first memory of Gadd was of being chided for entering the dance hall in sandals.[98] So the apolitical character of the dance evening, which reflected the apolitical character of the dances' own origins—or at least their origin stories—spoke to the chilling effect of the Cold War as much as the conservative, elite cast of the community prior to the 1960s.

The Second Revival, Phase Two: The 1960s in the United States

The Sixties (as a social and cultural movement that began around 1957 and carried through the early 1970s) transformed the second folk revival into a mass movement. A left-liberal "softening" of the oppositional character of the folk culture accompanied the popularization of folk repertoire and, in time, brought into CDSS (it added "Song" to its name in 1967) a new and vibrant young generation from the counterculture that appreciated the country dance community as a congenial alternative social space.

The Newport (Rhode Island) Folk Festival stands as one marker of the transformation of the folk "revival" into a folk "boom." The most important of a series of folk festivals that sprang up in the 1960s, the Newport Festival was held annually from 1959 (except for 1961–62) until 1969 (it was revived in 1985). As a public celebration led by the leading folk singers and folk bands in the country, an invitation to perform at the festival legitimized a group as "folk." Thus, to demonstrate the "significant role" that folk dance had played in the "urban dance revival in this country," CDSS's pride of place as the first permanent folk dance organization in the nation won it invitations in both 1959 and 1967 to perform at the festival.[99]

In both years, CDSS was not the only group invited to dance, however, and the other selections suggest the early priorities given to song and music, but they quite possibly also reflect the organizers' limited familiarity with the folk dance community. In 1959, the folk dance demonstration was placed just before the afternoon intermission in the middle of Sunday afternoon, after performances by Pete Seeger, the New Lost City Ramblers, Memphis Slim, and the Clancy Brothers. Two groups were lumped together as "New England Folk Dancers": the English CDS of Boston and the Scottish Country Dance Society of Boston. The program noted that both groups "immerse themselves in folklore" and "take great pride (and pains) to wear authentic costume," but it elided the history of Scottish dance as a regimented and invented twentieth-century dance tradition with more complicated if not dubious credentials as a folk tradition.[100]

Changes in folk dance programming at Newport between the two ECD appearances reflected transformations in the second folk revival that were, in the words of Bob Dylan's folk anthem for the Sixties, "Blowin' in the Wind." In contrast to the limited attention to dance in 1959, the 1967 festival reflected the growing place of both International and American folk dance in the revival. Organizers now allotted more extended time to folk dance and to a broadened range of groups that mirrored the increasing identity and appeal of International Folk Dance and contra/squares in the Sixties. The week-long festival now highlighted a full day (from ten in the morning to five in the afternoon) of participatory folk dance workshops, not mere performances pigeonholed into the middle of a music program. On this occasion, separate sessions, each running an hour or an hour and a half, were dedicated to Contra Dance, Balkan Dance, Square Dance, Lancers and Quadrilles, International Dance, and ECD. Ralph Page and Margot Mayo led the American squares and contras; the Hermans and their Boston equivalents, Cornell ("Connie") and Marianne Taylor, taught International and Balkan. Only CDSS, advertising itself as dedicated to persevering both American and English folk dance, was given two hours. Leading its demonstrations and teaching was May Gadd, with help from Boston's Art Cornelius.[101]

The 1967 attention to folk dance came, however, at a time when the festival—and the revival—had begun to lose its core left-wing political identity. To at least some devotees, this constituted a "decline." Many felt the transitional moment was the 1965 festival, when Bob Dylan plugged in his guitar, electrically transforming the acoustical "natural" sound that had characterized bluegrass and skiffle into a new genre tied to rock 'n' roll. Pete Seeger was particularly outraged, calling it "some of the most destructive music this side of hell." Thus, by 1967, Seeger believed that to the extent that the Newport Festival was a leading institutional symbol, the folk revival had passed its peak. Many folkies agreed, feeling that the more commercial genre diluted folk's oppositional role as the voice of the dispossessed; yet, for others, in merging with rock, the popular music of youth culture, the new sound developed mass popular appeal. As the historian David Dunaway observes, Dylan "left Newport's stage for good, [but he took] . . . with him most of the folk revival's audience." To be sure, as Ronald Cohen has noted, folk music remained a vital movement, albeit less visible and commercial. But the move out of Newport was not without political resonance, personal and social: Seeger gradually refocused his energy on an alternative social movement—

environmentalism—and many others embraced a growing popular folk-rock movement.[102]

The changes begun at Newport in 1965 corresponded to fundamental shifts in the cultural politics and the social base of the New Left and the second folk revival at the end of the Sixties. In the early years of the decade, red-diaper babies played a major role in joining with new left-wing activists to build a political protest movement around Students for a Democratic Society. By middecade, as the Vietnam War escalated and male college students in general became vulnerable to a draft, the social base of the movement broadened. A left-liberal coalition brought together radical sects of Maoists and Trotskyites with large numbers of social democrats and concerned liberal progressives. Folk-rock, which especially to some older folkies more emphasized the beat than topical issues, became the musical idiom of cultural protest for this Sixties version of the Cultural Front. Rebels, who had been marginalized as "freaks" in Washington Square Park a few years earlier, now became part of a mass social and cultural movement that brought together psychedelic hippies and activists. The folk events and the folk idioms helped unite these people as they sang and danced before, during, and after they marched.

This populist phase of the revival in the last half of the Sixties that broadened the social base of the folk community carried a political price. The folk tradition that nurtured the new revival could be both alternative and oppositional, and many in the hippie communes of Haight-Ashbury or the East Village or on back-to-the-land communes created anticapitalist, antimaterialist enclaves. But omnivorous cultural merchants were never shy of seeking profit in any cultural forms, and cultural elements could become, in their commodified form, more alternative than oppositional, diluting what had earlier been more explicit political messages.[103] The history of the "Hammer Song" is a case in point. The Weavers first performed their song "If I Had a Hammer" at a rally in support of eleven members of the Communist Party on trial in 1949 as "subversives." The lines "I'd hammer out a danger, I'd hammer out a warning" were warnings of the coming oppressive times. Peter, Paul, and Mary's rerecording of the song rose to the Top Ten in 1962, and subsequent versions by dozens of major popular artists in France, Britain, and the United States soon flooded the airways. The populist language of the song, which had left-wing political messages in the Cold War, however, was easily adapted to the political culture of the liberal democratic antiwar campaigns of Robert Kennedy and Eugene McCarthy in 1967–68. Thus, new pulsating folk-rock rhythms replaced what had been written as a radical anthem of peace, brotherhood, and social justice in the face of growing Cold

War intolerance with what left-folkies bemoaned as a celebration of the beat rather than of the meanings in the original words.¹⁰⁴

The Contra Boom and "Roots" Revival

Two secondary revivals during the later left-liberal stage of the second folk revival—one in contra and the other in ethnic "roots"—had an immediate effect on the American Country Dance movement, although the latter undoubtedly characterized EFDSS in England as well. The first of these revivals gained impetus from the counterculture's back-to-the-land movement that renovated the folkloric rural idyll. Young people, rebelling against a fast-paced, anomic culture of urban capitalism that they saw as waging an imperialist war abroad and sustaining anti-intellectual materialist culture at home, opted for what they imagined as the "simple" rural life. Moving to New England and Appalachia, they established collective communes and alternative communities where they tried to live off the land or from artisan skills in traditional folk arts such as woodworking. In the evenings and on weekends, they flocked to grange halls and barns to dance to the vibrant sounds of a new contra and square revival.

The contra revival of the late 1960s and early '70s was of course the second contra revival to transform CDS. In the preceding decades, CDS leaders had integrated American contra and squares, first celebrated in the "Running Set," into programs that mixed traditional and historical dances and included some ceremonial morris or sword dance as well. Ralph Page, the "dean of square dancing," had begun calling squares in Keene, New Hampshire, in the 1930s, and it will be recalled, Phil Merrill played a leading role in teaching square dance with Gadd in England. By 1943, Page was leading an urban revival as well, coming down to Boston weekly to call square and contras at the Boston YMCA. He attracted the young future contra callers Ted Sannella and Rickey Holden to contra and, the next year, founded the New England Folk Festival Association (NEFFA).¹⁰⁵ Dances from the initial square dance revival during World War II and the postwar era had also been quickly incorporated in the country dance repertory on both sides of the Atlantic. But by the mid-1950s, the postwar square dance boom had become Western or Club Squares, the more formal, choreographed dance form done in western dress that was closer to the conservative world of country music than to folk dance. Consequently, as noted earlier, the initial square dance revival recruited relatively few dancers into the ECD community, and those that did cross over looked little different from their predecessors.¹⁰⁶

Old-time square dance and contra dance continued to thrive in New England towns and Appalachian hollows, however, and by the late 1960s found a ready new audience in the back-to-the-land hippies. Rejecting club squares, they thrilled to the stirring old-time music and playful singing calls of new callers inspired by Page: Tony Parkes and Dudley Laufman. With Ted Sannella, these callers helped spread a contra dance craze. With a new smooth, grounded style, exciting improvisational clogging, and innovative dances with original patterns, a contra boom had swept the country by the end of the 1970s.[107]

During this period, another secondary revival, this one of "roots" music and dance, encouraged and valorized the move into a national dance tradition represented by English and American Country Dance. Coincident with the rise of the identity politics that increasingly dominated the cultural politics of the later Sixties, folkies had begun to move into groups organized to advance ethnic folk traditions, some becoming even fiercely nationalistic. International Folk Dance began to morph into Balkan Dance; Klezmer music and Israeli dance won new adherents following the 1967 Sinai War; and in dance, "Riverdance," Irish set dancing, and an expanding Scottish dance movement on both sides of the Atlantic reflected a Celtic revival.[108] The next chapter picks up this story, as the popularity of the 1977 *Roots* television miniseries further mobilized these revivals and, in response to the Celtic revival in particular, could sustain if not feed the nationalist strain of ECD. "Englishness" made EFDSS and CDSS unlikely ports for the Irish, for instance, but, in turn, it encouraged the Anglophile strains within the ECD communities. (It is worth remembering how fears of Irish militancy and bombs marked the mid-1970s in Britain.) So as International Folk Dance and the folk song movement waned for some people, and simply changed for others, dancers in the 1970s had many choices, and CDSS, an Anglo American national tradition with ties through contra back to the counterculture, won its share of them—though notably fewer of Irish descent.

The contra craze and "roots" revival did not immediately change ECD programming, but both had longer-term effects on the constitution and social profile of the ECD community in the United States as it was remade in the 1970s. By 1970, with Gadd celebrating her eighty-first birthday, it became increasingly evident to many people that it was time to bring in new leadership. The new leadership instituted challenging organizational and programming innovations, changes that upset some and thrilled others, but the country dance movement in the United States was never the same.

Conclusion

In sum, the second folk revival, though born in the United States, until the mid-1960s had greater impact on country dance in England then in the United States. International Folk Dance excited EFDSS leaders to rethink its tradition and the constrained style of the dancing body. Douglas Kennedy's response was to deemphasize the historical dances from the Playford publications in favor of traditional dances that he collected in the seven *Community Dance Manuals*. He built on this new direction with an adjunct of the revival from the United States: square dancing. The lively music and dance of square dancing captivated British young people who lined up to dance at Cecil Sharp House. At the same time, the folk music of the second revival—old-time, bluegrass, blues, jazz, and folk—swept the country in inventive new musical instrumentation of skiffle bands, folk clubs, and a new high-energy, kick-up-your-heels (i.e., *not* fussy) dance program: the ceilidh.

Kennedy's controversial couples-only policy uniquely shaped EFDSS's history. While the move especially upset older members steeped in the older historical dances, the policy inhibited the introduction of new single dancers into the community. Moreover, the policy put conditions in place that had serious implications for future growth of the movement; dancers who came to the dance as couples tended to dance as couples, and the community aged in place.

In contrast to England, the second revival's impact on CDS was to come only after the revival ended. If anything, through the 1960s, the CDS community continued to define, imagine, and normalize itself as other than the "freaks" in sandals and long hair that sang and danced in bohemian spaces. In the context of the particular virulence of the Cold War in the United States, CDS members had every reason to keep their distance from feared contagion by left-wing revivalists. In fact, the liberal political culture of these dancing elites was congenial with highbrow culture associated with a Brahmin Anglo-American and Victorian (reborn as bourgeois or "middle class") values, not with beatnik or hippie culture.

Folk dance in urban America divided into distinct social spaces for different groups, and in the demarcated geography of dance during the second revival, CDS occupied a relatively liminal place. In the period prior to World War II, urban recreational folk dance events in North America were generally either International or English.[109] In places such as rural New England or the southern mountains, local folk dance events continued to emphasize indigenous American squares and contras. But in urban centers such as postwar New York, May Gadd's New York Centre, like its parent organ, CDS, represented only country dance. In contrast, Cecil Sharp House, as both the home of English folk dance and folk dance in England, hosted International Folk Dance and groups from different national folk dance traditions.

In truth, during the postwar era, country dance programming in England and the United States did not look very different. A typical dance program in both New York and London, for instance, would mix historical dances with squares, contras, and traditional "community" dances. A program would also usually include a ritual morris or sword display. The different histories of the Cold War and folk dance revivals on each side of the Atlantic had a more subtle influence on programming during these years. The differences were, first, the gradual trend toward the ceilidh dance, with its "knees-up" informality, and the consequent deemphasis on programming and teaching historical dances in England, and second, the coupled attendance required at dance events in England. In fact, the women's movement in the late 1960s had much earlier and greater impact on dance in the United States than in England, so that although "gender balance" was a transatlantic issue, a pioneer of the Gay Liberation Movement in America, Carl Wittman, led the development in the United States of a movement diametrically opposed to Kennedy's couples policy: "gender-free" dance in which there were no gendered dance roles. The impact and differences between the two countries were set in motion during the postwar era and were more apparent at the end of the century, shaping the trajectories of programs and the style of dancing bodies in future decades. Ironically, the end of the second folk revival brought a new beginning for CDSS and country dance in the United States. Newport closed its doors in 1971 as CDSS opened its own.

7

Re-Generation

> It really depends on what you mean by "folk." I don't think origins matter very much. . . . Obviously, a lot of these dances have been composed at one time or another, so if the time happens to be the 20th century, why worry.
> —Pat Shaw, 1970[1]

> And in his own crazy English way of looking at American things, he [Pat Shaw] created American dances—so called American dances—that really were an English man's view of American dances. And so he shook the world up, and it [1974] was a great year.
> —Jacqueline Schwab, 1999[2]

Jacqueline Schwab, a self-described "nerd" who loved the folk trio Peter, Paul, and Mary and "the usual sixties," attended Pinewoods in 1971 for the first time. She found a world still rooted in a mainstream culture: "Women weren't allowed to ask men to dance. Men could ask women to dance. And women had to wear skirts to the dances. And there was even a bush patrol for scouring the bushes late at night so that there weren't any extracurricular activities going on . . . and etc." Schwab, who had been introduced to ECD through International Folk Dance, went on to have an illustrious career in CDSS and as a professional musician. She served as Pinewoods Camp manager, became the pianist for the leading ECD band Bare Necessities, and did the music for Ken Burns's blockbuster PBS television series *The Civil War*.[3]

In that same summer of 1971, future CDSS national director Brad Foster arrived for his first camp visit. It was the heyday of the sexual revolution in the counterculture, and he remembered that Gadd prohibited unmarried couples from rooming together. He recalled the year as "a very hormonal year at camp." "Some people said they got married so they could come and stay at Pinewoods in the same cabin," although he added what seemed more likely the case: others just quietly "changed roommates." No rules were posted, but "there were traditions that you had to be aware of. Even if you were never told, you had to follow these things."[4]

As these anecdotes suggest, the entrance of dancers such as Schwab and Foster who came of age in the Sixties into the urban dance communities and the pavilions at Pinewoods turned the world of country dance upside down in the 1970s. But at the same time as the social profile of the dance community changed, so did its repertoire—and it did so across the country as groups of converts to country dance in cities and college towns from the San Francisco Bay Area to the City of Brotherly Love and points in between made CDSS a robust national organization.

For many who remembered those years, the controversial 1974 visit to Pinewoods Camp of the pioneering dance choreographer and teacher from London—Pat Shaw—was the transformative symbolic moment. As Kate van Winkle Keller recalled, Shaw's call to innovation upset many traditionalists. Keller, who went on to become a leading historian of Playford and Colonial American dance, had her inaugural visit to Pinewoods that year and remembered the consternation that Shaw's visit occasioned among many CDSS leaders: "His ideas challenged their insistence that to have a uniform dance community there needed to be uniformity in teaching and dance interpretation. Pat's ideas undermined this uniformity but encouraged budding American choreographers . . . to follow his lead as he similarly inspired English teachers."[5] For many others, and most especially those of a new generation, Shaw's appearance was empowering. Typical is the view of the caller and musician Gene Murrow: "The effect of his prodigious talent, strong presence, and point of view was, in effect, to give us all permission to make this material our own."[6] For Shaw argued that the "folk" were as much expressions of contemporary and urban peoples as they were of "primitive" peoples in some distant, rural world; Shaw could not have been more forthright: folk origins do not matter very much.

Although Shaw was not an academically trained folklore theorist, his view reflected a profound and growing alternative among anthropologists and folklorists to the colonial, linear paradigm that had dominated folklore studies— and to the thinking of country dance revivalists. The formative work in folklore and modern anthropology at the end of the nineteenth century by Lewis Henry Morgan and James G. Frazier essentialized the peasantry and traced cultural evolution from peasantry to "civilization." Written from the donnish corridors of Cambridge (both in Massachusetts and in England), the "folk" origins of civilization were located in northern Europe; "race"—by which folklorists meant "not Anglo-Saxon"—was tied to tribal and not "folk" cultures. In this tradition, folk dance revivalists focused their travels on Scandinavia and the British Isles, and the folk revivals remained decidedly Eurocentric.[7]

Shaw's view of a contemporary, urban folk reflected a new, more dynamic, interactive, and reflective perspective on both culture and the folk that had been advanced in the first half of the century, notably, by cultural anthropologists at Columbia University: Franz Boas, Margaret Mead, and Ruth Benedict. Their work and that, subsequently, of anthropologists such as Clifford Geertz and Edmund Leach challenged the hegemony of the dominant paradigm. While they won many adherents in the scholarly world, their work penetrated popular discourse much less. Indeed, when Shaw visited the United States, the two views remained contested within folklore studies, and many traditionalists in organizations such as CDSS remained wedded to "peasant authenticity."[8]

Shaw's view of the folk, then, reflected struggles within folklore generally, and while it empowered some, it threatened others, most especially those committed to preserving what they imagined to be Sharp's legacy: the Playford tradition. To be sure, Shaw's view did little to reverse the Anglocentric character of ECD; it was, after all, a community dedicated to Anglo-American dance, not international dance. But Shaw set in motion the development of a new "modern" genre of dances in the spirit of historical English Country Dance, leaving it to choreographers to interpret how that historical "spirit" or "tradition" would be represented in the newly written "folk" dances. The result was the emergence by the century's end of a new subset of ECD: Modern English Country Dance (MECD).

Signs of Change

The last years of the second revival brought new people into CDSS well before Shaw's visit. Entering ECD in 1966, Gene Murrow remembered it as a moment of change that challenged the prudish Victorian tone that had been set by the older generation of upper-class women who led it: "It did loosen up in the '60s, as many other things did."[9] For although the majority of newcomers entered the ECD community in the 1970s and 1980s, well after the folk revival had ebbed, enough began to filter into it in the late '60s and early '70s to create a stir. The continuing role of longtime leaders and a familiar repertoire muted the changes for old-timers, at least for a while, but ultimately the entrance of left-liberal folkies of the second folk revival who found a new home in the Country Dance and Song Society of America in increasing numbers precipitated fundamental social changes in the history of the country dance community.

A survey conducted early in the twenty-first century of 171 dance enthusiasts at ECD national camps (on both coasts) and at special local events, which probably drew disproportionately large numbers of more committed CDSS members, provides a telling profile: a quarter of the sample had begun ECD prior to 1980, and 84.1 percent described themselves as liberal or left-wing. In fact, though the sample is small, four of the fourteen (28.6 percent) who began ECD before 1970 described themselves as left-wing. Equally significant, approximately three of every ten (29.5 percent) were Jewish or Italian. And while the data did not distinguish those of Irish descent, anecdotal evidence and dancer reminiscences note their relative absence, even in cities such as New York and Boston with large Irish American communities and Irish immigrants.[10]

Several developments coincident with the left-liberal "softening" of the oppositional character of folk culture at the end of the Sixties helped stimulate the move of many new people into CDSS. Some simply joined country dance groups where programming mixed historical ECD dances with traditional dance, contra, and squares. But for some others, the move was a lateral one from a world of English and American folk ballads or from a love of classical music. For many others, however, it was an extension of New Left political culture, a byproduct of the back-to-nature counterculture, and an alternative to the growing nationalism of ethnic groups that had displaced the International Folk Dance movement. In interviews, many longtime dancers at the end of the twentieth century told of having been introduced to English Country Dance through the folk revival in song or in contra or International Folk Dance. Typical of some who were first exposed to contra dance on campuses or from back-to-nature hippie sites of the counterculture were the experiences of the new leaders of the Boston ECD community, the musician Peter Barnes and the teachers Art and Helene Cornelius. Barnes, who authored the bible of ECD tunes (popularly known simply as "Barnes"), was singing in a Boston coffee house when introduced to contra dance; the Corneliuses found their way to ECD after introductions to square dance and international dance in the Cambridge area.[11]

The emergence of a contra revival in New England helped transform the U.S. country dance community, including that of ECD. Square dance introduced some people, like the Corneliuses, to ECD, especially in the immediate postwar era, but it played a relatively small role in the changes that rocked the ECD community in the 1970s. As noted earlier, the wartime and postwar square dance revival moved away from vernacular country dance and developed into the modern choreographed hybrid known as Western or Club Squares.

Instead, in the late '60s, Dudley Laufman, the head of the New England–based "contra boom," galvanized a vibrant young generation that had moved into New Hampshire and Vermont towns and villages with a new energy and attitude. "American" dance was hardly new, of course, and the Appalachian squares remained a popular and integral part of the country dance scene, especially of course in southern dance settlements such as at Brasstown and Berea. But the Dudley style, described by Gene Murrow as "'slow' with lots of clogging and a very grounded, earthy style," encouraged a particularly thrilling personal showmanship with "incredible variations" as individuals clogged, stepped, and twirled as they and their partners moved up and down the line. Young people flocked to "Dudley dances," and many of these folks, in turn, joined CDSS affiliates where they could do more of these dances and other kindred forms. The entry of these dancers onto the urban CDSS dance floors in the early '70s did more than change the profile of the typical dancer; their attendance brought new energy and expectations as well.[12]

Migrants from the contra boom infused what may have been an even larger number of new dancers who had moved laterally from International Folk Dance. The largest number of those interviewed traced their folk dance experience back to international dance on a college campus in the '60s and '70s.[13] While most also cited their participation in International Folk Dance as part of their more general involvement with the left-liberal political culture of the era, they were less explicit about why they had left that dance movement to start ECD—and most did eventually leave rather than do both. Reasons could be social, political, physical, aesthetic, or a combination of factors, but speaking years later when they danced on aged feet and knees, they lauded as attractions the Baroque, Renaissance, and classical music and ease of dance, all markers of their distinctive bourgeois class culture. Moreover, dancers' repeated celebration of the supportive dance community as a "haven from a heartless world"—to reprise the title of a popular 1977 book by the historian Christopher Lasch—suggests how politics of the dance space also informed their attraction to ECD.[14] For, as foreshadowed in the preceding chapter, International Folk Dance by the late 1960s increasingly changed its focus from proletarian to ethnic imaginings and, more particularly, to a fascination with an ethnic regional culture: the Balkans. Led by the charismatic and pioneering work of dance collector and teacher Dick Crum, "Balkan dance"—an amalgam of dances from southern and eastern Europe—increasingly came to dominate the International Folk Dance repertory after 1965. In the "Balkan craze," dances of other lands continued to be done, but coincident with the decline of the driving political concerns of the Sixties, dancers' delight increasingly came from mastering the intricate steps and identifying with the Balkan cultures. But learning the dances could be a challenge. The steps, often demanding and complicated, required concentration, regular practice, and some physical agility. In the International Folk Dance tradition, usually only a few dances were taught every evening, and dancers learned dances by standing behind experienced dancers and imitating the steps. For some dances and dancers, that process worked fine; for others, it was frustrating, especially as the Balkan craze led many groups to develop a cadre of exclusive experienced dancers who provided little encouragement to newcomers.

English and American Country Dance were welcome alternatives, albeit, with the nationalism of the Celtic revival, not so much for Irish or Scottish dancers. Yet, in the political culture of back-to-nature contra dance, the ECD dance floor was an alternative and oppositional space, a rural community retreat from fast-paced, materialist, urban capitalist culture. English Country Dance had no such political meaning, but to newcomers from International Folk Dance moving into CDSS, which represented both English and American dance, the ECD venue could be imagined as an extension of the contra boom and, for the more politically radical, a bridge back to the proletarian politics of international dance. Indeed, even as the ECD community lost its oppositional character, dancers saw it as an alternative left-liberal cultural space. But the nationalist imperatives of "Englishness" and "Americanness" and racial liberalism complicated this perspective and could ironically find the community reinforcing the dominant white, Anglo-Saxon national legacy.

But English and American dance held many aesthetic attractions as well. Some American dances such as "The Virginia Reel" were familiar, as were squares. English Country Dance was also famously "easy on the knees," an attribute not lost on dancers with aging joints. The dances required little more footwork than skipping and felt safe for newcomers who did not think of themselves as graceful or coordinated. The dances had a few intricate patterns that required geographic and geometric sense, which is accessible for academic types. New dancers might find the patterns disorienting, but they were regularly repeated in different dances, and as important, every country dance was taught and prompted. And finally, unlike the recorded music in the international dance, by the '60s, English and American dance was increasingly done to wonderful live music, with energetic contra bands and English musicians playing tunes drawn from classical and Baroque composers.[15]

As the survey suggested, many of the ECD newcomers were Jewish, and some of them undoubtedly came with background in Israeli dance. For as the international impulse behind the international dance community waned,

Re-Generation | 211

another national dance tradition was invented to coincide with the making of a new nation: Israeli dance. Doris Humphrey began Israeli dance at the 92nd Street Y shortly after the war, and by the 1960s, as the number of Jewish college students grew, Israeli folk dance grew on and around college campuses in cities such as Cambridge, Berkeley, and New York. In addition, the increasing identity that some Jews had with Israel after the 1967 Sinai War may help explain the increased popularity of Israeli dance in the 1960s. Contrarily, some left-wing "peace" Jews who had identified with Kibbutz socialism saw the post-1967 Israeli government's policy and its cultural politics as increasingly imperialist. For them, alternative recreational dance communities such as in country dance could represent a congenial alternative political and social space.[16]

The entrance of many Jewish dancers into the ECD community, both from Israeli dance and probably more so from International Folk Dance, in which they appear to have been disproportionately active, democratized what had been an Anglo-Saxon elite movement.[17] The newcomers gave ECD, which had been a fundamentally Anglo-American national tradition, an international characteristic: the new adherents were not necessarily doing their "own" ethnic dances; in English Country Dance, the dancers were increasingly white-ethnic transplants from the counterculture familiar with doing "other" people's dances. But embracing the Anglo-American dance tradition also testified to these white-ethnic Americans' assimilation. This tradition was now "theirs," not an "other's." Thus, the Anglo-Saxon elites that had dominated ECD leadership and constituted the backbone of the rank-and-file dancers now found themselves part of a more diverse but not unfamiliar white dance community, though one from a wider middle-income professional class. White ethnics entering the dance community confirmed their whiteness in making the white Anglo-American dance floor their own. At the same time, it is important to remember that in the 1970s, Jewish migration into the Anglo-American dance community coincided with the souring of Jewish–African American race relations (and the story was largely the same for Italians and other white ethnics entering the dance community). These conflicts provide a racial context to the place of race in the country dance community, which its adherents came to celebrate as a safe urban space in the following decades.[18]

Culture Clash

Reminiscing about the era, those who were new to the community offer a prevailing narrative that is less about change than about a culture clash.

Regardless of their point of entry to the ECD and American dance communities, with their apparent comfort with the whiteness of the country dance movement, post-1970 newcomers shared a sense that as children of the counterculture, they had found a safe haven. But newcomers and old-timers found that there was much that they did not share. ECD stalwarts greeted the white-ethnic newcomers with mixed feelings and a rather familiar set of traditional attitudes. The leadership had long sought to bring a younger generation into ECD and welcomed their addition to the movement. But old-timers also maintained a class and cultural distance from the youth culture that was not so different from the way they characterized the Sharp generation's paternal relationship to these young people's immigrant grandparents half a century earlier. In the first half of the century, EFDS and its American Branch had looked to ECD as an Anglo-Saxon tonic for immigrant customs and behavior that they found troubling. The counterculture, however, with its florid dress (or more provocatively, braless mini-dresses), long hair, bare feet, lack of deference, and "loose" morality, was equally a world apart from that of the Victorian/Georgian era in which Sharp's and Gadd's generation had been reared.

New dancers vividly remember arriving at Pinewoods or dancing in their local communities and confronting censorious old-timer leaders, and most notably Gadd, monitoring the dance floor and dance community. Dancers agreed that National Director Gadd, who celebrated her eight-first birthday in 1970, was personally puritanical. Stories of her patrolling the bushes to prevent any hanky-panky at summer dance camps in the early 1970s have become camp folklore.[19] Yet these stories as told by the younger generation have tended to minimize or forget that Gadd had been by all accounts a lovely dancer and guiding force for forty-five years in the establishment of the American Branch and CDSS.

Tradition and the burden of CDSS's proud history also made it difficult to implement changes, even as it became increasingly apparent by the late '60s to some CDSS leaders that the new era had brought a new constituency with its own expectations and interests. Age was catching up with the seemingly indomitable Gadd, and she was slowing down. Genny Shimer and Sue Salmons, who had been dancing since the 1940s, often shared the teaching responsibilities with Gadd. CDSS was Gadd's "life," however, and loyalty and a sense of decency made it difficult to move to replace her, even though it had become apparent to some members that she was continuing to teach "a little too long."[20] One of those who later succeeded Gadd summed up the problem CDSS faced in moving forward: Gadd was "an incredibly single-minded person . . . , [who was] resistant to new things and giving up control."[21] As a first step, in April 1970, CDSS created the new position of Assistant Director for Fieldwork and Special Services. Paul Skrobela, one of the several New York dance teachers, assumed the position as an interim appointment until, in November, CDSS appointed to the post a twenty-two-year-old young man fresh out of college: James E. Morrison.[22]

Morrison's social profile resembled that of the intellectual-artistic establishment that peopled CDSS; however, he broke the mold of the British-born matriarchy that had been running the American ECD show for fifty-five years: he was young and male, had been reared in both the American and English traditions, and was born in America. A graduate with a degree in English from Dartmouth, which was probably the most conservative school in the Ivy League at the time, gave him respectable bone fides. But Morrison was a musician and a dancer whose youth and "keen interest in both the American and English traditions" also made him an ideal bridge to new dancers. Morrison had been weaned on the Berkeley Folk Festival in 1963, and as a Dartmouth undergraduate, he fulfilled a "community service" requirement by attending the John C. Campbell Folk School to work with "the poor." The Campbell School nurtured in him a newfound love for both traditional and historical Playford dance and Appalachian squares, and afterward, back at Dartmouth, he sought out contra dances. Morrison became a regular in the "contra boom." In fact, at Dartmouth, he helped host a "Dudley dance." So CDSS, in adding Morrison to its staff, signaled its commitment to youth and an enhanced repertory. Gadd supported Morrison's appointment, although she had no way of predicting the changes that would ensue. But while Morrison brought into the leadership a particular passion for the contra dances that reoriented CDSS, he shared with traditionalists a love for the historical, traditional, and ceremonial dances.[23]

Morrison did not have long to wait before he could draw on his energy and vision in leading CDSS. When Gadd retired in 1972, Genny Shimer took the helm as national director, but with two understandings: First, Gadd had to agree to stay out of the executive office. Morrison remembers Gadd as competitive with women and agreed that though this decision must have been personally devastating for Gadd, it was necessary if any change was to take place. Shimer's second condition was only that her appointment be short-term, as her husband, Jack, was retiring, and they had plans to travel.[24]

Shimer, with the youthful Morrison as her assistant director, was an ideal choice to effect a transition within CDSS. She had been a stalwart within the New York dance community for over twenty-five years and a regular teacher at Pinewoods, at the Berea College's Christmas Country Dance School, and at the John C. Campbell Folk School. British born and trained in ECD, she was a familiar face to old-timers in CDSS, and at age sixty in 1973, she was one of their generation.[25]

Three developments in particular during Shimer's tenure as national director marked the beginning of a new participatory, democratic regime in which CDSS established itself in fact as well as in name as equally representative of American and English Country Dance. First, the council that had been running the local New York group, over which Gadd ruled, reorganized in 1973 as the New York Dance Activities Committee (NYDAC). According to Shimer, the change was made to allow "for more membership involvement."[26]

Second, a new generation of American dance callers and the infectious spirit of the contra revival became fixtures at Pinewoods and increasingly in local dance communities. Ted Sannella had begun regular Pinewood appearances in the late '60s, and Dudley Laufman arrived at camp a few years later to transform the dance floor. In that regard, Gene Murrow thought Pinewoods in 1973—the first year after Gadd's retirement—especially memorable. Sannella called contra one week, Laufman called it the second week, and Morrison called southern mountain squares both weeks. And the mood on the dance floor was electric: young, in some accounts libidinous, contra dancers brought a sexual energy of the counterculture with the new style and panache of the second contra revival. Wildly exuberant with high energy, the Dudley contras emphasized style very different from what young people perceived as the fussiness of ECD and the childishness of traditional community dances, but it was style nonetheless. The new place of American dance in CDSS was symbolized in the 1973 publication of Laufman's *Let's Try a Contra*. CDSS had previously published ECD recordings and two ECD books by Gadd; it now signaled to the growing community of contra dancers that it could be their home as well.[27] In 1976, Morrison added a sixth week to the Pinewoods summer program exclusively for American dance.

Dance forms, like all cultural forms, constantly evolve, of course, and are themselves changed by contact with one another. Thus, as the arrival of the contra revival transformed Pinewoods, Gene Murrow has suggested how Pinewoods in turn transformed Dudley dancing. "A high point for us dancers, imagine, was the 1st couple down the center and back—the 1s doing incredible variations on clog steps as they moved down and turned to move up—the inactive 2s relishing the opportunity to do solo clog routines on the sides." But Laufman and Sannella encountered "quick and light" English dancing, "vigorous traditional dances" being "encouraged" by Jim Morrison, and singling southern mountain squares and running sets. By the end of the summer, Murrow notes, Sannella was writing contras and triplets with English figures such as heys and gypsies, and Laufman was calling some English classics such as the three-couple set dance "Prince William" and the longways dance "Childgrove" at his Dudley dances. The result was a new blend of the communities and a new "zesty" contra form: "Soon the contra tradition, via Ted [Sannella] and Dudley and others, would embrace the figures, flow, and faster tempi of the English and Southern Mountain dances, culminating in the 'zesty contra' style."[28]

The third development during Shimer's tenure affected Pinewoods itself. Richard Conant announced in 1974 that the Conant family had decided it could no longer operate the facility and was prepared to sell it at a reasonable price to a nonprofit organization. The camp was, of course, a CDSS institution, and the original two-week programming in the 1930s had grown into summer-long use. Lily Conant had invited Boston-area groups to use the camp, the Country Dance Society's Boston Centre used the camp for annual weekends early and late in the summer, and the Royal Scottish Country Dance Society of Boston used it for a weekend as well. CDSS, however, was the major tenant. Not surprisingly, then, CDSS members responded enthusiastically to the opportunity to ensure that the camp—with its twenty-five unspoilt acres of woodlands, two ponds, and four open-air dance pavilions—would remain a CDSS fixture. A fund to raise $265,000 was begun, and in 1974, Pinewoods Camp, Inc.—a CDSS-led consortium of its previous users—assumed the deed.[29]

And then came Pat Shaw.

The Coming of Pat Shaw

The arrival of a well-established figure who was himself from the older generation cut right to the heart of the ECD tradition. The generational culture clash brought new attitudes, mores, and energy to CDSS dance floors, and especially to the American dance events, but the arrival of Pat Shaw at Pinewoods in the summer of 1974 constituted a revolutionary challenge to the Playford historical repertoire that had been the core of the movement's claim to represent Anglo-American folk culture.

Patrick (Pat) Noel Shuldham-Shaw, the leading musician, choreographer, and interpreter of English Country Dance of the mid-twentieth century, had never been to United States. Independently wealthy—recall his mother had chaired the fundraising committee for Cecil Sharp House—he led a life of modest gentility, residing quietly in an unpretentious house in North London's Hampstead Village, long the home to bourgeois intellectuals and artists. Sharp had lived not far away half a century earlier. Reared in a dancing family, he was devoted to country dance, and his talents were in wide demand, both in the United Kingdom and in Belgium and the Netherlands, to which he often traveled.[30] Shaw could be found calling a dance one night and playing his accordion the next. Moreover, unlike the dances Sharp had collected from villages or reconstructed from the Playford manuscripts in the British Library, many of the dances Shaw taught were from the approximately 141 of his own invention.

But as long as May Gadd was firmly in control, few of Shaw's dances made it onto dance programs. According to Sue Salmons, Gadd, ever the Sharp loyalist, disdained the "invented" dances and blacklisted "Maggot Pie," a pathbreaking 1932 book of twenty-five newly composed "contemporary dances in the Playford style."[31] But with Gadd's retirement from the scene, one of the new generation of dance teachers, Fried Herman, renewed her long-frustrated efforts to get Shaw invited to Pinewoods. As noted in chapter 6, twenty-five years earlier, as a Dutch émigré to England, Fried had lived in Shaw's home, where she did some light housekeeping. With the support of his friend and student, Shaw won his invitation to America, and Pinewoods was, as dancer folklore has it, never the same.[32]

The folklore surrounding Shaw and his visit is Bunyonesque. Jacqueline Schwab remembered him as a "great charismatic guy," "a creative force" with an "imposing large presence—physically and charismatically . . . [who] had us all sort of following him around like lemmings." Shaw stayed with Arthur and Helene Cornelius for a few days before and after camp, and Arthur remembered him as "amazing, a genius I would say. And he loved to drink, a definite drinker. But, he could do anything. He could sing. He composed dances [and tunes] on the spot, partly he played instruments and, of course, he was a tremendous influence on everything, not only on the dances he composed, but an influence on how to dance and the music."[33]

Shaw's iconoclastic views and teaching did not come as a complete surprise to Americans, however. Despite Gadd's best efforts, several of Shaw's inventive dances had found their way onto local U.S. dance floors prior to his visit. Art Cornelius had learned and "loved" two Shaw pieces from the mid-'60s, "Margaret's Waltz" and "John Tallis's Canon." "The latter was a clever musical and dance figure 'canon' where dancers on one diagonal perform the dance four counts behind the other two dancers and one musician plays for each pair of dancers. The complexity of the round, and the break

"Bottoms Up!" Pat Shaw with Genny Shimer at Pinewoods, 1974. (Photo: Helene Cornelius)

with partner-centered patterns signaled how Shaw was in fact reinventing and expanding ECD—indeed, faster and farther than many dancers found comfortable."[34] Indeed, Shaw had gone back to the Playford manuscripts and taken a fresh look at Sharp's interpretations, putting questions about style, authenticity, and the meaning of the folk back on the table. Moreover, Shaw had not masked his contrarian view that the folk were not simply a "peasant" tradition but could be an expression of a modern, twentieth-century people. Challenging Sharp and the traditionalists who adhered to his position, Shaw trumpeted his view that he did not "think origins matter very much" in a 1970 issue of the EFDSS journal.[35]

Thus, arriving at Pinewoods, an air of anticipation—excitement mixed with wariness—greeted Shaw. Kitty Keller, herself still a relative newcomer to Pinewoods, found herself between "two torrents of new information": "when he [Shaw] came to Pinewoods, I think people were afraid that he was going to change everything that we had learned, which turned out not to be the case. But, what he did was open our eyes. And we didn't know anything. So what Pat showed us made so much sense. But what we learned in Gay's

[Gadd] classes and other people's classes made such sense too." Many others fell into one camp or the other, but the abiding significance of Shaw's visit was it authorized new choreography, new ways of thinking about steps and figures, about bodily carriage, and about the division between American and English dance.[36]

Shaw's reinterpretation of a canonical step in English Country Dance called "siding" became a lightning rod for antipathy toward the changes that Shaw offered and that his visit represented. Cecil Sharp had reconstructed siding from his initial reading of the Playford manuscripts, and his instruction had been the gold standard since the 1910s. In Sharp's version, a couple face and swirl past each other by the left shoulder in four steps making a J-pattern (callers sometimes refer to this as "banana siding") and then pass back the same way they came. In fact, Sharp had himself suggested in the introduction to the sixth country dance book that he may have been wrong in his interpretation of the siding, but his choreography had become entrenched in the dance community, and Sharp chose not to reconsider the step.[37] But Shaw, returning to look at many of the same publications Sharp had studied, reached the opposite conclusion. In Shaw's version, which came to be called "Pat Shaw siding," partners came forward four steps to meet (not pass) by the right shoulder, retreat four steps, and then repeat the pattern to meet by the left shoulder. Sharp's sweeping version allowed for more movement, but, as the musician and choreographer Jacqueline Schwab notes, Shaw's way "has more musical art that's choreographically correct. . . . [It may be] less sensual, but [it is] stronger."[38]

Shaw's visit, though surrounded by controversy, had a profound impact on the dance community. Shaw left a legacy for dancers and choreographers, opening up a performative space in which new dance choreographers could experiment with style and tempo, footwork, and patterns. He also enriched the repertoire with theretofore unknown dances that he had collected or constructed.[39] But as important, his choreography and instruction for the dance punctured the rather rigid authorial cocoon that CDSS leaders such as Gadd had wrapped around English Country Dance in particular. Using inventive choreography that borrowed both from English and American dance styles, Shaw breached stylistic lines that had divided the two dance traditions, and often their respective devotees, into rival camps. Some of Shaw's dances had an American signature, in name, vigor, and patterns that particularly endeared him to many local dancers. During his American sojourn, Shaw wrote dances that commemorated people and places in the American dance community, dances subsequently published in two collections, *Between Two Ponds* and *Pat Shaw's Pinewoods*. Two dances are illustrative of his playful spirit and inventiveness: "Quite Carr-ied Away" was a pun on a beloved CDSS administrator who worked at Pinewoods, Joan Carr, and "Levi Jackson Rag," which celebrated Shaw's visit to Levi Jackson State Park in London, Kentucky, integrated "balance and swing" from American dance with a cake-walk-like rag more usually associated with American country music and introduced the dance into the English repertoire.[40]

Art Cornelius's memory of Shaw's transformative effect was typical: Shaw's dances and teaching gave ECD "a whole new sort of look. It was a lot of Anglo-American stuff. He incorporated a whole lot of American things, swinging and various other things in his dances, which was hardly done at all, before that. And also the kinds of complexities introduced in dancing, sort of taking various figures to a new level. Using different formations and stuff like that, and that's influenced every composer since then." Schwab's recollections mirrored those of Cornelius: "And in his own crazy English way of looking at American things, he created American dances—so called American dances—that really were an English man's view of American dances. And so he shook the world up, and it was a great year."[41]

Shaw not only "shook the world up," however, he created a new dance world. For Shaw's willingness to rethink what had been passed on as tradition opened the floodgates for a stream of new composers and choreographers on both sides of the Atlantic, one of the most influential and prolific of whom was his former housemate-cum-protégé and the sponsor of his American visit, Fried de Metz Herman. Shaw's views on the inventiveness and universality of folk traditions, which removed the sanctity of the "peasant" past and gave equal weight to the "folkie" present, gained popular currency among the new generation who made up the dance community. Thus, Gene Murrow, reminiscing twenty-five years later, noted that "every year, at the same time in the same place, we do certain dances here at Pinewoods. Certain people come to this and they do these dances, so I say we are the folk."[42]

Being constituted as the folk gave would-be composers and choreographers permission to express their own culture as much as that of the Playford era, but it also resurrected an age-old tension between folklore as the preservation or creation of tradition. How would the new dances be integrated into the English Country Dance repertoire if they were written in (sub)urban America or London in the late twentieth century and consisted of figures that bore at times only scant relation to "traditional" steps? Gene Murrow's answer—and as one of the leading callers, musicians, and record producers on both sides of the Atlantic, his view had considerable currency within the dance community—was that "for the present, what feels right to present-day twenty-first-century Americans preserves the essence of the aesthetic of the English country dance—the figures, the kinds of interactions."[43]

The "essence of the aesthetic" can be elusive and debatable, though, and the enthusiasm for the new made some anxious about preserving the old. The contrasting views of two of the grande dames of ECD in the late twentieth century United States—ironically, women who shared the teaching leadership of the suburban New York dance community in Westchester County—illustrated the conflict. Christine Helwig, who devoted herself to reconstructing the old Playford dances, worried in 1999 that the new choreography was jeopardizing the old repertoire: "there are many, many dances written today and some of them are lovely, but I'm very anxious to see the old dances from the Playford, you know, continue to be taught and enjoyed. I think it would be a tremendous loss if those early dances did not continue to be done and taught and relished for what they are."[44] Fried Herman, however, saw herself as part of what like-minded dancers increasingly referred to as a "living tradition." Fried insisted, "I always advocate . . . you should dance all the old dances," but in a 1999 interview she emphasized her own preference for the new dances: "I couldn't possibly understand people from the 1600s. . . . Inside I'm not from the 1600s—I'm from 1999. And so I think that we should really show ourselves the way we are and feel and that's what I'm trying to do" in writing "new movements from the old style" but "with a new name."[45]

On the difference between Helwig and Fried, the dance community voted with its feet and settled the matter largely in Fried's favor. Tensions around the issue continued, but the victory of the "new" was expressed in the emergence and eventual triumph of many new "historical" dances in a modern idiom. Ironically, however, for all their differences, in their teaching, choreography, and dance reconstructions, both women helped nurture the elegance, graciousness, and measured movements of a new Modern ECD, a dance style with its own tempi, embodiments, and character. Sharp, it will be recalled, recorded dances in 1915 with 134 beats per minute, a pace that had dancers leaning forward on the ball of the foot in the running step. In the MECD era, the same dances were typically played at approximately three-quarters that speed, with 104 beats per minute. And in keeping with the slower tempi, few dances were "danced" with the running step; rather, dancers walked and skipped. The dances also encouraged a more vertical, composed posture, rather than the Sharp demonstration teams' forward slant immortalized in the 1920 photographs (see page 151). Romantic and more languid waltz or triple-time dances increasingly predominated. These dances encouraged flowing arms and gliding, in most exaggerated form resembling Sharp's hated ballet style. Equally important to the success of the new dance form was its convergence with the taste of the younger generation. The generation of computer geeks who increasingly constituted a core constituency in the dance community took special delight in complicated figures, such as those advanced in Pat Shaw's new dances. Shaw's visit, then, marked the beginnings of MECD as a new dance form for the age. Shaw stimulated a passel of talented musicians and choreographers who developed its repertoire, and a new young audience stood ready to embrace it.

Becoming National

The change in leadership of CDSS had helped make Shaw's visit to Pinewoods possible, and in the wake of his visit, the new leadership moved energetically forward with the same spirit. Shimer, as she had promised, left the post of national director in September 1975 after less than three years, and James E. Morrison, at the age of twenty-seven, was appointed director.[46]

Morrison's elevation as director could not have come at a more auspicious time for CDSS. If CDSS was to hold the hundreds of new baby-boomer recruits from the folk revival, it had to find a way to honor their interests in contra dance and tolerate the cultural attitudes of the Sixties they brought with them. At the same time, of course, CDSS could not afford to alienate the older and more conventional (and sometimes prissy) members who had led the organization until then. It was not always easy, and in retrospect, it appears Morrison focused his energy and new programs on attracting and holding the new dancers.

Morrison's tenure was brief but momentous. Feeling that CDSS needed to become a truly national organization, he sought to move the national headquarters out of New York, where it had been based since 1915. For most of the century, the largest two groups had long been in New York and Boston, and Morrison felt the movement would never be seen as national as long as it remained under the de facto control of the local group. Morrison had personal reasons that were equally compelling though: a small-town and country boy reared in Berkeley, California, and schooled in New Hampshire, he had recently married and did not want to raise a family in the city. So, when CDSS refused to agree to move its national offices out of the city, Morrison resigned in June 1977 and moved his family to Charlottesville, Virginia.[47]

However brief, Morrison's tenure as national director coincided with what one member of the CDSS executive committee recalled as "the biggest expansion of country dancing in all its forms." The membership had stagnated for many years at about seven to eight hundred members in about twenty groups, mostly in and around East Coast cities; during the 1970s, the membership and number of groups doubled to nearly thirteen hundred members in some fifty centers. Like the youthful new director, the new members were also young and dynamic. Morrison consequently related well to the younger generation wearing "bell bottoms and with long hair" who were increasingly exploring country dance, and he created new programs in American dance and morris dance in particular, which appealed to them. He brought Dudley Laufman to Pinewoods, and when Laufman ran afoul of Gadd, Genny Shimer, and Marshall Barron—the ECD music and dance leaders—and wondered whether he should just pack up and go home, Morrison counseled him to "just ignore them."[48]

Morrison had an interest in historical dance as well, and during the bicentennial he spawned "a little movement" in colonial dance. But he remembered that his focus was to "invigorate programs" and "bridge contra dance and the old-time music scene" with CDSS's traditional emphasis on ECD. In addition to the enlivened weekly and weekend events that added more American dances, Morrison created a touring demonstration group, the American Country Dance Ensemble, and added an American Week at Pinewoods.[49]

The expansion of American dance in the late 1970s and 1980s had unintended but profound consequences for the unique shape of what came to be understood as English Country Dance in the United States. As the community of American dance enthusiasts grew, their numbers made it possible to sustain more dance events. As important, the contra dancers began to constitute a self-sustaining community of their own. Of course, many enjoyed English dance as well and did both; but many found the ECD pace too slow and style too formal. And their preference was matched by those favoring the Playford-style dances, among whom were older dancers who found the gentler dance tradition easier on tired feet and aching joints. As a result, the longstanding "English" dance evenings began to deemphasize American contras and squares (as well as the more active traditional dance rants, reels, and jigs). By the mid-'80s, while British country dance evenings continued to mix historical, traditional, and American dances, country dance communities across the United States had largely separated the two genres into separate evenings. For instance, in New York, "English" dance—reconstituted as largely only Playford-style dances—was done on Tuesday night, and Saturday night was reserved for American contras and squares.[50] Ten years earlier, an evening dance mixed the two forms, and some dancers probably never distinguished one set as English and another as American. Over time, the separation was sustained by instructional structures: dance teachers apprenticed only within each tradition, and as time passed fewer of the new generation of English teachers learned how to call American dances.[51]

In addition to Morrison's support for American dance, he helped stimulate a morris dance revival in the late 1970s. Morris dance had, of course, been the staple of early folk revival, and Sharp early established a demonstration morris team. It was traditionally an all-male tradition, but Sharp had broken with patriarchal tradition and supported women morris dance performances by Mary Neal's Espérance girls and by many of his female teachers, including May Gadd. Morris dance had continued to be taught as part of the ECD syllabus, and every weekly dance in New York and elsewhere typically began with a morris class. But many enthusiasts periodically desired to start morris teams that could perform on their own, not unlike the Headington Morrismen who first excited Sharp's interest in country dance in 1899. The Morris Ring was one such federation of enthusiasts, though Gadd and Kennedy generally resisted the idea of separate morris clubs, feeling they would dilute EFDSS and CDSS; they wanted all groups under their umbrella. The Morris Ring was also all male, which only excited further opposition from Gadd, who was herself a morris dancer. She supported morris dance for both men and women, but under CDSS auspices.[52]

Morrison reversed Gadd's longstanding opposition to independent morris teams. The Pinewoods Morrismen had existed in the previous decade, but their affiliation with the camp had facilitated their acceptance. The Village Morrismen, a local New York group that Morrison thinks Gadd saw as a "threat," dissolved in 1969 after only eighteen months and shortly before Morrison arrived in the city. Morrison initiated a new revival of the form with the creation of independent clubs across the country. As early as 1973, the Binghamton Morris Men and the Cambridge Morris Men started, and the next year, Morrison helped form the Greenwich Morrismen, a team that lasted until 2007. Four months later, Ring O'Bells, a women's team that also flourished, formed. Soon after, the Pinewoods Morrismen reorganized as a club and, serving as a training ground for morris dancers who passed through the camp, spawned a national movement of clubs. By the end of the decade, longsword and rapper performance teams were forming. Gadd remained skeptical of their independence—and even more of the women's "manly" attire in pants—but when the teams affiliated with CDSS, any residual reservations seemed to disappear.[53]

Perhaps the most fundamental change during these years was the explosion of country dance groups across the nation and the character of that growth. CDSS became the organization for a national leisure activity of an expanding professional-technical white-collar class that was of the city, and it was often located in the suburban periphery of it. ECD, with its vacation schools, balls, and dances, had long been a playground for the well-to-do and a major leisure activity. But by end of the century the core of dancers was drawn from a broader social swath of affluent professionals and technical workers. This class's investment in consumer accoutrements embraced and heightened the development of the country dance movement as a consumer industry. Starting in the 1970s, CDSS—and its behavior mirrored that of some International Folk Dance leaders such as Michael Ginsburg and Karl Finger—began to sell dance books and records and promote special local events to dancers from across the country, and the making of a "folk dance industry" grew apace in succeeding decades.

The role of what historians understand as the new middle class of white-collar professionals in CDSS also helped make the movement more national. Many Americans moved often, and even if these dancers and dance teachers were more settled in stable jobs than others of their class, those who resettled in new communities helped build a national movement with a national dance idiom and ties. But as CDSS became a truly national movement—and with Canadian members, in truth a North American movement—its members often had an attenuated relationship to the city: urbane, with a love, for instance, of the Baroque and Renaissance music used in ECD dances, new post-1980 dance groups drew from white ethnics (many of whom Anglo-American elites in the American Branch had not always considered white)[54] who worked in the city but had moved to suburban split-level and ranch homes to fulfill the middle-class dream. Not surprisingly, then, many of the new groups settled and danced in "safe" havens in the shadows of the city.

The Modern Country Dance Nation

While new groups appeared in many of the major urban centers between the late 1960s and the mid-1980s, unlike in New York, they more often centered in the suburban periphery near the dancers' homes. Substantial contingents sustained groups in cities such as Philadelphia, San Francisco, St. Louis, Washington, DC, and Baltimore, but it was in the suburbs such as Westchester and Western Ontario (near New York and Toronto, respectively) and around college towns where ECD had long been supported, such as Princeton, Swarthmore, Ann Arbor, Pasadena, Durham, Palo Alto, and Berkeley, that groups increasingly established roots. A brief history of four such sites gives a sense of the urbane but suburban pattern of development and the political impact of the new generation from the era of the second folk revival.

In Philadelphia, the dance community has moved back and forth over the city and suburban line. By the late '70s there were three Philadelphia groups that focused on ECD: Perdue's, Germantown Country Dancers, and Swarthmore English Country Dancers. The oldest group, Perdue's, was named for Perdue Cleaver, who initiated the group in 1946 (although it celebrated its fiftieth anniversary in 2004). The group met in Philadelphia at the home of a local dance couple. When their hosts moved to California, the group met in the barn owned by the uncle of another dancer, and from there it moved to churches in a suburb west of Philadelphia in Media, Pennsylvania.[55] Germantown Country Dancers was organized in 1971 by Hanny Budnick, a local ECD enthusiast. By the next year, the group had live music and a regular meeting place for its weekly dance: the Germantown Friends School gym in the Germantown section of Philadelphia. Budnick also promoted a performance team in middecade to dance at local events and spur interest in ECD. In 1976, the team was a natural choice to help celebrate the American bicentennial. Invited to perform at the Philadelphia Folk Fair and at the preopening of the Old City Tavern, a reconstructed colonial inn, the team developed a colonial repertoire and continues in the present as a colonial demonstration troupe, the Colonial Assembly. Germantown Country Dancers eventually moved to Calvary Episcopal Church, because one of the members knew the pastor and his wife, but as one Philadelphia dancer remembered it, because of "some minor crime incidents and a large perception of possible crime," the group moved to the Friends Meeting House in suburban Lower Merion, Pennsylvania.[56]

The location at a Friends facility was not happenstance. The location of many groups in houses of worship was often simply a matter of finding a cheap rental with a good wood floor, and someone with a connection to the church or temple might also be able to negotiate a good price. But the Society of Friends had a long association with the ECD dance movement: Quaker schools such as Earlham College (which Elizabeth Burchenal attended) and Swarthmore College, which tended to be internationalist in outlook and British identified, often hosted ECD groups, and in that regard, the third local Philadelphia group was based at suburban Swarthmore College. Proud that it was the oldest extracurricular institution at the college, the Swarthmore College Folk Dance Club taught Scottish, English, and contra dance. The club also sponsored longsword and morris classes and hosted the first of its annual Scottish and English country balls in 1971.[57]

Perdue Cleaver's Gilbert and Sullivan Night during Pinewoods' "Talent Night," 1963. Left to right: Perdue Cleaver, Jack Langstaff, Elizabeth Copstein. (Photo: probably by Stan Levy; Jack Shimer Collection, courtesy of Joan Shimer and David Millstone)

The history of the Bay Area Country Dance Society (BACDS) tells much the same story but, like the history of the American West, reflects also the role of migrant dancers. Song Chang and his postwar successors had incorporated English and square dancing into the international scene and into the Folk Dance Federation of California, and a Scottish group started as early as 1946. The Stanford community around Palo Alto seems also to have sponsored ECD events periodically over the years, and contra and Scottish groups met irregularly. A Stanford graduate student, Nick Harris, who had attended Dudley dances as an Amherst undergraduate, started a regular Stanford contra dance in 1974–75. Around the same time, Harris started an ECD dance in Berkeley. There also seem to have been longsword and rapper teams in the Bay Area. But these were local groups that operated in isolation from one another, or almost like private clubs, and it was the arrival in Berkeley of a dance enthusiast from Pasadena, Brad Foster, that transformed these fragments into a regional CDSS dance community.[58]

Foster had been taught country dancing as a high school student in Pasadena by Mary Judson, another of the grande dames of the ECD community, and she was the one who also arranged for his first visit to Pinewoods in 1971. Arriving to study architecture at Berkeley in the fall 1975, Foster plunged into the local country dance scene. Chuck Ward had started an ECD group in San Francisco in late 1968 or early 1969, which was taught by Tom Kruskal, a Pinewoods regular. Kruskal departed from the area in 1975, however, just as Foster arrived, and Foster became the new leader and teacher for the San Francisco Dance Society. At approximately the same time, a square dance group formed in Santa Cruz (which later morphed into a contra group), and an English group started up in San Jose. Foster called squares for the Santa Cruz dance, and in 1978 he took over the Stanford contra dance.[59]

Then, in 1980, the success of the first West Coast summer camp—Alta Sierra Camp near Kings Canyon National Park in the Sierras, in Mendocino, California, which had a week devoted to English Country Dance—set Foster thinking. If he, with his wife's help, could bring together dancers from the region for the camp, the same logic made sense for an umbrella regional organization. The small groups of dancers in Palo Alto, in Berkeley, and in the East Bay often did not constitute a critical mass needed for a successful dance. In 1980, though, the development of the interstate highway system and mass media gave the region a new coherence, and Foster proceeded to capitalize on it, creating a new federation of area dance groups, the Bay Area Country Dance Society (BACDS). BACDS helped network all the area dancers so they could attend one another's evenings of contra or English dance and also come together to sponsor special events that required greater numbers. In 1981, BACDS added an American Week to its summer program, and in 1986 it inaugurated a "No Snow Ball," a playful nod to the local climate and East Coast migrants' memories of Playford balls. At its founding, BACDS networked country dance groups in San Francisco, Berkeley, San Jose, Santa Cruz, and Palo Alto. Foster recalls, however, that by the mid-'80s the groups had mushroomed and sprung up along the peninsula and throughout the East Bay and North Bay. Like Foster, however, many of the musicians and callers during BACDS's early years had been trained at East Coast ECD centers. For instance, Bruce Hamilton, one of the leading area callers who also had a national reputation, was tutored by California's Mary Judson, but after learning to dance at Swarthmore. The musician Stan Kramer came from a longstanding country dance family with roots at Berea, and his wife, Susan, who has played flute for decades, grew up in Berea and then lived and danced in Philadelphia. The leader of the Palo Alto ECD dance, Bob Fraley and his wife, Ruthanne, met dancing in Princeton. And Jody McGeen, a transplanted New Yorker, apprenticed as a caller in New York under Genny Shimer and Christine Helwig.[60]

The history of the Princeton Country Dancers (PCD) is a more straightforward suburban tale, but its spinoffs document the canopy of supportive dance and extradance associations that nourished ECD members. In 1978, the caller David Chandler created the Princeton dance and called a mix of contra and English dances. Chandler, who was active on the CDSS executive committee, moved to central New Jersey to take a job at Rutgers University. He had been dancing in New York City and simply imported the mixed program model then in effect there to Princeton. Chandler's first exposure to contra dance, however, had been at the Fox Hollow Festival in upstate New York, where Dudley Laufman and the Canterbury Orchestra was the resident band.[61]

For the first year, Princeton dancers met at a school in Franklin Park, a town east of Princeton. "Somewhat later" the group named itself Princeton Country Dancers, quite possibly during the following year, when it briefly met on the university campus. But the need for a good wooden sprung floor and affordable rent required folk dance groups to be flexible about location, and for the first twenty years of the group's existence it moved constantly. Half the years were spent in churches in Belle Mead and Franklin Park; during the other half, the group met in a series of Princeton churches.[62]

Initially PCD danced to recorded music. Soon after, the group sponsored a pickup band, which nurtured a cadre of homegrown musicians in a community band, Rum and Onions, which explicitly drew on the Canterbury Orchestra as a model. Some local musicians formed a regular band, Tripping Upstairs, and in 1980–81, others served as the core of the band Hold the Mustard (HTM), a group that became one of the leading ECD bands of the era. HTM regularly performed at dance weekends and special events around the country and, with the release of its first recordings in 1987 and 1991, helped institutionalize a universal CDSS sound and tempo.[63]

The life of the PCD dance community only began on the dance floor. In addition to offering regular contra and English dances as well as an annual Winter Cotillion and special Halloween dance, PCD nurtured the flourishing of local ritual teams that usually met privately to practice. PCD dancers formed Millstone Ritual Morris (ca. 1980), Foaming at the Feet (a clogging team, ca. 1982), Shandygaff Longsword (1985), and the Griggstown (a neighboring town) Lock Rapper Team (1989). And in 1994, some members formed a Handsome Molly, a mixed team of men and women that reflected a radical political tradition. Molly Dance drew on an East Anglia tradition that PCD's twentieth-anniversary history described as "originally done by men, some dressed women (mollies), all dressed in working clothes and stout boots, with faces smudged with charcoal for disguise, who would stomp through the villages on Plough Monday, boisterously mocking the dances of the gentry." Bespeaking the affluence of its members, the continuing transatlantic character of the dance community, and the heightened place of leisure travel, within the first five years of its existence, Handsome Molly had performed in Toronto and East Anglia, England.[64]

PCD folk activities also extended beyond the dance, though, often drawing on other folk traditions. The Cotillion Singers, for example, with an "ever shifting repertoire of folk, rock and roll, seasonal and classical choral music," debuted at PCD's 1983 cotillion. Another group of dancers did Sacred Harp singing. The friendships forged during the dancing and singing, which in some cases even blossomed into love affairs, provided additional opportunities for dancers to come together to celebrate and support one another. In PCD's first ten years, it counted no fewer than eighteen marriages among dancers and fourteen babies born to dancer families. Members frequently met at one another's homes for potluck diners. The Dancing Needles Quilt Guild drew on the folk tradition of quilting to celebrate the marriages and births, and the sardonically named Ladies Who Lunch formed as a mothers' support group. During the '80s, PCD members also created a Gardeners Seed Exchange and inaugurated its most significant and enduring community dance event: the Head for the Hills (HFTH) retreat. Originating in 1984, HFTH met annually at the Hudson Guild Farm in western New Jersey (until its closing in 1995, when the weekend moved to the Pocono Mountains). Today it remains a weekend of country dancing, singing, and partying—an occasion for a celebration of community—the bonding of friendships radiating out from the dance floor.[65]

The final stop on this tour of new dance venues spawned by the folk and contra revivals focuses on an extraordinary individual who, drawing on the left-liberal legacy of the Sixties, compels a rethinking of the ECD tradition even as he advances it. Traversing the United States several times and through several of the aforementioned sites, his life also illustrates the stretch of the revitalized CDSS to the South. The individual, Carl Wittman, is remarkably little known to contemporary dancers beyond his development of gender-neutral dancing, but his work was in fact shaped by the larger progressive political project that animated the second folk revival.

Raised in the New York suburb of Paramus, New Jersey, Wittman was weaned on the politics and folk culture of the second revival and New Left: he was a red-diaper baby whose parents were communists. He then attended

Carl Wittman teaching morris dance (and holding a morris stick), at Duke University, ca. 1982. (Photo: Laura Dacy, courtesy of Allan Troxler)

Swarthmore College, where a member of the physical-education staff, Irene Moll, introduced him to English Country Dance and morris dance, as well as Scottish and international dance. Moll, in fact, introduced generations of Swarthmore students to ECD from the 1950s to the late '70s, many of whom, like Bruce Hamilton, played major roles in the dance community. Moll ran a Friday-night international dance but emphasized, as kindred forms, Scottish and English Country Dance, and both became Wittman's leisure-time passion and complement to the political activism that consumed him then.[66] He spent summers in the South working for civil rights, and in 1963 he became an early member of the National Council of the radical Students for a Democratic Society (SDS). He coauthored with Tom Hayden "An Interracial Movement of the Poor" and published an organizing pamphlet in 1964, "Seminar on Marxism." He then moved back to New Jersey, where during the day he worked on SDS's pioneering community-organizing project in Newark, New Jersey, the Newark Community Union Project (NCUP), and danced with May Gadd at Duane Hall in New York two evenings a week.[67]

Carl Wittman and back-to-the-land friends dancing on the front lawn, Wolf Creek, Oregon, ca. 1974. (Photo: Boyd Peters, courtesy of Allan Troxler)

Changes in the New Left in the mid-1960s, however, and Wittman's responses to them, in time transformed the way many people experienced ECD. Wittman had married a college friend, Mimi Feingold, in 1966, and moving to San Francisco around 1968, he joined a commune of antidraft activists. But immersed in the radical sexual counterculture of late-1960s San Francisco, Wittman began to address his sexual identity. He had started to have sexual relations with men at the age of fourteen and grew increasingly unhappy with the homophobia and machismo of SDS's male leaders.[68] Resigning from SDS, Wittman began to come out as a gay man to friends, and in 1969, the couple separated.

In the next decade, as a gay man of the Left, Wittman became an antiwar activist, a pioneer for gay rights, and a convert to the counterculture. He turned in his draft card and in 1968 published *Waves of Resistance*, a primer for antidraft resisters. His most significant writing, however, was a manifesto he published the next year that became a foundational text for the gay liberation movement. A call to arms, *Refugees from Amerika: A Gay Manifesto* rejected both capitalist and socialist repression of homosexuality and the medicalization of gay identity. Convinced that hegemonic American culture was inhospitable terrain, he bought some land in rural Wolf Creek, Oregon, where some gay men had been establishing communes, and moved there in 1971 with his lover, Steven McClave. Two years later, he began a long-term relationship with Allan Troxler, another conscientious objector (and Swarthmore graduate). In Wolf Creek, Wittman became an environmental activist and turned his attention to his longstanding passion for English Country Dance.

Wittman had never lost his love for country dance, and while in San Francisco, he and Feingold had attended Chuck Ward's English group and joined his Scottish team. In Oregon, Wittman began his own group in their commune, initially teaching it in the traditional coupled dance form. But, looking about them at the gay community of dancers, Wittman and Troxler began to speak of an alternative format that would make more sense for their group and be more inviting to them. So, drawing on a shared commitment to both gender and social equality, they began to experiment with a global language that substituted gender-free categories. Initially, to identify roles, they used the colors red and green on "pinnies" of cloth or paper (to "pin" to their shirts) as alternatives to the "men's line" or the "women's line." They later settled on the "left" and "right file." The focus was as much on gender-neutral language as on creating an inclusive environment, for they believed the problem of exclusion was as applicable to people who felt unwelcome in the dance community because of their race or class. Unfortunately, in the subsequent history, this latter thrust of the mission largely disappeared in practice; Wittman's efforts were known as "gender-free" dance.[69]

By 1978 internecine conflicts within Wolf Creek's gay and environmental communities had soured Troxler and, to a lesser extent, Wittman, and they had begun to think of greener pastures. In the next year, Troxler returned to Durham, North Carolina (he had been raised in Greensboro), where he had taken a production position with *Southern Exposure*, a progressive magazine committed to social justice in the South. Wittman followed him a year later, but not without having left behind the seeds of a gender-free movement that blossomed in Oregon and elsewhere. In 1980, Wittman choreographed for the Oregon Shakespeare festival in Ashland, where the lighting director was Chris Sackett and a member of the demonstration team was Michael Cicone. Sackett had cofounded Ashland Country Dance two years earlier, and the next year his wife, Brooke Friendly, helped found the Heather and Rose Country Dancers, a statewide federation of Scottish and English dance groups committed to teaching with "global dance" instructions that refer to people's positions rather than their gender. Cicone went on to lead the Boston Gender-Free English Country Dance in Jamaica Plain.[70]

The women's liberation and gay liberation movements were at the center of the identity politics that dominated left-liberal circles in the 1980s, but it would be misleading to suggest that gender-neutral dancing penetrated very far into the dance community. Even among the younger generation of dancers, patriarchal structures did not soften overnight. The idea of men dancing with men provoked reactions among many dancers that ranged from unease to consternation. Women, who often had to dance with one another because of the shortage of men, were more willing to dance with one another. But, as suggested earlier, Wittman won his share of admirers and followers. One of the straight old-time grande dames, Christine Helwig, was notably appreciative of both his work in reconstructing Playford dances and his inclusiveness. Moreover, to many women in particular, gender-neutral dance solved the problem of gender balance that had long been a problem in dance communities where men were frequently in short supply. And for others, Wittman's compelling personality and enthusiasm may have attracted them to the practice. In any case, though most CDSS affiliates never adopted gender-neutral terminology, gradually over the next decades, as a result of Wittman's influence, followers established several regular gender-neutral dance venues in the country, and the groups federated in 1988 as the Lavender Folk and Country Dancers.[71]

Perhaps the most famous local group was located in the city in which Wittman and Troxler settled: Durham, North Carolina. Located in the shadows of the Appalachian Mountains, Durham had a long and venerable history of country dancing—from southern mountain squares and clogging to contra dance. The Research Triangle of universities also provided a ready audience for folk dance. Arriving in 1981, Wittman continued his environmental gay rights activism, serving as codirector of North Carolina's Public Interest Research Group (PIRG) and cofounding the Durham Lesbian and Gay Health Project. But Wittman also turned his attention equally to ECD and Scottish dance, the twin forms he had learned two decades earlier at Swarthmore. Weekly he taught a class of Scottish and English dancing for the Durham Department of Parks and Recreation and then offered a biweekly separate class mostly for gay men. Both classes used global terminology for teaching. Within a year or two, the two groups merged into a single CDSS affiliate, the Sun Assembly Country Dancers. Taking its title from a popular Playford dance, the group was a mix of straight and gay dancers who did gender-neutral dancing.[72]

Carl Wittman died of complications resulting from AIDS in 1986. Just before his death, he finished a book called *Sun Assembly* that was published posthumously a decade later. The book provided instruction for teaching two hundred Scottish and English dances with global terminology. As significant, he also left behind a core of dancers committed to his idea, both in Oregon and in Durham. Troxler and Pat Petersen, a New York transplant to Durham in 1982, led Sun Assembly Country Dancers after Wittman's death. More than twenty-five years later, the group, which still has a mixed membership of straights and gays, remains one of three major groups in the United States committed to gender-neutral dancing. In Oregon, Brooke Friendly and Chris Sackett have continued to run a gender-neutral dance that by the twenty-first century has mostly straight couples, and Michael Cicone, one of the other dancers who had learned from Wittman in Oregon, is one of a team of teachers of a Boston group that has mostly gay participants.[73]

Making CDSS "North American"

When CDSS's board refused to move the national office from New York, Jim Morrison resigned to raise his children outside the city. His departure created an administrative vacuum in the organization, and CDSS decided to divide the job of national director into two positions. Morrison agreed to stay on as artistic director, largely to oversee Pinewoods programs. He operated from a "field office" in Charlottesville, Virginia; meanwhile the Executive Committee looked to hire someone from the arts management community who could function as an executive director. However, the hire, Nancy White Kurzman, neither danced nor seemed to the Executive Committee to understand it and was let go in 1980. Her successor, Bertha Hatvary, who had just joined the new New York Dance Activities Committee (NYDAC) teacher apprenticeship program, stepped down after a couple years as well, apparently by mutual agreement with the Executive Committee that the job was not one that suited her talents or interests. A search for a new director proceeded, and according to at least one member of the Executive Committee, the chair of the committee, Sue Salmons, functioned as de facto director until a new leader could be found. The Executive Committee scoured the membership and turned to one of the bright young stars of the movement who had already made his mark on the West Coast by building BACDS: Brad Foster.

On February 1, 1983, CDSS appointed Foster its national director. Foster both had taught in New York as a visiting caller and was a well-known Pinewoods regular. He was also a man with few ties to New York, and when the question of relocating the office arose again, he had less personal investment in keeping CDSS there. In fact, his family lived outside the city in Connecticut, and he had an hour or more daily commute to the office. So, in 1986, when the landlord announced that the rent on CDSS's Barrow Street office in Greenwich Village would double, the organization and its national director had practical reasons to look for new accommodations.

In 1987, CDSS moved to Northampton, Massachusetts, not far from the site of the early summer schools at the Agricultural College, and two years later it moved a few miles away to its present site in Haydenville. The move forced NYDAC, New York's local dance committee, which was technically a subcommittee of the CDSS Executive Committee, to reorganize as Country Dance * New York (CD*NY), an autonomous chapter with a status no different from other local groups.[74]

Western Massachusetts was not Middle America, but if CDSS's relocation meant to signal that the movement was no longer New York–centric, its location was less than two hours from Boston and Pinewoods Camp. To be sure, it was not in the city, and the "village" ambience of the semirural area and its location amid a network of five colleges sited CDSS in an area that had been a traditional source of support for both American and English Country Dance. By virtue of being *not* New York or Boston or in another of the East Coast cities, the site did help CDSS represent itself as *national*. But, in fact, that description was problematic for the Canadian members of the organization. So, as a gesture to Canadian members of the organization, Foster's title was changed in 1989 from national director to executive and artistic director.[75]

But while the kinds of dances in the ECD repertoire narrowed as CDSS entered the last decade of the twentieth century, the organization expanded geographically: CDSS did not just cross the country; it crossed national borders and become a North American organization. For example, Canadian Tom Seiss and Portland's Mary Devlin each served as president of CDSS in the coming years. The movement they led, however, had taken on a new character that began to lead to two very different understandings of English Country Dance in England and the United States. In the United States, English and contra dance had become segregated for most country dancers into separate evenings, and an evening of English Country Dance now consisted of almost exclusively Playford-inspired dances. Ritual dances became the province of teams that met privately, and in part because the dance community was aging, fewer and fewer of the traditional village dances were done.[76] English choreographers also composed new dances in the historical tradition, but in contrast, American squares and contras and English traditional rants, reels, and jigs remained an integral part of the British country dance evening, which often in its almost boisterous enthusiasm resembled a ceilidh or barn dance.[77] For as important as was the different repertoire, it was the new "modern" style and tempi of the Playford-inspired dances that characterized the new modern variant of ECD. The new mode informed the pace and style of how older dances were taught, as well those of the many newly written dances.

MECD both reflected and shaped the new generation of dancers reared in the second folk revival who had entered the dance community since 1970. Few had the activist pedigree of Carl Wittman, but many carried with them inherited left-liberal concerns with environmentalism, human rights, feminism, and social justice. For Wittman, the dance form and his political concerns had to be integrated; he demonstrated in his own life and work the radical position that the "personal is political." The next chapter expands on how the culture of liberalism informed the American MECD dance community more generally.

8

Modern English Country Dance and the Culture of Liberalism

> [There is an] alarming trend in the Dance Community; that is, the trend of everyone getting old. By "old," I mean, the fact that we regard anyone with more than two body piercings with suspicion; commercials featuring oat bran and medicinal sports crèmes suddenly fascinate us.
> —Alice La Pierre, Bay Area dancer, 1998

> [In their] sartorial choices . . . nerds . . . deny themselves an aura of normality . . . [and become] "hyperwhite" . . . [in their] rebellion against "cool white kids" and their use of black culture.
> —Benjamin Nugent, "Who's a Nerd, Anyway?"

Modern English Country Dance (MECD) blossomed after 1990 and transported its participants. In interviews, dancers repeatedly testified—and the religious meaning of the word resonated in their remarks—to how ECD took them to another social and emotional space. Thom Yarnal, a New York dancer who had moved to Wisconsin to manage a regional theater, well articulated this view. He loved ECD for its "otherworldly" quality. "It doesn't have anything to do with the 20th century, as far as I'm concerned. It takes you to a different place and it takes you mentally and physically."[1] Similarly, Glenn Fulbright, a retired professor of music from Kentucky, waxed over the music as the "most transporting experience I have." He characterized his typical feeling after doing a dance as "like I've been to church."[2] Invoking its access to a sacred place, such attitudes suggest how the music associated with highbrow culture—tunes by Corelli, Purcell, and other classical and Baroque composers—functioned as a signifier of this particular class fraction's "distinctiveness" and its status.[3]

The dance and music transported participants to what they repeatedly referred to as a "safe" social space as well. The heyday of the counterculture was past, but the CDSS community still served for many dancers as an alternative social space, a respite from a "speed-and-greed" dominant culture in which they thrived as affluent professional, technical and cultural workers, yet whose values they found alienating. Yarnal pointed out that people on the ECD dance floor could express themselves in ways that would be ridiculed elsewhere: "The kind of gestures that we do in dancing, you just don't do on the street." The dance might be "modern," but he appreciated that people were "not answering cell phones and running around." As Gene Murrow explained it, doing "English country dancing to beautiful acoustic music in a beautiful setting with people we feel comfortable with" made the ECD dance community "a haven" from "the hurly-burly of the 21st century American speed-and-greed culture."[4]

In their sense of the dance world as a safe haven, these overwhelmingly urbane and urban/suburban dancers repeated again and again the antimodern theme that could have been expressed thirty years earlier by countercultural back-to-the-land communitarians. According to Murrow, ECD was a refuge "from what many of us would agree is an increasingly depersonalized, stressful, high-speed world."[5] Sharon Green, a sixty-year-old leader of the Country Dance * New York community, saw the haven as a return to the "innocence and simplicity of childhood." And for Mary Alison (pseudonym), a forty-nine-year-old southern-based writer, "This is a refuge from the rest of the world. . . . People here are among their tribe, and out in the real world, you often are not. You're trying to find your way among a lot of people with different values, and people that don't necessarily share your interests and share your common history. . . . [Here] they're entering into a community that's accepting of them and that basically wants them here."[6]

Of course, "community" is a historically contingent experience, and by the 1990s its meaning had left behind some of the communitarian values of its countercultural expression in important ways. The musician and folklorist John Bealle describes this new sense of "community" in his insightful ethnography of the changing Cincinnati country dance scene from the late 1960s to the 1990s. In the beginning, the dance community was rooted in the counterculture. Dance was integral to the alternative cultural and political project of that age, and musicians and dancers organized local events organically. There was little planning; local dancers arrived and everyone pitched in to help set up; teaching and music was played at an open mike; someone passed the hat for rent. The groups' boundaries were informal, fraternal, and flexible—in a word, communitarian. By the '80s, Bealle, who was a participant-observer, bemoans how private family lives made dance a recreational rather than oppositional space. The Cincinnati dance became bureaucratized; fees were collected, a committee organized responsibilities and scheduled bands, including those from out of town. Dancers still felt a part of a community, but Bealle suggests that the loss of the communitarian democratic ethos created an individualized, contained, and commodified sense of community that befit the "me generation" in neoliberal America.[7] To be sure, Cincinnati's experience may have been more like that of the newer dance communities to organize then rather than the older centers in places such as New York and Boston. And even with the shift that Bealle describes, dance communities could sustain the considerable panoply of social associations seen in the Princeton dance community at the time. Still, Bealle's analysis accounts for a new supralocal geographic locus to community and new commercial (and impersonal) bonds of association: thus, by the 1990s, one could experience community by listening to a CD, join an exotic international and national dance vacation, or dance at fancy dress balls scattered about the land.

But as important as were the changed meanings of "community," its invocation also celebrated a bonding and coherence that often blurred the exclusionary social boundaries of the group. For community was as much about excluding as belonging. Murrow and other interviewees agreed with what survey data confirmed: they were elite or middle-class professionals with a sense of themselves as outsiders in a fast-paced urban world. Their average household income was about eighty thousand dollars, twice the U.S. average. They were a relative elite, however, neither upper crust nor independently wealthy. Fewer than one in ten (8.9 percent), as Murrow observed, were managers, and most of these were white-collar managers rather than corporate executives; rather, most were a peculiar social cut below. Part bohemian, part bourgeois—they resembled the "bobos" caricatured by the journalist-social critic David Brooks.[8] With one foot—perhaps only a large toe—back in the counterculture, they were those, as dancer and anthropologist Jennifer Beer observes, "who've dropped out of the achievement races and just want to hang out and dance and make music."[9]

The future of this haven, however, also gave the community pause, as many also worried about the ability of the community to re-create itself. The profile of the Princeton dance community in the preceding chapter illustrated the social network that enriched and sustained its members, but the ease of the dance especially attracted older people with spare time and money, and many people worried about the aging of the community. The second folk revival and the contra boom had brought young people such as Brad Foster and Jim Morrison into CDSS in the 1970s; yet one had only to look around the dance

White ethnics dancing a "hey" to music by Bare Necessities at the 2007 CD*NY Yuletide Cotillion. The women in their center are both Jewish. (Photo courtesy of Efraim Kohn)

floor two decades later to see that the process had not been replicated. Photographs of people at dance events confirmed ethnographic and survey data: the core of the Modern ECD community consisted of middle-aged postwar baby boomers entering their "golden" years. The extracurricular folk dance program at Swarthmore College, and that at other colleges such as Oberlin, perhaps because of their strong music conservatories, continued to bring college youth into ECD, but these programs were the college exception, not the rule. By the end of the century, the Anglo dominance of school cultural forms waned with the changing school demography. The nostalgia for Englishness held less appeal to African American and Hispanic students and the rainbow of ethnics in urban schools and college classes who were more likely to embrace Latin and ballroom dance than ECD.[10]

One source of younger newcomers—some twenty- and thirty-somethings—was the popularity of the television and film dramatizations of Jane Austen novels in which English Country Dance featured. Austen's independent women protagonists had long been a favorite of college women, and dramatizations created a boomlet that soon became a "revival." Films of *Per-*

suasion (1995), *Sense and Sensibility* (1995), and *Emma* (1996)—each with country dance scenes—appeared in rapid succession. But it was the award-winning 1996 coproduction by the British Broadcasting Company and the Arts and Entertainment channel (United States) of *Pride and Prejudice* that most captivated viewers. The impact of the Austen revival had perhaps its most dramatic impact in New York, after a CD*NY member and freelance reporter, Linda Wolfe, published a prominent article on the front page of the Weekend Arts and Leisure section of the *New York Times* highlighting where readers could go in New York to dance like Gwyneth Paltrow in *Emma*. The next weekly ECD dance found Duane Hall packed with several hundred newcomers, who found themselves at home amid a group that shared their social profile; all were well-educated professionals (and white). Not all returned another week, but a couple dozen found a new leisure-time hobby and became active members of CD*NY. Unfortunately, Austen-revival newcomers to ECD during the modern era did little to lower the age of the dance community. Two-thirds of the dancers surveyed remained age fifty or over, and only 20 of 171 were under forty.[11]

Dancers may have found the community "withering," but equally of concern to many members was what Shakespeare found "staling" Cleopatra: the lack of "infinite variety." To be sure, modern Americans typically segment themselves into associations of like-minded peers, and against this insular tendency, it is notable that the community *had* broadened its ethnic base. Those who found themselves at home in this Anglo-American tradition, however, conformed to those groups that historians have noted "became white." For the changing history of the ECD community is yet another lesson in the history of whiteness in the twentieth-century United States. Recall that until midcentury the ECD community had never been especially welcoming to such ethnics, even if only in the subtle demeanor and attitudes of its members. But since the Sixties, second- and third-generation ethnic folks such as Gene Murrow, Pat Ruggiero, Sharon Weiner Green (and myself) had become integral members of the community.[12] A cursory review of 2008 CDSS membership lists or enrollees at Pinewoods discloses the prevalence of ethnic Italian and Jewish names in the dance community, members who seemingly have little ancestral connection to England. Survey data from early in the new millennium confirmed this impression: only 36.9 percent of respondents claimed British ancestry; Jews, who were largely absent half a century earlier, now made up 27.5 percent of the group.[13]

This diversity did not mask, at least to some dancers, the class and racial homogeneity of the community: members were still overwhelmingly profes-

"In Step with Austen: English Country Dance." Gwyneth Paltrow as Emma Woodhouse and Jeremy Northam as Mr. Knightly dance in *Emma* before an insert of June Fine and the author dancing at CD*NY's weekly Tuesday-night dance in New York, February 1997. (From the *New York Times*, March 7, 1997, C1; used with permission)

sional and technical workers—and white. Aside from a few African Americans and people of East Asian descent, everyone at dances was white.[14] Of course, the meaning of whiteness had changed over the course of the century, as northern and eastern European ethnics had, as Mathew Jacobson has demonstrated, become white in postwar American culture and immigration policy.[15]

In addition, although the class background of dancers had broadened somewhat since Cecil Sharp's visit, it had not changed profoundly. The ethnic and more middle-class base of the community did make the dance community a somewhat more democratic and less elite space. Indeed, CDSS affiliates generally ended graded classes in early 1990s, albeit as much to hold new members as from some democratic impulse. But if the class composition had become a tad less elite, it remained preeminently bourgeois and urbane, from affluent suburbs and urban areas. In the survey, most "folk" were professional-technical workers or in the arts—the majority (56.3 percent) were (and are today) professors, teachers, librarians, social workers, nurses, and doctors, but there was also a fair representation (14.3 percent) of crafts, theatrical and musical people. In a reflection of the changing character of work in the late twentieth century, a substantial number (10.1 percent) worked in the computer world. Not surprisingly, this professional-technical group was older, well established and highly educated. As noted earlier, the average dancer reported a comfortable household income nearly twice the national average, virtually all were college educated (88.3 percent), and more than half (60.2 percent) had graduate degrees.[16]

The class fraction represented in the dance community was also a cultural slice defined by age in important ways: for if youth was to be served, it was not by ECD. As noted, the ease of the dance partially explained the attraction of older people to ECD. But the ECD community also embraced a "distinctive" culture with class signifiers that stood in opposition to central elements of a more lusty cross-class and intraethnic alternative youth culture. Part of the answer as to why this may have been so lies in the emergence of a transcontinental Modern English Country Dance and the liberal body carriage that its music and style promulgated.

Transcontinental MECD

In the last decade of the twentieth century, MECD became a robust transcontinental and transatlantic leisure activity of postwar baby boomers. Although the typical English Country Dancer was aging, CDSS could nonetheless take pleasure in their increasing numbers. CDSS membership rose to nearly three thousand early in the new century. Approximately three hundred of the memberships were held by dance groups, but nearly six hundred more groups listed themselves in the annual CDSS directory. The list included sword and morris teams, contra groups, and the occasional swing, Cajun, or folk song group, although a few of these groups also did English Country Dance. Formal membership in CDSS represented only a small fraction, however—perhaps a quarter—of the numbers who did English or one of its fraternal forms of country dance. MECD during this era became a continental movement, both in its geographic stretch and in its development of a mobile transcontinental and transatlantic community with shared passions and a shared emergent new dance practice. As discussed earlier, MECD was as much a new spirit, tempo, and style of dancing as it was a corpus of newly written dances that advanced that spirit.[17]

Pat Shaw died in 1978, and his approximately one hundred new dances were but the tip of the proverbial iceberg. The warm reception that many of his dances received encouraged more than a dozen others on both sides of the Atlantic (including Belgium as well as the United Kingdom) to compose, by dance historian and musician-caller Allison Thompson's count in 2006, over nineteen hundred new dances since the mid-1970s. Thompson uncovered at least twelve people who had composed more than fifty each, of whom Americans best knew Fried de Metz Herman and Gary Roodman in the United States and Colin Hume, Pat Shaw, and Charles Bolton in England.[18]

The playfulness, challenge, and innovation in Pat Shaw's new dances excited dancers. New MECD choreographers often similarly invented new steps and patterns that drew on patterns in the historical tradition but often, as Thompson notes, included "quirky or novelty" formations and music that could as likely be by Scott Joplin as by Handel. Moreover, the new compositions, appealing to the late twentieth century's diminished attention span, avoided choreography in which some couples were occasionally passive (which had been welcome interludes for flirting in the seventeenth and eighteenth centuries), in favor of creating complex dance "puzzles" that kept all dancers moving at once. These were modern dances for a modern temperament.[19]

But, significantly, the emergent modern style was often applied as well to older dances previously done at a much faster tempo and, accordingly, with the forward-leaning "running step." Variations in any dance existed from community to community, of course, and local teachers, having learned their new folklore lessons, would justify the differences to queries from outlanders as "our village's variation." But the new MECD style persisted across the variants and across the nation, as the community no longer consisted of isolated villages.

The new modern form spread as MECD took root across North America. Many U.S. dance groups continued to congregate in the urban metropoles of New York, Boston, Philadelphia, Seattle, Portland, and San Francisco, but they had numerous suburban branches. By 2005, for example, the New York area had lively ECD groups in Manhattan, Westchester, Princeton/Lambertville, North Jersey, Round Hill (Connecticut), and New Haven, as well as newer groups on Staten Island and Long Island. But groups could be found in virtually every state in the Union and several Canadian provinces, and some, in places such as Little Rock, Durham, Chicago, Portland, and Amherst, had leaders who also often taught at summer dance camps and served on various CDSS committees. A tabulation of some seventy local dances in 2007 (contacts at another twenty-three did not respond to the call for information) showed that some groups struggled to sustain a weekly or bimonthly dance and often had to rely on recorded music, but groups averaged twenty to thirty people at a dance, and large groups had live music.[20] In truth, a dancer could visit almost any metropolitan area and find a country dance on one of several nights of the week.

Live music was one of the features that attracted newcomers to MECD, and the popular bands in the modern era reflected as much as created a modern tempo and sound. Of course, live music was not entirely new. Kimber had played for Sharp in 1899, and Sharp himself played the piano or hired musicians when he taught. But, as in the earlier era in particular, many groups had neither the local musical talent nor the money to support live music and relied on recordings. Sharp had early recognized this situation and had taken care to oversee early recordings. In midcentury, Phil Merrill, as CDSS musical director, had worked to nurture country dance musicians. But the new generation of musicians that came into the dance community starting in the 1960s, most notably Marshall Barron and Eric Leber, quickened the appreciation for live music. By the 1970s, Gene Murrow, Jacqueline Schwab, Chuck Ward, and Peter Barnes, among many others, had made live music the new standard at events. Barnes's publication of a compilation of ECD dance tunes facilitated the new standard, soon becoming the required manual for musicians across the land.

Some groups and, in the era of the "personal listening device," many individuals, continued to rely on recordings, however. Like the recordings Sharp had produced, cassettes and, later, CDs gave a transportable uniformity to dance tempi and orchestration, both for group and individual listeners. Whereas Sharp's recordings initially had to rely on bands organized by the record companies, in the last third of the century several bands organized to perform professionally at dance events for fees. The most influential of the bands was Bare Necessities (BN), a renowned quartet consisting of Jacqueline Schwab (piano), Peter Barnes (flute and whistles), Earl Gaddis (violin), and Mary Lea (viola) that formed in 1978 (see fig. 8.3). Taking its name from a Pat Shaw dance, the band was one of several to copy the MECD repertoire onto CDs. Princeton's Hold the Mustard and the Assembly Players, a British group, were two notable others. But BN, by dint of its output (by 2008, the band had recorded music for 177 English Country Dances on twelve CDs), its popularity at regional events,

Bare Necessities. Left to right: Peter Barnes, Jacqueline Schwab, Mary Lea, and Earl Gaddis. (Photo courtesy of Peter Barnes and Bare Necessities)

and its success at reflecting the MECD spirit, had enormous influence. CDSS distributed the CDs through its online store and catalogue.[21]

BN, as noted earlier, recorded dances at what had become the new MECD standard of 104 beats per minute, 25 percent slower than Sharp had recorded them eighty years earlier. The recordings also became music as much for listening to as for dancing, with playful switching of chords and lead instruments. BN's prodigious output, distribution, and popularity had the effect of authorizing a modern repertoire that alongside the Playford dances gave equal place to recent compositions disproportionately in triple time with tunes characterized more by elegance than by liveliness.[22] The band's tempi and the lyrical melodic register in which it recorded, however, had the tendency to transform both the older and newer compositions into MECD. BN's power to standardize all dances to their tempi was not lost on the prominent English caller and choreographer Colin Hume, and he asked that BN not record one of his dances. He was convinced the group would play it too fast or change his chords, and its version would "become the de facto standard."[23] In truth, cultural change and transmission is more complicated and dialectical, and BN reflected the tempi and melodic style that dancers loved as much as it shaped them. But Hume's concern spoke to the increasing musical hegemony evidenced in BN's many recordings and widespread appeal. In the year 2004 alone, in addition to BN's performing up and down the East Coast and at dance camps, Peter Barnes remembered that the band played for local and regional dance events or for dance tour groups in Sweden, Austria, Italy, Hungary, Peru, Hawaii, England (for two weeks), California, and Wisconsin (on three successive weekends).[24]

The transcontinental and transatlantic circulation of dance paraphernalia—recordings, bands, callers, and book compilations of new choreographers' dances—and, as important, of dancers, helped standardize MECD. Dance paraphernalia—costumes and the collectibles—reflected the growing commodification of country dance as a saleable leisure-time activity that one could literally wear on one's sleeve. And a round of dress-up balls provided the occasion to do so. The local New York group had held a festive ball as early as 1917, and Sharp had held summer and Christmas dance camps as early as 1911. But with more disposable income and time, the professional, semiprofessional, and technical people who populated each local dance community began to run annual Playford balls and sponsor dance weekends in the 1970s and 1980s, not unlike those held by the Princeton Country Dancers. By the 1990s, dance enthusiasts could attend a Playford ball or a special dance weekend event in one city or another on virtually any weekend of the fall, winter, or spring. The summer afforded dancers even more extended opportunities for dance vacations. They could, for instance, attend a Family Week at CDSS's Ogontz Camp in New Hampshire, an English Week at Pinewoods, and an American Week at Mendocino, California. If they were not sated, dancers could also enroll for a dancing tour in England or for a week in St. Croix or Hawaii. There they would mix beach, barbeque, and country dance. After a day at the beach or shopping in town, they would gather with friends for an evening of country dance to a group such as Bare Necessities, which toured to play for these events.[25]

The perambulations of dancers were central to the geographic reach of this national community. Dance "gypsies" traveled from one dance event to another. For instance, there were few opportunities to dance in Glenn Fulbright's Kentucky community, but as a retired Kentucky music professor, he had time and the means to travel, especially as he could often stay with friends from around the country. In an interview, he spoke of travel that many others undoubtedly did in smaller doses:

I prefer to call myself a trapsichorean traveler, but dance gypsy is sort of the equivalent. In Western Kentucky, where I'm now living, there are no local dance groups. So if I want to dance, I do have to travel. And becoming acquainted with the various centers of dancing through meeting people at Pinewoods camp has given me access to a much wider range of city contacts, so that I've been able to go from Portland, Oregon to Vermont and all the places in between. And down to the Christmas Dance School in Berea, and also to the John C. Campbell School, where the dance tradition is well-preserved.[26]

Dance gypsies reinforced the spread of the MECD repertoire and style, but so too did dancers and callers who moved and resettled from one dance group to another. Typically, late-twentieth-century Americans moved every few years, following new jobs or personal relationships, and this was especially true of professional and technical workers. Dancers, most of whom held stable professional jobs, may have been an exception, but they did their share of moving, and the migratory patterns of the American Country Dancer enhanced the dance community's transcontinental character. Brad Foster and Carl Wittman migrated from the West Coast eastward; others, such as Jody McGeen, Lise Dykeman, and Sharon Green, all of whom apprenticed as ECD teachers in New York, moved westward and became callers in the San Francisco Bay Area. Bruce Hamilton traveled from his Bay Area home to run teacher workshops on the East Coast; Gene Murrow reversed the pattern to lead weekends on the West Coast. Both men had careers in the computer industry. And as Pat Shaw had come to the United States in 1974, so Fried Herman, a teacher by profession, made four trips to England starting in the 1990s to teach her Modern ECD dances and encourage a style that she, ironically, found lacking in the tradition's home country.

By the end of the twentieth century, then, a transnational community of dancers had gained increased coherence as part of a commodified leisure-time dance industry. The dance form they expressed in their music and dance merged elements of the antimodern with modern sensibilities: the fetish for the new and dances that often resembled challenging mathematical puzzles. MECD—both its music and its dance—also encouraged certain bodily expressions that dancers thought appropriate to the form. For these bourgeois, urbane, antimodern dancers, the sounds and body carriages contrasted with urban sounds and bodies and exposed a racial and classist underbelly in the culture of liberalism that bedeviled many in the community.

Imaginings and the MECD Dancing Body

The commodification of MECD changed the experience of the dancer and the dancing body. A revival of ballroom dance and afternoon "tea dances" at hotels in the 1990s nurtured an increased love for the waltzes and triple-time dances that became one hallmark of MECD. Dancers also migrated into CDSS from Scandinavian dance, a coupled dance form that included a good deal of waltzing and that had a revival in the 1980s as an "international" dance done by people of diverse backgrounds.[27] By the 1990s, many country dance evenings often ended with one or another dances from these traditions: CD*NY traditionally ended both its middance break and evening with waltzes; contra dance bands around the country often played a Swedish hambo during the break; and Beginners' Night at Cecil Sharp House in London ended with a polka.[28]

It was the Austen revival in film and video, however, that many dancers cited as having excited their imaginings of the dance the most. In interviews, two respondents reflected how the 1996 BBC/A&E version of *Pride and Prejudice* served as a popular reference point for newcomers and how such productions shaped the way some dancers imagined themselves dancing English Country Dance. Bob Archer, a British caller visiting Pinewoods, found the Austen films "very useful because [he] can say it's the dancing that was done in the Jane Austen films. An awful lot of people saw the *Pride and Prejudice* films and enjoyed it thoroughly and in fact, there was a lot of interest in the dancing after that."[29] But equally telling was how Pat Ruggiero, a fifty-three-year-old book indexer from Palmyra, Virginia, modeled her dancing on media representations: "The little that I've picked up from novels of the period, from TV mini-series, like the George Washington mini-series or the Jane Austen movies, or from workshops, the sense that I get from that is something that I've tried to use to affect the way I move through space."[30]

The imaginings gleaned from the Jane Austen dramatizations were but one of twin roots of the ECD tradition on which dancers drew, however. Austen's novels depicted gentry dances set in the manor houses of early-eighteenth-century England, and this representation stood alongside older imaginings of a "peasant" past inherited from Cecil Sharp and the legacy of traditional folklore studies. These two foundational roots of the English Country Dance—in the medieval village circle dances and the gentry dances of the eighteenth century (with their own roots in Renaissance dance)—allowed modern dancers to develop different stories about the folk they emulated and express those stories in their dancing body.[31]

Thom Yarnal, for instance, expressed the attraction of each "history" well. Asked who he thought he was emulating when he danced, Yarnal opined, "I think more of the country bumpkin than I do of the aristocrats just because that's the kind of egalitarian spirit I like to think I embody. But I know that it was mostly an activity for the rich, and I know that I'm a very privileged person in my current society, so maybe I'm just kidding myself to say this is a country activity. But I think of the country manor house and the people in the kitchen; not the people in the front parlor." As a person interested in community theater, Yarnal wanted the dance to express the folk "downstairs"; when pressed, however, he reluctantly identified ECD as an "upstairs" style "more like the aristocrats, definitely more like the aristocrats."[32]

At least one other dancer did not think Yarnal "kidded himself" by seeing his connection to the agrarian past. Mary Alison, drawing on the medieval strain in the tradition, picks up some of the themes that had animated Gene Murrow in the 1960s. She puts garlands in her hair and imagines herself as "a middle class girl being a peasant maiden." Alison sees dancers "connecting with an agrarian past that probably doesn't exist anymore." The dances "speak" to her as she sees fellow dancers "becoming plowmen and shepherds, shepherdesses, threshers."[33]

But in practice, the traditional rants, reels, and hornpipes that were fast disappearing from U.S. English dance programs gave "peasant" imaginings little traction; it was the Austen imaginings that more matched the flow, tempi, and style of MECD. Thus, Ruggiero agreed with Yarnal's recognition that it was the aristocrats and not the country bumpkins that the "privileged" class of dancers today reflected. And Ruggiero's view, which coincided with popular media representations of the dance as a gentry and aristocratic activity that shaped her sense of the ECD, came closest to expressing the MECD dancing body.[34]

In Ruggiero's thinking about how she moved through space—how she embodied the dance tradition—she invoked a traditional older understanding of the folk as a rural peasantry. Such "folk" did country, line, and circle dances, "simple" dances that, presumably expressing the "natural" life of these people, did not have to be taught. However, she distinguished these from the dances "we do" that were and are taught by dancing masters—these "were done by, in the eighteenth century, by the middle class, and in the seventeenth century, just by the gentry and aristocracy." And it was these latter folks who shaped how Ruggiero "moved through space": her "sense of their having a social reticence in their interactions, an erect carriage, a dignified carriage, an economy of motion."[35]

In Ruggiero's interview with me, she candidly detailed the constrained sexual narrative in ECD dancing that made it a safe place for her in an imagined earlier time:

> I start with a dignified demeanor, arms quiet at the side, economy of motion, move through the space without any flailing of arms, without any embellishment to the figures, without any unnecessary gestures. Oh, and in body motion, I try to eliminate from my own motion, dancing or not, a lot of 20th century ways of conducting ourselves that I no longer care for. Either [the] smarmy sort of gliding across the floor, or jiggles or thrusts, or little coy affectations of the head, and I try to eliminate all of those so I don't look like a 20th century person dancing. I don't like it.
> Q: *Why? What don't you like about it?*
>   ... It's very overtly physical, and I prefer a reticence in my interactions with people. And so rather than thrust some limb or do some coy or flirtatious thing that would draw someone toward me—that's not what I want in my interactions, so I want to be honest in my interactions with people, and I prefer a certain aloofness, a certain reticence—so I keep my body tight. So I hold my body in reticence.[36]

In interviews, then, dancers expressed a range of voices with multiple referents, and most were less explicit than Ruggiero about the style and its sexual meanings. But as I observed them dance as a participant and as a part of the Smithsonian Folklife and Cultural Heritage Center's Video Documentation Project, they spoke a remarkably uniform language with their bodies. On the dance floor, Ruggiero's dignified carriage was the predominant body language. To be sure, dances and dancers differed in tempo, stepping, exuberance, carriage, and more. Some dances were sappy waltzes; others were exuberant—even aerobic—with chase patterns, reels, and ranting steps. But as Ruggiero's concern for holding her "body in reticence" suggests, as they "moved through space," MECD dancers' bodies told a gendered class story.

The class and gender signifiers of this story could be seen and heard in dress, carriage, and music. The music, drawn from highbrow, classical composers, may have been the most overt signifier of class: that of the northern European, white bourgeoisie and court. The dress was also more bourgeois and formal than "country." Some women did wear garlands in their hair, but they accompanied ball dresses or designer "peasant" dresses à la Laura Ashley. Although most men at balls simply wore white, ruffled shirts with knickers, some put on tuxedos or elaborate eighteenth-century aristocratic costumes.

Finally, while the dance form, especially in the United States, where eye contact has been stressed, encouraged sociability and flirtation, the unwritten rules of the dance culture and its music sent structured messages that spoke more to propriety than tussles in the country hay. The dance form, as noted earlier, limited physical contact, but—and this was especially the case in the United States—there were explicit expectations that dancers not pre-book dances and that they change partners after every dance. Indeed, dancing with any partner more than once an evening (except perhaps for the final waltz) was frowned upon. Marriages within the dance community were not uncommon, but coupling was expressed in community sociability and the intimacy of eye contact, and less so from intimate physical contact on the dance floor. In MECD, except for the final waltz, the couple generally danced at arms' length.

One dancer was unusually articulate and vocal about the related sexual and class meanings of the dance. Jennifer Beer, drawing on her professional background as an anthropologist, described Ruggiero's views on styling as "gendered whiteness."[37] Beer also placed the body language in a class context: "There's a certain containment in the way you handle your body all the time that is definitely a class mark. . . . It's a structure that allows sexuality, but in a very middle class, contained kind of way, a safe way." Then in a particularly revealing comment, she added, "You don't show off your butt or your breasts the way you might in, say, in some African dances, where you let it all hang out."[38]

Beer's observations also highlight the heterosexual character of this professional class, and she notes how gender roles (in this class) can be exhibited on the dance floor. Attitudes, she reminds us, have evolved over time, of course, and more men and women play with the conventions now then before. Still, she notes that heterosexual conventions concerning appropriate feminine and masculine behavior persist in overt and subtle ways. First, the coupled nature of the dance form structures the dance. Many people who attend the dance are single, but as you cannot get on the dance floor until you have a partner, the subtle message is that the goal of the dance is to be coupled. Second, the tradition of women wearing flowing skirts rather than trousers (or jeans) affects how they move—how they twirl their hips to make their skirt swing out. As one woman told Beer, "I feel like I don't dance correctly unless I have a dress on." Third, body language is deeply gendered. As Beer thought about how she and her lesbian friend related to male partners—the small nuances in how each moved on the floor—she characterized it as a "moment of awakening": "Wow, I really am deeply heterosexual in the way I move my body in this dance form.... The thing I notice the most is the smiling and the tilt of the head on the part of women, myself in particular. I think smiling obviously is a wonderful thing, but it is also an act of submission, as is a tilted head. And the tilted head is in the older Cecil Sharp dance style. If you look at the photographs, almost every woman is like this [she tilts her head]."[39]

The influence of second-wave feminism on dancers, however, led some in the dance community, such as Carl Wittman and his protégés, to seek to break gender stereotypes and create a more inclusive dance. Although the percentage was lower for men than for women, almost all respondents I surveyed (82.5 percent) described themselves as moderately or strongly influenced by feminism. (As one person wrote, "It has shaped my life experience in how people relate to one another.") Indeed, the previous chapter described how, coincident with the rise of second-wave feminism and the gay liberation movement, the last few decades of the twentieth century saw the emergence of gender-free dances in a few locations. And at least three communities held regular gender-free dances at the end of the twentieth century, but of course, that meant about a hundred more did not. In fact, in bending gender, ECD remained below the curve; many American cities had gay square dance and gay contra dance groups.[40] In MECD, the traditional coupled country dance form continued to rely on a heterosexual community. Some gay men and women were undoubtedly closeted, but the community has always been mostly heterosexual (93.3 percent surveyed identified themselves as heterosexual, and about two-thirds listed themselves as partnered). Still, some form of gender balance persisted in admission to special dance events such as balls and dance weekends that required advance registration. While gender-blind admission was a subject of great debate, gender-balance admission policies began to wane only in the 1990s. There was an increasing willingness to break with gender roles, but it was mostly among the women (who also tended to be in extra numbers). Men have always been less comfortable partnering with other men, although in the new millennium attitudes loosened, and a few men could be seen dancing with other men as partners.[41]

Some dancers may have felt more comfortable playing with gendered roles in the dance, but Beer insightfully suggests how their efforts could bump up against the limits of gender and the nuances of class within the liberal imaginary. One of the things that draws her to English dance is the relatively egalitarian roles of men and women in the coupled dance form: "You're mostly doing parallel or mirror image movement that doesn't have to be led by one person or another." Beer's experience, however, is that on a less visible microlevel, "men do most of the leading." Beer finds men leading with subtle signals that she hypothesizes video might detect: men determine the precise timing of when hands touch, of the angle of a two-hand turn, of how you do the swing, and so forth. My own experience confirms Beer's impression that men "get irritated with women who are taking initiative too often, or not doing it the way they're comfortable doing it." Beer notes, with irony, that in this relatively enlightened feminist community, some women tell her, "You know I can't say this in public, but I really love being a follower." Beer's problem is the reverse: "My problem is I really love being a leader! And I would say I probably follow about 80 percent of the time, and I'm considered aggressive on the dance floor. So my guess is that most women are following most of the time, but not consciously so. But unconsciously, the man sets the shape and tone of the interaction that happens between the two. . . . I would love to actually test that out with some real video sample."[42]

Expressions of feminism and gender-inclusiveness are evident in other displays of the dancing body, however. Some men have been known to wear skirts at dances, and gay male dancers delight in wearing kilts. Women customarily wear flowing dresses, so lesbian dancers occasionally adorn themselves in pants or tuxedos. Often it is hard to read whether the dress is carnivalesque, an expression of identity, or a merging of the two. But the prominent married male musician Peter Barnes regularly cross-dresses at dances as a personal expression of his other identity as "Kate," which was his grandmother's name. As Kate, Barnes often dances the woman's role, and usually with female partners as men, for on the whole, women seem more comfortable dancing with Kate than men do. One of those partners is sometimes his wife, who also dances and has always been comfortable with this part of his life. To Beer, as a beloved member of the community, Kate has had a "pivotal role in broadening people's willingness to play with gender on the dance floor."[43]

Feminism has many meanings, of course, and the testimony of a gay dance leader suggests some of the limits to its expression on the dance floor, limits that Beer had suspected were quite evident to gay men and women. In a 2004 interview, Allan Troxler, Wittman's former lover, who continued to promote gender-neutral teaching, ruefully notes that gay men and women remain woefully absent or invisible in the dance community. Acknowledging that some men wear dresses at contra dances and that, of course, Scottish dances have men in kilts, he sees no one "political savvy" enough "to take things to the next place." "We're still inhabiting different worlds."[44]

Put together, Troxler's and Beer's comments illustrate how the dance floor has remained gendered, racialized, and classed. Dancers may be responsive to feminism and may be from diverse ethnic backgrounds, but on the dance

Modern English Country Dance and the Culture of Liberalism

Kate (with decades-long traveling companion Hamish Monk) before a dance event at Blair Castle, Scotland, July 16, 2007. (Used with permission of Peter Barnes)

floor the legacy of traditional gender roles and Anglo-Saxonism could be seen in the contours of this heterosexual professional class fraction as it performed gender, propriety, and whiteness in the Anglo-American way.[45]

Race and the Liberal Dancing Body

Race, as many historians have emphasized, has been a core problem for liberalism in the twentieth-century United States, and as if on cue, in interviews, many people in the country dance community addressed the lack of diversity in the community.[46] Thus, as Gene Murrow reflected at the turn of the new century, the inability of the dance community to attract others concerned and perplexed him: "Why are there no, in today's terms, why are there no six figure high-powered corporate executives among us, and why are there no plumber's assistants among us?" Others emphasized the particular lack of racial diversity, noting the absence of black and Hispanic faces at the dances. The answer for many was that these folks had their "own interests"; they averred that ECD/MECD was a cultural expression of a particular social group. This obvious answer, however, belied the fact that the social profile of the community had changed dramatically in the past thirty years and that newcomers had been made to feel welcome: white ethnics, whose parents earlier had not encountered the Anglo-American dance community or found it an appropriate or welcome place, now embraced the tradition. Doing "other people's" dances in the international tradition changed how some felt; the changing character of "whiteness" made others feel more "American"; and the new generation of CDSS leaders, many from the Sixties, made others feel more welcome. Still, neither executives nor working-class people graced the country dance floor in the 1990s or afterward.[47]

The lack of racial minorities, however, was the more self-evident problem. The problem was especially vexing to many in the MECD community who came out of the counterculture and held progressive political views on race and class. Dance communities consistently welcomed African Americans, Asians, and Hispanics—on the few occasions when any of them did appear at a dance. But few who came made a return appearance. Reflecting on why they do not come back, Pat Ruggiero candidly admitted, "I don't think much about it." And although others do think about it, Bourdieu's lessons on the potential for class dominance in cultural forms are lost on them. Jenny Beer notes, "It's pretty esoteric, what we do." And Gene Murrow follows this logic in noting, "I don't think it speaks to them [black people]," to which Mary Alison adds, "I guess this kind of dancing is not part of their particular tradition."[48]

But we have seen how the Anglo-American tradition had expanded to incorporate Jews and other white ethnics.[49] Their inclusion had changed the meaning of the "tradition"; the expansion of whiteness to include ethnic Americans coincided with a changed sense of the folk in MECD. The folk early in the last century were part of the imagining of a national (Anglo-American) identity; at the end of the century, the imagining had come to define the identity of white, heterosexual, and (reluctantly) modern urbane and urban denizens. True, a preponderance of the dancers at the end of the century may have lived in suburbs, but it is important to remember that these suburbs had themselves been constructed as white spaces in relation to cities. Not surprisingly, MECD was white dancing in white spaces.[50]

Vestiges of the radical political impulses from the 1930s and 1960s folk traditions can be seen in the twenty-first-century MECD community, especially in its role as a haven for those who reject the dominant cultural rhythms—the "speed-and-greed" culture. The more contemporary movement was also a countercultural form, but as a site, not as a political or cultural movement. Thus, the social spaces provided by CDSS offered dancers a comfortable alternative to mainstream culture, most especially in the years of Reagan-Thatcherism, but with a fundamental difference from how such spaces served counterculture and New Left folkies two decades earlier. In the Sixties, the social spaces of folk song and dance were alternative and oppositional political spaces; in the modern era of Reagan-Thatcherism and its later neoliberal expressions, country dance spaces were alternative but not oppositional. In fact, in another commentary on the changed meaning of community, MECD dancers built and celebrated community, but they did so in private, white spaces.

The CDSS community thrived in increasingly commodified "safe spaces" as expressions of the culture of liberalism. Folk seeking antiurban spiritual renewal while engaged in urbanity, these urbane, educated urban professional MECD dancers were an elite distancing themselves from, not engaging with, the city, by creating dance spaces as antimodern places of respite from black urban youth hip-hop culture, whose constituency the liberal MECD community could not attract or hold at its dances. Computer geeks, Birkenstock-clad and vegetarian bohemians, countercultural refugees, or simply iconoclasts, MECD dancers did not always feel they "fit in" with the dominant culture. Many could appreciate the appeal of MECD to dancemates such as Jacqueline Schwab, who explained her embrace of the community as a "really shy, part nerdy high school kid." But as one recent cultural critic points out, in creating a hyperwhite "safe" space, "nerds" rejected black hip-hop music and dress. According to the same logic, MECD as a respite from modern urban America was a hyperwhite Anglo-American liberal rejection of the urban culture informed by the popular music forms of the late twentieth century.[51] Thus, MECD music, as several dancers were quick to note, contrasted with the driving beat of popular music often rooted in working-class and minority cultures, and their comments suggested how sexual and class subtexts underlie their response to the music as much as race does. For Pat Ruggiero, "Popular music has a very strong beat underneath, and a lot of sexual overtones. And, you know, [MECD] is not hip-hop." Similarly, Thom Yarnal compared MECD movements and music with that of the more aerobic popular music: "The [popular] music is way too loud, number one. And the movements tend to be really violent; it's very staccato kind of stuff. And our, you know, the kind of dancing we do here is aerobic, but it doesn't have that kind of jarring. I think it's more centered on a heartbeat than the driving rhythms of a machine, which is what I think drives modern music."[52]

Conclusion

Beer's comparison of MECD with some forms of African dance, where "you let it ["breasts and butts"] all hang out," though not meant to be about race per se, highlights a fundamental element of the MECD community's sense of itself in the new millennium as it relates to race: its class identity. All interviewees agreed that the dance community was "middle class," but most were also more specific. Ruggiero's and Yarnal's appraisals are typical: "We're just educated professionals," notes Ruggiero, and "Caucasian heterosexuals"; Yarnal simply adds, "We're a pretty affluent group of people, [and] we're pretty white." As Murrow succinctly puts it, "We are a group of lily-white, middle-class, urbanized Americans."[53]

For these white folk, the MECD community is at once reminiscent of what Christopher Lasch has called the search for a haven in a heartless world and the search for an alternative to feared licentiousness of "rough dancing" and music hall culture at the turn of the last century.[54] There are some important immediate differences though: contemporary antimodernists have neither the cultural capital of the founding generation nor their sense of agency and mission. They do not use their movement to retrain the working class or to invoke a nationalizing folk, and the MECD community might better be characterized as a haven in an overly wrought world.

But the MECD community is not so much antimodern as reluctantly modern—these dancers are not technophobes; actually, as noted earlier, there are disproportionate numbers of computer programmers and scientists in the community.[55] While some of the more intricately patterned dances seem to appeal to those who are mathematically inclined, others such as Harvard biochemistry professor George Whitesides find that MECD "serves to provide some humanity in the overall [scientific] enterprise" that is his professional life.[56] Some, however, find the "humanity" in imagining the pastness of the present. And in this way, the ECD community's imagining of itself as a gentry "folk" may be another commentary on the crisis of modern liberalism, one that is not so removed from Sharp's Fabian worldview (though the late-twentieth-century community was not committed to Sharp's imperial-national vision). As has been noted, the more contemporary MECD movement remained Anglo-American, but with lots of second- and third-generation ethnic Americans—at least Jewish, eastern European, and Italian Americans—who had become "white." That this urban folk identity had no blacks or Hispanics should not be so surprising. The MECD community was in conscious escape from the music and rhythms of the culture—

even if only as a metaphor for fast-paced modern life. In so doing, it appears that the political culture or racial urban liberalism in which the MECD community was embedded at the turn of the century had unintended political consequences for its future growth and any alternative polity its members might seek to advance.

In sum, white, heterosexual, and isolated from the culture of working people and racial minorities who make up the urban majority of U.S. cities, relatively affluent MECD dancers inhabited a countercultural space that echoed with the contradictions of liberalism. They remained antimaterialist. A majority of respondents claimed no religious affiliation, but a surprising number went out of their way to add how "spiritual" they were. Hobbies focused disproportionately on crafts and gardening; rather than competitive sports or working-class activities such as bowling, preferred sports activities were hiking and biking, both distinct class signifiers. What passed for social activism was a kind of civic associational environmentalism—membership in the Sierra Club, for example, a largely white, middle-income advocacy group with class markers congenial to those of the MECD community. Feminists, environmentalists, "spiritual" folk, these left-liberals inhabited a distinctive class sector, affluent yet not elite, alternative but also bourgeois. The world of the MECD dancer likely had little resonance with the working class or racial minorities whose absence on the dance floor they lamented. Ultimately, one can only speculate on the reasons for their absence, but the dances were held in spaces marked as white and middle class to which these others did not necessarily have easy access or in which they did not feel comfortable. In fact, the cultural messages in the space and the dancers' bodies signified to those they missed how much these others did not fit. In such ways, the history of the modern folkies of Modern English Country Dance suggests the extent to which exclusionary messages of modern liberal culture undermined the liberal political project to lessen inequity and injustice.

Conclusion

> I hate to admit it, but I do think English Country Dancing is thriving more in the States.
> —Colin Hume, British ECD choreographer and teacher, 2002

> I certainly hope . . . [for] a third revival in folk music. . . . A very encouraging thing is that there are some young musicians now. . . . Now if they can find a dance audience to play for of their own age—that would be the best thing.
> —Peter Barnes, ECD dance musician, 2004

London, June 2005.
It is Thursday evening, "Beginners' Night" for English Country Dancing at Cecil Sharp House in Camden Town, a North London district with a lively and youthful punk nightlife. The House—an impressive, heritage-listed, three-story, Georgian, purpose-built edifice—sits a few blocks away from the tube station in a prosperous, leafy residential area midway between Regents Park and Primrose Hill. Positioned on a triangle formed by the diagonal intersection of Regents Park Road with Gloucester Avenue, the House prominently faces outward from the triangle.

As the national organization committed to folk song and dance from around the world, Cecil Sharp House hosts a range of folk dances, and this night is no exception. Downstairs in the basement, one room is packed with perhaps forty to fifty young people doing lively Irish set dances to recorded music; another small room is filled with a heterogeneous crowd of perhaps fifteen taking a flamenco dance class. But as the home of English Country Dance, the Folk Song and Dance Society reserves the main dance hall on the ground floor—a spacious, chandeliered Grand Ball Room—for its country dance session. The venue could not contrast more with the dances downstairs. There are about a dozen dancers milling about the hall, which is large enough to accommodate several hundred dancers; a few more will trickle in, but the small "crowd" accounts for the low level of energy in the room—and in the dance. Most dancers are forty-something to sixty-something, although a couple of young people who are local college students hover anxiously on the sides. They are clearly neophytes. A small platform erected in the middle rear hosts the "band"—a fiddler or accordion player with a person on a keyboard—and the caller, a sprightly, older woman, Brenda Godrich, who is married to the fiddler. (Later a somewhat younger man takes a turn at calling.) Beginners' Night is meant to welcome new dancers, but at least half the dancers are familiar to me from past years.

The caller focuses her teaching on patterns of the dance, not the styling or body carriage. And the music has a raw energy that is mirrored in the repertoire, which alternates American squares, traditional village dances, and older, statelier dances from the seventeenth and eighteenth centuries. The mixture of country dances—English and American and historical and traditional—and the apparent indifference to styling make the evening resemble a "kick-up-your-heels" ceilidh or barn dance, though the presence of such a small group in the vast hall makes the tenor of the evening much more sedate than a barn dance.

New York, November 2005.

The entrance to the weekly English Country Dance sponsored by Country Dance * New York (CD*NY), the lineal descendant of the New York branch of the English Folk Dance Society founded by Cecil Sharp in 1915, is quite unassuming and easy to miss. Located on Seventh Avenue on the northwest corner of 13th Street at the margins of the West (Greenwich) Village and Chelsea, the entrance to the dance is through a weathered side door of the Metropolitan-Duane Methodist Episcopal Church. Located across from a Gay-Lesbian Cultural Center in the politically progressive Village, the church describes itself as a "reconciling congregation." Taped to the church door is a notice printed from someone's home computer on a plain piece of paper announcing that there is dancing downstairs. One enters, ascends a few steps, and then passes ten yards down a hallway to a staircase. Descending the stairs two flights, music begins to be heard: it is lyrical and schmaltzy in three-quarters time, and one can discern the sound of a violin, piano, and recorder. The music is Baroque, with an elegant, smooth pace, perhaps 100 beats per minute. (Square or contra dance—American Country Dance—is usually more like 120 beats per minute.)

Reaching the basement, one enters a gym. More formally called Metropolitan Duane Hall, the room is bare and the flooring is in need of repair, but the hall is quite full, with about fifty men and women (in about equal numbers) in three longways sets of lines up and down the hall. Two parents have brought their children along to dance, and while thirty-year-old dancers partner with those in their seventies, most seem to be between the ages of forty-five and sixty-five.

Basketball rims and nets hang at either end of room. The elevated stage at the far end hosts three musicians, some sound equipment, and a standing microphone at which the caller, Beverly Francis, leads the dancers through their paces. The evening, which runs from 7:00 to 10:15, has a theme. This evening is the Gotham Assembly, with a program of thirteen dances that the dance community has voted as its favorites. More than half the dances—seven—were composed in the past half century, six by Americans and one by a Belgian choreographer. Equally noticeable is the tempo of the favorites: the majority are in triple time (and are often florid waltzes). There are no traditional rants or reels or any American contra dances. Rather, the evening consists of all Playford-style "gentry" dances. The older repertoire emphasizes dances in 2/2 and 4/4 time, and the triple-time dances consist of three steps of even length and contain a more languid, emotive style. One Washington, DC, dance wag describes the dances as "ooey-gooey."[1] The dancing has a modern feel, with lots of flirtation and intense eye contact during the dance, and the waltz time encourages exaggerated balletic gestures and flow.

In all, the atmosphere is festive, almost boisterous. The social atmosphere and conviviality extends to a back-room kitchen where juice, cookies, cakes, and candy treats are laid out for the middance break, much as if it were a Sunday after-church event. Chocolate seems to be the flavor of choice.

The Modern Conundrum

As the preceding portraits illustrate, English Country Dance thrives in New York (and the United States) today, while, comparatively, it languishes in London (and the United Kingdom). In interviews, two leading British choreographers and dancing masters, who have danced in the United States, bemoan the current state of ECD in the United Kingdom. Nicolas Broadbridge, the leader of the ECD community in Scotland, sums up the problem: "There's very little dance technique taught in Britain now which is very sad. But in the days when dance technique was taught, when I grew up, people learned to dance carefully and properly. And that is the kind of dancing I found in Berea [College, the folk arts center in Kentucky]."[2] Colin Hume, a computer programmer by day and leading choreographer and caller by night, gets right to the point: "I hate to admit it, but I do think English country dancing is thriving more in the States."³

The ease of travel in the late twentieth century has meant that the difference in the two dance communities has become common knowledge on both sides of the Atlantic. The dismal state of the beginners' class at Cecil Sharp House in Camden Town, London, the EFDSS home, is apparent to visitors from abroad who stop by to dance, although it is important to note that local dance groups in and outside London report more robust regular ongoing biweekly or monthly dances. And, as suggested earlier, ceilidh dances do attract a crowd. Still, Broadbridge's and Hume's assessments speak to the general poor state of the older ECD historical tradition in the United Kingdom.

As important, though, is the emergence of distinct styles in these two countries, in both the sound and the styling of the dance and in what is constituted as ECD. Colin Hume summarizes some differences that were also reiterated many times in interviews with dancers across the United States who had danced in England. In the United States, ECD offers a narrower repertoire of dances in the historical Playford style. As Hume notes,

> We have a much wider definition of English Country Dance in England. In the States, when people say English they usually mean Playford Style, and they usually mean slow and gentle in three-time with a beautiful tune, and they drift through it. And sure, that is part of the English, but there are a lot of other parts of English. Traditional English dances and traditional style dances. And also we saw the Flamborough dance, which is another aspect of English dancing, which is just as English as the Newcastle and the Playford dances. So it's quite a varied thing here. Much more varied than in the States.⁴

Thus, the range of dances that British and American dancers imagine to be "English" differs; but so, too, does the style and interactions on the floor. Eye contact and partnering are the two areas of difference often noted. As Hume observes,

> In the States, they are taught you must have eye contact, you must look at people, and you must change partners every dance. And people in England are not good at either of these because it's not what we're taught. So you find a lot of people get embarrassed and stare at the floor, especially if you give them the "American stare." Then they really don't know; they think, is this woman after me or what?⁵

It should be noted that, as country dance in England continues to mix contras and squares with Playford dances, the difference in style in the two countries extends to contra dance as well. The British variant is more sedate: swinging is done without the flourishes and extra twirls common in the United States, and balance steps—performed as a step right, lift left, step left, lift right in England—are energetically weighted forward-and-back partner balances with body swizzles in the United States.[6]

So, while an Anglo-American folk dance tradition emerged on both sides of the pond, it did so with national inflections. Observers point, for instance, to differences in social interactions on and off the dance floor which they attribute to national character: British reserve or American brashness (i.e., American dancers look their partners in the eye more than their British equivalents do). "National character" does not, however, account for the apparent similarly in the dancing for the first two-thirds of the twentieth century. Neither does it account for a difference in the politics of sound: the tempi, orchestration, and the energy, pace, and flow of the dance as mirrored in the energy, pace, and melodic line in the music. In the United Kingdom, according to dance caller Michael Barraclough, "As audiences dwindle and clubs have to cut costs there is a significant trend towards 2 piece bands for club dances. This will typically be a violin + accordion or piano or keyboard." The dwindling dance scene, in fact, compelled Barraclough to emigrate to the United States in 2008. In contrast, U.S. dancer and dance historian Allison Thompson notes that the "typical band line-up" at an American dance event consists of a "piano plus a few melody instruments (violin, concertina, flute/recorder, clarinet) with sometimes guitar/mando[lin] filling in the middle but also acting from time to time as melody. Percussion, if any, is typically hand-percussion (bodhran, bones, triangle)."[7] The relatively robust American dance band allows instrumentalists to trade lead roles playfully and to energize the dancers with riffs and tune variants while the band creates a strong melodic line. In contrast, the English dance band sound, which has traditionally been dominated by the accordion (and often with percussion from a drum), sounds relatively thin and places greater emphasis on the beat. The raw energy it produces does feel more in keeping with the less fussy "knees-up" dancing of Britain that mixes the Playford historical dances with traditional village dances and squares.

The "decline" of Playford-inspired dance in England can be traced to the differing responses to changes there in midcentury. Kennedy's imposition of his couples-only rule after World War II coincided with his deemphasis on Playford dances. This shift also meant that there was less attention to and encouragement of the training of historical ECD teachers and musicians. Cecil Sharp had worked tirelessly to train a corps of teachers who could carry on his work, and the summer and vacation schools continued that project into midcentury. But EFDSS never developed the formal apprentice programs for teachers and musicians that subsequently arose in American dance communities such as New York, Boston, and Philadelphia and carried on throughout the twentieth century.

In place of Playford dances, Kennedy substituted a new focus on traditional village dances, squares and reels, many of which he published in seven volumes of the *Community Dance Manuals*. In the process, he reshaped the EFDSS repertoire and a typical country dance evening in midcentury England. The second folk revival brought American square dancing to England and spurred the rise of a folk song culture of folk clubs, folk festivals, and traditional "popular" village dances. The passion for square dancing easily morphed into the new emphasis on traditional reels and jigs to create a boisterous ceilidh-like "knees-up" atmosphere with little concern for dance styling. As important as the transformation of the country dance, though, were changes in the dance community. EFDSS had been an elite group since its inception, but the entry of young folkies in the 1950s and 1960s democratized the English folk movement and, in time, the dance community as well. By the 1960s, the country dance community in England was younger and represented a broader social base than it had in the past. Ironically, at the same time as ECD was a national English (and not British) dance tradition with less apparent traction for young people attracted to the Celtic nationalist revival, the second revival became the cultural expression of a British counterpolitics, of young people who marched for nuclear disarmament and identified with American jazz and radical folk singers while opposing American (and British) Cold War politics.

Change, however, does not take place overnight, nor is it necessarily all-encompassing. Playford enthusiasts persevered in England. The key is that EFDSS's move away from Playford dances and its couples-only policy meant newcomers encountered less teaching of the older historical dances and fewer experienced partners from whom to learn. In practice, the community of Playford dancers aged in place over time, leading to ever-diminishing numbers. At the end of the century, the scene at the monthly Saturday-night Cajun dance at the Cecil Sharp House contrasted sharply with that at the monthly Friday Experienced ECD class, which a group of veteran dancers had sustained. The former overflowed from the large upstairs Kennedy Hall with several hundred young people, whereas the latter labored to sustain one longways set in the smaller room downstairs. The ECD dancers were mostly octogenarians who had danced since midcentury. Without an infusion of new dancers, the group had become an increasingly small and insular band, numbering perhaps two dozen, if they all ever came on the same night. In 1998, unable to find a musician (in all London!) to replace their accordionist, who had tired of commuting in from Oxfordshire, the group folded.

In the United States, in contrast, the ECD community remained fairly stable into the 1960s. It began to change only in the late 1960s and 1970s with the infusion of dancers from international song and dance and the countercultural "contra boom." In the latter stages of the second folk revival, the U.S. country dance movement added many younger members with diverse ethnic backgrounds and built strong local communities of dancers. As in England, CDSS became a more democratic organization with a somewhat broader social base. Early in the century, members were mostly New England and East Coast elites; in the last third of the century, while CDSS remained a relatively privileged group, the new generation of members were drawn mostly from the professional-technical class with upper-middle-class incomes. Representatives of both the working class and corporate echelons were notably absent. Moreover, while virtually all members were still "white," by the end of the century they included ethnics who often would not have felt at home in the Anglo-Saxon culture of the prewar American Branch of the EFDSS.

The Culture of Liberalism

The problem of whiteness (and its contrary, the absence of other racial groups) in the country dance community is implicated in the history of liberalism in the twentieth-century United States. The Progressive Era, of which the folk revival was an integral part, inaugurated the era of modern liberalism—the point at which the word separates from its nineteenth-century classical form, which was associated with laissez-faire capitalism, and takes on its new associations with state intervention to support greater social equality. For modern liberals, reforming "bad" capitalism would allow the "good" variety to provide opportunity for all. Earlier leaders such as Sharp, Karpeles, and Burchenal were Fabians and Progressives who advanced liberal reform agendas. They were at home with conservative Anglophiles such as Helen Storrow whose considerable beneficence shaped the American ECD community in its first fifty years.

The elites who dominated the years of the American Branch and the affluent professional-technical-artist-intellectual group who make up the more recent membership constitute a social class fraction that has occupied a specific liberal political space. The ethnic profile of this fraction has changed over the course of the century, however (and with it, imaginings of these ethnics' "whiteness"). The new members who came out of the second folk revival more often had Jewish, Italian, or another eastern or southern European heritage. Liberalism, blossoming in the Depression years, focused on how economic abuses restricted individual opportunity, and many of those who entered CDSS after the 1960s were reared or shaped by the left-liberal political culture of the second folk revival. Thus, spanning as it does the better part of the twentieth century, ECD in the United States provides a window onto the political valences of liberalism and social relations during the last century.

There has been a substantial, impressive literature that traces the development of modern liberalism and its apotheosis in the New Deal state's commitment to reforming capitalism. This scholarship then follows liberalism into its postwar "decline" with a weakened state. Although Alan Brinkley's *The End of Reform* (1995) is arguably the best statement of this thesis, his view has been refined by Judith Stein, David Plotke, and others in important ways: they demonstrate how New Deal liberals drew on an antimonopolist tradition that restructured industries and actually set in motion patterns of deindustrialization that emerged out of the civil rights era of the 1950s. Thus, since liberals believed they had solved industrial problems, and did not see either the first signs of deindustrialization (in steel) or their collusion in it, they understood the United States' postwar "race problem" as one of educational opportunity, not structural change. As Stein observes, black people were educated for jobs that did not exist or were downsized.[8]

Liberals came to believe that the solution to the "race problem" lay outside the economy. They put cultural reform at the center of the liberal project in the United States, a project to incorporate shared values and priorities through associational life (e.g., folk dance groups). But in contrast to the rich literature on liberalism as economic state policy, liberal cultural policy is a relatively untouched subject. Andrew Camberlin Reiser has caught the spirit of this liberalism in his description of the history of the Progressive Era Chautauqua movement as "inchoate liberalism [whose] embodiment of participatory democracy resonated with those [Jews, Catholics, and immigrants] whom . . . [reformers] hoped to keep on the margins."[9] Progressive Era liberals similarly embedded economic and political reforms in cultural forms such as folk dance to make immigrant workers "democratic" and "productive." Left-liberals carried these cultural traditions forward into the postwar era; they hoped that cultural reforms—whether in Great Society programs such as Head Start or in the counterculture—would become the engine of change. Across the century, English Country Dance fully embodied this liberal cultural expression. As a cultural text, it inscribes the body as a form and product of the expression of liberal class consciousness and the disposition of power in society.[10]

Today, Modern English Country Dancers express the politics of contemporary liberalism in their communities and in the social relationships that define them. Almost exclusively white and affluent, MECD groups provide a sanguine view of the putatively democratic politics of associational life.[11] MECD members welcome all and speak of themselves as a family. But, of course, families discipline their members and mark out deviants. And though the censors are not always visible, their effects are, and it compels analysis of the content of the relationships in the dance community—who stays home, who joins, and what happens on the dance floor—and the politics of the dancing body.

In the new millennium, children of the counterculture, a core group within CDSS and its MECD constituency, celebrate their dance community as a "safe" alternative to a fast-paced material world to which they are often tethered in their day jobs. It remains for a historian of country dance in England to determine whether or not the MECD dance floor as a "safe" space is a uniquely American phenomena. It seems likely that as a transatlantic and transnational movement, English and American dance communities do share many of the social and political characteristics of the MECD world. Still, contemporary MECD dancers on both sides of the Atlantic increasingly look for inspiration to the United States, where the dancing is thought to thrive.

By the mid-1980s, MECD in the United States had become an almost exclusively Playford-style dance form. The contra community was large enough to sustain itself, and not enough dancers in either the MECD or contra community wanted to do the other's dances. Ritual morris and sword teams also had lives of their own and were no longer taught at weekly community dances. And many people in the MECD community rejected traditional rants and reels: for some, they were too exhausting or hard on aging joints; for others, the lack of style beyond the stepping made them uninteresting.

As the new millennium dawned, MECD relatively thrived in the United States, but not without internal contradictions, and many of its leaders continued to worry about its ability to re-create itself. Two aspects of MECD as a cultural formation, however, suggest how liberalism as a political culture both shaped the social relations of members and might affect CDSS's future prospects. First, with a core of dancers who had come from the counterculture, at the opening of the twenty-first century, the broader CDSS membership sought and could frequently be heard celebrating a sense of "community"—a space they saw as "spiritual," "feminist," ecologically friendly, peaceful, and inclusive. It was a space that provided a respite from much they found alienating in the highly technological world that they ironically served in their day jobs. The language and idealization of "community," however, may have reflected post-1980s foci on the private sphere and consumer identities more than a countercultural communitarianism. "Community" in the new millennium obscured the workings of racial and class exclusiveness and commercialized leisure activities that defined the boundaries and interactions of the community.

Second, MECD was a bodily and aural expression of a "reluctantly modern" liberalism. The classical music's romantic and lyrical tones and the dances' "easy" walking and skipping style at a slow pace contrasted with the "thrusting hips" and "jarring" aerobic music that MECD devotees associated with urban sounds. Ironically, then, MECD dancers' discomfort with the materialist "speed-and-greed" culture represented in the cultural expressions of black urban youth highlighted the contradictions of their urban racial liberalism. Increasingly viewed as an alternative "safe" social space, the MECD community served its members' need for sociality, not for English national identity.

For the ethnic members of MECD, the exclusive nature of this sociality represented the promise of liberal Americanness as Englishness. In this version of Americanness, the community negotiated race with a set of attitudes that ranged from multiculturalism to assimilationism. At times their attitudes resembled the attitudes of ECD proselytizers in the settlements and playgrounds a century earlier, albeit with one major difference: Sharp, Burchenal, Gulick, and others sought to transform urchins into "proper" boys and girls; MECD dancers mostly sought refuge from the "jarring" music of youth culture.[12] As an alternative, MECD offered its members contained sexual physicality limited to hand holds and eye contact, reliance on classical music, and the privileging of English dance as the root of Anglo-Americanness. The physical and cultural space of the dance, then, was an alternative urban space, but one that ironically advanced Anglo-Saxon cultural hegemony.

A Third Revival?

A new round of transatlantic crossings that began at the end of the twentieth century hint that a third folk revival may be dawning—and, like the second, it is one drifting eastward to revitalize London ECD. Rather than crossing the Atlantic, however, geographic compression and cultural convergence may better locate this next revival as transnational. The urban sociologist Harvey Molotch, ever the wordsmith, uses the acronym NYLON—an amalgamation of New York and London—to suggest the embeddedness of the two experiences, or the emergence of the transnational city.[13] To be sure, national inflections remain, but they are increasingly muted. This cultural exchange also mirrors the political mimicry of Reagan-Thatcherism, New Democrats and New Labour, and the importation of people such as New York financier and urban planner Richard Ravitch to "repair" London transit, while the Australian-born media mogul Rupert Murdoch communicates to New Yorkers through tabloid print and television journalism his personally inflected version of their "news."

The influence of the BBC and Hollywood may be one source of the cultural amalgam, and international travel is another. We have seen how, when American dancers described ECD to strangers at the end of the twentieth century, they referred to the BBC's Jane Austen dramatizations; in the past their reference was more often to square dancing. In the international perambulations of folk dancers and country dance bands such as Bare Necessities, however, we have also seen the emergence of MECD as a transcontinental and transatlantic dance form. To be sure, it has been the prerogative of dance leaders and the social elite to transport the dance across the sea since the early decades of the twentieth century. By the end of the twentieth century, however, international travel had become common for people of modest means. Increasingly, British dance tourists combined vacation travel to the United States with visits to dance camps and local city dances, while Americans appeared to reverse the pattern in even larger numbers, including through package dance tours.[14]

Even as international travel began to create an international dance community, differences remained. Traveling Americans in search of a familiar Playford-style dance evening found the Thursday Beginners' Dance at Cecil Sharp House in London, the longstanding traditional EFDSS program, dispiriting, and if they could, until 2008 they attended a new biweekly Wednesday advanced MECD dance at the House. Various prominent British and visiting American teachers took their turn running these classes, although in my occasional visits they were often hard-pressed to gather two dozen dancers with modest training.

The revival of the ECD group for experienced dancers started in 2004. Admission was by invitation, which the leader extended only to advanced dancers. The history behind the new group once again suggests the impact of the New World on the Old. During the previous decade, EFDSS leaders such as Colin Hume invited leading American MECD teachers, notably Fried de Metz Herman and Gene Murrow, to England to teach English Country Dance. Herman took her first of four visits to England to teach dance in 1993, and Murrow arrived almost a decade later. As was her wont, Herman railed at dancers' lack of style and pressed them to relate to one another better on the dance floor—to look at one another and to dance with different partners.[15] Her memorable personal style and provocations, however, whetted British dancers' appetites for more-advanced dancing and greater attention to styling.

The two British leaders of this third revival of dance in the United Kingdom were a new dancer, Judith Hanson, and the British dance leader and choreographer Colin Hume. Each had been transformed less by the visiting Americans than by the melodious and full sounds of a New York and U.S. MECD experience. Both also had the money or professional position that gave them the time and means to travel or relocate.

Judith Hanson, a child of empire, had immigrated to the United Kingdom from New Zealand (and her family had immigrated beforehand from Hong Kong).[16] Introduced fleetingly to ECD in Britain, she discovered that she loved the historical Playford dance and wanted to do more of it. She found Beginners' Night at Cecil Sharp House inadequate, and hearing of superior dancing in the United States, she traveled to New York. There she danced at the annual New York Ball and with Fried Herman at her annual dance weekend in the Berkshire Mountains. Transformed by the quality of dancing, Hanson returned to London and resolved to start a new experienced Playford-style dance in the city. The caller she enlisted, Colin Hume, had himself had a similar American experience.

Colin Hume had moved to the States in 1997, originally planning to settle there to partake of its more vibrant dance community. Fortunately for the prospect of a revived ECD dance community in London and England more generally, Hume met a woman whom he married just before leaving for the United States, and he returned to London, where he has played a major role in trying to revitalize ECD, not the least by arranging for tours to England by Gene Murrow. Thus, two Londoners, transformed by dance in New York, returned to remake ECD at the Cecil Sharp House in the American image as MECD. Hanson, elected to the EFDSS National Council in 2004, and Hume—programmer by day, renowned teacher and choreographer by night, and itinerant transnational dance master—have sought to seed a growing core of transatlantic English MECD dancers. Less than five years later, the fruit of their efforts remains uncertain at best. Both remain committed to a revitalized English Country Dance movement that includes a robust number of well-danced Playford-inspired dances in London at Cecil Sharp House and in England more generally. Hume, however, has largely withdrawn from teaching the advanced class, and for weekly recreational dancing in London, Judith Hanson and her husband, Michael, have turned to Scottish dance.[17]

What do developments in the new millennium portend for MECD in the United States and the nagging concern among its devotees for younger and more numerous recruits? Earlier sources of dancers offer one hope: contra dance could produce another generation of young dancers who segue across that fraternal CDSS tradition; or maybe they could benefit from the penumbra effect of the ballroom revival. ECD foremothers and forefathers fled from the "tango craze" a century ago, but could not the contemporary passion for Argentinean tango and ballroom dance lead people to try country dance, including MECD?

Of course, there was another source for the first folk revival that could be reprised to rebuild enthusiasm for an Anglo-American dance form, although it would fundamentally alter the transnational trend of the past half century: nationalism. The politics of the folk have been mobilized to serve national chauvinism before, and there is no reason to believe it could not happen again, however much one hopes it is unlikely.

Finally, what of the legacy of the culture of liberalism in which MECD is embedded? The solution to the problem of sustaining or growing the movement need not lie in a missionary project to "reform" black urban youth culture. Indeed, as many "nerds" recognize, that culture deserves and merits its own autonomous expression. If the changed relationship of white ethnics to MECD is any basis, a more likely answer than simply flight to a "safe" insular space may come from the rise of a black middle class for whom MECD signifiers no longer appear alien. To make this more possible, CDSS—and the United States—has a challenge: to the extent that CDSS means to represent American (or Anglo-American) national culture, it must think about broadening those dance forms it shelters under its umbrella, without presuming they must be "whitened" or made "respectable."

This latter possibility is not as outlandish as it may seem. Cecil Sharp's "discovery" of the "Kentucky Running Set" as an "authentic" link to English Country Dance effectively obliterated two centuries of complex cultural exchange among African Americans and back woodsmen of diverse origins. A century later, CDSS preserves a sanitized "American" legacy without reference to dance of Native Americans, free blacks, the plantation, or the reservation, although occasional folk dance texts recognize some of the African American influence in clogging. The challenge for CDSS will be to incorporate dances with "thrusting hips" as an integral part of the folk dance tradition within the Country Dance and Song Society of America. In doing so, CDSS will further realize the ambitions of members such as Carl Wittman to make the community more inclusive and, in the process, may begin to ensure its future.

Notes

NOTES TO THE PREFACE

1. The transformation of International into "Balkan" dance is a complex subject requiring its own historian, but it may also have been shaped by Middle Eastern politics and the emergence of Israeli dance groups, which may have drawn some of the Jewish constituency away from International dance. Israeli dance repertoire became increasingly "modern," as well, emphasizing newly written dances in the Israeli style that International dancers rejected as inauthentic folk dances and found too tied to growing Zionist nationalism.

NOTES TO THE INTRODUCTION

1. Mary W. Hinman, letter dated February 18, 1909, reprinted in Gulick, *The Healthful Art of Dancing*; Margaret Knox, letter to Gulick, in ibid., 66–69.
2. The roots of "The Virginia Reel" in "Sir Roger de Cloverly" had been disclosed in American publications but did not seem to have been widely known publicly. See Rath, *The Folk Dance in Education*, 25.
3. Buckland, "English Folk Dance Scholarship," 6; and Buckland, "Definitions of Folk Dance."
4. Frazer, *The Golden Bough*.
5. Lears, *No Place of Grace*, 9.
6. Ibid.; Reiser, "Secularization Reconsidered," 138; Moskowitz, "Public Exposure," 172–73.
7. Howkins, *Reshaping Rural England*, 231.
8. See Buckland, "English Folk Dance Scholarship"; and Sharp, *The Country Dance Book, Part II*, 8–9.
9. Hobsbawm and Ranger, *The Invention of Tradition*; C. Briggs, "The Politics of Discursive Authority"; Dunaway, "Music and Politics in the United States."
10. Buckland, "English Folk Dance Scholarship"; Buckland, "Definitions of Folk Dance"; Sughrue, "Some Thoughts on the 'Traditional versus Revival' Debate"; Kennedy, "Tradition."
11. Boyes, *The Imagined Village*; Filene, *Romancing the Folk*; Tomko, *Dancing Class*.
12. Gary Gerstle has averred that war was the "crucible" in which modern liberalism was molded around a blend of civic and racial nationalism and demonstrates that popular and conventional texts—the "stuff" of cultural work—can be read as attempts to define the social order. See Gerstle, *American Crucible*, 6–9 and passim.

13. Dunaway, "Music and Politics in the United States," 215–19, illustrates this with folk songs such as "The Hammer Song." Originally composed on the occasion of the trial of Communist Party leaders during the McCarthy era, the song became popular in the 1960s in the general spirit of peace and justice associated with civil rights and the peace movement, but without its original political context.

NOTES TO CHAPTER 1

1. Addams, *Spirit of Youth and the City Streets*, cited in a wonderful doctoral dissertation by Lausevic, "A Different Village," 30.
2. Strangways and Karpeles, *Cecil Sharp*, 27.
3. Ibid., 27–28.
4. Harker, *Fakesong*; Boyes, *The Imagined Village*, 77; Shapiro, *Appalachia on Our Mind*, 255.
5. Whisnant, *All That Is Native and Fine*, 126–27. Whisnant also provides the references to Shapiro, *Appalachia on Our Mind*, 255, and Archie Green, "A Folklorist's Creed and a Folksinger's Gift."
6. Karpeles, *Cecil Sharp*, 16–20, 68.
7. Evelyn Sharp to Cecil Sharp, August 8, 1913, from 15 Mount Carmel Chambers, Duke's Lane, Kensington, London, Box 3, Sharp Collection, VWML.
8. Cecil Sharp to Maude Karpeles, June 10, 1915, Pittsburgh, Pennsylvania, MK/3-66, Karpeles Collection, VWML.
9. Malcolm Taylor, the VWML librarian, made this point in an interview with the author at Cecil Sharp House, in London, November 8, 2002.
10. On "Satan's Strongholds," see E. Thompson, *Making of the English Working Class*; Samuel, "Workshop of the World," 6–72; and Wilentz, *Chants Democratic*.
11. Braverman, *Labor and Monopoly Capital*.
12. Howkins, *Reshaping Rural England*, 223.
13. Ibid.
14. Turner, "The Significance of the Frontier in American History."
15. Rothman, *The Discovery of the Asylum*; Foucault, *Discipline and Punish*.
16. Peiss, *Cheap Amusements*.
17. Cavallo, *Muscles and Morals*.
18. See descriptions in the *Oxford Dictionary of National Biography*, www.oxforddnb.com.
19. Cavallo, *Muscles and Morals*.
20. See D. Walkowitz, *Working with Class*, chap. 1, where I recount the vast literature on settlement houses. See, in particular, Crocker, *Social Work and Social Order*. For the relationship between the settlements and folk dance, see Tomko, *Dancing Class*, 81–86; Whisnant, *All That Is Native and Fine*, 21.
21. Cavallo, *Muscles and Morals*, 32.
22. See biographical sketch of James Naismith on the Kansas Heritage website, http://www.kansasheritage.org/people/naismith.html.
23. Rainwater, *The Play Movement in the United States*, 20–23; Gulick, *A Philosophy of Play*, 32.
24. Curtis, *The Play Movement and Its Significance*, 45.
25. Tomko, *Dancing Class*, 184–85.

26. Gulick, *A Philosophy of Play*, 8.

27. Cavallo, *Muscles and Morals*, 38. Cavallo notes that Gulick opposed Lee's support for immigration restriction and presumably could work with him because they could all support Americanizing the immigrants who were already in the country.

28. Gulick, *A Philosophy of Play*, 4–6.

29. Ibid., 54–63; Tomko, *Dancing Class*, 11–18.

30. Established in *turnverein*—associations for mutual assistance and recreation—the discipline incorporated calisthenics with "heavy emphasis on apparatus work" such as vaults, horses, rings, and ladders. Tomko, *Dancing Class*, 11; Gulick, *A Philosophy of Play*, 56–57; and "Friedrich Ludwig Jahn: Father of Gymnastics," GYMmedia.com, www.gymmedia.com/jahn/e_index.htm (July 19, 2005).

31. The Swedish system built on a gymnastics routine led by an American health and temperance lecturer, Dio Lewis (1823–1886), that was popular in the 1860s. Lewis advocated for physical exercise as a part of public education and, to that end, founded the Boston Normal Physical Training School in 1863 to build a corps of instructors. Tomko, *Dancing Class*, 12–16; "Dio Lewis," Virtualology website, www.famousamericans.net/diolewis/ (July 19, 2005).

32. Tomko distinguishes Sargent as seeking the "toned" rather than the muscular body, combining strength and suppleness. Tomko, *Dancing Class*, 16–18; Gulick, *A Philosophy of Play*, 61. Thanks, too, to Allison Thompson for the observation about the individualism of the exercise regime.

33. Clarke, *Sex in Education*, 33, 154–55.

34. Tomko, *Dancing Class*, 18–19; Nancy Lee Chalfa Ruyter, "Genevieve Stebbins," *American National Biography*, www.anb.org; Jack Hrkach, "Steele MacKay," *American National Biography*, www.anb.org. See also Shapiro, *Appalachia on Our Mind*, 255.

35. Gulick, *A Philosophy of Play*, 56–62; Tomko, *Dancing Class*, 17. Thanks again to Allison Thompson, too, for her unromantic perspective on the YMCA programs.

36. Tomko, *Dancing Class*, 42–62; James Ross Moore, "Loie Fuller," *American National Biography*, www.anb.org; Deborah Jowitt, "Ruth St. Denis," *American National Biography*, www.anb.org; Ann Daly, "Isadora Duncan," *American National Biography*, www.anb.org.

37. Buckland, "English Folk Dance Scholarship"; Buckland, "Definitions of Folk Dance."

38. Filene, *Romancing the Folk*, 9–10. Filene notes that scholars date the "first explicitly historical collection" of ballads to 1723, though John Playford's publications of the *English Dancing Master* are ample evidence of seventeenth-century collecting.

39. This background is nicely summarized in R. Cohen, *Folk Music*, chap. 1.

40. Szczelkun, *The Conspiracy of Good Taste*, 41–45.

41. Ibid.; Strangways and Karpeles, *Cecil Sharp*; Brenda Collins, "Sabine Baring-Gould," *Oxford Dictionary of National Biography*, www.oxforddnb.com/view/article/30587. Baring-Gould died with £16,132 in probate.

42. Szczelkun, *The Conspiracy of Good Taste*, 41–45; Dorothy de Val, "Lucy Broadwood," *Oxford Dictionary of National Biography*, www.oxforddnb.com/view/article/57238. Broadwood died with £8,949 in probate.

43. Filene, *Romancing the Folk*, 12–15; Benjamin Franklin, "James Francis Child," *American National Biography*, www.anb.org.

44. Filene, *Romancing the Folk*, 12–15, cites Child's use of this language in his "Ballad Poetry"; Harker, *Fakesong*, 113–14.

45. Filene, *Romancing the Folk*, 12–15.

46. Whisnant, *All That Is Native and Fine*, 23–25; Filene, *Romancing the Folk*, 15–16.

47. Filene, *Romancing the Folk*, 16; Whisnant, *All That Is Native and Fine*, chaps. 1–2; and the feature film *The Songcatcher* (2001).

48. Four historians of the folk in particular have made this point central to their analyses: Harker, *Fakesong*; Howkins, *Reshaping Rural England*; Filene, *Romancing the Folk*; and Boyes, *The Imagined Village*. The phrase "invention of tradition" is most famously used by Hobsbawm and Ranger, *The Invention of Tradition*.

49. M. Smith, "Dancing through English Literature." Smith notes that Pepys's diary entry for December 31, 1661, refers to "Cockolds All Awry." Thanks, too, to Allison Thompson for her clarification of the political meaning of the new name.

50. Boyes, *The Imagined Village*, 101–2.

51. Kennedy, "Tradition," 196–97; Howkins, *Reshaping Rural England*, 41.

52. Rodgers, *Atlantic Crossings*, 3.

53. Burchenal, *Folk-Dances and Singing Games*.

54. Rodgers, *Atlantic Crossings*, 354–59.

55. Burchenal, *Folk-Dance Music*; Burchenal, *Folk-Dances and Singing Games*; Burchenal, *Folk-Dances of Finland*; Burchenal, *Folk-Dances of Denmark*.

56. Ruskin, "The Nature of the Gothic," 14; Ruskin, "Modern Manufacture and Design," 16:338–44; Robert Hewison, "John Ruskin," *Oxford Dictionary of National Biography*, www.oxforddnb.com/view/article/24291; Boris, *Art and Labor*, 4–7; Tomko, *Dancing Class*, 86. For illustrations of the Arts and Crafts style, see Lambourne, *Utopian Craftsmen*.

57. Morris, "How We Live and How We Might Live," 171, 177; Morris, "Innate Socialism," 84–104; Morris, "The Worker's Share of Art," 140–43; Boris, *Art and Labor*, chaps. 1–2; E. Thompson, *William Morris*; Fiona MacCarthy, "William Morris," *Oxford Dictionary of National Biography*, www.oxforddnb.com/view/article/19322?docPos=3.

58. Whisnant, *All That Is Native and Fine*, 58; Lambourne, *Utopian Craftsmen*, 157–58; Boris, *Art and Labor*, chaps. 3–9.

59. Whisnant, *All That Is Native and Fine*, 58–61; Tomko, *Dancing Class*, 87–89; Alan Crawford, "C. R. Ashbee," *Oxford Dictionary of Biography*, www.oxforddnb.com/view/article/30465; Shi, *The Simple Life*, especially chap. 8, "Progressive Simplicity," 175–214; Lambourne, *Utopian Craftsmen*, chaps. 8–11; Boris, *Art and Labor*, chaps. 3–10. On the rural crisis in England, see Howkins, *Reshaping Rural England*.

60. Tomko, *Dancing Class*, 87–88; D. Walkowitz, *Working with Class*, chaps. 1–2.

61. Curtis, *The Play Movement and Its Significance*, 45.

62. Ibid.

63. Gulick, *A Philosophy of Play*, 122; Gulick, *The Healthful Art of Dancing*, 4–5; Gulick, *Physical Education by Muscular Exercise*, 63.

64. Gulick, *A Philosophy of Play*, 263, 265.

65. Ibid., 236, 242.

NOTES TO CHAPTER 2

1. See de Mille, *Martha*, 22.

2. Burchenal, "Folk-Dancing as a Social Recreation for Adults," 9–12; emphasis in the original.

3. Isaac, *The Transformation of Virginia*, 77–87, 301–2.

4. See "contredanse" in Pugliese, "Country Dance," 255–56. For example, Washington danced a minuet with Lucy Knox, the wife of General Knox, to open a Philadelphia ball in 1779, inspiring a local news account to wax that "when this man unbends from his station, and its weighty functions, he is even then like a philosopher, who mixes with the amusements of the world, that he may teach it what is right, or turn trifles into instruction." *Pennsylvania Packet*, March 6, 1779, quoted in Keller and Hendrickson, *George Washington*, 15.

5. Keller and Hendrickson, 20–21.

6. Ibid.

7. Ibid. In a triple minor formation, three couples in the longways sets of perhaps ten couples dance together, the first couple (the first, fourth, seventh, etc. couples) dancing a round with the next two couples, and all first couples ending progressed one place to dance the next round with the two couples now in the next places, who will have alternated the second- and third-couple roles.

8. Hilton, *Dances of Court and Theater*, 3–50.

9. Carson, *Colonial Virginians at Play*, 28–29; Hilton, 250.

10. Claude Blanchard, chief commissary for the French in 1780, quoted in Bonsal, *When the French Were Here*, 57.

11. Ibid., 58.

12. Skip Gorman, *New Englander's Choice*, CD listed at www.folk-legacy.com.

13. Keller and Hendrickson, *George Washington*, 55, 60; Gardner, "Contradances and Cotillions."

14. Keller and Hendrickson, *George Washington*, 22; Pugliese, "Country Dance," 257; Aldrich, *From the Ballroom to Hell*; Millstone, "Continuity and Change in American Country Dance." Thanks to David Millstone for sharing his research with me.

15. Gorman, *New Englander's Choice*, text accompanying CD.

16. Jay Cook, in a conversation, shared his research with me for his forthcoming book on Jacksonian New York immigrant culture.

17. Krause, "Morris Dancing and America," 2–13; Brickwedde, "The History of Morris in America." The dance historian Allison Thompson has noted, in correspondence with the author, that these were early morris performances, not sides.

18. Krause, "Morris Dancing and America," 3.

19. Three figures that initiate each of the three parts of many early dances—up a double, siding, and arming—all have origins in Renaissance dance.

20. Keller and Hendrickson, *George Washington*, 22–23, 81.

21. Karpeles, *Cecil Sharp*, 128–29; Cecil Sharp, diary, April 29, May 7, 1915, Sharp Collection, VWML.

22. Karpeles, *Cecil Sharp*, 116–18, 135. Karpeles provides lovely short obituaries of these men. They were remarkably talented individuals who are deserving of their own histories.

23. Jennifer Beer suggested this term, and it seems to capture the ambivalent and liminal location of the embrace of the folk by so many contemporary professionals and technologists.

24. Addams, *Spirit of Youth and the City Street*, cited in Lausevic, "A Different Village," 30.

25. Hammack, *Power and Society*, 33; McNickle, *To Be Mayor of New York*, table 1.1, p. 13; Hacker, "Looking Backward—and Forward," 203–6; "City of New York: Population History," Demographia website, http://www.demographia.com/db-nyc4.htm.

26. Osofsky, *Harlem*, 220; Rischin, *The Promised City*, 271; McNickle, *To Be Mayor of New York*, 13.

27. Riis, *How the Other Half Lives*, 17; Hammack, *Power and Society*, 62–63. Riis's conservatism is well documented in Yochelson and Czitrom, *Rediscovering Jacob Riis*.

28. Hacker, "Looking Backward—and Forward," 205-6.

29. Bender, *Sweated Work, Weak Bodies*.

30. Greenwald, *The Triangle Fire*.

31. Dorothy Ross, in *Origins of American Social Science*, 25, 390, sees World War I as the trigger for this modernist crisis. The characterization of it in the text is from Hornstein, *A Nation of Realtors*.

32. Gordon, "A Pleasure Which They Can Find Nowhere Else."

33. Stansell, *American Moderns*.

34. O'Neill, "The Dodworth Family and Ballroom Dancing in New York," 88–99.

35. Ibid., 95.

36. Judith R. Walkowitz, "The 'Vision of Salome.'" Ruth St. Denis and Isadora Duncan both performed in New York City during the winter of 1916-17.

37. Allen, *Horrible Prettiness*, 245.

38. Lasky quoted in Erenberg, *Steppin' Out*, 146.

39. Peiss, *Cheap Amusements*; Aldrich, *From the Ballroom to Hell*.

40. Peiss, *Cheap Amusements*.

41. Schultz, *May I Have This Dance?* 4, 99.

42. Erenberg, *Steppin' Out*, 79–80.

43. Ibid., 151–52; Schultz, *May I Have This Dance?* 18–20.

44. O'Neill, "The Dodworth Family," 99.

45. Erenberg, *Steppin' Out*, 126, 162–64.

46. Ibid., 167.

47. Schultz, *May I Have This Dance?* 20–21. Schultz describes the Castle walk as a dance of eight little steps, slightly rising on the balls of the feet on the downbeat and doing little side-to-side patterns, the woman going backward in a large circle that grows smaller.

48. Quoted in Erenberg, *Steppin' Out*, 126, 164.

49. Rainwater, *The Play Movement in the United States*, 132.

50. J. Ross, "The Feminization of Physical Culture," 97.

51. Public Schools Athletic League, Girls' Branch, and Elizabeth Burchenal, *Official Handbook of the Girls' Branch of the Public Schools Athletic League, 1909–10*, frontispiece photo and p. 14.

52. "Schoolgirls Seen in Folk Dancing," *New York Times*, February 28, 1914, 9; *New York Times*, June 9, 1914, 11.

53. *New York Times*, June 9, 1914, 11; A. Thompson, *May Day Festivals in America*, chaps. 5–7 and the appendix; Burchenal, "May Day Celebrations." See also Lincoln, *The Festival Book*. Lincoln, who directed the Physical Education program at the University of Illinois, began her study of May Day in 1900.

54. Thompson, *May Day Festivals in America*; Rivers, *A Full Description of Modern Dances*; Rivers, *New Dances*; Grant, *The American National Call Book*.

55. Thompson, *May Day Festivals in America*, 100.

56. Three of these students were George Z. Medalie, Jacob Zeitlin, and Edward Sapir, who subsequently became, respectively, a district attorney and judge, a University of Illi-

nois professor of English, and a distinguished Columbia University linguistic anthropologist. The three were suspended under dubious circumstances—teachers claimed they were "unclean" or "disrespectful," but given how distinguished all three became, one suspects the problem may have been uppityness and a dose of anti-Semitism. See Pertilla, "Class Exercises."

57. Burchenal, *Folk-Dances and Singing Games*.
58. "The Chalif School of Dancing," pamphlet, Dance Collection, New York Public Library (NYPL); Lausevic, "A Different Village," 15–22.
59. "Skansen Dancers' Tour of America, 1906–07," 224–34.
60. Bergquist, *Swedish Folk Dances*. The translation was funded by Stockholm's Friends of Swedish Folk Dance.
61. Tomko, *Dancing Class*; Lausevic, "A Different Village," 10.
62. Burchenal, *Folk-Dances and Singing Games*.
63. J. Ross, "The Feminization of Physical Culture," 97.
64. Mary W. Hinman, letter dated February 18, 1909, reprinted in Gulick, *The Healthful Art of Dancing*.
65. Mary B. Stewart, quoted in Gulick, *The Healthful Art of Dancing*, 70.
66. Helen Storrow, letter quoted in Gulick, *The Healthful Art of Dancing*, 73–74.
67. Public Schools Athletic League, Girls' Branch, and Burchenal, *Official Handbook of the Girls' Branch of the Public Schools Athletic League, 1908-9*; "Elizabeth Burchenal," Phantom Ranch website, www.phantomranch.net/folkdanc/teachers/burchenal_e.htm.
68. Margaret Knox, letter to Gulick, in Gulick, *The Healthful Art of Dancing*, 66–69.
69. Gulick, *A Philosophy of Play*, 263–65.
70. Burchenal, "Folk-Dancing as a Social Recreation for Adults," 9– 12; emphasis in the original.
71. Rodgers, *Atlantic Crossings*; Shapiro, *Appalachia on Our Mind*; Whisnant, *All That Is Native and Fine*.
72. Burchenal, preface to Burchenal and Burchenal, *American Country-Dances*.

NOTES TO CHAPTER 3

1. From the title of Drew's autobiography, *I'll Try Anything Once—Except Incest and Morris Dancing* (London: Blake, 1993). Boyes, in *The Imagined Village* (147n. 16), notes that the remark is "popularly attributed" to Beecham but cites Arnold Bax in *Farewell My Youth* (London: Longmans, Green and Co., 1943), 17, who in turn cites "a Scot."
2. Tomko, *Dancing Class*, 192–93; also see "Elizabeth Burchenal," Phantom Ranch website, www.phantomranch.net/folkdanc/teachers/burchenal_e.htm.
3. For James Dawson Collery, see Charles Alexander Rook, ed., *Western Pennsylvanians* (Pittsburgh: Western Pennsylvania Biographical Association, 1923), available online at www.libraries.psu.edu/do/digitalbookshelf/29440461.
4. Tomko, *Dancing Class*; also see "Mary Wood Hinman," Phantom Ranch website, http://www.phantomranch.net/folkdanc/teachers/hinman_mw.htm.
5. Country Dance Society, Boston Centre, "A Brief History."
6. Pethick-Lawrence, *My Part in a Changing World*, 74–75.
7. Judge, "Mary Neal and the Espérance Morris," 546–47. Ellen Ross also generously provided helpful information on Pethick-Lawrence and Neal.

8. Roy Judge, "Mary Clara Sophia Neal," *Oxford Dictionary of National Biography*, http://www.oxforddnb.com/view/article/40485; also Judge, "Mary Neal and the Espérance Morris"; Dommett, "How Did You Think It Was?" 47–52.

9. Neal, *As a Tale That Is Told*, 136; and Dowling, "So Who Was Mary Neal Anyway?"

10. Neal, *As a Tale That Is Told*, 138.

11. Ibid., 138–45.

12. Strangways and Karpeles, *Cecil Sharp*, 33. Karpeles deletes the reference to English as the author of this comment in the 1967 revised second edition of her biography.

13. Neal, *As a Tale That Is Told*, 138–45.

14. Ibid., 146.

15. Ibid., 149; Judge, "Mary Neal and the Espérance Morris," 552–53.

16. Neal, *As a Tale That Is Told*, 139; see also Boyes, *The Imagined Village*.

17. Michael Heaney, "Cecil Sharp," *Oxford Dictionary of National Biography*, http://www.oxforddnb.com/view/article/36040.

18. Cecil Sharp, typescript from lecture before the Small Queen's Hall, April 3, 1906, Sharp Correspondence, Box 5, Folder G, Sharp Collection, VWML. This reference is also in Judge, "Mary Neal and the Espérance Morris," 551.

19. Dommett, "How Did You Think It Was?" 49; Judge, "Mary Neal and the Espérance Morris," 558.

20. Evelyn Sharp to Cecil Sharp, August 8, 1913, Box 3, Sharp Collection, VWML; Dowling, "So Who Was Mary Neal Anyway?"; E. Sharp, *Unfinished Adventure*.

21. Boyes, *The Imagined Village*; Neal, *As a Tale That Is Told*, 168. Neal makes this case in her autobiography, *As a Tale That Is Told*. She saw her conflict with Sharp arising from her putting women in the traditionally male morris dance, an error that she had come to believe—and it was her theosophy speaking here—had "broken a law of cosmic ritual."

22. Neal, *As a Tale That Is Told*, 139.

23. Krause, "Morris Dancing and America Prior to 1913," 13–14.

24. Neal, *As A Tale That Is Told*, 155–56; Dowling, "So Who Was Mary Neal Anyway?"

25. Judge, "Mary Neal and the Espérance Morris," 552.

26. Dommett, "How Did You Think It Was?" 51; Judge, "Mary Neal and the Espérance Morris," 558.

27. Sharp, *The Country Dance Book, Part II*, 9.

28. Karpeles, *Cecil Sharp*, 104–6.

29. Many scholars have made this observation. See, for example, Buckland, "English Folk Dance Scholarship," 3–18; Boyes, *The Imagined Village*. See also Sharp's introductions to *Folk Song: Some Conclusions* and *The Country Dance Book, Part II*.

30. *Daily Telegraph*, December 6, 1917.

31. Sharp, *English Folk-Song*, 174–75.

32. Neal, *As a Tale That Is Told*, 159; Karpeles, *Cecil Sharp*, 73. Karpeles (*Cecil Sharp*, 74) quotes Neal from her letter to the *Saturday Review*, April 11, 1908.

33. Cecil Sharp to Mary Neal, March 7, 1909, Sharp Correspondence, Box 5, Folder A, Sharp Collection, VWML, and as quoted in Judge, "Mary Neal and the Espérance Morris," 557.

34. Judge, "Mary Neal and the Espérance Morris," 560.

35. Ibid., 559.

36. Neal to Sharp, July 22, 1909, Sharp Correspondence, Box 5, Folder A, Sharp Collection, VWML.
37. Sharp to Neal, July 26, 1909, Sharp Correspondence, Box 5, Folder A, Sharp Collection, VWML.
38. For the gendered and class dimensions of the professionalizing project of the era, see D. Walkowitz, *Working with Class*.
39. Judge, "Mary Neal and the Espérance Morris," 560; see also E. Burrows to Sharp, October 18, 1909, Sharp Correspondence, Box 5, Folder F, Sharp Collection, VWML.
40. Karpeles, *Cecil Sharp*, 76–77; Michael Heaney, "Maud Pauline Karpeles (1885–1976)," *Oxford Dictionary of National Biography*, http://oxforddnb.com/view/articles/54870.
41. Karpeles, *Cecil Sharp*, 81; "The Progress of Folk Song and Dance," *Musical Herald*, April 1913.
42. Karpeles, *Cecil Sharp*, 79–81, quoting the *Morning Post* and *Vanity Fair*, April 14, 1910.
43. Neal to Archibald Flower, October 25, 1910, Neal Correspondence, Box 5, Folder A, Sharp Collection, VWML, quoted in Judge, "Mary Neal and the Espérance Morris," 565.
44. Karpeles, *Cecil Sharp*, 80–81; Sharp's "invention" and "particularist" use of Kimber is noted by Douglas Kennedy in "Tradition."
45. Krause, "Morris Dance and America Prior to 1913," 1–17.
46. Boyce, *The Imagined Village*; Judge, "Mary Neal and the Espérance Morris."
47. Karpeles, *Cecil Sharp*, 85.
48. Ibid., 78–81.
49. Brickwedde, "A History of Morris in America," 8, cites Sharp's diary, February 15, 1918, Box 7, misc., Sharp Collection, VWML; "George P. Baker," obituary, *EFDS News* 40 (IV), no. 6 (May 1935).
50. Neal, *The Espérance Morris Book*; Kidson and Neal, *English Folk-Song and Dance*; L. Phillips Barker's review of Kidson and Neal's book appeared in the *Musical Times*, November 1, 1915.
51. "The Progress of Folk Song and Dance," *Musical Herald*, April 1913.
52. Karpeles, *Cecil Sharp*, 82, 88; Neal, *As a Tale That Is Told*.
53. Broadbridge, interview with the author, November 2002, London, UK, ECDDP.
54. Strangways and Karpeles, *Cecil Sharp*, 114; Karpeles, *Cecil Sharp*, 114.
55. *EFDS News* 9 (May 1925): 278; Judge, "Mary Neal and the Espérance Morris," 570.
56. *EFDS News* 9 (May 1925): 279.
57. Karpeles, *Cecil Sharp*, 116–18.
58. *EFDS News* 9 (May 1925): 279.
59. Ibid., 282.
60. Strangways and Karpeles, *Cecil Sharp*, 106.
61. Michael Heaney, "Maud Pauline Karpeles (1885–1976)," *Oxford Dictionary of National Biography*, http://oxforddnb.com/view/articles/54870.
62. Neal, *The Espérance Morris Book*, introduction.
63. Strangways and Karpeles, *Cecil Sharp*, 90.
64. Boyes, *The Imagined Village*; also see the introduction to Reeves, *The Idiom of the Peasant*; and Harker, "May Cecil Sharp Be Praised?"

NOTES TO CHAPTER 4

1. Karpeles, *Cecil Sharp*, 21.
2. Elizabeth Burchenal to Cecil Sharp, September 1, 1908, Burchenal Correspondence, Sharp Collection, VWML.
3. Burchenal to Sharp, December 15, 1911, in ibid.
4. *New York Times*, December 20, 1911, 13:3, and December 21, 1911, 2:3; Mary Neal to Clive Carey, December 30, 1911, Carey Correspondence, Sharp Collection, VWML; Neal, *As a Tale That Is Told*, 160–61. This material is pulled together nicely by Krause, "Morris Dancing and America," 7.
5. Hobsbawm and Ranger, *The Invention of Tradition*. For a review of the social constructionists writing since Hobsbawm and Ranger who have emphasized the ways contemporaries "construct," "make," or "invent" traditions, see C. Briggs, "The Politics of Discursive Authority," 435–69. Briggs criticizes these usages by hegemonic social scientists that demean the legitimacy of the indigenous groups who they study. I understand traditions as constantly changing, and I see those doing revived folk dances as a folk themselves.
6. Krause, "Morris Dancing and America," 8.
7. *New York Times*, January 23, 1911, 7; Krause, "Morris Dancing and America," 8.
8. *The (London) Times*, July 22, 1911, quoted in Krause, "Morris Dancing and America," 10. Krause quotes the Boston paper reviews as well.
9. *Times Union* (Albany), June 1911, quoted in Krause, "Morris Dancing and America," 10.
10. Ibid., 10–11. Krause relates the romantic story of the relationship as told by Brown to his children (ibid., 14).
11. A full account of Wright's life and American tours is given by Brickwedde, "A. Claud Wright."
12. Baker obituary, *EFDS News* 40 (IV), no. 6 (May 1935).
13. Brickwedde, "A. Claud Wright," 31.
14. Wright was a popular and regular presence at the Stratford summer and Christmas vacation schools, and his classes for boys and girls in gymnastics, country dances, sword dances, and Morris dances at the Chelsea school were thriving. That Easter, he had helped demonstrate country dance and morris at the International Congress and Exhibition of Physical Education in Paris as part of the English team. And in April, a dance course he initiated in north London in Tottenham had attracted nearly two hundred students. Claud Wright to George P. Baker, March 4 and April 16, 1913, George P. Baker Collection, HTC.
15. Wright taught classes that averaged fourteen enthusiastic students four hours a day on the Storrow lawn: from 10 to 11 a.m., they learned country dances such as "Peascods"; from 11 a.m. to noon, they practiced morris dances such as "Bean Setting"; and in the afternoon, they had hour-long lessons in jigs and sword dancing. Wright to Baker, October 11, 1917, in ibid.
16. Wright to Baker, October 11, 1914, in ibid.
17. Wright is summarizing Hinman's reassurance to him. Wright to Baker, n.d. ("Tuesday morning," ca. mid-July 1913), in ibid.

18. Wright to Baker, September 18, 1913, in ibid.
19. Ibid.
20. Wright to Baker, January 12, 1914, in ibid.
21. Wright to Baker, October 12, 1913, in ibid.
22. Wright to Baker, December 12, 1913, and March 15, 1914, in ibid.
23. Wright to Baker, March 15 and May 27, 1914, in ibid.; Cecil Sharp to Helen Storrow, October 15, 1913, Storrow Correspondence, Box 3, Sharp Collection, VWML. For a fuller discussion, see Brickwedde, "A. Claud Wright."
24. Wright to Baker, June 16 and October 11, 1914, Baker Collection, HTC.
25. Brickewedde, "A. Claud Wright," 21; and Wright to Baker, June 12, 1914, Baker Collection, HTC.
26. Wright to Baker, October 11, 1914, Baker Collection, HTC.
27. Wright to Baker, November 9, 1914, in ibid.
28. Wright to Baker, December 27, 1914, and January 1 and April 11, 1915, in ibid. Also see Brickwedde, "A. Claud Wright."
29. Cecil Sharp to Maud Karpeles, December 25, 1914, MK/3-36 (2), Maud Karpeles Collection, VWML.
30. Karpeles, *Cecil Sharp*, 17, 82, 131.
31. Strangways and Karpeles, *Cecil Sharp*, 131.
32. "Police Notebooks," Book 13LB357, *Charles Booth Online Archive*, http://booth.lse.ac.uk/images/notebooks/b357.
33. Strangways and Karpeles, *Cecil Sharp*, 185.
34. Cecil Sharp to Paul Oppé, November 24, 1922, quoted in ibid.
35. Karpeles, *Cecil Sharp*, 131.
36. Cecil Sharp to Constance Sharp, December 25, 1914, quoted in Karpeles, *Cecil Sharp*, 124.
37. Sharp to Karpeles, December 25, 1914, MK/3-36 (2), VWML.
38. Ibid.
39. Cecil Sharp, diary, January 22, 1915, Sharp Collection, VWML.
40. Sharp to Karpeles, January 8, 1915, MK/3-40, VWML.
41. Ibid.
42. Sharp to Karpeles, January 18, 1915, MK/3-45, VWML.
43. Ibid.; and Keller and Shimer, *The Playford Ball*.
44. Karpeles, *Cecil Sharp*, 129.
45. Sharp to Karpeles, January 25 and 29, 1915, MK/3-45, VWML.
46. Strangways and Karpeles, *Cecil Sharp*, 124.
47. Sharp, diary, January 23 and 30 and February 3, 4, and 6, 1915; Sharp, quoted in Strangways and Karpeles, *Cecil Sharp*, 124; Sharp to Karpeles, February 2, 1915, MK/3-48, VWML. Sharp taught dances such as "Newcastle," "Peascods," "Hey Boys," "Rufty Tufty," Parson's Farewell," "Bo Peep," and "Merry Conceit" at Columbia University and at Gilman's dance studio. The capstone performance was a Saturday-evening dance lecture at the Plaza Hotel in which Sharp lectured with slides, played the pipe and tabor, performed a number of morris tunes on the piano, accompanied Mattie Kay on the piano when she sang some folk songs, and then took the floor himself to dance a couple of two-couple dances. He danced with Burchenal ("pulling Miss B. through"), while Ferris danced with Charles Rabold, a musician.

48. Sharp to Karpeles, February 7, 1915, MK/3-50, VWML.
49. Sharp to Karpeles, February 5, 1915, MK/3-49, and Sharp to Karpeles, February 14, 1915, MK/3-52, VWML.
50. Sharp to Karpeles, February 7 and 12, 1915, MK/3-50, VWML.
51. Sharp to Karpeles, February 14, 1915, MK/3-52, VWML.
52. Sharp to Karpeles, March 15, 1915, MK/3-58, VWML.
53. Burchenal to Sharp, January 15, 1915, Burchenal Correspondence, Sharp Collection, VWML.
54. Ibid.
55. Sharp, dairy, January 3, 1915; Sharp to Karpeles, January 5, 1915, MK/3-39, VWML; Conant, "Interview with Jocelyn B. Reynolds, May 12, 1991."
56. Sharp to Karpeles, March 11, 1915, MK/3-57, VWML.
57. Sharp to Karpeles, February 21, 1915, from Lincoln, MA, MK/3-53, VWML; Sharp, dairy, February 16, 17, 1915. Sharp and Barker also went to see Duncan perform *Oedipus* in April. See Sharp, diary, April 17, 1915.
58. Sharp to Karpeles, March 11, 1915, MK/3-57, VWML. The running step is the basic country dance step, walked energetically while leaning forward on the front of the foot, usually in 2/4 time.
59. Sharp to Karpeles, March 23, 1915, MK/3-59, VWML.
60. Sharp to Karpeles, March 11, 1915, MK/3-57, VWML; emphasis in the original.
61. Sharp to Karpeles, February 26, 1915, MK/3-54, VWML.
62. Sharp did not conceal his anger, even if Karpeles tried after the fact to do so: "Between ourselves, I am not over fond or over trustful of him. . . . Imagine an English Prof. doing such a thing!" Sharp to Karpeles, March 11, 1915, MK/3-57, VWML. The truth of the allegations remains unclear, but what is clear is that the arrangement would also undermine Sharp's prospects.
63. Sharp to Karpeles, January 25, 1915, MK/3-46, VWML.
64. Sharp to Karpeles, April 8, 1915, MK/3-63, VWML.
65. "Cecil Sharp in Boston," *Boston Herald*, February 28, 1915, clippings file, Sharp Collection, VWML.
66. Sharp notes "Mrs. Shaw" as the Wellesley "head," but Ellen Fitz Pendleton was the Wellesley president at the time. "Hey-Days & Holidays," History of Wellesley website, http://www.wellesleyhistory.com/things/tree.html (accessed July 16, 2008). Sharp to Karpeles, March 23, 1915, MK/3-59, VWML.
67. After three "delightful" days in Boston, where he and Storrow became "most chummy," he was off to Pittsfield, Massachusetts. Mira Hall, the headmistress of a fashionable girls' school, had invited him to teach ECD there. He taught his now usual repertoire of traditional older Playford dances, but Sharp suddenly found himself in yet another social league. He was used to teaching the professional middle class and the intellectual bourgeoisie and their children; Miss Hall's students were "the daughters of very rich parents—mostly millionaires—and they were all being prepared to come out at New York and other fashionable centers." In Pittsburgh, Callery had arranged a full four-day schedule of lectures and classes for Sharp. Sharp to Karpeles, March 4 and 15, 1915, MK/3-56, VWML; Sharp, diary, March 2 and 20, 1915.
68. In fact, he had admitted such thoughts in a letter to Maud Karpeles a month earlier. At the time, he wrote that he felt, happily one presumes, "pressed on all sides to stay &

do" the work, hinting then that additional trips might be in the works. Sharp to Karpeles, March 15, 1915, MK/3-56, and February 21, 1915, MK/3-53, VWML.

69. Sharp to Karpeles, March 23, 1915, MK/3-59, VWML.

70. Sharp to Karpeles, March 11, 1915, MK/3-57, and March 15, 1915, MK/3-58, VWML.

71. Sharp to Karpeles, March 11, 1915, MK/3-57, VWML.

72. Ibid.

73. Sharp to Karpeles, February 21, 1915, MK/3-53, VWML.

74. Sharp to Karpeles, March 23, 1915, MK/3-59, VWML; A. Thompson, *May Day Festivals in America*, and personal correspondence with the author.

75. Sharp to Karpeles, March 23, 1915, MK/3-59, and March 26, 1915, MK/3-60, VWML.

76. Sharp taught long hours in each city and, before running out of certificates, awarded a total of twenty-seven to dancers able to meet his exacting standards. Sharp to Karpeles, April 5, 1915, MK/3-62, VWML; Strangways and Karpeles, *Cecil Sharp*, 126.

77. Sharp, diary, June 7, 1915; Karpeles, *Cecil Sharp*, 129; Sharp to Karpeles, June 10, 1915, MK/3-66, VWML.

78. Sharp, diary, 1915; Strangways and Karpeles, *Cecil Sharp*, 126.

79. Karpeles, *Cecil Sharp*, 116. "English Society at Swiss Resorts," *New York Times*, January 11, 1911, C3.

80. *New York Times*, February 23, 1912, 11, and February 24, 1912, 11.

81. Wright to Baker, October 11, 1914, Baker Collection, HTC.

82. Thanks to Tom Bender for reminding me of the fascist resonance for 1920s nationalism.

NOTES TO CHAPTER 5

1. Maud Karpeles to "Aunt Helen," February 2, 1928, EFDSS Correspondence, 1923–1929, Box 1, f. 21, Kate Van Winkle Keller Papers, UNH-MC.

2. Filene, *Romancing the Folk*, 17–21.

3. Sharp to Karpeles, March 11, 1915, MK/3-57, VWML; Burchenal to Sharp, January 12, 1915, Burchenal Correspondence, Sharp Collection, VWML (emphasis in original).

4. Burchenal and Howells Burchenal, *American Country-Dances*, title page and p. v.

5. Strangways and Karpeles, *Cecil Sharp*, 129–30; Shapiro, *Appalachia on Our Mind*, 254–55.

6. Langdon to Olive Dame Campbell, June 4, 1915, John C. and Olive Dame Campbell Papers, Southern Historical Collection, University of North Carolina, quoted in Whisnant, *All That Is Native and Fine*, 113.

7. Whisnant, *All That Is Native and Fine*, chap. 2; Shapiro, *Appalachia on Our Mind*, 254–55; Karpeles, *Cecil Sharp*, 142–43. For a full account of Sharp's trips, see Michael Yates, "Cecil Sharp in America: Collecting in the Appalachians," a "second draft," dated December 23, 1999, of an article that initially appeared in the *Folk Music Journal* (available online at http://www.mustrad.org.uk/articles/sharp.htm). Cecil Sharp with Campbell, *English Folk-Songs from the Southern Appalachian Mountains*.

8. Sharp to Karpeles, March 15, 1916, MK/3-75, VWML, on $50 from Russell Sage; Sharp to Storrow, December 3 and 6, 1916, Storrow Correspondence, Box 3, Sharp Collection, VWML, on the hope for major Russell Sage support; Karpeles, *Cecil Sharp*, 131–32, 155. Sharp, diary, December 17–18, 1917. Sharp wrote that the rejection left him "very depressed."

9. Karpeles, *Cecil Sharp*, 157–58.

10. Malcolm Taylor, librarian of the Vaughan Williams Memorial Library, notes that an old friend of Karpeles's said there was "certainly love" in the relationship, "but it was only one way" (personal communication, December 3, 1997). Karpeles moved her cot into Sharp's room when he nearly died of an asthmatic attack during one of his trips at high altitude in the mountains, and she wrote on her diaries, "Please Destroy." See also Kennedy's obituary, "Maud Pauline Karpeles," 192–94.

11. Karpeles, *Cecil Sharp*, 141, 168.

12. Sharp, diary, August 23, 1916; Daron Douglas, interview with the author, ECDDP, Pinewoods Dance Camp, August 1999.

13. Sharp, dairy, August 1917; Maud Karpeles, diary, May 5 and September 16 and 17, 1918, Maud Karpeles Collection, VWML.

14. Sharp, diary, July 26 and August 13, 1916.

15. Karpeles, *Cecil Sharp*, 169, and quoting Sharp, from the introduction to *English Folk-Songs from the Southern Appalachian Mountains*.

16. Sharp, quoted in Filene, *Romancing the Folk,* 25, who, in turn, cites Harker, *Fakesong*, 202, for the citation for Sharp's diary in 1918.

17. Filene, *Romancing the Folk,* 26.

18. Sharp, introduction to *The Country Dance Book*, part V, quoted in Karpeles, *Cecil Sharp*, 163–64.

19. Sharp to Storrow, September 11, 1917, Storrow Correspondence, Box 3, Sharp Collection, VWML. Sharp wrote of it as a six-couple set, but it appears to have been most often performed with four couples.

20. Karpeles, *Cecil Sharp*, 163.

21. Sharp, introduction to *The Country Dance Book*, part V, 9–10, 13; see also E. Sharp, *Here We Go Round*.

22. Karpeles, *EFDS News* 6 (November 1923): 71.

23. Sharp, quoted from *English Folk-Songs of the Southern Appalachian Mountains*, in Karpeles, *Cecil Sharp*, 169.

24. Sharp to Storrow, December 6, 1916, Storrow Correspondence, Box 3, Sharp Collection, VWML.

25. Gadd, "Lily Roberts Conant," 11–15.

26. Sharp to Karpeles, June 10, 1915, MK/3-66, VWML; Conant, "Interview with Jocelyn B. Reynolds," 18–26.

27. Sharp to Lily Roberts, July 24, 1915, Sharp Collection, VWML; Sharp to Mrs. Roberts (Lily's mother), August 26, 1915, in ibid.

28. Gadd, "Lily Roberts Conant."

29. Following Lily's marriage, Louise Chapin became the head teacher of the Boston Centre, a role she filled for half a century. Chapin, who had learned to dance on the Storrow lawn in 1913–14, probably under Claud Wright, had subsequently attended the Stratford summer school, where Sharp had certified her. See Country Dance Society, Boston Centre, "A Brief History."

30. Sharp to Storrow, March 22, 1922 (in response to her letter to him dated February 27, 1922), Storrow Correspondence, Box 3, Sharp Collection, VWML.

31. Boyes presents evidence that the choice of Kennedy reflected a continuing pattern of prejudices against women and toward male leadership among the EFDS leaders. Sharp

personally asked Kennedy to take the reins after his death, but in practice, after his death, the EFDS Board of Artistic Directors sought someone with administrative talents and bypassed the person who was higher in the dance "hierarchy": Maud Karpeles. The board asked Sharp's friend Paul Oppé to take the post, and when he declined, Douglas Kennedy, described by Boyes as mostly a "weekend dancer," gave up his university post as a biologist to take the position. See Boyes, *The Imagined Village*, 177, 194n. 76.

32. In Pittsburgh, teacher Nora Parkes Jervis, an Englishwoman herself who had recently moved to the States, had a falling out with Mrs. Callery, the grande dame and patron of the Pittsburgh dance community. Barnett was based in New York, where the American Branch was housed. But Barnett was also an accomplished musician. Melville Smith, director of the Eastman School of Music in Rochester, New York, and one of a group of four accomplished brothers who had become English dance enthusiasts, enticed her to join him at Eastman. Barnett found the offer too good to pass up. Sharp to Lily Roberts, September 21, 1915, Sharp Correspondence, VWML; Gadd, "History of the Country Dance Society of America," 40–42.

33. *EFDS Report*, no. 13, January 1927, and no. 15, September 1917, VWML. Barnett's departure as national director opened the door to new leaders who shaped the fortunes of the American movement for the next half century. Barnett also helped firm up the ECD community in Rochester and raised expectations that the American movement might yet become national in more than name. By 1929, within a year of Barnett's arrival, Rochester, with a flourishing group of sixty-five dancers based at the Eastman School of Music, was the third-largest group in the country. Unfortunately for the local group, Barnett only remained in Rochester for two years, returning to England to marry, and by 1930 the branch there collapsed. But her move to Eastman had another impact with broad significance for the American movement: she made one of the Eastman students a convert to English dance: Phil Merrill. Merrill took to morris, sword, and country dance and within a decade emerged as one of the stalwarts of the New York dance community and the national summer dance camp programs, as well as becoming the longtime CDSS musical director. The 1930 *EFDS Report* notes that the branch had collapsed and become an affiliate center. After Barnett's marriage, she moved to South Africa, where she also organized English Country Dance. See also Gadd, "History of the Country Dance Society of America."

34. See Ginsberg, *Women and the Work of Benevolence*. Women often did forge relationships akin to marriage with other women, of course—"Boston marriages." but after her boyfriend died, Gadd never appears to have had a lifetime partner. CDSS became the abiding passion of her life. James E. Morrison, phone interview with the author, November 10, 2007. Also see Gadd's biography in *Who's Who of American Women* (Chicago: Marquis, 1968), 456.

35. See obituaries for Gadd in 1979 issues of *Country Dance and Song*. See also "May Gadd," Phantom Ranch website, www.phantomranch.net/folkdanc/teachers/gadd_m.htm.

36. Karpeles, *Cecil Sharp*, 137.

37. Sharp wrote his wife several times a week long chatty letters in which he shared all his concerns and successes. There are no copies of her letters to him to assess how she felt about his long absences and priorities, but his and Maud Karpeles's letters suggest that Sharp's wife was always supportive of him and his work.

38. Karpeles, *Cecil Sharp*, 135.

39. Culbertson, "Sixty Years of Song and Dance"; Sharp's visits to Berea and Pine Mountain Settlement are described in Karpeles, *Cecil Sharp*, 157–58, 161–62. The songs from Berea appear in Sharp and Campbell, *English Folk-Songs from the Southern Appalachian Mountains*.

40. See Sharp's and Karpeles's diaries for references and accounts of these trips. Chicago is mentioned in Sharp to Storrow, February 14, 1918, Storrow Correspondence, Box 3, Sharp Collection, VWML.

41. A. Thompson, *May Day Festivals in America*; Burchenal, "May Day Celebrations." See also Lincoln, *The Festival Book*. Lincoln, who directed the Physical Education program at the University of Illinois, began her study of May Day in 1900. Louise Freer, a younger member of the faculty, was a regular participant at Sharp's summer classes. Freer hosted Sharp, with Karpeles and Rabold on hand to assist him, for a week-long set of classes at the university in March 1917, and Urbana became a regular stop on Sharp's Midwest itinerary (see Sharp, dairy, March 19, 1917). So, too, did Madison, Wisconsin, home of the University of Wisconsin, which had established a Women's Physical Education Program there in 1910 and had introduced annual maypole dancing festivities. A faculty member, Blanche M. Trilling, had established a "booming" folk dance program by 1910, and Sharp, visiting it on several occasions, always found a welcome at the university. J. Ross, "The Feminization of Physical Culture."

42. Sharp, quoted in Karpeles, *Cecil Sharp*, 133.

43. *St. Louis Post-Dispatch*, May 30, 1916, and *St. Louis Times*, May 30, 1916, clipping file, Sharp Collection, VWML. Sharp, dairy, June 2–5, 1916.

44. Sharp, dairy, June 5, 1916.

45. *St. Louis Post-Dispatch*, May 30, 1916, and *St. Louis Times*, May 30, 1916. Sharp, dairy, June 2–5, 1916.

46. Karpeles, *Cecil Sharp*, 128.

47. By 1924, the Boston Centre reported only 110 members. It sponsored six parties that year attended by an average of 52 participants. See Country Dance Society, Boston Centre, "A Brief History."

48. Eighty-six people had on average attended New York Centre parties. The Centre held a dance every other Tuesday, and on alternate Tuesdays it provided lessons. In addition to its annual May Parties, Twelfth Night Revel, and numerous demonstrations before groups around the city, *EFDS Report*, the annual publication of the EFDS in London, took particular pride in noting that seven Centre members had won certificates, raising the Centre's total number to thirty-seven. *EFDS Reports*, 1924–45; *EFDS News* 5 (November 1923): 164.

49. Leaflet from the Montclair EFDS Group, misc. clippings from the *Newark Evening News*, 1932–33, Scrapbook 1, CDSS Archive, New York Branch, UNH-MC.

50. May Gadd, "English Folk Dancing as Recreation," *Recreation* (April 1932), copy in Scrapbook 1, CDSS Archive, UNH-MC.

51. *EFDS Reports*, 1924–45.

52. Three delegates from each branch and two at-large delegates constituted the federation's steering committee. One at-large delegate was Rabold, who was seen as representing Fairhope, Alabama, and other areas he had visited, and the other was Olive Whitworth, a longtime Cleveland dancer. Gadd, "History of the Country Dance Society of America," 41.

53. Ibid.

54. Ibid., 42.
55. Sharp to Karpeles, March 3, 1916, MK/3-71, VWML; also see *EFDS Reports*, 1924–36.
56. Sharp to Storrow, October 30, 1916, Storrow Correspondence, VWML.
57. Sharp to Storrow, December 7, 1915, in ibid.
58. Sharp to Lily Conant, July 7, 1918, Conant Correspondence, VWML.
59. Rabold to Conant, October 22 and November 11, 1920, in ibid.; Sharp to Burchenal, February 3, 1916, Burchenal Correspondence, VWML.
60. Rabold to Conant, November 11, 1920, VWML; Karpeles to Conant, August 13, 1922, Conant Correspondence, VWML. Karpeles notes that Sharp was very ill then.
61. Teachers included Gilman and another woman, Sydney Parsons, and a trio of men: Milton Smith, Kenneth Wheeler, and W. Harry Curwen. *EFDS Reports*, 1924–39; Gadd, "History of the Country Dance Society of America."
62. Typical was Sydney Parsons, the secretary in 1925, who resided at 186 Prospect Place in fashionable Brooklyn Heights. A woman named Miss Blanchard, the 1928 secretary, had an even more exclusive address at 100 Central Park South. Ibid.
63. *Newark Evening News*, 1932–39, Scrapbook 1, CDSS Archive, UNH-MC.
64. *EFDS Reports*, 1924–36; Gadd, "History of the Country Dance Society of America."
65. George Baker retired as president of the American Branch after only one year; largely disappearing from the local dance scene, he did apparently continue his summer dance program at Chocorua for a few years. Wilfert, "Pinewoods Fifty Years Ago," 1.
66. Gibbs, Storrow's friend and associate, presided over Storrow's School of Dance and helped steer it away from International dance to English Country Dance. It is thought that Gibbs may have even helped introduce Storrow to Claud Wright. Dorothy Bolles, who went with Chapin to Stratford before the war and learned ECD from Sharp himself, also taught at the Boston Centre. Country Dance Society, Boston Centre, "A Brief History"; *EFDS News* 41 (IV), no. 7 (June 1935).
67. Wells was one of several women to be introduced to English dance at Wellesley College, where she later joined the faculty. She was on the staff of the Pine Mountain Settlement School for over a decade. Present when Sharp arrived there and discovered the "Running Set," Wells established a robust tradition of morris, sword, and country dance among the children at the Settlement School. Karpeles, *Cecil Sharp*, 161–62, 170; "Pine Mountain Settlement School, History, 1929," Box 54, Evelyn K. Wells Papers, CDSS Archive, UNH-MC. Wells attended the Vacation School at Stratford in 1923, along with Olive Dame Campbell. *EFDS News* 6 (November 1923): 164.
68. Milton was in New York, and Melville, who began in Rochester, moved to the Langly School in Cambridge by the late 1930s, joining his brothers Everett and Albert as members of the Boston dance community. Gadd, "Lily Conant Roberts," 12.
69. Gadd, "Lily Conant Roberts"; EFDS, Boston Branch, 1930, "Schedule of Classes, 1930–1931," CDSS Collection 140, Series I d., Scrapbook, Box 4, CDSS Archive, UNH-MC.
70. Karpeles to "Aunt Helen," February 2, 1928, Box 1, f. 21, Kate Van Winkle Keller Papers, UNH-MC.
71. Alden, "The Revival of Country Dance," 50.
72. See Roberta Frankfort, *Collegiate Women: Domesticity and Career in Turn-of-the-Century America* (New York: New York University Press, 1977), 83.
73. Tedesco, "Making a Girl into a Scout," 19–39; S. Mitchell, *The New Girl*; Inness, *Intimate Communities*.

74. Sharp to Karpeles, March 11, 1915, MK/3-57, VWML.

75. Burchenal to Sharp, January 15, 1915, Burchenal Correspondence, VWML.

76. Recall that Burchenal thought "all things good in dancing are in the folk dances of all countries." Sharp to Burchenal, January 12, 1915, Burchenal Correspondence, VWML.

77. Sharp to Storrow, January 1, 1916, Storrow Correspondence, VWML; Sharp to Karpeles, February 5, 1915, MK/3-49, and March 15, 1915, MK/3-58, VWML.

78. English Dance Society (New York Branch), published materials, 1919–1925, Stanley Watkins Papers, CCDS Archives, UNH-MC. Watkins taught the grade 1 morris dance class. Mary Smith and Susan Gilman taught grades 1 and 4 of country dance, respectively, and Sydney Parsons taught a class in sword dancing as well as grade 2 of morris dance. Fifty cents a lesson was a tidy recreational sum to put out regularly; a movie cost twenty-five cents or less, and subway fare was a nickel.

79. Personal experience of the author. The change was a democratic impulse combined with the desire to welcome younger new dancers to an ever-aging dance community.

80. Sharp to Karpeles, March 11, 1915, MK/3-57, VWML.

81. Program, "Annual Ball of the English Folk Dance Society of New York, Program of Dances," Box 1, Stanley Watkins Papers, UNH-MC. The program notes were written by Milton Smith, a leader of the New York Centre.

82. Wilfert, "Pinewoods Fifty Years Ago."

83. The school was to be the first of many for the EFDS American Branch. Sharp had asked his American organizers to guarantee him a hundred registrants; only sixty enrolled, but although the weather did not cooperate, all involved thought the event a success. Maud Karpeles, Norah Jervis, and Lily Roberts assisted Sharp at the school, and it was there that Charles Rabold was formally initiated into Sharp's American demonstration team.

84. Strangways and Karpeles, *Cecil Sharp*, 129; Sharp to Karpeles, March 26, 1915, MK/3-60, VWML, on wanting one hundred entrants.

85. Sharp also ran what he and Karpeles referred to as summer schools in New York, to accommodate New Yorkers. But because the New York programs were neither advertised as national "schools" nor organized as residential retreats away from the city, historians have reserved pride of place in the history of the EFDS American Branch's history for the Amherst summer schools. Sharp, diary, June 30, 1916.

86. Sharp, diary, June 29–July 20, 1917; Sharp to Storrow, July 16, 1916, quoted in Karpeles, *Cecil Sharp*, 134.

87. Sharp chose to interpret what he called the "failure" of the summer schools as a commentary on the character of Americans, rather than blaming it on the war. The New York Centre did run its regular three-week summer school at Gilman's Studio in the city in late June and early July 1918, and its disappointing attendance may have occasioned or confirmed the decision to cancel the Amherst school: only nine or ten students attended, and Karpeles had only four in her morris class. With the meager attendance, Sharp despaired that "there never will be more than a few people in America who will give the necessary time to be proficient." He had complained to Rabold at one point that "the average American dancer seems to me to be incurably superficial." "They like everything equally well, good, bad and indifferent." Sharp, dairy, June 21–July 13, 1918; Karpeles, diary, June 24, 1918; Sharp to Rabold, n.d., quoted in Strangways and Karpeles, *Cecil Sharp*, 135; Sharp to Lily Roberts, July 7, 1918, Conant Correspondence, VWML.

88. Sharp, diary, June 28, 1916, and June 15–16, 1918; Karpeles, diary, July 15, 1918.

89. From the first, Louise Chapin, the Boston Centre's head teacher, also taught there. Wilfert, "Pinewoods Fifty Years Ago," 3.

90. Ibid.

91. Flyer announcing the second season of the English Folk Dance Camp of the New York Branch, Box 1, English Folk Dance camp, 1925, Watkins Papers, UNH-MC; Wilfert, "Pinewoods Fifty Years Ago," 3.

92. Gadd, "History," 41; Wilfert, "Pinewoods Fifty Years Ago," 3; eight-millimeter tape of ECD in the United States, 1927–1950s, VWML.

93. Storrow's improvement included two-person cabins rather than tents, the separation of the two Girl Scouts camps to various ends of the campsite, camp electrification, and a separate Storrow family compound, with private cabins for the Conant family, to whom she had become deeply attached. Wilfert, "Pinewoods Fifty Years Ago," 3.

94. See the website for the Association of Research Libraries, www.arl.org/pp/ppcopyright.

95. One critically divisive event was Sharp's displeasure at Burchenal's reported behavior at the fall meeting of the EFDS branch in Boston to plan the 1916 summer school. According to the minutes of the discussion, Burchenal had urged that the school not rely on Storrow's largess and be discontinued if enrollment was insufficient. She pleaded to Sharp that this misrepresented her position; she had only proposed that plans be "scaled down." Storrow to Sharp, n.d. (ca. late January 1916), Storrow Correspondence, VWML.

96. Sharp to Karpeles, January 8, 1915, MK/3-40, VWML.

97. Rabold, quoted in Sharp to Karpeles, February 29, 1916, MK/3-70, VWML.

98. At the formation of the EFDS American Branch in March 1915, participants agreed formally to locate it in New York, but Boston was made the de facto headquarters, as it was there that Baker and Storrow, its two principal officers, resided. In New York, Gilman, a woman named Miss Young (who, according to Karpeles, inexplicably left the dance community after a few years), and Rabold became Sharp's principal dancers and contacts. Sharp to Storrow, January 1, 1916, Storrow Correspondence, VWML. Karpeles penciled a note on Sharp's Correspondence file (as executor of his estate) that "Miss Young dropped out of things." Sharp to Storrow, July 16, 1916, in ibid.

99. Burchenal to Sharp, n.d. (ca. late January 1916), Burchenal Correspondence, VWML.

100. Sharp to Burchenal, February 3, 1916, in ibid.; Sharp to Karpeles, February 25, 1916, MK/3-69, VWML.

101. "Race Records," PBS website, www.pbs.org/jazz/exchange/exchange_race_records.htm.

102. Samuel, "'Quarry Roughs,'" 162, 191, based on information from Kimber and Sharp.

103. Lausevic, "A Different Village," 53.

104. Paul Stamler, e-mail to the author, July 3, 2007, and to the ECD listserv, June 30, 2007.

105. Sharp to Karpeles, February 7 and 14, 1915, MK/3-50, 3-52, VWML.

106. Sharp to Karpeles, March 23, 1915, MK/3-58, VWML.

107. Sharp listed the following dances he had recorded as of March 1916: "My Lady Cullen," "Black Nag," "Grimstock," "Mage a Cree," "If All the World," "The Old Mole," "Hundsdon House," "Rufty Tufty," "Parson's Farewell," "Hey Boys," "Merry Conceit," "Sell-

inger's Round," "Gathering Peascods," "Newcastle," "Sweet Kate," "Jenny P[luck].P[ears]," "Oranges & Lemons," "Confess," "Lady in the Dark," "Chelsea Reach," and "Live Companion." He noted that his earliest recordings were of "Flamborough Sword Dance," "Tideswell Processional Dance," "Three Meet," "The Butterfly," "Goddesses," "Jamaica," "Keibly & Sleights's Sword Dance," and "Row Well Ye Marines." Sharp to Karpeles, March 6, 1918, MK/3-73, VWML.

108. Sharp to Karpeles, March 23, 1915, MK/3-58, VWML.

109. Sharp to Karpeles, March 15, 1916, MK/3-75, VWML; Sharp, diary, 1916, July 19–21 and October 27–28, 1916; *EFDS News* 4 (1922); Mike Wilson-Jones, "Listen to the Band," program notes for the two-CD set of dance tunes from the EFDSS Archive (December 2006).

110. Sharp to Karpeles, March 26, 1916, MK/3-60, VWML.

111. Sharp to Karpeles, March 6, 1916, MK/3-73, VWML.

112. Wilson-Jones, "Listen to the Band."

113. Ibid.

114. "Rufty Tufty" is track 1 on "Listen to the Band." Thanks to Gene Murrow for timing the recordings for me. The 1911 notation is reprinted in Keller and Shimer, *The Playford Ball*, 92.

115. Boyes, *The Imagined Village*, 95, 106–8.

116. Gadd, "English Folk Dance as Recreation," n.p.

117. To which the first speaker responded, "Ah! Well, we do all 'ave our vailin's." Strangways and Karpeles, *Cecil Sharp*, 36.

118. Minutes of the Executive Committee Meeting, January 6, 1928, IaB1f21, CDSS Archives, UNH-MC, quoted in Gordon, "A Pleasure Which They Can Find Nowhere Else."

119. Conant, "Interview with Jocelyn B. Reynolds," 16–23. The role of the English folk dance movement in providing public leadership roles for women is well developed in Tomko, *Dancing Class*.

120. Boyes, *The Imagined Village*, 96, 98, 101–2.

121. The "House"—more resembling a manor estate—is a substantial Georgian three-story building on a comfortable residential block on Regents Park Road in Camden Town, half a mile south of Primrose Hill. Patrick Schuldham Shaw, *Pat Shaw Collection, Book II*, compiled by M. Fennessey (London: H. E. Styles, 1986). Marjorie Fennessey email, kindly forwarded to the author by Stephanie Smith.

122. Ford, *"Good Morning"*; Boyes, *The Imagined Village*, 157–63. British fascists actually wore black shirts. Some have doubted Gardiner's sympathy with fascism, but the prevailing view of historians is convincing. See, for instance, Frank Trentmann's biography in the *Oxford Dictionary of National Biography* at http://www.oxforddnb.com/view/article/59314.

123. "Two Folk Dance Societies Claim Kentucky Running Set," *Herald Tribune*, May 10, 1931. R. Cohen, in *Folk Music* (15–17), notes the German, Irish, and African roots of folk music, as well as the fact that collectors such as Sharp often elided these various origins.

124. Leonard Elsmith to the Editor, *Herald Tribune*, May 17, 1931.

125. Burchenal and Howells Burchenal, *American Country-Dances*; Burchenal, *Dances of the People*; Burchenal and Crampton, *Folk-Dance Music*; Burchenal, *Folk-Dances and Singing Games*; Burchenal and Howells Burchenal, *Folk-Dances of Germany*; Burchenal, "May Day Celebrations"; Burchenal, *Folk-Dances of Finland*; Burchenal, *Folk-Dances of Denmark*; Burchenal and Howells Burchenal, *Rinnce Na Eirann*.

126. Rath, *The Folk Dance in Education*. Rath, who was the director of Physical and Health Education, Indianapolis Public Schools, earlier published *Folk and School Dances* (Indianapolis, 1929).

127. Sharp to Karpeles, March 11, 1915, MK/3-57, VWML.

128. Karpeles, "The International Folk Music Council," 14–32; Kennedy, "Maud Pauline Karpeles," 292–94. Perhaps Karpeles's German-Jewish background also made her more receptive to "other" folk traditions.

129. Brochures and clippings from 1932, the English Folk Dance Society, New York Branch, Scrapbook 1, CDSS Archive, UNH-MC.

130. Graff, *Stepping Left*.

131. Gadd, "English Folk Dancing as Recreation," n.p.

NOTES TO CHAPTER 6

1. Gene Murrow Oral History, Pinewoods Dance Camp, Plymouth, Massachusetts, August 2000, ECDDP.

2. Tom Seiss Oral History, Pinewoods Dance Camp, August 1999, ECDDP.

3. Newbold Morris to Samuel M. While, March 13, 1961, reproduced in Pertz, "The Jewgrass Boys," 107.

4. For a wonderful account of this protest and rise of bluegrass in the park, see Pertz, "The Jewgrass Boys."

5. See ibid., 112.

6. Von Schmidt and Rooney, *Baby, Let Me Follow You Down*. This lovely illustrated collection is based on nearly a hundred oral histories with men and women who gathered in the Cambridge folk clubs and in Washington Square Park, including a young college girl named Joan Baez.

7. Bealle, *Old-Time Music and Dance*. Thanks to Stephanie Smith for drawing my attention to Bealle's terrifically smart book.

8. As I have suggested elsewhere, however, this liberal political orientation was not so new. Fabian socialists such as Sharp and Progressive reformers were at the center of the first revival. See D. Walkowitz, "The Cultural Turn and a New Social History."

9. Cantwell, *When We Were Good*; R. Cohen, *Rainbow Quest*.

10. See Brocken, *The British Folk Revival*; Mitchell, *The North American Folk Music Revival*; Weissman, *Which Side Are You On?*

11. Ibid.

12. Miller, "Segregating Sound"; L. Cohen, *Making a New Deal*.

13. Filene, *Romancing the Folk*, chaps. 1–2; Malcolm Taylor Oral History, London, November 2002, ECDDP.

14. Filene, *Romancing the Folk*, chaps. 2 and 3.

15. Ibid., 39–49.

16. Ibid., chap. 2; Baggelaar and Milton, *Folk Music: More Than a Song*; Bealle, *Old-Time Music and Dance*; Harris, *The New Folk Music*.

17. Pertz, "The Jewgrass Boys," 11; Rosenberg, *Bluegrass, A History*; Oakley and Ripic, *A History of Bluegrass in New York and Northeastern Pennsylvania*. Bealle, in *Old-Time Music and Dance*, draws on his experience in the Bloomington, Indiana, contra community to emphasize the role of old-time music in contra, but my experience at my sister's

commune in West Virginia at the time and my sense of urban folk communities suggest that bluegrass and more commercial forms of folk-rock were woven through the folk communities.

18. On folk song as an established part of left-wing functions with the rise of the Popular Front, see Filene, *Romancing the Folk*, 70; Denning, *The Cultural Front*; Mishler, *Raising Reds*, 6, 136.

19. International Folk Music Conference, July 17–21, 1950, and "Members," November 1970, 1915–, Collections 140, Series III, Box 2, Folder: International Folk Music Council (Conferences), 1950–1975, Evelyn K. Wells Papers, CDSS Archives, UNH-MC.

20. Denning, *The Cultural Front*.

21. Geduld, quoted in email correspondence with the author, February 13, 2009; Geduld, "Performing Communism in the American Dance," 39–65; Graff, *Stepping Left*.

22. Denning, *The Cultural Front*; Mishler, *Raising Reds*, 6, 136; Graff, *Stepping Left*.

23. To be sure, the historian Georgina Boyes hints at a British version of liberalism, and it merits further study. See in particular the last chapters in Boyes, *The Imagined Village*.

24. Greene, *Square and Folk Dancing*, 16.

25. T. L Cotton, vice chairman of the Folk Festival Council (of New York), noted the "just criticism" of "dissatisfied" audience members and stated that the council was "organizing [its] next affair so that everybody can dance and sing together." Cotton to "Dear Friend," October 17, 1932, Scrapbook 1, EFDS, New York Branch, CDSS Archive, UNH-MC. See also Parmelee, "New York Folk Festival Council," 57–60.

26. Lausevic, "A Different Village," chap. 4; "Vyts Beliajus," Phantom Ranch website, www.phantomranch.net/folkdanc/teachers/beliajus_v.htm.

27. *Federation Folk Dancer* (Folk Dance Federation of California, San Francisco; later called *Let's Dance*) 10 (August 1944): 1, describes Chang; Chang, "International Folk Dance in the West," 1–3.

28. Box 1, folders 18–25, Virgil Morton Papers, SFPALM. Also see Lausevic, "A Different Village," chap. 3; Gretchell, *A History of the Folk Dance Movement in California*; *Federation Folk Dancer* (Folk Dance Federation of California, San Francisco; later called *Let's Dance*) 1–2 (1944–45), and *The Folk Dancer* (Chang's International Folk Dancers; became *The Record* in 1944) 1–4 (1941–44), SFPALM.

29. Lausevic, "A Different Village," 43–53; "Michael & Mary Ann Herman," Phantom Ranch website, http://www.phantomranch.net/folkdanc/teachers/herman_mm.htm; Howard, "Mary Ann and Michael Herman."

30. *New York Times*, November 1941 (Sunday edition); clippings, CDSS Archives, UNH-MC.

31. Lausevic, "A Different Village," chap. 5, p. 26, and chaps. 3 and 4.

32. Michael Herman, *The Folk Dancer* 1 (1941): 1, quoted in Lausevic, "A Different Village," 43–44.

33. Roediger, *The Wages of Whiteness*; Brodkin, *How Jews Became White Folks*; Ignatiev, *How the Irish Became White*; Lipsitz, *The Possessive Investment in Whiteness*; Jacobson, *Whiteness of a Different Color*.

34. Dachant, "These Folk Dancers—Who Are We Anyhow?" Averaging in their late twenties and early thirties, half the respondents were married, and half were born in the United States (though many more were undoubtedly sons and daughters of immigrants).

35. Box 1, Folder 20, Folk Dance Federation, 1950s, Virgil Morton Papers, SFPALM.

36. Lausevic notes that Walter Kalaidjian made this claim for radical magazines between the wars in his book *American Culture between the Wars*. Lausevic describes International Folk Dance as "apolitical." I admire much in her dissertation, but this characterization treats International Folk Dance as one political formation and does not appreciate the left-liberal politics that underlies "apolitical" positioning.

37. Personal observation of the author; and Lausevic, "A Different Village," part 2.

38. Belle Bernstein, telephone conversation with the author (her nephew), October 4, 2007. Bernstein had been secretary of the Communist Party in New Jersey. Also see the annual conference reports of the Catskill Institute: catskills.brown.edu/hcc.html.

39. Gornick, *The Romance of American Communism*.

40. Mishler, *Raising Reds*; and personal observation by the author as a "red diaper" baby who attended these camps. My parents both folk danced in the 1940s and 1950s at these "red" resorts and with friends at their homes and at the YMHA in Paterson, New Jersey.

41. Greene, *Square and Folk Dancing*, 174; Gilbert, *International Folk Dance at a Glance*. In a Sicilian circle dance such as "St. Bernard's Waltz," couples begin in a double circle with the man's back to the center and with his partner facing in. This is a traditional dance in which couples do not change partners.

42. Mishler, *Raising Reds*. My parents and many of their friends were in and around the Communist Party until 1956 in northern New Jersey, and these included Al Shadowitz, a physicist brought before the McCarthy Committee. Al had a disability and did not folk dance, but his wife, Edith, joined in regular dances I witnessed among this group.

43. Ironically, what Kennedy witnessed was closer to the spirit championed by Sharp's British rival, Mary Neal, but that is another story. The best account of the relationship between Sharp and Neal is in Boyes, *The Imagined Village*. See, too, Kennedy, *English Folk Dancing*, 20–21.

44. Kennedy, *English Folk Dancing*, 21. Kennedy's introduced the concept of what he called "anacrusis" to infuse a new spirit in the dance. Debunked by Boyes as "a confused principle of rhythmic momentum which was deployed talismanically as a cure for the Society's self-conscious arty style," anacrusis seems to have been less significant than other changes in the repertoire (*The Imagined Village*, 179).

45. Boyes, *The Imagined Village*, 179.

46. Sweers, *Electric Folk*; G. Mitchell, *The North American Folk Music Revival*. The Clancy Brothers and Tommy Maken were at the center of the nationalist Celtic revival in the 1970s and 1980s.

47. Boyes emphasizes the misogyny and sexism she see within EFDSS (*The Imagined Village*, 167–73).

48. Readers wanting to read Kennedy's explicit assault on single women and to witness its misogyny, should see ibid., 152, 206–10.

49. Ibid., 204.

50. *Christian Science Monitor*, August 16, 1948, Clippings, CDSS Archives, UNH-MC.

51. Kennedy, *English Folk Dancing*, 28; and Taylor Oral History.

52. Miss Reed, P.T. Organizer, and Miss Tolley, Youth Organizer in Hants, March 7, 1947, quoted in "Report on Six Months Experimental Scheme: Feb. to Aug. 1947," Kathleen Atkins (née Church-Bliss) Papers, VWML.

53. "Report on Six Months Experimental Scheme."

54. Nicolas Broadbridge Oral History, London, November 6, 2002, ECDDP.

55. Anonymous dancer described in Minutes, April 6, 1948, Atkins Papers, VWML.

56. Boyes, *The Imagined Village*, 185; and Judith R. Walkowitz's forthcoming book on Soho in the interwar years and the role of the Windmill Theatre in reconstructing Englishness.

57. Boyes, *The Imagined Village*, 201.

58. March 2, 1950, monthly reports by Church-Bliss and Whiteman to Kennedy, Atkins Papers, VWML. "Modern style" as referring to community dance was clear from the context in which it appears in the report.

59. Kennedy, *English Folk Dancing*, 28; Minutes of Sussex District Annual Meeting, November 8, 1947, Atkins Papers, VWML.

60. Boyes, *The Imagined Village*, 214–15.

61. Taylor Oral History. Taylor traces the second revival back to the 1920s with the arrival in England of gramophone records of American jazz, which after the war fed into the skiffle clubs and folk clubs. Skiffle, according to Taylor, "was a form of music very much based on people like Lonnie Donegan . . . listening to records of people like Lead Belly and putting them in the intervals between the jazz bands." See also R. Cohen, *Folk Music*, 89–97; Boyes, *The Imagined Village*, 214–15.

62. Filene, *Romancing the Folk*, 118.

63. Boyes, *The Imagined Village*, 213–15.

64. Ibid., 216.

65. Ibid.; Brocken, *The British Folk Revival*, chap. 5; R. Cohen, *Folk Music*, 98–100.

66. Taylor Oral History.

67. Ibid.; Brocken, *The British Folk Revival*; Boyes, *The Imagined Village*, 216, 231–34; R. Cohen, *Folk Music*, 133–36.

68. Sawyers, *Celtic Music*, chap. 6.

69. Schofield, "Ceilidh Roots"; Bearman, "Knees Up at Cecil Sharp House."

70. Fried de Metz Herman, on Paul B. Ross, *Fried de Metz Herman, Conversation with Paul B. Ross* (CD); see also Fried de Metz Herman Oral History, August 1999, ECDDP.

71. Allison Thompson to the author, February 28, 2008. Thompson reminded me of strong objections by one dance historian on the ECD listserv to any effort to distinguish recent dance as "modern." This dance historian considers Baroque and Renaissance dance to be "historical" and all reconstructions of country dance a "modern" activity of "hobbyists." Even if I could accept the distinction between the work of Renaissance dance "historians" versus ECD "reconstructor-hobbyists" (which I do think problematic), I use the term to distinguish the modern choreography *and* new tempi and style of contemporary dancing of older dances as "modern."

72. Personal observation by the author from the late 1970s to the early 1990s when the center closed its dance hall on Varick Street; also see Lausevic, "A Different Village."

73. "A Chronology of Country Dance & Song in New York City, 1915–1997," Country Dance * New York website, www.cdny.org/chronology.html.

74. "Genevieve Shimer," Phantom Ranch website, www.phantomranch.net/folkdanc/teachers/shimer_g.htm.

75. Art and Helene Cornelius Oral History (August 1999), Emlen Cressen Oral History (August 1999), Kitty Keller Oral History (May 5, 2001), and Brad Foster Oral History (August 1999), ECDDP; and conversation-interviews by the author with Peter Fricke,

Glen Echo, Maryland, December 12, 2001, and (via telephone) February 10, 2002, and John Bremer, Glen Echo, Maryland, December 12, 2001. The 1999 interviews are at Pinewoods Dance Camp in Plymouth, Massachusetts.

76. Helwig, "Pinewoods Camp," 60–61; Shimer, "Country Dance and Song Society," 42–43; Foster Oral History; Wilfert, "Pinewoods Fifty Years Ago"; Sue Salmons, phone interview with the author, November 10, 2007.

77. Salmons interview.

78. Murrow Oral History; Conant, "Interview with Jocelyn B. Reynolds," 16–23.

79. Josie Giarratano, for instance, joined the New York dance community after reading a February 7, 1952, *New Yorker* profile of Gadd. Giarratano interview with the author, New York City, ca. 2002.

80. Fricke, Bemer, Richard Wilson, and Giarratano conversations and oral histories with the author, 2001–7. For Shimer, who had been a schoolteacher in England during the war, see "Genevieve Shimer," Phantom Ranch website, www.phantomranch.net/folkdanc/teachers/shimer_g.htm (accessed September 27, 2007).

81. Elizabeth Burchenal published her collection of contras in 1918, and Sharp's and Karpeles's experiences attested to the continuing presence of these dances in indigenous rural communities.

82. Greene, *Square and Folk Dancing*, 12–14; Damon, *The History of Square Dancing*, 50. Thanks also to David Millstone for the discussion of the modern Western Squares.

83. Program, "Silver Jubilee Festival, 1915–1940," CDSS Archive, UNH-MC.

84. "Swing Your Lady for a Dos a Dos!" *Cue* (Jersey Section), September 27, 1941, J1, form Clippings, CDSS Archive, UNH-MC.

85. "Swing Your Lady"; Country Dance Society, Boston Centre, "A Brief History."

86. Murrow Oral History.

87. Country Dance Society, Boston Centre, "A Brief History."

88. Gadd, "Adventure into Television"; Gadd, "Television and the Folk Dance"; Gadd, "Television News"; Gadd, "Television Adapts to Wartime"; Gadd, "Defense Recreation"; Gadd, "Recreational Dancing and the U.S.O."; Gadd, "Country Dancing with the Services."

89. "A Chronology of Country Dance & Song in New York City, 1915–1997." Dancers were drawn from New York, Boston, and New Jersey centres but also included a few people from Kentucky (presumably Pine Mountain) and Pennsylvania as well.

90. Geduld, "Performing Communism in the American Dance," 61–65. In correspondence to the author (February 13, 2009), Geduld notes that the budget for the recreational dancers was in the range of twenty thousand dollars, about one-tenth that allocated to the high-modern troupes.

91. Casey, introduction to *International Folk Dancing, U.S.A.*, 7–8.

92. See Prevots, *Dance for Export*, 117.

93. Robert F. Jordan, quoted in ibid., 159; and Shimer, "Country Dance and Song Society," 42–43.

94. Fricke interview.

95. Graff, *Stepping Left*, 113. As early as the 1930s, New York's *Dance Observer* also employed Gadd to write on folk dance.

96. Tony Hiss, telephone interview with the author, October 14, 2007, New York. These gatherings appear to have taken place from the early 1950s through the 1960s, as Alger Hiss got out of jail only in 1954, and Tony recalls being there while his father was still in

jail. Hiss also recalls the evenings as lively, exciting affairs full of "interesting people" and hosted by Gadd and her female housemate (about which he knew nothing more).

97. Fricke interview; Bremer interview.

98. Anonymous comment to the author, True Brit Dance Weekend, Hopewell Junction, October 7, 2007.

99. *Country Dance and Song* 1 (1968): 4; also programs of the 1959 and 1967 Newport Folk Festival, Misc. Papers, CDSS Archives, UNH-MC.

100. Newport Folk Festival, July 11–12, 1959, Gadd Papers, UNH-MC.

101. Newport Folk Festival, 1967, Gadd Papers, UNH-MC. Connie Taylor and his wife, Marianne, started teaching International Folk Dance in Boston in 1953 and in the next years opened the Boston Folk Arts Center, which played a parallel role to that of the Hermans' Folk Dance House in New York. "Conny Taylor, Co-Founder of FAC," Folk Arts Center of New England website, http://www.facone.org/about/conny.htm.

102. Rosenberg; *Bluegrass, a History*, 196; Dunaway, *How Can I Keep Singing?* 247–50; Neff, "The Folk Revival"; R. Cohen, *Folk Music*, 157–62; R. Cohen, *A History of Folk Music Festivals in the United States*, 91–99. When Dylan plugged in his guitar, there was a chorus of boos from the audience, but some remember this as directed at the poor PA system and the short time given to Dylan to perform. "Dylan Goes Electric in 1965: 50 Moments That Changed the History of Rock & Roll," *Rolling Stone* online, www.rollingstone.com/news/story/6084576/dylan_goes_electric_in_1965 (reference courtesy of David Millstone). Cohen graciously commented on the complexity of this moment in correspondence with the author, March 2009.

103. The sociologist Richard Flacks decoded the different profiles of the pre- and post-1965 New Left, with red-diaper babies playing a major role in the earlier period: Flacks, *Youth and Social Change*. Among the many books on the social history of the 1960s, see Farber, *The Age of Great Dreams*; Gitlin, *The Sixties*.

104. Dunaway, *How Can I Keep from Singing?* 138–39; "If I Had a Hammer," Wikipedia, http://en.wikipedia.org/wiki/If_I_Had_a_Hammer. Similarly, in subsequent years, staples of the civil rights and labor movement such as "We Shall Not be Moved" were taken on by even conservative protest movements such as the Right to Life campaign against abortion.

105. Pittman, Waller, and Dark, *Dance A While*, 189–90.

106. Ibid.

107. Ibid.; on the new contra style, see Gene Morrow, March 15, 1998, email to the ECD listserv, reprinted online by Alan Winston, http://www-ssrl.slac.stanford.edu/~winston/ecd/gmurrow.htmlx (accessed December 25, 2005).

108. Sawyers, *Celtic Music*; Sweers, *Electric Folk*; Jackson, *Converging Movements*.

109. Fourteen dances were listed in the *New York Times* for the first week of November 1941, of which four were country dance (English and/or American), nine were International dance, and one was a Scottish Country Dance. Scottish dance mirrors English dance patterns and is also a couples dance, but it is almost wholly a twentieth-century invention with a style that is "approved" and monitored by the Royal Scottish Dance Society. The flowering of modern dance in New York of the 1930s owed a debt to either "ethnic" or English dance. For example, the socialist dancer Edith Segal drew on her experiences as a young girl with "ethnic dance" at the Henry Street Settlement. In contrast, when the radical dancer Sophie Maslow choreographed her *American Folk Suite* (1938), she took the title and inspiration for the second part from Cecil Sharp's foundational "discovery": the "Running Set." See Graff, *Stepping Left*, 26–27, 138.

NOTES TO CHAPTER 7

1. Pat Shaw, in Rippon, "The English Country Dance."
2. Jacqueline Schwab Oral History, Pinewoods, August 1999, ECDDP.
3. Ibid.
4. Foster Oral History. Gadd required Dillon Bustin and his wife, who had different last names, to produce a marriage license before she would allow them to come to Pinewoods. See Millstone, *The Other Way Back* (DVD).
5. Keller Oral History. See, too, S. Smith, "Revival, Revitalization, and Change."
6. Murrow Oral History; S. Smith, "Revival, Revitalization, and Change."
7. Frazer, *The Golden Bough*; Morgan, *Ancient Society*. Also see, Buckland, "Definitions of Folk Dance," 315–332.
8. Boas, *Race, Language, and Culture* and *Anthropology and Modern Life*; Mead, *Coming of Age in Samoa*; Benedict, *The Chrysanthemum and the Sword* and *Patterns of Culture*; and Geertz, *The Interpretation of Cultures*. I witnessed the contested nature of folklore studies in a discussion of guidelines with a program officer responsible for folklore with the New York Council for the Arts. The officer averred that CDSS, as a group of people of diverse origins doing revival dancing, was ineligible for a folklore grant; they were not English villagers. In conversation with the author, the folklore scholar Barbara Kirschenblatt-Gimlett noted that such views remain strong within the folklore community.
9. Murrow Oral History; Foster Oral History.
10. D. Walkowitz, "ECD Dancer Survey." Irish Americans and new Irish immigrants were disproportionately in blue-collar construction families who would not have felt at home among the professional-technical dance community, but historians also point to the "fierce nationalism" of the Irish Celtic revival (Sweers, *Electric Folk*, 253). Gene Murrow remembers few ethnic Irish dancers and recalls May Gadd's displeasure when he naively invited some Irish set dancers to demonstrate a dance at New York's regular Tuesday-night ECD dance. Gadd politely but firmly let him know that the evening was only for English dance and that they were not to return. Gene Murrow, conversation with the author, New York, NY, March 2009.
11. Peter Barnes Oral History, Lincoln, Massachusetts, April 1, 2004, ECDDP; Art and Helene Cornelius Oral History.
12. James E. Morrison, telephone interview with the author, November 10, 2007.
13. Among the many who began in International Folk Dance were Gene Murrow, Anand Hingorani, Peter Ogle, Yonina Gordon, Bob Morris, Kathy Terzi, Beth Lewis, Lucy Weinstein, Gary Roodman, and the author. See ECDDP.
14. Lasch, *Haven in a Heartless World*.
15. Thanks to Jenny Beer for her help with this description.
16. Jackson, *Converging Movements*; Michael Frisch, email to the author, March 19, 2008. Shifting attitudes toward Israeli dance corresponded to my own experience and that of several others with whom I have spoken.
17. Jackson, *Converging Movements*. Jewish involvement in International Folk Dance can be partially attributed to the Jewish political culture and the socialist commitment of many urban Jews.

18. The final chapter will return to these origin stories. See Barnes Oral History and Tom and Anne Seiss Oral History. Their experiences and views were repeated in many other interviews.

19. Schwab Oral History and Foster Oral History, among others.

20. Salmons went to Pinewoods as a teenager right after the war as a babysitter for Bob and Kathleen Hider. She took her first morris class with Louise Chapin, and when she returned to dance in New York in the 1960s after a decade's hiatus, she soon started to teach morris, in particular. Her background was in physics and systems analysis, but later in life, she became a physiotherapist. Salmons, telephone interview with the author, November 10, 2007.

21. Morrison interview.

22. Ibid.; Shimer, "Country Dance and Song Society," 42–43.

23. Morrison interview.

24. Ibid.

25. "Genevieve Shimer," Phantom Ranch website, www.phantomranch.net/folkdanc/teachers/shimer_g.htm.

26. Shimer, "Country Dance and Song Society," 42–43.

27. Gene Murrow, email to the ECD listserv, March 15, 1998, reprinted online by Alan Winston, http://www-ssrl.slac.stanford.edu/~winston/ecd/gmurrow.htmlx (accessed December 25, 2005); and Shimer, "Country Dance and Song Society," 43–44.

28. Murrow email to the ECD listserv, March 15, 1998.

29. In 1973, the Royal Scottish Country Dance Society initiated a Scottish Dance Week. CDSS added a third week in 1950 for teachers and singers, which became two weeks in 1962 that were split into chamber (Early Music) and folk music weeks. In 1967, Family Week began. Helwig, "Pinewoods Camp"; Shimer, "Country Dance and Song Society," 45.

30. Belgium's thriving ECD community, with its well-regarded and internationally acclaimed choreographer-caller Philippe Callens, can be traced to Shaw's visits.

31. Salmons interview; Heffer and Porter, *Maggot Pie*.

32. Fried had met Shaw when he was teaching ECD in Amsterdam in 1948. Emigrating in 1961, she sought a place to live in London and a modest income, and Shaw invited her to stay with him. She emigrated to the United States two years later in 1963 and in the subsequent decades became a teacher for dance groups in Westchester County (a northern suburb of New York) and New York City. She was among the most prolific and arguably was the leading choreographer of the last quarter of the twentieth century. Herman Oral History; Fried de Metz Herman, on Paul B. Ross, *Fried de Metz Herman, Conversation with Paul B. Ross* (CD).

33. Schwab Oral History; Arthur and Helene Cornelius Oral History.

34. Thanks to Jenny Beer for the description of the "canon." Beer, email to the author, July 30, 2008.

35. Pat Shaw, in Rippon, "The English Country Dance."

36. Keller Oral History.

37. Schwab Oral History; Helene Cornelius in Arthur and Helene Cornelius Oral History. Helene noted that Sharp discussed his concern that he got siding wrong in the introduction to the sixth country dance book.

38. Schwab Oral History; Helene Cornelius, in Arthur and Helene Cornelius Oral History; Kitty Keller Oral History.

39. Helene Cornelius recalled, for instance, "[He] taught us all these wonderful country dances, many of which he'd written or he researched himself. And he also taught this amazing sword dance from the Shetland Islands, called 'Papa Stour,' and that was the first we had ever seen of that, a dance for seven people." Helene Cornelius in Arthur and Helene Cornelius Oral History. Thanks, too, to David Millstone and Allison Thompson for clarifying the oral transcription. More typically, longsword dances such as those Sharp had collected have six or eight dancers.

40. John Ramsey commissioned the dance. Glenn Fulbright Oral History, Lenox, Massachusetts, June 13, 1999, ECDDP. Fulbright was at Pinewoods in 1974 and at the premiere of the dance in 1975.

41. Schwab Oral History; Arthur Cornelius in Arthur and Helene Cornelius Oral History. Uncannily, Schwab repeated almost word for word much of what Cornelius said about Shaw's impact.

42. Murrow Oral History.

43. Ibid.

44. Christine Helwig Oral History, New Haven, Connecticut, June 1999, ECDDP.

45. Herman Oral History. ECD as a "living tradition" was repeated in several interviews, for example, Tanya Rotenberg Oral History, Pinewoods, August 1999, and Andreas Horton Oral History, Pinewoods, August 1999, ECDDP.

46. Shimer, "Country Dance and Song Society," 42–43.

47. Ibid., 46; Morrison interview.

48. Dudley Laufman, quoted in Millstone, *The Other Way Back* (DVD). David Millstone, the producer of the DVD, reminded me of the reference.

49. David Chandler, email communication to the author, November 9, 2007; Morrison interview.

50. Brad Foster, telephone interview with the author, December 4, 2007. Foster's view was largely confirmed in interviews and communications with Sue Salmons and David Chandler.

51. Salmons interview; David Millstone, email communication with the author, July 15, 2008.

52. Salmons interview; Boyes, *The Imagined Village*; Morrison interview; Chandler communication.

53. Salmons, Chandler, Millstone, and Morrison interviews and communications; "Princeton Country Dancers: The First Twenty Years," generously donated to the author by Judy Klotz. For a good overview of pre-1980 morris dance in North America, see Morris Dancing Wiki, http://morrisdancing.wikia.com/wiki/Pre-1980s_morris_in_North_America.

54. There is a rich literature on whiteness, notably, Roediger, *The Wages of Whiteness*; Lipsitz, *The Possessive Investment in Whiteness*; Jacobson, *Whiteness of a Different Color*; and Brodkin, *How Jews Became White Folks*. In research I did in the 1960s for a graduate essay, I recall a Baptist newspaper justifying U.S. imperialism in 1898 by observing that Italians were "not quite white folks altogether."

55. The Philadelphia ECD teacher, choreographer, and dancer Scott Higgs is developing a history of the Philadelphia story on the Internet, "An Informal History of Perdue's English Dance," http://scotthiggs.com/perdhist.htm (accessed February 2009).

56. Liz Snowden, email to Jenny Beer on behalf of the author, July 2008. Although Germantown Country Dancers meets weekly in suburban Lower Merion, it also holds monthly meetings at a Presbyterian church in the Mount Airy section of the city. The move to the suburbs in cities where narratives of crime carry racial subtexts seems also to have been replicated in other urban areas, where white, middle-class dance groups met in poor, black neighborhoods. The Baltimore group, for instance, also moved to a suburban location from Lovely Lane Church in downtown Baltimore because of fears of crime.

57. Rachel Winslow Oral History, Peter Ogle Oral History, and Ellie Nicklin Oral History, conducted with Stephanie Smith, Landsdown and Philadelphia, Pennsylvania, June 19 and 20, 2004, ECDDP.

58. Foster, conversations with the author, December 2007; BACDS Papers, SFPALM.

59. Foster, conversations with the author, and Foster Oral History; "An Interview with Jody McGeen"; and Miscellany, BACDS Papers, SFPALM.

60. Foster, conversations with the author, and Foster Oral History; Jenny Beer, email communication with the author, July 30, 2008; and interview with Jody McGeen, *Bay Area Country Dancer*.

61. David Millstone, email communication to the author, December 2007.

62. Princeton Country Dancers, "10th Anniversary Celebration," and "Princeton Country Dancers: The First Twenty Years," both in the possession of the author, courtesy of Judy Klotz.

63. Ibid.

64. Princeton Country Dancers, "Princeton Country Dancers: The First Twenty Years."

65. Ibid.; Princeton Country Dancers, "10th Anniversary Celebration."

66. Beer, email communication with the author, May 2007. Swarthmore students learned Scottish from others as well. For instance, a Swarthmore chemistry professor, Bob McNair, had Scottish dance parties in his house. For a fuller account of folk dance at Swarthmore during the folk revival and the impact of the counterculture, see "If I Had a Song . . . ," *Swarthmore Bulletin,* March 1997, available online at http://www.swarthmore.edu/Admin/publications/bulletin/archive/97/mar97/folkfestivals.html.

67. Allan Troxler, telephone interviews with the author, December 8–9, 2007; Duberman, *Stonewall*; "Carl Wittman," *The Knitting Circle* (website sponsored by the Lesbian and Gay Staff Association, South Bank University, London), n.d.; Highleyman, "Who Was Carl Wittman?"

68. The machismo reflected an abiding paternalism among the male SDS leadership that also stimulated radical women to form women's liberation groups.

69. Troxler described the process as a result of joint conversation between himself and Wittman, although Wittman as teacher put it into practice and authored the book on it. Troxler interviews. Also see Wittman, "A Report on One Group's Pursuit of English Dance in a Non-Sexist Context." Thanks, too, to Jenny Beer for the reference to "pinnies."

70. Troxler interviews; "About the Heather and the Rose Country Dancers," The Heather and the Rose Country Dancers, http://www.opendoor.com/heatherandrose/about.html (accessed December 9, 2007).

71. Troxler interviews; Helwig's support for Wittman is noted by Allan Troxler in his oral history: Allan Troxler Oral History, interview with Stephanie Smith, Durham, North Carolina, September 16, 2004, ECDDP.

72. Pat Petersen Oral History, interview with Stephanie Smith, Durham, North Carolina, September 17, 2004, ECDDP; Troxler interviews.

73. Ibid.

74. "A Chronology of Country Dance & Song in New York City, 1915–1997," Country Dance * New York website, www.cdny.org/chronology.html.

75. Foster interview, December 2007.

76. Jenny Beer argues that the reason these dances are no longer done is a function of "class-based 'taste,'" noting that "we have lots of people who sit down when a rant is on the program but who are Scottish dancers and seem to have no trouble doing skip change (the same step really) for 32 bars in THAT context!" Beer Oral History, Pinewoods, August 30, 2000, ECDDP.

77. Chandler, email to the author; personal observation by the author.

NOTES TO CHAPTER 8

1. Nugent, "Who's a Nerd, Anyway?"

2. Fulbright Oral History.

3. Ibid.

4. Thom Yarnal Oral History with the author, Pinewoods, August 28, 2000, ECDDP; Murrow Oral History.

5. Murrow interview.

6. Sharon Green Oral History with the author, Pinewoods, August 28, 2000, and Mary Alison (pseudonym) Oral History with the author, Pinewoods, August 29, 2000, ECDDP.

7. Bealle, *Old-Time Music and Dance*.

8. Brooks, *Bobos in Paradise*.

9. Jennifer Beer, email to the author, December 11, 2000.

10. The documentary film *Mad Hot Ballroom* (2005) illustrated exactly that appeal. The film also showed how ballroom dance was used by middle-class teachers to uplift "urban urchins" and transform them into "little ladies and gentlemen" in ways both Cecil Sharp and Jane Addams would have understood.

11. D. Walkowitz, "ECD Dancer Survey."

12. See *Country Dance and Song Society 2000–2001 Members List* (Haydenville, MA: Country Song and Dance Society: 2000). The society lists about thirty-six hundred individual and family members spread over every state in the Union and every province of Canada. It has members in fifteen other countries, though mostly in England and Denmark.

13. D. Walkowitz, "ECD Dancer Survey."

14. My survey found one person who listed herself as mixed race, and she was dancing for only the second time. Ibid.

15. Jacobson, *Whiteness of a Different Color*.

16. D. Walkowitz, "ECD Dancer Survey." Although some had since retired, only a single person interviewed had an occupation outside this profile. Christine Helwig had been a town manager in Westchester County, New York.

17. Robin Hayden, email to the author, October 13, 2002.

18. The estimated twenty-five hundred new dances written since 1930 must be seen against the estimated twenty-seven thousand country dances and tunes that were published in England between 1700 and 1830. Thompson, "Exploring Modern Choreographies in English Country Dance," 16, and posting to the ECD listserv, February 21, 2006. Thompson starting using the term MECD around the same time as I did, and she uses it in this listserv posting.

19. Thompson, "Exploring Modern Choreographies," 6–7.

20. Paul Stamler, tabulation posted on the ECD listserv, July 25, 2007.

21. Barnes Oral History; Schwab Oral History. See also the Canis Publishing website, www.canispublishing.com/.

22. Thompson, in "Exploring Modern Choreographies," writing as a musician, dancer, and historian, describes the modern dance style.

23. Colin Hume, email to Gene Murrow, June 5, 2007. Thanks to Gene Murrow, who produced Bare Necessities' recordings, for sharing Hume's email with me.

24. Barnes Oral History.

25. See back-page advertisements in *CDSS News*, ca. 1995–2009.

26. Fulbright Oral History.

27. In conversations with me at the Stanford Humanities Center in 2001–2, the ethnomusicologist Mark Perlman usefully suggested distinguishing national dance traditions from those in which people do "other" people's dances. My sense of the diverse and non-Scandinavian background of this dance community in the 1980s and 1990s comes as a participant-observer in Southern California, New York, and elsewhere.

28. Participant observation by the author.

29. Bob Archer Oral History, Pinewoods, August 1999, ECDDP.

30. Pat Ruggiero Oral History, Pinewoods, August 2000, ECDDP.

31. My collaborator on the ECD Documentation Project, Stephanie Smith, develops this discourse further in a coauthored essay, Smith and Beer, "The Dancer Within," 1–7.

32. Yarnal Oral History.

33. Alison Oral History.

34. Ruggiero Oral History.

35. Ibid.

36. Ibid.

37. Jennifer Beer, conversations with the author, July 2008, New York City and email.

38. Beer Oral History.

39. Ibid.

40. Godwin, in "City Folk Who Feel the Call of the Do-Si-Do," describes gay square dancing in New York City. In 2008, gay square dances flourished in Boston, New York, and San Francisco, but the International Association of Gay Square Dance Clubs (IAGSDC; website www.iagsdc.org) listed sixty-one clubs across the United States, ranging from Phoenix and Seattle to Milwaukee and Memphis and Burlington and Ft. Lauderdale. Gay contra dances were less extensive but still outpaced those for English Country Dance. Again, Boston, New York, and San Francisco were mainstay groups, but the Lavender Country and Folk Dancers website (www.lcfd.org) also listed groups in Albany, Syracuse, and Atlanta.

41. D. Walkowitz, "ECD Dancer Survey."

42. Beer Oral History.

43. Barnes Oral History; and participant observation by the author of Barnes's dancing and reactions of the community for the past fifteen years. Also Beer, in various conversations with the author.

44. Troxler Oral History.

45. Beer Oral History and conversations with the author.

46. Much has been written on the relationship between race and liberalism. See, for example, Stein, *Running Steel, Running America*; Fraser and Gerstle, *The Rise and Fall of the New Deal Order*; and Stromquist, *Reinventing "The People."*

47. Murrow Oral History. Also see Ruggiero Oral History; Green Oral History; Broadbridge Oral History; Alison Oral History; Beer Oral History.

48. Ruggiero Oral History; Beer Oral History; Murrow Oral History; Alison Oral History.

49. Roediger, *The Wages of Whiteness*; Lipsitz, *The Possessive Investment in Whiteness*; Jacobson, *Whiteness of a Different Color*; Brodkin, *How Jews Became White Folks*.

50. I develop the idea that the cities were "blackened" in public imaginings in the 1950s with the rise of suburbs as safe white alternative spaces in Walkowitz, *Working with Class*, chap. 7.

51. Nugent, "Who's A Nerd, Anyway?"

52. Ruggiero Oral History; Yarnal Oral History.

53. Yarnal Oral History; Ruggiero Oral History; Green Oral History; Murrow Oral History; Alison Oral History; Beer Oral History.

54. Lasch, *Haven in a Heartless World*; Peiss, *Cheap Amusements*.

55. Thanks to Jennifer Beer for the formulation of these people as "reluctantly modern."

56. George Whitesides Oral History, Lenox, Massachusetts, June 14, 1999, ECDDP.

NOTES TO THE CONCLUSION

1. Stephanie Smith, in one of many conversations with the author.
2. Broadbridge Oral History.
3. Colin Hume Oral History, London, November 6, 2002, EDDDP.
4. Ibid.
5. Ibid.
6. Participant observation by the author, confirmed in conversation with many dancers on both sides of the Atlantic.
7. Allison Thompson, posting on the ECD listserv, March 30, 2006, with a response from Michael Barraclough, March 31, 2006.
8. Brinkley, *The End of Reform*; Stein, *Running Steel, Running America*; Plotke, *Building a Democratic Political Order*. Also see Hartz, *The Liberal Tradition in America*; Fraser and Gerstle, *The Rise and Fall of the New Deal Order*; Gerstle, *American Crucible*.
9. Reiser, "Secularization Reconsidered," 143.
10. See Tompkins, *Sensational Designs*, xi, xvi; Foucault, *History of Sexuality*. These citations appear in Volpe, "Cartes de Visite," 157–69.
11. Putnam, "Bowling Alone," 65–78, and *Bowling Alone*. In the defining anecdote of the introduction to Putnam's book, a thirty-three-year-old accountant, Andy Boschma, presumably with little in common with John Lambert, a retired hospital worker almost twice his age, "casually" learns of the latter's need for a kidney and donates one of his. The two men knew each other only through their participation together in a bowling league. Putnam's punch line: the bowling association allows Boschma, a white man, to traverse the United States' racial chasm in aiding Lambert, an African American.
12. In the award-winning documentary film *Mad Hot Ballroom* (2005), which chronicles a ballroom dance competition among New York City schoolchildren, teach-

ers' descriptions of the dance floor as an alternative to the enticing pitfalls of street life echo language used by Cecil Sharp and Jane Addams almost a century earlier about the palliative effects of folk dance on urban immigrant youth. The teachers gently prod the eleven-year-old boys and girls into the formal postures, dance holds, and etiquette of the ballroom dance. As the children dance, bow and curtsy, and walk arm in arm onto and off the dance floor, one teacher proudly and tearfully summarizes their transformation from urban street toughs to "ladies and gentlemen."

13. Molotch coined the term NYLON to describe the three-year, twice-annual seminar of London and New York urbanists that met between 2004 and 2007. Molotch and the author organized the American participants. The sociologist Richard Sennett ran a parallel graduate seminar at the time that may have used the same acronym.

14. Many British dancers pass through New York City and show up at the CD*NY dance that I attend. There are also regular tours to England and elsewhere by at least three American dance leaders. Advertisements come through email solicitations and can be found on the back page of the *EFDS News* and the *CDSS News*.

15. Herman Oral History.

16. Judith Hanson and her husband, Michael, and their two sons live in St. Johns Wood, a fashionable north London inner suburb a couple miles from Cecil Sharp House. Michael was a Labour government economist; Judith took primary responsibility for child rearing.

17. Judith Hanson, in conversation with the author at CD*NY's Weekend Whirligig in Spring Lake, New York, October 2008. Judith and Michael had returned to the States to experience higher-quality English Country Dance.

Bibliography

ARCHIVES

Country Dance and Song Society Archive, Milne Special Collections and Archives, University of New Hampshire Library, Durham, NH (CDSS papers, scrapbooks, photographs, miscellany)
    May Gadd Papers
    Kate Van Winkle Keller Papers
    Evelyn K. Wells Papers
    Stanley Watkins Papers
Harvard Theatre Collection, Houghton Library, Harvard College, Cambridge, MA
    George P. Baker Collection, Claud Wright Correspondence
Jerome Robins Dance Division, New York Public Library, Lincoln Center Library, New York, NY
    American Folk Dance Society Collection
San Francisco Arts Library and Museum, San Francisco, CA
    Rolfe and Mime Theatre Collection
    Bay Area Country Dance Society Papers
    Virgil Morton Papers
Vaughan Williams Memorial Library, Cecil Sharp House, London, England (journals, scrapbooks, photographs, videos)
    Cecil James Sharp Collection
        Elizabeth Burchenal Correspondence
        Clive Carey Correspondence
        Lily [Roberts] Conant Correspondence
        Mary Neal Correspondence
        Helen Storrow Correspondence
    Maud Karpeles Collection
    Kathleen Atkins (née Church-Bliss) Papers

JOURNALS

Country Dance and Song, 1968–
CDSS News, 1966–
Country-Dancer, 1943–1967
EFDS News, 1921–36

EFDS Reports, 1924–45
Federation Folk Dancer, 1941–44
Journal of the English Folk Dance and Society, 1932–64

ORAL HISTORIES AND INTERVIEWS

Smith, Stephanie, Daniel J. Walkowitz, and Charles Weber. *English Country Dance Video Documentation Project*. Washington, DC: Center for Folklife and Cultural Heritage, Smithsonian Institution, 1999–2009. Video oral histories with the following:
    Mary Alison (pseudo.)
    Bob Archer
    Peter Barnes
    Jenny Beer
    Nicolas Broadbridge
    Arthur and Helene Cornelius
    Emlen Cressen
    Mary Devlin
    Brad Foster
    Glenn Fulbright
    Sharon Green
    Christine Helwig
    Fried de Metz Herman
    Anand Hingorani
    Andrea Horton
    Colin Hume
    Kitty Keller
    Bob Keller
    Beth Lewis
    Bob Morris
    Gene Murrow
    Ellie Nicklin
    Peter Ogle
    Pat Peterson
    Gary Roodman
    Tanya Rotenberg
    Patricia Ruggiero
    Jacqueline Schwab
    Ann and Tom Seiss
    Malcolm Taylor
    Kathy Terzi
    Allison Thompson
    Allan Troxler
    Lucy and Mark Weinstein
    Rachel Winslow
    George Whitesides
    Thom Yarnal

INTERVIEWS AND WRITTEN COMMUNICATIONS WITH THE AUTHOR

Belle Bernstein
John Bremer
David Chandler
Margherita Davis
Brad Foster
Peter Fricke
Josie Giarratano
Tony Hiss
James E. Morrison
Allan Troxler
Sue Salmons
Richard Wilson

AUDIO-VISUAL MATERIAL AND SURVEYS

CDSS 8 mm historical dance footage at summer dance camps in the United States, ca. 1927–1960. 58 min. VWML and CDSS Archives, Milne Special Collections, University of New Hampshire.
ECD Documentation Project, Smithsonian Center for Folklife and Cultural Heritage, 1999–2008. Ambient dance community footage, dance footage.
Millstone, David. *The Other Way Back: Dancing with Dudley.* DVD. 99 minutes, plus two-hour bonus disk with stories, music, and dance. Westmoreland, NH: Great Meadow Music, 2004.
———. *Paid to Eat Ice Cream: Bob McQuillan and the New England Contra Dance.* DVD. 70 min. Westmoreland, NH: Great Meadow Music, 2001.
Ross, Paul B. *Fried de Metz Herman, Conversation with Paul B. Ross.* CD. Summer 2007.
Walkowitz, Daniel J., with the assistance of Mary Devlin, Robin Hayden, Sharon Green, and Irv Kass. "ECD Dancer Survey," 2001–2. Spring Dance Weekend in Hopewell Junction, NY; the Playful Ball in Ridgewood, NJ; Pinewoods Dance Camp, Plymouth, MA; BACDS ECD Camp, Mendocino, CA; Berkeley English Country Dance, Berkeley, CA.

BOOKS, ARTICLES, AND UNPUBLISHED WRITTEN MATERIAL

Addams, Jane. *The Spirit of Youth and the City Streets.* New York: Macmillan, 1910.
Alden, Francesca. "The Revival of Country Dance." *Dance Magazine* (August 1928): 41–50.
Aldrich, Elizabeth. *From the Ballroom to Hell: Grace and Folly in Nineteenth-Century Dance.* Evanston, IL: Northwestern University Press, 1991.
Allen, Robert C. *Horrible Prettiness: Burlesque and American Culture.* Chapel Hill: University of North Carolina Press, 1991.
Anderson, Hugh. "Virtue in a Wilderness: Cecil Sharp's Australian Sojourn, 1882–1892." *Folk Music Journal* 6, no. 5 (1994): 545–91.
Baggelaar, Kristin, and Donald Milton. *Folk Music: More Than a Song.* New York: Thomas Y. Crowell, 1976.

Bealle, John. *Old-Time Music and Dance: Community and Folk Revival*. Bloomington: Indiana University Press, 2005.
Bearman, Florence. "Knees Up at Cecil Sharp House." *English Dance and Song* (Autumn 2006): 24–25.
Bender, Daniel E. *Sweated Work, Weak Bodies: Anti-Sweatshop Campaigns and Languages of Labor*. New Brunswick, NJ: Rutgers University Press, 2004.
Benedict, Ruth. *The Chrysanthemum and the Sword*. Boston: Houghton Mifflin, 1946.
———. *Patterns of Culture*. New York: Penguin Books, 1946.
Bensel, Elise van der Ven-Ten. "Aspects of Folk Dance in Different Stages of National Development." *Journal of the English Folk Dance and Song Society* 2 (1935): 17–24.
Bergquist, Nils W., trans. *Swedish Folk Dances*. Introduction by C. Ward Crampton. New York: A. S. Barnes, [1906] 1928.
Boas, Franz. *Anthropology and Modern Life*. New York: Norton, 1928.
———. *Race, Language, and Culture*. New York: Macmillan, 1940.
Bonsal, Stephen. *When the French Were Here*. Garden City, NY: Doubleday, Doran, 1945.
Boris, Eileen. *Art and Labor: Ruskin, Morris, and the Craftsman Ideal in America*. Philadelphia: Temple University Press, 1986.
Boyes, Georgina. *The Imagined Village: Culture, Ideology and the English Folk Revival*. Manchester: Manchester University Press, 1993.
Braverman, Harry. *Labor and Monopoly Capital: The Degradation of Work in the Twentieth Century*. Foreword by Paul M. Sweezy. New York: Monthly Review Press, 1975.
Brickwedde, James C. "A. Claud Wright: Cecil Sharp's Forgotten Dancer." *Folk Music Journal* 6, no. 1 (1990): 4–36.
———. "The History of Morris in America." *American Morris Newsletter* 10, no. 3 (November–December 1986): 6–12.
Briggs, Asa, ed. *William Morris: Selected Writings and Designs*. London: Penguin Books, 1962.
Briggs, Charles L. "The Politics of Discursive Authority in Research on the 'Invention of Tradition.'" *Cultural Anthropology* 11, no. 4 (1996): 435–69.
Brinkley, Alan. *The End of Reform: New Deal Liberalism in Recession and War*. New York: Knopf, 1995.
Brocken, Michael. *The British Folk Revival, 1944–2002*. Burlington, VT: Ashgate, 2003.
Brodkin, Karen. *How Jews Became White Folks and What That Says about Race in America*. New Brunswick, NJ: Rutgers University Press, 1998.
Brooks, David. *Bobos in Paradise: The New Upper Class and How They Got There*. New York: Simon & Schuster, 2000.
Buckland, Theresa. "Definitions of Folk Dance: Some Explorations." *Folk Music Journal* 4, no. 4 (1983): 319–32.
———. "English Folk Dance Scholarship: A Review." Paper presented at the Traditional Dance Conference, Crewe and Alsager College of Higher Education, Cheshire, England, March 28, 1981. Crewe and Alsager College of Higher Education, 1982.
Burchenal, Elizabeth. *Folk-Dances of Denmark; Containing Seventy-Three Dances*. Selected, edited and translated by Elizabeth Burchenal. Translation authorized by the Danish Society for the Promotion of Folk-Dancing. New York: G. Schirmer, 1915.
———. *Folk-Dances of Finland*. New York: G. Schirmer, 1915.
———. *Folk-Dances and Singing Games: Twenty-Six Folk-Dances of Norway, Sweden, Denmark, Russia, Bohemia, Hungary, Italy, England, Scotland and Ireland*. New York: G. Schirmer, 1909.

———. *Folk-Dancing as a Popular Recreation; A Handbook by Elizabeth Burchenal*. New York: G. Schirmer, 1922.

———. "Folk-Dancing as a Social Recreation for Adults." *The Playground: Journal of the Playground and Recreation Association of America*, October 1920, 9–12.

———. *Folk Dancing as Social Recreation for Adults*. New York: Playground and Recreation Association of America, 1920.

———. "May Day Celebrations." New York: Department of Child Hygiene of the Russell Sage Foundation, n.d. [1909].

———. *Official Handbook of the National Committee on Women's Athletics of the American Physical Education Association, Containing the General Policies of the Committee and the Official Rules for Swimming, Track and Field Soccer*. New York: American Sports Publishing, 1923.

Burchenal, Elizabeth, and Emma Howells Burchenal. *American Country-Dances*. New York: G. Schirmer, 1918.

———. *Folk-Dances of Germany, Containing Twenty-Nine Dances and Singing Games*. New York: G. Schirmer, 1938.

———. *Rinnce Na Eirann, National Dances of Ireland*. New York: A. S. Barnes, 1924.

Burchenal, Elizabeth, and C. Ward Crampton. *Folk-Dance Music*. New York: G. Schirmer, 1908.

Cantwell, Robert. *When We Were Good: The Folk Revival*. Cambridge, MA: Harvard University Press, 1996.

Carson, Jane. *Colonial Virginians at Play*. Williamsburg, VA: Colonial Williamsburg, 1965.

Casey, Betty, ed. *International Folk Dancing, U.S.A.* Garden City, NY: Doubleday, 1981.

Cavallo, Dominic. *Muscles and Morals: Organized Playgrounds and Urban Reform, 1880–1920*. Philadelphia: University of Pennsylvania Press, 1981.

Chang, Soon. "International Folk Dance in the West." *Let's Dance*, no. 10 (December 1944): 1–3.

Clarke, Edward H. *Sex in Education: A Fair Chance for Girls*. Boston: Houghton Mifflin, 1873.

Cohen, Lizabeth. *Making a New Deal: Industrial Workers in Chicago, 1919–1939*. Cambridge: Cambridge University Press, 1990.

Cohen, Ronald D. *Folk Music: The Basics*. New York: Routledge, 2006.

———. *A History of Folk Music Festivals in the United States: Feasts of Musical Celebration*, American Folk Music and Musicians Series. Lanham, MD: Scarecrow, 2008.

———. *Rainbow Quest: The Folk Music Revival and American Society, 1940–1970*. Amherst: University of Massachusetts Press, 2002.

Conant, Ricky. "Interview with Jocelyn B. Reynolds, May 12, 1991." *American Morris Newsletter* 19, nos. 1&3 (March–April/November–December 1996): 18–26 (no. 1), 16–23 (no. 3).

Country Dance Society, Boston Centre. "A Brief History." http://www.cds-boston.org/history.html.

Crocker, Ruth. *Social Work and Social Order: The Settlement Movement in Two Industrial Cities, 1889–1930*. Urbana: University of Illinois Press, 1992.

Culbertson, Anne. "Sixty Years of Song and Dance: The John C. Campbell Folk School in Brasstown, North Carolina, from 1925 to the Present." *Country Dance and Song* 17 (1987).

Curtis, Henry S. *The Play Movement and Its Significance*. New York: Macmillan, 1917.
Czarnowski, Lucile. *Dances of Early California Days*. Palo Alto, CA: Pacific Books, 1950.
Dachant, Clarice E. "These Folk Dancers—Who Are We Anyhow?" *Let's Dance* 3, no. 1 (January 1946): 1–2.
Damon, S. Foster. *The History of Square Dancing*. Barre, MA: Barre Gazette, 1957.
de Mille, Agnes. *Martha: The Life and Work of Martha Graham*. New York: Vintage, 1992.
Denning, Michael. *The Cultural Front: The Laboring of American Culture in the Twentieth Century*. London: Verso, 1997.
Dommett, Roy. "How Did You Think It Was? The Political Background to the Folk Revival, 1903–1912." *Country Dance and Song* 11–12 (1981): 47–52.
Douglas, Ann. *Terrible Honesty: Mongrel Manhattan in the 1920s*. New York: Farrar, Straus and Giroux, 1995.
Dowling, Janet. "So Who Was Mary Neal Anyway?" Shave the Donkey website, http://www.thedonkey.org.
Duberman, Martin Bauml. *Stonewall*. New York: Plume, 1994.
Dunaway, David King. *How Can I Keep from Singing? The Ballad of Pete Seeger*. New York: McGraw-Hill, 1981.
———. "Music and Politics in the United States." *Folk Music Journal* 5, no. 3 (1987): 268–94.
Erenberg, Lewis. *Steppin' Out: New York Nightlife and the Transformation of American Culture, 1890–1930*. Westport, CT: Greenwood, 1981.
Farber, David R. *The Age of Great Dreams: America in the 1960s*. New York: Hill and Wang, 1994.
Filene, Benjamin. *Romancing the Folk: Public Memory and American Roots Music*. Chapel Hill: University of North Carolina Press, 2000.
Flacks, Richard. *Youth and Social Change*. Chicago: Markham, 1971.
Ford, Henry. *"Good Morning": Music, Calls and Directions for Old-Time Dancing, as Revived by Mr. and Mrs. Henry Ford*. 4th ed. Edited by Benjamin Lovitt. Dearborn, MI: Henry Ford, 1943 [1926].
Foucault, Michel. *Discipline and Punish: The Birth of the Prison*. Translated by Alan Sheridan. New York: Pantheon, 1973.
———. *The History of Sexuality*. Translated by Robert Hurley. New York: Vintage, 1980.
Frankfort, Roberta. *Collegiate Women: Domesticity and Career in Turn-of-the-Century America*. New York: New York University Press, 1977.
Fraser, Steve, and Gary Gerstle, eds. *The Rise and Fall of the New Deal Order: 1930–1980*. Princeton, NJ: Princeton University Press, 1989.
Frazer, James George. *The Golden Bough: A Study in Comparative Religion*. London: Macmillan, 1890.
Gadd, May. "Adventure into Television." *Country Dancer*, November 1941, 5, 14.
———. "Country Dancing with the Services." *Dance Observer*, October 1943, 89–90.
———. "Defense Recreation." *Country Dancer*, January 1942, 6; March 1942, 32.
———. "English Folk Dance as Recreation." *Recreation*, April 1932, n.p.
———. "History of the Country Dance Society of America, Part Two." *Country Dancer* 12, nos. 3&4 (Spring 1957): 40–42.
———. "Lily Roberts Conant: A Memorial." *Country Dance and Song*, no. 6 (Spring 1974): 11–15.
———. "Recreational Dancing and the U.S.O." *Country Dancer*, November 1942, n.p.

———. "Television Adapts to Wartime." *Country Dancer*, March 1942, n.p.
———. "Television and the Folk Dance." *Country Dancer*, December 1941, 134–35.
———. "Television News." *Country Dancer*, January 1942, 21, 39.
Gammon, Vic. "Song, Sex, and Society in England, 1600–1850." *Folk Music Journal* 4, no. 3 (1982): 208–39.
Gardner, John. "Contradances and Cotillions: Dancing in Eighteenth-Century Delaware." *Delaware History* 22, no. 1 (1986): 39–47.
Geduld, Victoria Phillips. "Performing Communism in the American Dance: Culture, Politics and the New Dance Group." *American Communist History* 7, no. 1 (2008): 39–65.
Geertz, Clifford. *The Interpretation of Cultures: Selected Essays*. New York: Basic Books, 1973.
Gerstle, Gary. *American Crucible: Race and Nation in the Twentieth Century*. Princeton, NJ: Princeton University Press, 2001.
Gilbert, Cecile. *International Folk Dance at a Glance*. Minneapolis: Burgess, 1969.
Ginsberg, Lori D. *Women and the Work of Benevolence: Morality, Politics and Class in the Nineteenth-Century United States*. New Haven, CT: Yale University Press, 1990.
Gitlin, Todd. *The Sixties: Years of Hope, Days of Rage*. New York: Bantam Books, 1987.
Godwin, Joy. "City Folk Who Feel the Call of the Do-Si-Do." *New York Times*, July 15, 2008.
Gordon, Leah. "'A Pleasure Which They Can Find Nowhere Else': The Country Dance Society, Ralph Page and the Complexity of Nostalgia, 1915–1965." Undergraduate thesis, History Department, Brown University, 1997.
Gornick, Vivian. *The Romance of American Communism*. New York: Basic Books, 1977.
Graff, Ellen. *Stepping Left: Dance and Politics in New York City, 1928–1942*. Durham, NC: Duke University Press, 1997.
Grant, H. N. *The American National Call Book*. Buffalo, 1893.
Green, Archie. "A Folklorist's Creed and a Folksinger's Gift." *Appalachian Journal* 7 (Autumn–Winter 1979–80): 37–50.
Greene, Henry. *Square and Folk Dancing: A Complete Guide for Students, Teachers and Callers*. New York: Harper & Row, 1989.
Greenwald, Richard A. *The Triangle Fire, the Protocols of Peace, and Industrial Democracy in Progressive Era New York*. Philadelphia: Temple University Press, 2005.
Gretchell, Larry. *A History of the Folk Dance Movement in California, with Emphasis on the Early Years*. San Francisco: Folk Dance Federation of California, 1995.
Gulick, Luther Halsey. *The Healthful Art of Dancing . . . Illustrated from Photographs*. Garden City, NY: Doubleday, Page, 1911.
———. *A Philosophy of Play*. New York: C. Scribner's Sons, 1920.
———. *Physical Education by Muscular Exercise*. Philadelphia: P. Blakiston's Son & Co., 1911.
Hacker, Andrew. "Looking Backward—and Forward." In *New York Unbound: The City and Politics of the Future*, edited by Peter D. Salins, 203–6. New York: Blackwell, 1988.
Hammack, David C. *Power and Society: Greater New York at the Turn of the Century*. New York: Russell Sage Foundation, 1982.
Harding, Arthur, and Raphael Samuel. *East End Underworld: Chapters in the Life of Arthur Harding*. London: Routledge & Kegan Paul, 1981.
Harker, David. *Fakesong: The Manufacture of British "Folksong" 1700 to the Present Day*. Milton Keynes, UK: Open University Press, 1985.

———. "May Cecil Sharp Be Praised?" *History Workshop* 18 (Autumn 1982): 44–62.
Harris, Craig. *The New Folk Music*. Crown Point, IN: White Cliffs Media Company, 1991.
Hartz, Louis. *The Liberal Tradition in America*. New York: Harcourt, Brace and World, 1955.
Heffer, Marjorie, and William Porter. *Maggot Pie: A Book of Country Dances*. Cambridge, UK: W. Heffer & Sons, 1932.
Helwig, Christine. "Pinewoods Camp." In *International Folk Dancing, U.S.A.*, edited by Betty Casey, 60–61. Garden City, NY: Doubleday, 1981.
Highleyman, Liz. "Who Was Carl Wittman?" *Letters from CAMP Rehoboth* 16, no. 4 (May 5, 2006).
Hilton, Wendy. *Dances of Court and Theater: The French Noble Style, 1690–1725*. Princeton, NJ: Princeton Book Company, 1981.
Hobsbawm, Eric J., and Terence O. Ranger, eds. *The Invention of Tradition*. Cambridge: Cambridge University Press, 1983.
Hornstein, Jeffrey M. *A Nation of Realtors: A Cultural History of the Twentieth-Century American Middle Class*. Durham, NC: Duke University Press, 2005.
Howard, Carole. "Mary Ann and Michael Herman." In *International Folk Dancing, U.S.A.*, edited by Betty Casey, 22–29. Garden City, NY: Doubleday, 1981.
Howkins, Alan. *Reshaping Rural England: A Social History, 1850–1925*. London: HarperCollins Academic, 1991.
Ignatiev, Noel. *How the Irish Became White*. New York: Routledge, 1995.
Inness, Sherrie A. *Intimate Communities: Representation and Social Transformation in Women's College Fiction, 1895–1910*. Bowling Green, OH: Bowling Green Popular Culture Press, 1995.
"An Interview with Jody McGeen." *Bay Area Country Dancer* 42 (Fall 1999): 13–15.
Isaac, Rhys. *The Transformation of Virginia, 1740–1790*. Chapel Hill: University of North Carolina Press, 1982.
Jackson, Naomi M. *Converging Movements: Modern Dance and Jewish Culture at the 92nd Street Y*. Hanover, NH: University Press of New England, 2000.
Jacobson, Matthew Frye. *Whiteness of a Different Color: European Immigrants and the Alchemy of Race*. Cambridge, MA: Harvard University Press, 1998.
Jaffe, Nigel Allen. *The World of English Country Dance*. Skipton, North Yorkshire: Folk Dance Enterprises, 1992.
Judge, Roy. "Mary Neal and the Espérance Morris." *Folk Music Journal* 5, no. 5 (1989): 545–91.
Karpeles, Maud. *Cecil Sharp: His Life and Work*. Chicago: University of Chicago Press, 1967.
———. "The International Folk Music Council: Twenty-One Years." In *1969 Yearbook of the IFMC*, 14–32. International Folk Music Council, 1969.
Keller, Kate Van Winkle, and Charles Cyril Hendrickson. *George Washington: A Biography in Social Dance*. Sandy Hook, CT: Hendrickson, 1998.
Keller, Kate Van Winkle, and Genevieve Shimer. *The Playford Ball: 103 Early Country Dances, 1651–1820: As Interpreted by Cecil Sharp and His Followers*. 2nd ed. Northampton, MA: Country Dance and Song Society, 1994.
Kennedy, Douglas. *English Folk Dancing: Today and Yesterday*. London: G. Bell and Sons, [1949] 1964.
———. "Maud Pauline Karpeles." *Folk Music Journal* 3, no. 3 (1977): 292–94.

———. *Sixty Years of Folk*. London: EFDSS, 1971.
———. "Tradition: A Personal Viewpoint of Douglas Kennedy, Vice-President of the Society." *Folk Music Journal* 4, no. 3 (1982): 195–207.
Kidson, Frank, and Mary Neal. *English Folk-Song and Dance*. Cambridge: Cambridge University Press, 1915.
Krause, Rhett. "Morris Dancing and America Prior to 1913." *American Morris Newsletter* 25, no. 4 (December 2005): 1–17.
Lambourne, Lionel. *Utopian Craftsmen: The Arts and Crafts Movement from the Cotswolds to Chicago*. London: Astragal Books, 1980.
Lasch, Christopher. *Haven in a Heartless World: The Family Besieged*. New York: Basic Books, 1977.
Lausevic, Mirjana. "A Different Village: International Folk Dance and Balkan Music and Dance in the United States." PhD diss., Wesleyan University, 1998.
Lears, T. J. *No Place of Grace: Antimodernism and the Transformation of American Culture, 1880–1920*. Chicago: University of Chicago Press, 1994.
Lincoln, Jennette. *The Festival Book: May-Day Pastime and the May-Pole*. New York: A. S. Barnes, 1912.
Lipsitz, George. *The Possessive Investment in Whiteness: How White People Profit from Identity Politics*. Philadelphia: Temple University Press, 1998.
Lowenthal, David. *The Past Is a Foreign Country*. Cambridge: Cambridge University Press, 1985.
McNickle, Chris. *To Be Mayor of New York: Ethnic Politics in the City*. New York: Columbia University Press, 1993.
Mead, Margaret. *Coming of Age in Samoa*. New York: W. Murrow, 1928.
Miller, Karl Hagstrom. "Segregating Sound: Folklore, Phonographs, and the Transformation of Southern Music, 1888–1935." PhD diss., Department of History, New York University, 2002.
Millstone, David. "Continuity and Change in American Country Dance." Socorro: New Mexico FolkMADS Camp.
Mishler, Paul C. *Raising Reds: The Young Pioneers, Radical Summer Camps, and Communist Political Culture in the United States*. New York: Columbia University Press, 1993.
Mitchell, Gillian. *The North American Folk Music Revival: Nation and Identity in the United States and Canada, 1945–1980*. Burlington, VT: Ashgate, 2007.
Mitchell, Sally. *The New Girl: Girls' Culture in England, 1880–1915*. New York: Columbia University Press, 1995.
Morgan, Lewis Henry. *Ancient Society, or, Researches in the Lines of Human Progress from Savagery through Barbarism to Civilization*. New York: H. Holt, 1877.
Morris, William. "How We Live and How We Might Live" (1888). In *William Morris: Selected Writings and Designs*, edited by Asa Briggs, 117–35. London: Penguin Books, 1962.
———. "Innate Socialism." In Briggs, *William Morris*, 84–104. Originally a lecture, "The Lesser Arts" (1878).
———. "The Worker's Share of Art." In Briggs, *William Morris*, 140–43. Originally appeared in *Commonweal*, April 1885.
Moskowitz, Marina. "Public Exposure: Middle-Class Material Culture at the Turn of the Twentieth Century." In *The Middling Sorts: Explorations in the History of the American*

Middle Class, edited by Burton J. Bledstein and Robert D. Johnston, 172–73. New York: Routledge, 2001.

Munro, Ailie. *The Democratic Muse: Folk Music Revival in Scotland.* Aberdeen: Scottish Cultural Press, 1996.

Neal, Mary. *As a Tale That Is Told: The Autobiography of a Victorian Woman.* In *Mary Neal.* London: Vaughan Williams Memorial Library, n.d.

———. *The Espérance Morris Book: A Manual of Morris Dance, Folk Song and Singing Games.* 2 vols. London: J. Curwen and Sons, 1910, 1912.

Neff, Maryl L. "The Folk Revival: The Late 1950s–1960s." Course syllabus, University of Florida. http://www.coe.ufl.edu/courses/edtech/folk/revival.htm (accessed October 19, 2001).

Nugent, Benjamin. "Who's a Nerd, Anyway? Someone Very, Very White for One Thing." *New York Times Magazine*, July 29, 2007, 15.

Oakley, Ken, and Carol Ripic. *A History of Bluegrass in New York and Northeastern Pennsylvania.* Deposit, NY: R&C Publications, 1999.

O'Neill, Rosetta. "The Dodworth Family and Ballroom Dancing in New York." In *Chronicles of the American Dance,* ed. Paul Magriel, 81–100. New York: Henry Holt and Company, 1948.

Osofsky, Gilbert. *Harlem: The Making of a Ghetto.* New York: Harper & Row, 1964.

Parmelee, Patricia. "New York Folk Festival Council." In *International Folk Dancing, U.S.A.*, edited by Betty Casey, 57–60. Garden City, NY: Doubleday, 1981.

Peiss, Kathy. *Cheap Amusements: Working Women and Leisure in Turn-of-the-Century New York.* Philadelphia: Temple University Press, 1986.

Pertilla, Atiba. "Class Exercises: How Teachers College's 'Model Schools' Modelled Bodies, Space and Identity, 1887–1915." Unpublished seminar paper, Department of History, New York University, 2008.

Pertz, Timothy Josiah Morris. "The Jewgrass Boys: Bluegrass Music's Emergence in New York City's Washington Square Park, 1946–1961." Undergraduate thesis, History and Literature, Harvard College, 2005.

Pethick-Lawrence, Emmeline. *My Part in a Changing World.* London: Victor Gollancz, 1938.

Pittman, Anne M., Marlys S. Waller, and Cathy L. Dark. *Dance A While.* 9th ed. San Francisco: Pearson Education, 2005.

Plotke, David. *Building a Democratic Political Order: Reshaping American Liberalism in the 1930s and 1940s.* Cambridge: Cambridge University Press, 1996.

Prevots, Naima. *Dance for Export: Cultural Diplomacy and the Cold War.* Middletown, CT: Wesleyan University Press, 1998.

Princeton Country Dancers. "Princeton Country Dancers: The First Twenty Years." Princeton, NJ: Princeton Country Dancers, May 22, 1999.

———. "10th Anniversary Celebration." Princeton, NJ: Princeton Country Dancers, May 20, 1989.

Public Schools Athletic League New York, Girls' Branch, and Elizabeth Burchenal. *Official Handbook of the Girls' Branch of the Public Schools Athletic League.* New York: American Sports Publishing, 1908–10.

Pugliese, Patri J. "Country Dance." In *International Encyclopedia of Dance*, edited by Selma Jane Cohen et al., 255–56. New York: Oxford University Press, 1998.

Putnam, Robert D. "Bowling Alone: America's Declining Social Capital." *Journal of Democracy* 6, no. 1 (January 1995): 65–78.

———. *Bowling Alone: The Collapse and Revival of American Community*. New York: Simon & Schuster, 1999.

Rainwater, Clarence E. *The Play Movement in the United States: A Study of Community Relations*. Chicago: University of Chicago Press, 1922.

Rath, Emil. *The Folk Dance in Education*. Minneapolis: Burgess, 1939.

Reeves, James. *The Idiom of the Peasant: English Traditional Verse*. London: Heinemann, 1958.

Reiser, Andrew Camberlin. "Secularization Reconsidered: Chautauqua and the De-Christianization of Middle-Class Authority, 1880–1920." In *The Middling Sorts: Explorations in the History of the American Middle Class*, edited by Burton J. Bledstein and Robert D. Johnston, 136–50. New York: Routledge, 2001.

Riis, Jacob. *How the Other Half Lives*. New York: Avon, 1890.

Rippon, Hugh. *Discovering English Folk Dance*. Aylesbury, UK: Shire, 1975.

———. "The English Country Dance: An Interview with Pat Shaw." *Country Dance and Song* 3 (1970): 4–11.

Rischin, Moses. *The Promised City: New York's Jews, 1870–1914*. New York: Harper & Row, 1962.

Rivers, C. H. *A Full Description of Modern Dances*. Brooklyn, NY, 1885.

———. *New Dances*. Brooklyn, NY, 1891.

Rodgers, Daniel T. *Atlantic Crossings: Social Politics in a Progressive Age*. Cambridge, MA: Belknap Press of Harvard University Press, 1998.

Roediger, David. *The Wages of Whiteness: Race and the Making of the American Working Class*. London: Verso, 1991.

Rosenberg, Neil V. *Bluegrass, a History*. Urbana: University of Illinois Press, 1993.

Ross, Dorothy. *Origins of American Social Science*. Cambridge: Cambridge University Press, 1991.

Ross, Janice. "The Feminization of Physical Culture." PhD diss., Stanford University, 1997.

Rothman, David. *The Discovery of the Asylum: Social Order and Disorder in the New Republic*. Boston: Little, Brown, 1971.

Ruskin, John. "Modern Manufacture and Design." In *The Works of John Ruskin*, edited by E. T. Cook and Alexander Wedderburn, 338–44. New York: Longmans, Green, 1905.

———. "The Nature of the Gothic." In *On Art and Life*. London: Penguin, 1953.

———. *On Art and Life*. London: Penguin, 2004 [1853].

Samuel, Raphael. "'Quarry Roughs': Life and Labour in Headington Quarry, 1860–1920; An Essay in Oral History." In *Village Life and Labour*, edited by Raphael Samuel, 162–91. London: Routledge & Kegan Paul, 1975.

———. "Workshop of the World: Steam Power and Hand Technology in Mid-Victorian Britain." *History Workshop* 3 (Spring 1977): 6–72.

Sawyers, June Skinner. *Celtic Music: A Complete Guide*. New York: Da Capo, 2001.

Schmidt, Eric von, and Jim Rooney. *Baby, Let Me Follow You Down: The Illustrated Story of the Cambridge Folk Years*. Garden City, NY: Doubleday, 1979.

Schofield, Derek. "Ceilidh Roots." *English Dance and Song*, Spring 2006, 20–26.

———. "'Revival of the Folk Dance: An Artistic Movement': The Background to the Founding of the English Folk Dance Society in 1911." *Folk Music Journal* 5, no. 2 (1986): 215–19.

Schultz, Mari Helen. *May I Have This Dance? A Social Dance Digest*. New York: Vantage, 1986.
Shapiro, Henry D. *Appalachia on Our Mind: The Southern Mountains and Mountaineers in the American Consciousness, 1870–1970*. Chapel Hill: University of North Carolina Press, 1978.
Sharp, Cecil James. *The Country Dance Book, Parts I and II*. London: Novello, 1909, 1911.
———. *English Folk-Song: Some Conclusions*. London: Novello, 1907.
Sharp, Cecil James, and George Butterworth. *The Country Dance Book, Parts III and IV*. 2 vols. London: Novello, 1912, 1916.
Sharp, Cecil James, and Maud Karpeles. *The Country Dance Book, Parts V and VI*. 2 vols. London: Novello, 1918, 1922.
Sharp, Cecil James, with Olive Dame Campbell. *English Folk-Songs from the Southern Appalachian Mountains*. Putnam, NY, 1917.
Sharp, Cecil James, and Herbert C. MacIlwaine. *The Morris Book, Part I*. London: Novello, 1907.
———. *The Morris Book, Part II*. London: Novello, 1909.
Sharp, Evelyn. *Here We Go Round*. London: Gerald Howe, 1928.
———. *Unfinished Adventure: Selected Reminiscences from an Englishwoman's Life*. London: John Lane, 1933.
Shi, David E. *The Simple Life: Plain Living and High Thinking in American Culture*. New York: Oxford University Press, 1985.
Shimer, Genevieve. "Country Dance and Song Society." In *International Folk Dancing, U.S.A.*, edited by Betty Casey, 42–43. Garden City, NY: Doubleday, 1981.
"Skansen Dancers' Tour of America, 1906–07." *Swedish-American Historical Quarterly* 34, no. 3 (1983): 224–34.
Smith, Milton M. "Dancing through English Literature." *English Journal* 9, no. 6 (June 1920): 305–17.
Smith, Stephanie. "Revival, Revitalization, and Change in English Country Dance." Paper presented at the World Conference of the International Council for Traditional Music, Sheffield, England, August 2005.
Smith, Stephanie, and Jennifer Beer. "The Dancer Within: Identity and Imaginings in English Country Dance." Paper presented at the Proceedings of the 23rd Symposium, International Conference on Traditional Music, Monghidoro, Italy, 2004.
Stansell, Christine. *American Moderns: Bohemian New York and the Creation of a New Century*. New York: Henry Holt, 2000.
Stein, Judith. *Running Steel, Running America: Race and Economic Policy and the Decline of Liberalism*. Chapel Hill: University of North Carolina Press, 1998.
Strangways, A. H. Fox, and Maud Karpeles. *Cecil Sharp*. London: Oxford University Press, 1933.
Stromquist, H. Shelton. *Reinventing "The People": The Progressive Movement, the Class Problem and the Origins of Modern Liberalism*. Urbana: University of Illinois Press, 2006.
Sughrue, Cynthia M. "Some Thoughts on the 'Traditional versus Revival' Debate." *Traditional Dance* 5–6 (1985–86): 184–90.
Sweers, Britta. *Electric Folk: The Changing Face of English Traditional Music*. New York: Oxford University Press, 2005.
Sykes, Richard. "The Evolution of Englishness in the English Folksong Revival, 1890–1914." *Folk Music Journal* 6, no. 4 (1993): 446–90.

Szczelkun, Stefan A. *The Conspiracy of Good Taste: William Morris, Cecil Sharp, Clough William Ellis and the Repression of Working-Class Culture in the 20th Century*. London: Working Press, 1993.
Tedesco, Laureen. "Making a Girl into a Scout: Americanizing Scouting for Girls." In *Delinquents and Debutants: Twentieth-Century American Girls' Culture*, edited by Sherrie A. Inness, 19–39. New York: NYU Press, 1998.
Thompson, Allison. "Exploring Modern Choreographies in English Country Dance." Unpublished mss. in possession of the author. Pittsburgh, 2006.
———. *May Day Festivals in America, 1830 to the Present*. Jefferson, NC: McFarland, 2009.
Thompson, Edward Palmer. *The Making of the English Working Class*. London: Victor Gollancz, 1963.
———. *William Morris: Romantic to Revolutionary*. London: Lawrence & Wishart, 1955.
Tomko, Linda J. *Dancing Class: Gender, Ethnicity, and Social Divides in American Dance, 1890–1920*. Bloomington: Indiana University Press, 1999.
Tompkins, Jane. *Sensational Designs: The Cultural Work of American Fiction, 1790–1860*. New York: Oxford University Press, 1985.
Turner, Frederick Jackson. "The Significance of the Frontier in American History." Chapter 1 in *The Frontier in American History*. New York: Henry Holt, 1921 [1893].
Volpe, Andrea. "Cartes de Visite Portrait Photographs and the Culture of Class Formation." In *The Middling Sorts: Explorations in the History of the American Middle Class*, edited by Burton J. Bledstein and Robert D. Johnston, 157–69. New York: Routledge, 2001.
Walkowitz, Daniel J. "The Cultural Turn and a New Social History: Folk Dance and the Renovation of Class in American History." *Journal of Social History* 39 (Spring 2006): 781–802.
———. *Working with Class: Social Workers and the Politics of Middle-Class Identity*. Chapel Hill: University of North Carolina Press, 1999.
Walkowitz, Judith R. "The 'Vision of Salome': Cosmopolitanism and Erotic Dancing in Central London, 1908–18." *American Historical Review* 108, no. 2 (2003): 337–76.
Weissman, Dick. *Which Side Are You On? An Inside History of the Folk Music Revival in America*. New York: Continuum, 2005.
Whisnant, David. *All That Is Native and Fine: The Politics of Culture in an American Region*. Chapel Hill: University of North Carolina Press, 1983.
Wilentz, Sean. *Chants Democratic: New York City and the Rise of the American Working Class, 1788–1850*. New York: Oxford University Press, 1984.
Wilfert, Ed. "Pinewoods Fifty Years Ago." *Country Dance and Song* 19 (June 1989): 1–37.
Wittman, Carl. "A Report on One Group's Pursuit of English Dance in a Non-Sexist Context." *CDSS News* 26 (May 1976): 3–6.
Yochelson, Bonnie, and Daniel Czitrom. *Rediscovering Jacob Riis: Exposure Journalism and Photography in Turn-of-the-Century New York*. New York: New Press, 2008.

Index

Page numbers in italics refer to illustrations.

accompaniment, 2, 147, 179, 211, 246, 265. *See also* instruments; music; recordings
Acocella, Joan, 59
Addams, Jane, 15, 25, 50, 137
aesthetic dance. *See* modern dance
African Americans, 51, 52, 273–74
   influence of, on American dances, 42–43, 47, 58, 59, 274
aging, 204, 223, 240–41, 266–67
Albany, N.Y., 93–94
Alison, Mary (pseudonym), 239, 251, 257
Allen, Maud, 56
Almanac Singers, 166, 167, 184
Alta Sierra Camp, 228
American Branch, 2, 125–29, 132–37, 153, 154, 189, 213
   Cecil Sharp's goals for, 111–12
   Elizabeth Burchenal and, 118, 146, 154
   founding meeting of (1915), 113, 293n8
   leaders of, 125–29 (*see also* Gadd, May)
   membership of, 132–33, 134
   planning for, 108–13
   renaming of, 133
   separation of, from EFDSS, 133, 156–57, 189
   see also Boston Centre; New York Centre
American Country Dance, 1, 189, 202, 215, 223–24
   difference of, from English Country Dance, 2
   see also contra dancing; square dancing
American Country Dance Ensemble, 223
American Folk Dance Society, 63, 118, 154
American Folk Lore Society, 110
"Americanization," 65–66
Anglo-American identity, 116, 118, 154
   CDSS and, 2, 46, 192–93, 195, 204, 273–74
   Cecil Sharp and, 117, 122–25
   reformers' goal of "sharing" with immigrants, 32–33, 68

Anglo-Saxon cultural hegemony, 8, 19, 211, 213, 270
"antimodernism," 3–4, 239
anti-Semitism, 191
Appalachia, 39, 130–31, 188
   Cecil Sharp's collecting in, 19, 117, 119–25
Archive of American Folk-Dance, 118
aristocrats, 85–86, 151
Arts and Crafts Movement, 37–40
Ashbee, C. R., 39
Assembly Players, 246
Austen revival, 241–42, 243, 250–51
"authenticity," 4–5, 36
   quarrels over, 89, 111, 115
   and second folk revival, 165, 166, 175

Baker, George P., 110, 291n65
   and A. Claud Wright, 94, 96, 98, 99, 106, 109
   classes led by, 94, 141, 142
   and founding of American Branch, 110, 112
   travel to England by, 69, 84, 94
Balkan dance, 203, 210–11
ballroom dancing. *See* social dances
balls, 56, 138–40, 248, 252
Bancroft, Jessie, 27
Bare Necessities, 150, 206, 241, 246–48
Baring-Gould, Sabine, 33–34, 36, 72
Barker, Granville, 87, 102, 104, 129
Barnes, Peter, 209, 246, 247, 248, 255, 256, 261
Barnett, Marjorie, 128, 133, 143, 144, 289n32
Barraclough, Michael, 265
Barron, Marshall, 223, 246
Bay Area Country Dance Society (BACDS), 227–29
Bealle, John, 162–63, 239–40
"Bean Setting," 16, 72
Beard, Daniel Carter, 25

| 323

Beer, Jennifer, 240, 253–55, 257, 259
Beliajus, Vytrutus ("Vyts"), 170–71
Bender, Daniel, 53
Benedict, Ruth, 208
Bennett, Samuel Augustus, 25
Berea College, 39, 130, 188, 197, *198*, 214
Berlin, Irving, 58
blackface, 46–47
bluegrass, 166
Boas, Franz, 208
bodies, 23–27, 48–50, 52–53, 55–59
    Progressive reformers' concern with, 23–31, 55–56
    see also bodily expression
bodily expression, 137, 252–54
    Cecil Sharp on, 88, 97, 109, 115–16
    and gender roles, 137, 253–54
    see also eye contact
Bolles, Dorothy, 69, 136, 142, *144*, 291n66
Bolton, Charles, 245
Boston, 9, 93, 110, 162, 188, 235
    banning of tango in, 57
    Helen Storrow's role in, 64, 93, 107, 110
    importance of, in U.S. English Country Dance, 32, 110, 188, 222
    travelers to England from, 69
    see also Boston Centre
Boston Centre, 132, 133, 140, 142, 290n47
    women's leadership in, 135–36, 288n29
Bourdieu, Pierre, 257
Boxing Day revelation, 8, 15–16, 19, 41
Boyes, Georgina, 18, 36, 75, 153, 154, 183
boys, 1, 25, 26, 64
Boy Scouts, 25
Brickwedde, James C., 46, 94
Brinkley, Alan, 268
Broadbridge, Nicolas, 180–81, 263
Broadwood, John, 33
Broadwood, Lucy, 33–34, 72
Brown, Arthur H., 94
Buckland, Theresa, 3
Budnick, Hanny, 226
Burbank, Emily M., 83, 94
Burchenal, Elizabeth, 64–67, 68, 168, 173, 188, 267
    and American Branch, 118, 146, 154
    and American Folk Dance Society, 63, 135, 154
    background of, 61–62, 63
    early cooperation of, with Cecil Sharp, 67, 92, 103, 106, 131, 146

    folk collections published by, 37, 63, 66–67, 68, 155
    on folk dancing as path to Americanization, 42, 65
    and International Folk Dance, 118, 137, 155, 170
    and Mary Neal, 92, 93, 106
    and New York youth programs, 60, 61, 62–63, 64–65
    as pioneer in folk dance revival, 1, 27, 41, 61, 62–63
    rivalry of, with Sharp, 19, 90, 112, 118, 134, 137–38, 145–47, 148, 149, 293n95
Burnaby, Andrew, 42–43
Burrows, Edward, 80, 81, 83
Butterworth, George, 48, 84, 86, 130

cabarets, 56–57
cafés, 57, 58
Callery, Mrs. James Dawson, 68, 108, 130, 131
Campbell, John C., 35–36, 119
Campbell, Olive Dame, 17, 35–36, 119, 145
Canadians, 225, 236, 245
Carey, Clive, 76, 82, 85, 92
Carnegie Hall, 93
Carr, Joan, 220
Castle, Irene, 58–59
Castle, Vernon, 58, 59
CD*NY. *See* Country Dance * New York
CDS. *See* Country Dance and Song Society of America, adding of "and Song" to name of
CDSS. *See* Country Dance and Song Society of America
Cecil Sharp House, 153
    broadened dance programs at, 10, 177, 179–81, 186, 204, 205, 261–62, 266–67
    English Country Dance at, 261–62, 266–67, 271–73
    lack of a U.S. counterpart for, 187–88
    square dancing at, 9–10, 179–81, 204
ceilidh dancing, 185–86, 264
Celtic revival, 185, 203
censorship, 36, 88
certificates (issued by English Folk Dancing Society), 87
    in U.S., 103–5, 108, 138, 140, 141, 142, 287n76
Chalif, Louis H., 63, 170
Chandler, David, 229
Chang, Song, 227, 171, 172

Chapin, Louise, 20, 69, 142, 152, 190, 288n29, 293n89
  at Amherst summer school, 143, *144*
  as head teacher of Boston Centre, 135, 136, 194
Chaplin, Nellie, 76
Charity Organization Society, 26
Chester, Susan, 39
Chicago, 64, 111, 131, 170-71. *See also* Hinman, Mary Wood; Hull House
Child, Francis James, 34-35, 36, 168
children, 1, 24-31, 59-66. *See also* boys; girls; public schools, folk dancing in
Chocorua, N.H., 94, 131, 141, 142
Chubb, Percival, 98
Church-Bliss, Kathleen (later Atkins), 180, 183
Cicone, Michael, 233, 235
Clarke, Edward H., 28-29
class composition:
  of English folk dance community, 5-6, 81-82, 114-15, 151, 177
  of U.S. folk dance community, 68-69, 93-94, 114-15, 134, 151, 174-75, 194, 240, 259 (*see also* "new middle class")
Claxton, Philander P., 37
Cleaver, Perdue, 226, *227*
clogging, 36
Cohen, Ronald, 200
Cohn, Francis, 53
Coit, Stanton, 25
Cold War, 162, 169, 195-99
  and International Folk Dance, 169, 174, 195-96
  and U.S.-U.K. differences in folk dance, 9, 163, 164, 187
collecting, 33-36. *See also* Sharp, Cecil: collecting by
colleges, 131, 241. *See also* Swarthmore College; Wellesley College
colonies, American, 42-44
Columbia Gramophone Company, 148-49
Columbia Record Company, 184
"community," 238-40, 270
community ("traditional") dance, 46, 182-83
Conant, Constance, 136
Conant, Lily Roberts, 20, 125-27, 136, *144*, 191
  background of, 86, 125, 190
  and Cecil Sharp, 20, 113, 125-26, 134, 190
  as dance teacher, 134, 135, 141, 143
  as leader of American Branch, 126-27, 135
  and Pinewoods, 216

Conant, Richard, 126, 136, 216
Conant, Ricky, 152
contra dancing, 66-67, 265, 306n40
  CDSS and, 2, 9-10, 202, 223-24, 269
  in England, 265
  origins of, 44, 46, 47
  revival of, 9-10, 202-3, 209-10
Cook, Tom, 186-87
Copland, Aaron, 168
copyright law, 144-46, 149
Cornelius, Arthur, 190, 194, 200, 209, 217-18, 220
Cornelius, Helene, 190, 191, 194, 209
costumes, 142, *173*, 175, *193*, 252
Cotillion Singers, 230
counterculture, 238-40, 269
  and CDSS's social conservatism, 162, 190, 202, 206-7, 213
  and eventual rejuvenation of CDSS, 199
Country Dance and Song Society of America (CDSS), 2, 235-36, 244, 258, 273-74
  adding of "and Song" to name of (1967), 199
  and American Country Dance (contra and square dancing), 2, 9-10, 46, 157, 189, 191-94, 202, 211, 223-24, 269
  and Anglo-American identity, 2, 46, 192-93, 195, 204, 273-74
  Canadian members of, 225, 236, 245
  and contra dancing, 2, 9-10, 202, 223-24, 269
  leaders of, 189-90, 191, 213-16, 222-23, 235-36
  membership of, 2, 222-23, 244
  and morris dancing, *196*, 224
  in New York, 162, 172-73, 192-93, 205, 222
  political orientation of, 162, 195-96, 204
  rejuvenation of, in 1970s, 207, 208-9, 210, 216-25, 267
  and second folk revival, 162-63, 176, 191, 199, 200, 203
  social conservatism of, into 1970s, 162, 204, 301n4
  as successor to American Branch, 2, 8
  see also ECD community: in U.S.; Pinewoods Camp
Country Dance * New York (CD*NY), 138, 236, 239, 242, 250, 262-63
"couples only" policy, 178-79, 183, 204, 265, 266
Crum, Dick, 210
Curtis, Henry S., 26-27, 40

Index | 325

dance "gypsies," 248–49
dance halls, 56–57
Delsarte, François, 28
Delsarte system, 28–30, 40
de Mille, Agnes, 169, 196, 197
Denning, Michael, 168
Devlin, Mary, 236
Dewey, John, 64
Dodge, Grace, 27
Dodworth, Allen, 56
Dodworth, T. George, 56, 58
Dodworth Dancing Academy, 56, 58
Donegan, Lonnie, 184–85
Douglas, Daron, 121
Drury, Nelda, 197
Duane Hall. *See* Metropolitan-Duane Methodist Episcopal Church
"Dudley dances," 210, 214, 215–16
Dunaway, David, 200
Duncan, Isadora, 30, 55, 56, 108
Durham, N.C., 234, 235
Dvořák, Antonin, 34
Dykeman, Lise, 249

ECD community:
IN ENGLAND:
  aging of, 204, 266–67
  class composition of, 5–6, 81–82, 114–15, 151, 177
  gender dynamics in, 178–79, 288–89n31
  politics in, 89, 154, 177
  see also English Folk Dance and Song Society; English Folk Dance Society;
IN U.S., 5–7, 9–11, 19
  aging of, 223, 266–67
  class composition of, 68–69, 93–94, 114–15, 134, 151, 174–75, 194, 240, 259 (*see also* "new middle class")
  ethnic composition of, 9, 191, 203, 209, 211, 212, 242, 259, 268
  gender dynamics in, 8, 19–20, 135–37, 152, 178–79, 205, 252–56
  newcomers to, from 1970s onward, 9–10, 163, 208–13, 241–42
  politics of, 10, 153–54, 162, 169, 176, 197–99, 257–58, 266
  and race, 242–43, 256–58, 259–60, 267, 269, 270, 273–74
  and "safe spaces," 7, 225, 238–39, 258, 269
  see also American Branch; Country Dance and Song Society of America

Edwards, Lila W., 35
Elgar, Edward, 34
Elizabeth, Princess, 10, 180–81
Elsmith, Leonard, 154
Engel, Carl, 34
England, John, 72, 89, 145
English Country Dance (ECD):
  in American colonies, 42–47
  distinction of, from American Country Dance, 2
  in folk dance revival, 6–7, 41, 65, 94–109 (*see also* American Branch; English Folk Dance Society)
  imagined roots of, 48, 66–67, 124–25, 154
  and International Folk Dance, 9, 169, 174–75, 176–77, 191
  U.S.–U.K. differences in, 163–64, 182, 187, 265
  writing of dances for, 43–44, 152–53 (*see also* Shaw, Pat)
  see also ECD community; Modern English Country Dance; Playford-style historical dances
English Country Dance and Song Society of America, 133. *See also* American Branch
English Folk Dance and Song Society (EFDSS), 85, 177–83, 187, 266, 272
  couples-only policy adopted by, 10, 179, 204
  and International Folk Dance, 155, 177–78
  Maud Karpeles and, 155
  place of Playford-style dances in, 186, 187, 266–67, 272–73
  social profile of, 177
  and square dancing, 10, 204, 178–82, 192
  see also Cecil Sharp House
English Folk Dance Society (EFDS), 85–87, 176, 213
  and American Branch, 142, 143
  bypassing of Maud Karpeles by, 288–89n31
  Cecil Sharp as leader of, 85, 86–87, 88, 101, 127
  certificates issued by, 87, 103–5, 138, 140, 141, 142, 287n76
  Douglas Kennedy as leader of, after Sharp, 127–28, 288–89n31
  merger of, with Folk Song Society (1932), 85
  see also English Folk Dance and Song Society
"Englishness," 6, 9, 122, 154, 178
Erenberg, Lewis, 57, 59

Espérance Club and Social Guild, 70–72, 76.
  See also Espérance girls
Espérance girls, 71–73, 76, 85, 94, 115, 188
  Cecil Sharp and, 72, 79, 80, 82, 89
  see also Warren, Florence "Florrie"
Ethnic Arts Center (New York), 189
ethnicity, 268
  and U.S. English Country Dance, 9, 191, 203, 209, 211, 212, 242, 259, 268
  and "whiteness," 52, 225, 242, 267
  see also EDC community, in U.S.: ethnic composition of
eye contact, 164, 253, 263, 264, 265

Fabianism, 155
  Cecil Sharp and, 16, 17–18, 77, 89, 267
Farwell, Jane, 197
fascism, 116, 153–54
Feingold, Mimi, 232, 233
feminism, 254–55. See also suffrage movement
Fennessey, Marjorie, 153, 186
Filene, Benjamin, 124, 165, 166
Finger, Karl, 225
Fireside Industries, 39
"folk," 36, 251
  competing meanings of, 3–4, 9, 206, 207–8, 220
  romanticizing of, 77–78, 156, 167
Folk Arts Center (New York), 189
folk clubs (Britain), 185
Folk Dance Federation of California, 171, 174–75
Folk Dance House (New York), 172
folk dance revival, 8, 31–37, 47–49, 163
  and Arts and Crafts movement, 37–40
  in England, 15–16, 33, 68–88
  and imagined roots of English Country Dance, 36, 48, 66–67, 124–25
  missionary goals of, 19, 88
  pioneers of, 1, 41 (see also Burchenal, Elizabeth; Hinman, Mary Wood; Neal, Mary; Sharp, Cecil)
  and Progressive reformers, 6–7, 24, 40–41, 59–66
Folk-Dance Society. See American Folk Dance Society
Folklore Society (U.K.), 33
folklorists, 3, 31–36, 207–8, 301n8
folk music, 161–63, 164–69, 184, 204, 266
folk-rock, 201–2

Folk-Song Society (U.K.), 34, 72, 73–74, 85
folk tales, 37
Ford, Henry, 4, 116, 153–54, 192
Foster, Brad, 206–7, 227–28, 235–36, 249
Foucault, Michel, 23
Fraley, Bob, 228–29
Fraley, Ruthanne, 229
Francis, Beverly, 263
Frazer, James G., 3, 207
French influence, 42, 43, 44–45
Fricke, Peter, 197–98
Fried. See Herman, Fried de Metz
Friendly, Brooke, 233, 235
Fulbright, Glenn, 238, 248–49
Fuller, Loie, 30
Fuller, Rosalind, 119
Fullers, the, 119

Gadd, May, 20, 128, 162, 168, 198, 200, 223, 231, 289n34, 301n10
  at Amherst summer school, 143, 144
  background of, 129
  and Cecil Sharp's heritage, 129, 189–90
  in International Folk Music Council, 168, 198
  as leader of English Country Dance in U.S., 129, 155, 156, 189–90, 191, 203, 213–14
  and morris dancing, 224
  and Pat Shaw, 217, 218–19
  recollections by, 133–35, 136, 151
  social conservatism of, 168, 189–90, 198–99, 206, 213, 301n4
  and square dancing, 179, 180, 191, 192, 193–94
  in World War II, 194–95
Gaddis, Earl, 246, 247
Gardiner, Rolf, 154, 177
"Gathering Peascods," 103, 148, 285n47
Gavit, John P., 35
"gay simplicity," 2, 6, 41, 77, 131
Geduld, Victoria, 168, 196
Geertz, Clifford, 208
gender dynamics:
  Cecil Sharp and, 105, 115
  in English folk dancing community, 178–79, 288–89n31
  in U.S. folk dancing community, 8, 19–20, 135–37, 152, 178–79, 205, 252–56
Genee, Adeline, 83, 93
Gentry, Mrs. Jane, 121, 125
Gershwin, Ira, 168

Index | 327

Gibbs, Emma Wright, 136, 147, 291n66
Gilman, Susan, 103, 113, 133, 147
Ginsburg, Michael, 225
girls, 1, 26–27, 40, 60, 64, 65, 137
Girl Scouts of America, 25, 136–37
Glass, Henry, 175
Glenn, John, 17–18, 120
Gordon, Robert Winslow, 165
Gowing, Gene, 172
Graham, Martha, 156, 169, 196
Gray, H. W., 102
Great Depression, 133, 165, 167
Green, Archie, 17
Green, Sharon Weiner, 239, 242, 249
Grieg, Edvard, 34
Grimm brothers, 37
Gulick, Charlotte, 25
Gulick, Luther Halsey, Jr., 25, 26–28, 29–30, 106, 277n27
  and folk dancing, 40–41, 61, 63, 65
Gursay, Elba, 170
Guthrie, Woody, 166, 167, 184

Hamilton, Bruce, 228, 231, 249
Hammack, David, 51
Handel, George Frederick, 2
Handsome Molly, 229–30
Hanson, Judith, 272–73, 308n16
Harker, David, 17
Harris, Nick, 227
Hartford, Conn., 93
Hatvary, Bertha, 235
Hausman, Laurence, 72–73
H'Doubler, Margaret, 60
Helwig, Christine, 190, 191, 221, 229, 234
Hendrickson, Charles, 43, 44
Henry Street settlement, 63
Herder, Johann Gottfried, 33
Herman, Fried de Metz, 191, 302n32
  as composer, 186, 245
  in emergence of Modern English Country Dance, 186, 187, 220, 221, 249
  and Pat Shaw, 186, 217
Herman, Mary Ann, 171–72, 197, 200
Herman, Michael, 171–74, 191, 197, 200
"Hey Boys, Up We Go," 36, 88, 103, 285n47
Hider, Robert, 193, 196
Hindman Settlement School, 35–36, 39
Hinman, Mary Wood, 20, 84, 131, 170
  and A. Claud Wright, 96, 98

  social standing of, 69, 131
  as teacher of folk dances to children, 1, 62–63, 64, 111
Hiss, Alger, 198
Hiss, Priscilla, 198
Hobbes, Mrs. May Eliot, 90, 97
Hobsbawm, Eric, 4
Holden, Rickey, 197, 202
Hold the Mustard (HTM), 229, 246
Holmes, E. G. A., 81, 83
Holst, Gustav, 84
Holst, Imogen, 149
Horace Mann School, 62, 63
Howkins, Allan, 4
Hull House, 1, 25, 40, 64
Hume, Colin, 245, 247–48, 261, 263–64, 272–73
Humphrey, Doris, 69, 98, 156, 212

immigrants, 21
  influence of, on American folk dancing, 46, 188–89
  in New York, 21, 51–54, 65–66, 188–89
  Progressive reformers and, 6–7, 30–31, 40, 50, 65–66
industrialization, 37–38
Industrial Workers of the World (IWW), 54–55
instruments, 43, 149–50, 166, 179, 184, 246, 265
International Folk Dance, 9, 156, 169–77, 225
  and Cold War, 174, 195–96
  decline of, 203, 209, 210–12
  Elizabeth Burchenal and, 118, 137
  in England, 155, 177, 178, 204, 205
  and English Country Dance, 9, 116, 174–75, 176–77, 191
  politics of, 156, 173–74, 175–76, 297n36
International Folk Music Conference, 155
International Folk Music Council, 168, 170, 198
"internationalism," 9, 167–69, 173–74, 197–98. See also International Folk Dance
International Ladies Garment Workers' Union (ILGWU), 53–54
Irish Americans, 9, 203, 209, 301n10
Isaac, Rhys, 42–43
Israeli dance, 211–12, 275n1
Italian Americans, 53–54, 191, 209, 212, 242, 259, 268
Ives, Burl, 167, 168, 198
Ives, Charles, 168

328 | *Index*

Jacobson, Mathew, 243
Jahn, Friedrich Ludwig, 28
jazz, 183
Jensen, Jonathan, 2
Jervis, Nora, *127*
Jewish Americans, 52, 53–54, 211–12
   in English Country Dance groups, 191, 209, 211, 242, 259, 268
jigs, 42–43, 46, 47
John C. Campbell Folk School, 130–31, 188, 214, 215
Journal of American Folklore, 33, 117
Judge, Roy, 80, 93
Judson, Mary, 228

Karpeles, Helen. *See* Kennedy, Helen Karpeles
Karpeles, Maud, 20, 81, *127*, 129, *144*, 267
   on Appalachian music, 117, 124–25
   background of, 81, 87–88, 113
   as Cecil Sharp biographer, 16, 18, 77, 86, 123, 132
   and international folk traditions, 155, 168
   as secretary and confidante to Sharpe, 97, 100, 102, 103, 104, 105, 108, 109, 113, 120–21, 130
   with Sharp on U.S. travels, 120–22, 129, 130, 132, 141, 142
Kay, Mattie, 72, 102–3, 106, 285n47
Keller, Kate van Winkle "Kitty," 43, 44, 207, 218–19
Kennedy, David, 128
Kennedy, Douglas, 97, 128, 154, 204, 265–66, 297n44
   and broadening of English folk dance, 177, 179–80, 182–83, 186, 187, 204, 265–66
   "couples only" policy instituted by, 178–79, 183, 204, 265, 266
   as EFDS leader after Cecil Sharp's death, 127–28
   family background of, 128
   and morris dancing, 36, 82, 86, 224
   recollections by, 151, 177
   in U.S., 143, *144*
Kennedy, Helen Karpeles, 81, 86–88, 97, 179
   at Amherst summer school, 143, *144*
   as Sharp's first choice for representative in U.S., 104, 113, 125
Kennedy, Peter, 184, 185
Kennedy-Fraser, Marjorie, 128

"Kentucky Running Set," 124, 125, 139, 154, 163, 166
Kidson, Frank, 84
Kilborn, Miss Marjorie, 139
Kimber, William, Jr., *17*, 36, 71, 82, 91
   and Cecil Sharp, 16, 71, 72, 145, 165, 246
   and Mary Neal, 71, 82, 92, 165
Kingston Trio, 184
Kittredge, George Lyman, 34
Koch, Edward I., 161
Koenig, Martin, 189
Kramer, Stan, 228
Kramer, Susan, 228
Krause, Rhett, 46, 47, 94
Kurzman, Nancy White, 235

Langdon, William Chauncey, 119
La Pierre, Alice, 238
Lasch, Christopher, 210, 259
Lasky, Jesse, 57
Laufman, Dudley, 210, 215–16, 223, 229. *See also* "Dudley dances"
Lausevic, Mirjana, 170, 173–74
Lawrence, Frederick, 70, 74–75
Lea, Mary, 246, 247
Leach, Edmund, 208
"Lead Belly" (Huddie Ledbetter), 165, 166, 167, 184
Leber, Eric, 246
Lee, James, 27, 277n27
leisure industries, 49–50, 56
Lett, Olive, 86
Lewis, Perceval, 130
liberalism, 5–7, 10–11
   class basis of, 5, 10, 267–68
   exclusionary aspects of, 7, 10–11, 249, 256–60
   and MECD, 237, 249, 256–60, 269–70, 273–74
   paternalism of, 16, 100
   and race, 256–58, 268, 273–74
Library of Congress, 165
Ling, Peter Henry, 28
Log Cabin Settlement, 39
Lomax, Alan, 125, 161, 165–66, 167, 168, 184
Lomax, John, 165–66
Lomax, John, Jr., 165–66
London, 32, 39, 187–88. *See also* Cecil Sharp House; Espérance Club and Social Guild
Longley, Mary E., 136

Index | 329

Low, Juliette Gordon, 25, 137
Lucas, Perceval, 48, 86

MacColl, Ewan, 184
MacIlwaine, Herbert, 71, 73, 75–76, 80
MacKaye, Steele, 29
Mad Hot Ballroom, 307–8n12
Maitland, John, 34
Maslow, Sophie, 156, 169, 196
May festivals, 59–60, 131, 136
Mayo, Margot, 200
McGeen, Jody, 229, 249
Mead, Margaret, 208
MECD. *See* Modern English Country Dance
"Merrie England," 34, 78, *79*
Merrill, Phil, 180, 189, 194, 202, 246, 289n33
Metropolitan-Duane Methodist Episcopal Church (New York), 162, 189, 224, 242, 262–63
Mills, C. Wright, 4
minstrelsy, 46–47
minuets, 42, 43, 44
modern dance, 30, 56, 107–8
  use of folk themes in, 169, 197
  see also de Mille, Agnes; Duncan, Isadora; Graham, Martha
Modern English Country Dance (MECD), 7, 238, 250–56
  Austen revival and, 241–42, *243,* 250–51
  and class, 240, 242–44, 256–57
  and culture of liberalism, 237, 249, 256–60, 269–70, 273–74
  exclusionary boundaries of, 7, 240, 242–44, 256–60, 269–70, 273–74
  and gender roles, 252–56
  music for, 246–48
  and new choreography, 44, 153, 221–22, 244 (*see also* Shaw, Pat)
  origins of, 187, 208
  and race, 7, 256–58, 273–74
  "safe spaces" provided by, 7, 238–39, 258, 269
  transcontinental, 10, 244–49
modernism, 55–56
Moll, Irene, 231
Molly Dance, 229–30
Molotch, Harvey, 271
Morgan, Lewis Henry, 207
Morland, David, 135
Morris, Newbold, 161–62

Morris, William, 38–39
morris dancing, 75–76, 86, 92–93, 224
  conflicts over, 69, 78–85, 88–89, 92, 106, 115, 141, 165, 282n21
  demonstration teams for, 48, 86–87, 94, 99, 128, 130
  differences of, from country dances, 91–92
  Elizabeth Burchenal and, 68
  and minstrelsy, 46–47
  in U.S., 46–47, 91–94, 106, 269
  by women, 92, 242, 282n21 (*see also* Espérance girls)
  see also Sharp, Cecil: and morris dancing
Morrison, James E., 214, 215–16, 222–24, 235
Morris Ring, 224
Moskowitz, Marina, 4
Mouvet, Maurice, 57
Muller, Maggie, 86
Murrow, Gene, 207, 208, 242, 249, 272
  on dancing styles, 210, 215–16, 220–21
  as musician, 246
  on social atmosphere of country dancing, 161, 194, 208, 239, 240, 256, 257, 259
music:
  English–American differences in, 2
  for MECD, 246–48
  see also accompaniment; folk music; instruments; recordings
music halls, 6, 40

National Cultural Center (NCC), 197
nationalism, strident, 116, 153–54
Neal, Mary, 41, *70,* 76, 84–85, 88, 89
  background of, 69–71, 73, 81
  conflict of, with Cecil Sharp, 19, 69, 78–85, 88–89, 92, 106, 115, 141, 165, 282n21
  early cooperation of, with Sharp, 71–73, 75–76
  and Espérance girls, 71–73, 94
  pioneering role of, 41, 71–72
  and Stratford-on-Avon Summer School, 81, 82–84
  and suffrage movement, 74–75, 84, 136
  and theosophy, 72, 73
  U.S. trip of, 53, 54, 83, 91–93, 106
New England Folk Festival Association (NEFFA), 202
"new middle class" (professional-technical-managerial), 4, 5–6, 10, 49, 174–75, 225, 240, 242–44, 267–68
  in England, 5–6

330 | Index

New Moon Sword Team, *140*
Newport Folk Festival, 199–201, 205
New York, 9, 50–56, 161–62, 222, 223–24
  CDSS in, 162, 172–73, 192–93, 205, 222
  class conflict in, 53–55
  importance of, in U.S. English Country Dance, 32, 110, 188, 222
  International Folk Dance in, 170, 171–73
  immigrants in, 21, 51–54, 65–66, 188–89
  varieties of dancing in, 56–66
New York Centre, 132–35, 138–40, 142–43, 152, 155–56, 205, 290n48
New York Dance Activities Committee (NYDAC), 215, 235, 236. *See also* Country Dance * New York
New York Dancers' Council, 189
New York Folk Festival Council, 170, 171, 172
New York Public Schools Athletic League (PSAL), 26, 27
New York Society of Teachers of Dance, 58
New York Times, 92–93, 172, 242
nightclubs, 56–57
Nugent, Benjamin, 238

Ogontz Camp, 248

Page, Ralph, 197, 200, 202
Palo Alto, Calif., 133
Parkes, Tony, 203
Partridge, Bernard, 78
Paterson, A. James, 86, 99
Peabody, Dr. Charles, 110, 136
Peabody, Trixie, 136
Peiss, Kathy, 57
Percy, Thomas, 33
Peterson, Pat, 235
Pethick-Lawrence, Emmeline, 69, 70, 71, 74–75, 76
Petit, Katherine, 35
Philadelphia, 226
Philip, Prince, 10, 180–81
phonographs, 147. *See also* recordings
physical culture movement, 27–31, 107
physical education, 61–62
Pine Mountain Settlement, 35, 39, 124, 130, 136, 188
Pinewoods Camp, 143, 188, 215–16, 223, *227,* 248
  Pat Shaw at, 207, 216, 217–19
  and perpetuation of Cecil Sharp's legacy, 143
  social conservatism of, 206–7, 213, 301n4

Playford, John, 33, 36, 76–77
Playford manuscripts, 76–77, 124, 219
Playford-style historical dances, 47, 91, 192, 223–24, 264, 269, 273
  in American colonies, 44
  Cecil Sharp and, 86, 149, 182
  decline of, in England, 164, 182, 187, 265
  distinction between, and traditional dances, 149, 153, 182
  new choreography for, 44, 150, 186–87, 221–22, 236, 237, 263
  see also Playford manuscripts
Playground Association of America (PAA), 26, 27, 63, 112
Plotke, David, 268
politics:
  in English ECD community, 89, 154, 177
  of International Folk Dance, 156, 173–74, 175–76, 297n36
  in U.S. ECD community, 10, 153–54, 162, 169, 197–99, 257–58, 266
Popular Front, 168
Porter, Grace Cleveland, 85
Pride and Prejudice films, 242, 250
Prince, Charles, 148
Princeton Country Dancers (PCD), 229–30, 248
professional-technical workers, 5–6, 225. *See also* "new middle class"
Progressive reformers, 23–31, 50, 89
  concern of, with healthy bodies, 23–31, 55–56
  hopes of, for folk dance, 6–7, 24, 40–41, 64–66
  ideas of, on gender, 26–27, 28–29, 55–56
  and immigrants, 6–7, 30–31, 40, 50, 65–66
  see also Settlement House movement
public schools, folk dancing in:
  in U.K., 73–74, 79–80
  in U.S., 1–2, 64–65, 188
Public Schools Athletic League (New York), 60, 61
Purcell, Henry, 2

quadrille, 45

Rabold, Charles, 113, 129, 135, 139, 146, 147
  and Amherst summer school, 142, 143, *144*
  Cecil Sharp's trust in, 113, 129, 134–35
race:
  and ECD community, 242–43, 256–58, 259–60, 267, 269, 270, 273–74

Index | 331

race (*continued*):
   and liberalism, 267, 268, 270
   see also African Americans; racism; "whiteness"
racism, 52, 123
ragtime dances, 58
Raim, Ethel, 189
Ranger, Terence, 4
Rath, Emil, 155
recording machines, 165–66
recordings, 143–50, 221, 246, 247
Reiser, Andrew Camberlin, 3, 268
Riis, Jacob, 27, 52
Ritchie, Jean, 165
Ritson, Joseph, 33, 36
ritual dances, 46, 229–30, 236. *See also* morris dancing; sword dancing
Rivers, C. H., 60
Robbins, Jerome, 196
Roberts, Lily. *See* Conant, Lily Roberts
Robeson, Paul, 176
Robinson, Earl, 169
Rochester, N.Y., 289n33
Rodgers, Daniel, 5, 37
Roodman, Gary, 245
Roosevelt, Eleanor, 156
Roosevelt, Franklin D., 156
Roosevelt, Teddy, 27
"roots" music and dance, 203
Ross, Janice, 59
"Rufty Tufty," 104, 138, 150, 285n47
Ruggiero, Pat, 242, 250, 251
   on dancing style, 251–52, 253
   on social composition of country dance community, 257, 258, 259
"Running Set." *See* "Kentucky Running Set"
Ruskin, John, 37–38
Russell Sage Foundation, 119, 120
Russian Revolution, 156

Sackett, Chris, 233, 235
"safe spaces," 7, 225, 238–39, 258, 269
St. Denis, Ruth, 18, 30, 56, 156
St. Louis, Mo., 131–32
Salmons, Sue, 191, 213, 217, 235, 302n20
Sandburg, Carl, 165
San Francisco, 133, 171
Sannella, Ted, 194, 202, 203, 215–16
Sargent, Dudley A., 28, 29
Scandinavian dance, 250

Scandinavian folk traditions, 62–63
schools. *See* public schools, folk dancing in
Schwab, Jacqueline, 206, 217, 220, 246, 247, 258
Scott, Sir Walter, 33
second folk revival, 163, 164–69, 187–90, 202–5
   and Cold War, 187, 190–99
   differences of, from earlier folk dance revival, 163–64
   in England, 177–87
   and folk music, 164–69
   in 1960s, 199–202, 204, 205
   phases of, 165
   politics of, 166–68
   see also International Folk Dance
Seeger, Pete, 166, 167–68, 176, 184, 198, 200–201
Segal, Edith, 156, 168–69
Seiss, Tom, 161, 236
"Sellenger's Round," 104, 138, 148
Settlement House movement, 25–26, 39–40, 63, 64 (see also Hull House)
settlements, rural, 35, 39 (*see also* Hindman Settlement School; John C. Campbell Folk School; Pine Mountain Settlement)
Shapiro, Henry D., 17
Sharp, Cecil, 15–19, 36, 41, 91, 127, 130, 248
   and A. Claud Wright, 94–99, 108–9, 115
   background of, 15, 73, 100
   censorship by, 36, 88
   as dance teacher, 55, 103–5, 106, 106, 108, 131–32, 141–42, 285n47, 286n67
   death of, 127
   finances of, 75, 100–104, 106, 114
   first trip of, to U.S. (1914–15), 48, 90, 100–114
   health problems of, 83, 90, 119, 120
   and Helen Storrow, 18, 97, 107, 108, 120, 126, 127, 129, 131, 141–42
   lasting influence of, 8, 90, 109, 266
   paternalism of, 19, 77–78, 122
   and Playford historical dances, 76–77, 86, 149, 182, 218, 219
   recordings by, 143–50, 221, 246, 247
   BELIEFS OF:
      on Anglo-American identity, 117, 25
      on "authenticity," 89, 111, 115
      on Fabian socialism, 16, 17–18, 77, 89, 267
      on female suffrage, 18, 75, 152
      on gender roles, 105, 115
      on peasant origins of country dances, 4, 6, 274

Sharp, Cecil (*continued*):
  BELIEFS OF:
    political, 16, 17–19, 77, 89, 267
    on proper bodily expression for ECD, 88, 97, 90, 109, 115–16
    on race, 122–24, 125
    on superiority of English folk dance, 155
  COLLECTING BY:
    in Appalachia, 19, 35, 117, 119–25, 152
    in England, 46, 72, 102
  AND ELIZABETH BURCHANEL:
    early cooperation with, 67, 92, 103, 106, 131, 146
    later conflict with, 19, 90, 112, 118, 134, 137–38, 145–47, 148, 149, 293n95
  AS ENGLISH FOLK DANCE SOCIETY LEADER, 86, 88, 101, 106, 124–25
    and American Branch, 104, 108–14, 117, 129–30, 131, 132, 134, 137–38, 140–42
    certificates issued by, 87, 103–5, 138, 140, 141, 142, 287n76
  AND MARY NEAL:
    early cooperation with, 71–73, 75–76
    later conflict with, 19, 69, 78–85, 88–89, 90, 92, 106, 115, 141, 165, 282n21
  AND MORRIS DANCING: 36, 68, 72, 75–76, 80, 81–82, 224
    demonstration team of, 48, 86–87, 94, 99, 128, 130
    and Espérance girls, 72, 79, 80, 82, 89, 224
    and Headington Morrismen, 8, 16, 71, 72
    (*see also* Boxing Day revelation)
Sharp, Charles, 48, 130
Sharp, Constance, 101
Sharp, Evelyn, 18, 75
Shaw, Lloyd, 191–92, 197
Shaw, Pat, 152–53, 186–87, 216–20
  impact of, on English Country Dance in U.S., 153, 206, 207–8, 216, 219–20, 245
  on meaning of "folk," 206, 207–8, 220
"Shepherd's Hey," 72, 139, 148
Shimer, Genevieve (Genny), 189, 191, 213, *218*, 223, 229
  as CDSS director (1972–75), 214–15, 222
Shuldham-Shaw, Patrick Noel. *See* Shaw, Pat
Shuldham Shaw, Winifred Holloway, 153
"siding," 219
Simkovitch, Mary, 25, 27, 156
Sinclair, Marjory, 86
"Sir Roger de Cloverly," 2, 43

Skansen Dancers, 63
skiffle, 184–85
Skrobela, Paul, 214
Sloackum, Maury, 184
Smith, Ada, 36
Smith, Everett, 136
Smith, Joseph, 57
Smith, Margaret Dean, 184
Smith, Melville, *144*, 147
Smith, Milton, 135, 142–43, *144*
Smith brothers, 135, 136, *144*, 291n68. *See also* Smith, Melville; Smith, Milton
Smithsonian Folklife and Cultural Heritage Center, 252
social dances, 56–59, 250, 273. *See also* tango
Speyer, Ellen, 27
"spieling," 57
square dancing, 4, 209, 306n40
  in England, 10, 178, 179–82, 183, 204, 266
  origins of, 46, 47
  revival of, starting in 1930s, 176–77, 191–94, 202
"standards," 137–40
Stansell, Christine, 55
Starr, Ellen Gates, 25, 40
Stebbins, Genevieve, 29
Stein, Judith, 268
Stewart, Mary B., 64
Stone, May, 35
Storrow, Helen Osborne, 143, 154, 156, 194, 267
  and A. Claud Wright, 95–96, 97, 98
  Boston dance academy of, 64, 110
  and Cecil Sharp, 18, 97, 107, 108, 120, 126, 127, 129, 131, 141–42
  certification of, as dancer, 108, 129
  conservative views of, 18, 107, 136, 152, 267
  country estate of, as dance site, 95, 98, 126
  death of, 190
  early interest of, in ECD, 64, 84, 93
  and founding of American Branch, 110, 112–13
  important role of, in U.S. ECD, 20, 64, 267
  as president of American Branch and its successors, 133, 135
  social standing of, 68, 131
Storrow, James Jackson, 68
Strangways, Fox, 18
Stratford-on-Avon Summer School, 81, 138, 140–41
  Americans attending, 105, 135, 141
  conflict over, 82–84, 141

suburbs, 135, 225, 245, 257, 304n56
suffrage movement, 74–75
    Cecil Sharp's hostility to, 18, 75, 152
    Mary Neal and, 74–75
    in the U.S., 53–54, 107, 152
summer schools, 112–14, 119, 134, 140–43, *144*, *151*, 292nn85,87. *See also* Stratford-on-Avon Summer School
Swarthmore College, 226, 231, 241
sword dancing, 139, *140*, 148, 269
Szczelkun, Stefan, 34

Tamaris, Helen, 156, 169
tango, 57–58, 65, 273
Taylor, Cornell ("Connie"), 200
Taylor, Malcolm, 184–85
Taylor, Marianne, 200
tempo, 149–50, 221–22, 247, 263
theosophy, 72, 73
Thompson, Allison, 60, 61, 245, 265
Tiddy, Reginald, 48, 86, 130
Times, The (London), 93
Tomko, Linda, 30, 40, 136
Townsend, Kathleen, 135
Toynbee Hall, 25
"traditional" (community) dance, 46, 182–83
Trefusis, Lady Mary, 85–86
Trevelyan, Lady, 151
Triangle Shirtwaist Factory fire, 54
Troxler, Allan, 233, 235, 255
"Turkey in the Straw," 176
Turner, Frederick Jackson, 23

upper class, 68. *See also* aristocrats; Callery, Mrs. James Dawson; Storrow, Helen Osborne
urbanization, 20–23, 27–28

vacation schools, 85, 86
Victor Company, 147–48, 149
Victor Military Band, 150
"Virginia Reel, The," 1–2, 43, 176, 193, 211
Voorhis, Flora, 58

Wagner, Robert F., Jr., 162

Wald, Lillian, 25, 27, 63, 156
Ward, Chuck, 228, 233, 246
Warren, Florence "Florrie," 76, 80, 94, 106
    in U.S., 53, 54, 83, 91, 92–94
Washington, Booker T., 39
Washington, George, 43, 45
Waters, Muddy, 165, 166
Weavers, 166, 167, 184, 201
Welch, Archibald, 93
Wellesley College, 18, 110, 112–13, 126, 131, 136, 152
Wells, Evelyn, 136, 152, 291n67
Western (or Club) Squares, 192, 209
Wheeler, Kenneth, 139
Whirligig, 186
Whisnant, David, 17, 39
Whiteman, Elsie, 180, 183
"whiteness," 11, 242–43, 257, 267
    changing character of, 242–43, 257
    and new-immigrant ethnic groups, 52, 225, 242, 267
Whitesides, George, 259
Wilde, Oscar, 38–39
Wilfert, Ed, 142
Wilkinson, George, 48, 86, 130
Williams, Ralph Vaughan, 34, 84, 149, 168
Winston, Louise, 194
Wittman, Carl, 205, 230–35, 237, 249, 254, 274
Wolfe, Linda, 242
Women's Social and Political Union (WSPU), 74–75
World War I, 48, 99, 116, 130
World War II, 157, 178, 194–95
Wright, A. Claud, 94–99, 141, 284n14
    athleticism of, 94, 95, 98
    background of, 86, 96, 115
    rivalry of, with Cecil Sharp, 94–99, 106, 108–9, 115–16
    warm U.S. reception for, 94, 95–96, 98, 109, 284n15

Yarnal, Thom, 238, 239, 251, 258, 259
YMCA gyms, 29–30

Ziegfield, Florenz, 56

About the Author

DANIEL J. WALKOWITZ is Professor of History and Social and Cultural Analysis at New York University. He is the author and editor of several books, most recently *Working with Class: Social Workers and the Politics of Middle-Class Identity* (1999) and, as coeditor, *Memory and the Impact of Political Transformations in Public Spaces* (2004) and *Contested Histories in Public Space: Memory, Race, and Nation* (2009).

www.ingramcontent.com/pod-product-compliance
Lightning Source LLC
Chambersburg PA
CBHW071147070526
44584CB00019B/2699